Heavenly Merchandize

Heavenly Merchandize

HOW RELIGION SHAPED COMMERCE
IN PURITAN AMERICA

Mark Valeri

PRINCETON UNIVERSITY PRESS

PRINCETON AND OXFORD

Copyright © 2010 by Princeton University Press
Published by Princeton University Press, 41 William Street,
Princeton, New Jersey 08540
In the United Kingdom: Princeton University Press, 6 Oxford Street,
Woodstock, Oxfordshire OX20 1TW

Library of Congress Cataloging-in-Publication Data

Valeri, Mark R.
Heavenly merchandize : how religion shaped commerce
in Puritan America / Mark Valeri.
    p.   cm.
Includes bibliographical references and index.
ISBN 978-0-691-14359-0 (hardcover : alk. paper)
  1. Puritans—Doctrines—History—17th century.
  2. Puritans—Doctrines—History—18th century.
  3. United States—Religion—To 1800. 4. Puritans—
  Influence. 5. Business—Religious aspects—
  Christianity. I. Title. BX9323.V35 2010
  261.8′5097409032—dc22   2009039606

British Library Cataloging-in-Publication Data is available

This book has been composed in Janson

Printed on acid-free paper. ∞

press.princeton.edu

Printed in the United States of America

1   3   5   7   9   10   8   6   4   2

For my brothers,
Doug, Bob, and John, and in memory of Richard;
and for my sons,
J.P. and Jamie

CONTENTS

ILLUSTRATIONS

PREFACE

THIS BOOK EXPLAINS how transformations in religious thought contributed to the creation of a market culture in early America. It narrates the worldviews of colonial New Englanders yet describes economic dilemmas that resonate today: the nature of debt, the problems of speculation, the dependence of the market on adequate supplies of credit, the role of external regulation over business, and the obligations of individuals to the common good. The final touches were put on this study in the midst of a global recession that has made the morality of commerce a subject in the daily headlines.

This project nonetheless took shape long before the current crisis. Throughout, I have attempted to fathom the interrelationships among religious doctrine, moral teaching, and economic practice in the terms used by early Americans. My narrative begins with Reformed communities in late-Elizabethan England, moves through the settlement of puritan Boston and expansion of New England's commercial order, and ends with the activities of revivalist-oriented Protestants during the mid-eighteenth century. The importance of religious convictions to economic decisions appears at every turn in the story.

In covering so much material and so many issues, my work has depended on the counsel and support of many people and institutions. Authors often speak of incurring debts in the midst of their labors. My debts are too extended to make a full accounting, but I will provide what ledgers I can, with gratitude.

Several conversation partners have sparked reflections on my argument and presentation. For the past decade, members of the Fall Line Early American Studies group (FLEAS) of Richmond have pushed for clarity in conception and prose. A conference titled "The Worlds of John Winthrop" at Millersville University, ably organized by Frank Bremer, allowed me an opportunity to present my initial soundings. The Omohundro Institute of Early American History and Culture provided a forum for friendly scholarly critique at an early stage of writing; within the institute, Fredrika Teute especially helped me to see that this book should not be about Max Weber but about New England merchants and their self-understandings. Respondents to paper presentations at the University of North Carolina at Chapel Hill, Southern Methodist University, the Princeton University Department of Religion and Center for the Study of Religion, Union Theological Seminary in Virginia, and the Program in Early American Economy and Society at the Library Company of Philadelphia offered sound criticism along with encouragement. Fred Appel at Princeton University Press gave a sympathetic reading to the manuscript. He and his coworkers have eased the publication process with friendly expertise throughout.

Some colleagues have read drafts of the whole book or parts of it. Doug Winiarski has made valuable suggestions over the long haul, shared research tips, and provided copies of manuscripts. Mark Noll and Mark Peterson made trenchant comments on the complete manuscript. Others have contributed insights, from their own areas of expertise, to scattered proposals and individual chapters: Rick Cogley, Laurie Maffly-Kipp, Cathy Matson, and Mark McGarvie in particular.

A book that has much to do with money has taken its share from organizations that generously support scholarly work such as this. The Lilly Endowment provided funds for a leave as part of the History of American Christian Practice Project and for an Association of Theological Schools faculty fellowship. The American Academy of Religion, the American Society of Eighteenth-Century Studies, the Boston University Institute for the Study of Economic Culture (now the Institute on Culture, Religion, and World Affairs), the Louisville Institute, and the National Endowment for the Humanities gave fellowships. Many thanks are due to distinguished scholars who took time out of their busy schedules to read parts, provide direction, and recommend this project for funding, including Joyce Appleby, John Murrin, Leigh Schmidt, and Harry Stout.

Several research institutions sustained this project with access to archives, professional advice, and funding for travel to their sites: the Baker Library at Harvard Business School, the Huntington Library, the Library Company of Philadelphia, and the Massachusetts Historical Society. The American Antiquarian Society (AAS) deserves special mention in this regard. Dear to the heart of any American historian who uses it, it has served as a resource and friendly home away from home several times. The AAS also granted permission for the republication of much of an essay that originally appeared in their *Proceedings*, which now appears in chapter 3 here. I wish to acknowledge also my home institution, Union Theological Seminary, for its support, from providing excellent library services and research expenses to sabbaticals from the classroom. In addition, the Institute for Reformed Theology at Union has underwritten a subvention for publication.

Family and friends have offered encouragement in different modes: constant concern, unfailing patience, and gentle wisdom. Anthony and Julie Strange, and Bob and Lynnie Parker, gave me quiet spaces near the water for reflection. Scott Armisted, Tom and Elizabeth Barila, John Callahan, David and Pam Clarke, Becky and Braxton Glasgow, Steve Hartman, Doug Hicks, Anna Kim and Walt Stevenson, Fritz and Val Kling, Bill and Kathy Morgan, Nelson Ould, and Jerry Parker have been hearing about this book for a long time. Lynn Valeri has endured the whole process of research and writing with her usual grace. Such kind support cannot be repaid; it can be only an occasion for gratitude.

Many of the merchants discussed in this book found identity, and moral meaning, in being part of a dispersed network of like-minded souls. Sometimes separated by distance, they often thought themselves linked by shared moral sentiments. So too with those to whom this book is dedicated. I trust that we are linked together by deep affection despite sometimes long distances. I wish you joy and true calling in all that you do and will do.

Heavenly Merchandize

HEAVENLY MERCHANDIZE

IN 1686 the pastor of Boston's Old South Church, Samuel Willard, delivered a series of sermons on the importance of spiritual wisdom in times of crisis. The past year had unnerved the residents of Boston. Newspapers and letters from abroad had spread rumors of war on the northern frontier. Trade imbalances, piracy, bad credit, and navigation regulations issued from London had stifled commerce. Most alarmingly, the Crown had revoked the colony's long-cherished charter and established a royal dominion administered by an appointed governor whose Anglican practices and courtly style betrayed long-established customs. In the midst of such trials it was "seasonable," as Willard put it, to urge devotion to New England's religious traditions.[1]

The most accomplished divine of his day, Willard knew how to shape his message to his audience. In the pews of Old South sat many of Boston's prominent merchants: powerful civic leaders with well-known names such as Gibbs, Brattle, Sewall, Oliver, Savage, and Wharton. They had joined other overseas traders struggling to transform Boston into a commercial power. Willard spoke their language. In a remarkable performance, later published under the title *Heavenly Merchandize, or The Purchasing of Truth Recommended*, he used the idioms of commerce to exhort his people. The wise merchant, he preached, bought divine revelation as the most valuable commodity in the marketplace of ideas. The perceptive dealer extended all his credit, mortgaged his estate, and signed any bond to get the truth because heaven insured it to deliver fantastically high returns. Willard did not bother to untangle the logical mess of metaphor, analogy, and literal reference, but his conflation of economic and spiritual images is striking nonetheless. Willard piled one market trope on another, for 170 pages. Bills of exchange, interest rates, credit ratings, usury, accounts, reserves, stocks, abatements, contracts, insurance, factors, attorneys, customers, trading companies: he omitted no conceivable tactic or instrument from what he called the "Worlds Market" to drive home his evangelistic message.[2]

Willard clearly knew how to descend beneath cloudy platitudes about religion and the economy. He did not portray the market as a monolithic power and moral force unto itself. It consisted of the discrete and contingent decisions of its participants. Willard spoke of actual transactions made by his parishioners in Boston's countinghouses, coffeehouses, lanes, wharves, and shops: dependence on book credit and credit instruments such as mortgages and bonds, speculation in commodities the value of which rose and fell by demand, prediction of long-range economic needs, reliance on agents and factors to arrange complicated deals, and the use of civil law to adjudicate disputes. The "Worlds Market" meant the collection of quite specific techniques by which local traders and overseas merchants exchanged goods and credit for a profit.[3]

Willard also avoided stark dichotomies between piety and profit; he understood commerce to be a mundane reality infused with transcendent meaning. His evocation of everyday exchanges reflected deep assumptions about trade, the nation, and society. He preached during a period when Boston merchants believed that their occupation was essential to the commonweal—to England's prosperity and therefore to Protestantism and liberty. Their strategies to convey goods, credit, and power throughout the British Atlantic proved them to be patrons of the empire.[4] Many moralists, Willard included, valorized them in such terms. His successors, leading Boston pastors of the 1710s, 1720s, and 1730s, went further. They, along with their parishioners, sanctioned the practices that guaranteed economic success as moral mandates, and the rules that governed commercial exchange as natural and divine laws. Their convictions informed a market culture that, by many accounts, came to maturity by 1750 and provided motives for rebellion against the British Empire after the cessation of war with France.[5]

Many of the leading original settlers of Massachusetts Bay, imbued with ideals from their puritan teachers in England, had thought of economic matters quite differently than did Willard.[6] Along with their counterparts in other Protestant communities throughout Europe—Geneva, parts of France, and the Netherlands—they often pitted Christian identities against political and commercial loyalties. They did not gainsay the worth of trade and prosperity. Yet they relied on a discourse of Scripture and Reformed doctrine that rarely accommodated the language of market exchange. Fastened on local social relationships and the religious congregation, they sought to constrain new techniques, such as usury or civil litigation, that they perceived to be impersonal and vicious. They intended to institute religious discipline over all forms of social interaction. They thought that their task was to teach merchants the grammar of faith, not to conform their speech to the rules of commerce.

It took a great deal of intellectual change, from the early seventeenth century to the eighteenth, for leaders in the congregational churches of Massachusetts to imagine the collection of practices evoked by Willard as anything but a corruption of trade. How did such a transformation take place? What transitions in church practices, preaching, devotional habits, and moral instruction allowed professors of godliness to embrace economic behaviors that the puritan founders rejected? How was it that self-identified believers distanced themselves from earlier suspicions and came to promote distant, indirect, and rationalized transactions as divine mandates? In sum, how did pious New Englanders come to revere the market as it developed in their day?

The answers given in this book presume that the market was not a fixed system over this period. Before their departure for the New World, puritans encountered in London a complex and dense mercantile order: a confusion of new and old trading companies and overseas ventures, innovative yet controversial credit instruments, and competition for power in the midst of political upheaval. The first settlers of Massachusetts Bay organized a localized market, dependent on new immigrants and capital imported from England. Their economy collapsed during the 1640s with a decline in migration and increased isolation. After several years of depression, Boston merchants established new lines of trade. From the beginning of the 1650s through the 1680s, they created a commercial network, including inland towns, that extended through other American colonies, across the Caribbean, to London. After the 1680s, merchants integrated New England into England's modern transatlantic system, yet again reshaping the meaning of the market for its participants.

The following narrative accordingly traces change in religious discourse in the context of what appeared to contemporaries to be a sometimes breathtaking economic passage. It begins with an account of the first generation of Boston's puritan merchants and ministers, especially the overseas trader Robert Keayne, his associates, and the leadership of Boston's First Church, such as Pastor John Cotton and Governor John Winthrop. The first two chapters describe Keayne's professional training and religious conversion in London, puritan teaching about exchange, and godly purposes for the settlement of New England. During the 1630s and 1640s, the First Church in Boston mounted a disciplinary campaign against merchants such as Keayne, whose commercial practices conformed to humanist dictates yet violated puritan proscriptions against usury and overpricing.

Early restraints on trade in Massachusetts represented social agendas developed over the course of half a century of puritan teaching in England. Some historians have argued that restrictive measures such as price controls were temporary and aberrant concessions to the expediencies of a fledgling colony,[7] but the puritan immigrants to New England had long aspired to institute discipline that chastened economic rationality with scriptural rules and shaped business decisions to local needs. Informed by godly dictates, puritans such as Keayne were in fact deeply ambivalent about their participation in England's burgeoning market.

Over the course of the seventeenth century and into the first decades of the eighteenth, puritan leaders—lay and religious—displaced received notions of discipline and muted critiques of tactics previously condemned under the rubrics of usury, oppression, and profane litigation. Chapter 3, covering the period from 1650 to 1680, is pegged to the story of the silversmith and trader John Hull. During Hull's career, a chain of social calamities, controversies in Boston's churches, and military crises provoked him and his pastors to reconsider the meaning of providence for New England. Ministers such as Increase Mather and Samuel Willard came to portray the civic order of New England as a special subject of divine rule. As they did so, they invested commercial proficiency and expansion—the means of a prosperous commonwealth—with providential purpose. Legitimating many innovations in exchange, they gave Hull and his colleagues reason to understand their ventures in the market as compatible with their spiritual duties.

Chapter 4 extends this account through the stories of the magistrate and merchant Samuel Sewall and his near contemporary Thomas Fitch. From 1680 through the 1710s, New England's merchants developed their trade into a regional economy and extended it into the Atlantic basin. Leading members of Boston's Old South Church, Sewall and Fitch also undertook their careers during the unsettling political affairs evoked in Willard's *Heavenly Merchandize*. They witnessed the accession to the English throne of a new dynasty deemed to be the patrons of true Protestantism in a worldwide contest with Catholic tyranny.

Ministers such as Willard, along with Cotton Mather, identified the English nation—the metropolis and its colonial extensions—as the chief instrument of divine providence in the world. They described pious Bostonians as patriotic Englishmen, whose efforts to secure a place in Britain's transatlantic market system amounted to religious duty. In the process, they adopted the conventions of England's political economists: thoroughgoing pragmatists who analyzed the nation's commerce through mathematical and scientific methods. Puritans such as Willard and Mather were convinced that the vocabularies of political economy, often deployed by popular commentators such as Daniel Defoe, constituted a dialect of divine truth. In continuity with their predecessors, they arraigned dishonesty, ostentatious consumption, disregard for the poor, and slave trading as evidences of avarice and selfish materialism. They nonetheless made decided changes in economic teaching. They provided moral sanctions for usury, trading in securities, new forms of paper money, and market pricing. Sewall and Fitch embodied those teachings. They conducted their businesses with moral sensibilities infused with transformed convictions about providence and the end of history.

Chapter 5 shows how Boston ministers such as Thomas Foxcroft of First Church, Ebenezer Pemberton of Old South, and Benjamin Colman of the Brattle Street Church, along with their merchant followers, implemented yet another form of moral discourse during the first three decades of the eighteenth century. They replaced previous critiques of exchange practices with exhortations to reasoned sentiment, right affection, and proper decorum in the midst of those practices. They made these changes for thoroughly religious reasons. They addressed themselves to an intellectual contest between critics and defenders of orthodox Protestantism in England, all of whom claimed to represent the cause of reason and virtue. Concerned to promote Christian belief among their parishioners, Boston pastors described providence as divine rule over a natural order through a natural law that promoted sociability and society.

Adopting fashionable moral vocabularies of reason and refinement, divines such as Colman urged merchants to an interior, affective piety that displayed the virtues of politeness in the midst of assiduous competition in the Atlantic market. A new generation of overseas merchants, in this case represented by one of New England's prominent slave traders, Hugh Hall, understood their commercial activities from this reasoned, naturalized Protestantism. Marking a transition out of puritan and into postpuritan Protestantism, Hall's career illuminates the near complete consonance between religious and commercial discourses in early New England. His story marks the final stage in the accumulation of changes within puritanism—slow, partial, and gradual transformations in language and practice—that explain the alliance between Protestant and market culture from the settlement of Boston through the early eighteenth century.

There are contrasting interpretations of religion and the economy in this period, against which *Heavenly Merchandize*—this book, that is— should be read. First, several economic and political historians have contended that systematic economic forces triumphed over moral customs and sheared away religious ideas from commercial practice. Merchants, as this argument goes, founded New England as a for-profit venture and overwhelmed conservative-minded ministers and farmers during the seventeenth century.[8] Market realities thus compelled preachers such as Willard, when they bothered to make economic statements, to domesticate their criticisms, jettison old-fashioned communal morals, and conform their ideas to imperial and bourgeois values. By this reading, religious language functioned merely as an ex post facto legitimization of commercial expansion and justification for economic elites. Ministers offered a veneer of propriety covering an economic culture more solidly constructed of class and individual interests.

This tale of secularization fails on several accounts. An impressive sociological tradition calls into question the bundle of unexamined assumptions and circular logic reflected in many such arguments.[9] A straightforward observation of historical sequence reinforces this critique: only after the religious transformations of the late seventeenth and early eighteenth centuries did New England's market system come to fruition, indicating at least some influence of the former on the latter. In addition, an understanding of religion as a cultural system—a complex of ideas, family practices, ritual, and communal expectations rather than merely a logic of doctrines set against social forces—suggests multiple connections between religion and business practice.[10]

Reducing the story to purely economic mentalities, moreover, mutes the voices not only of preachers but also of the merchant parishioners in Boston's puritan churches. Traders often sounded pious resolutions, moral perplexity, and genuine concern for the spiritual meaning of their businesses. Merchants and ministers, to be sure, were sometimes irresolute, displaying an ambiguous mixture of high intentions and quite mundane ambitions. Yet many of them described the purpose of commerce in thoroughly religious terms, reading the latest techniques as instruments of providence or the market system as designed by God for human felicity. The makers of New England's market claimed to be church members, devout believers, and successful merchants at the same time. They defined their interests by moral and cultural vocabularies that accommodated a mélange of spiritual, material, and economic goods. Their comments reveal a complexity obscured by the assertion that economic interests determined religious teaching in New England.

This book uncovers the relationship between the ways merchants did business and their beliefs. It reveals the extent to which religious convictions, from ideas about providence and political sentiments to regimens of moral discipline in local congregations, informed commercial decisions. *Heavenly Merchandize* relies on merchants' accounts and ledgers, business correspondence and personal letters, diaries and spiritual ruminations, autobiographical claims and the records of churches in which they participated. Such a thick description requires selectivity; each chapter focuses on one or two Boston traders who had suppliers and customers in different parts of the Atlantic world (so-called overseas traders) and who identified themselves as members of the puritan-congregational order of Massachusetts, joined prominent congregations in the town, and wrote about their spiritual lives. These cannot stand for all merchants in early New England. There were other traders with different religious sensibilities, Anglican, Quaker, and indifferent included. Yet the merchants discussed here offer particularly telling instances of the interdependencies among religious tenets, moral languages, and commercial behaviors. In some cases, their mentalities help to explain how a certain kind of economic pragmatism—what might appear to our modern eyes as mere profit seeking—gained religious legitimacy among the most tenaciously devout New Englanders. Principled expedience was not the same thing as unbridled materialism, at least by their lights. They articulated reasons for choosing what we might characterize as a pragmatic approach to commerce. Religious ideas, communal habits, and material conditions formed an ensemble of cultures in early New England.

A second interpretive dilemma shadows the following chapters. Many historians who admit to the importance of religious ideas for New England's economy rely on Max Weber's influential thesis in *The Protestant Ethic and the Spirit of Capitalism* and other essays. Weber recognized that the market represented an "absolute depersonalization" of social exchange, and therefore a challenge to the organic and interpersonal ethics—the "regulation"—prized by Christian tradition. Referring to the same kinds of economic instruments that Willard evoked, Weber observed that "it is not possible to regulate" the complicated and impersonal relations between holders of bonds, notes of exchange, or mortgages and their distant debtors. So, "where the market is allowed to follow its own autonomous tendencies, its participants" necessarily violated customary "obligations of brotherliness or reverence."[11]

Weber conceded that early Calvinists resisted the individualistic and materialistic implications of a market economy; yet he also claimed that Calvinist teaching implicitly invested rationalized, bureaucratic regimes with divine purpose. He described the essence of Reformed belief to include the spiritual validity of secular vocations, the pursuit of wealth as an indication of otherwise mysterious divine favor, and the primacy of diligence, industriousness, and frugality as moral virtues. Such teaching, according to Weber, helped to create the ethos of early capitalism. It molded a truly modern economic personality, driven to prove itself through diligence and frugality in a rational system regardless of conventional notions of interpersonal obligation. Without a close reading of puritan texts, or an examination of transformations between early Reformers and late seventeenth-century and early eighteenth-century puritans, Weber jumped to latter-day Protestants who embodied this personality even as they rejected Calvinist doctrine. Once shorn of its theological tenets and customary hedges on outright individualism, puritanism flowered into an economic culture of autonomy, rational discipline, entrepreneurialism, and specialization. Benjamin Franklin and John Wesley, by Weber's reading, perfectly signified the Protestant ethic.[12]

Weber's thesis is complex enough to sustain various interpretations and applications to early New England. Nothing in this book amounts to a wholesale attack on Weber. Surely there was something within Reformed thought, especially the sanctification of worldly labor and the belief that providence gave transcendent purpose and meaning to everyday social exchange, that propelled Protestants into commerce with moral confidence.[13] Weber only hinted, however, at the immense shifts required to displace older modes of discipline, validate the actual transactions performed in the market, and accordingly transform puritan disdain into sanction for the new economy. The importance of such changes for individual merchants, whose moral choices made the market, lay shrouded in Weber's mist of theoretical generalizations.

As a result, many historians have compressed Weber's argument into a single dictum: puritans were protocapitalists in their genes, by constitution, bursting out of the cocoon of religious tradition.[14] This has become something of a default explanation for religion and commerce in early New England. Echoing a parallel sounding of English puritanism, many interpreters have maintained that the whole story can be encapsulated in a simple formula equating the religion of New England's founders and successors to bourgeois, market-driven industriousness: New England was born capitalist and Protestant. If this book serves as a corrective, then it is in part to critique this misuse of Weber and complicate the narrative.[15]

Other studies have provided a much more suitably nuanced plot. One strand of interpretation has modified Weber by describing an inherent tension between a traditional social ethic and economic rationality within the puritan movement. Only the social and political changes brought about by the Restoration of the Stuart monarchy in 1660—outside incursions into New England's order—resolved these tensions in favor of market dictates.[16] English and Scottish historians, meanwhile, have issued warnings against general characterizations of the puritans as either wholly sympathetic with or antipathetic toward the emergent market. Radical Protestants in different locales, and in different times, responded to commercial opportunities with different degrees of enthusiasm, a variation that in itself diminishes the power of any single theory of Calvinism and the market.[17]

Yet again, a more recent turn has marked an appreciation for the persistence of a dense spirituality, even as New England's ministers and merchants moved into an expanding market. Several works have tracked shifting agendas, played out differently in various regions, that allowed puritans and their eighteenth-century successors to understand commercial exchange as a conduit for genuine religion. Understood as a divine gift, the market appeared to be a mode of social solidarity, a new and expansive means of community, and a benefactor of churches and their evangelistic work.[18]

Even these quite useful histories, however, foreshorten the long intellectual journey traveled from the puritan settlers to their mid-eighteenth-century heirs. Recent works minimize internal diversity and changes within New England puritanism. They continue to slight the intentional alterations that puritans made, for theological reasons, in their moral teaching. This book attempts to recover this distance by attending to the sermons and treatises, along with the personal writings, of religious leaders who addressed economic developments. These sources show the importance of transformations in ideas about providence, moral discourses, and rules for specific commercial practices.

The merchants examined in *Heavenly Merchandize* observed, recorded, and absorbed these innovations. Their reflections make this clear: the less they embraced the tenets of first-generation leaders such as Cotton and Winthrop, the more they entered into, and created, the world of the market. The more they adopted the idioms of civic loyalties, imperial identities, and enlightened rationalities, the more they embraced the mandates of the emergent economy. As Boston's ministers conformed their teaching to the latest transatlantic intellectual fashions, they gave their merchant parishioners a language to bridge piety and commercial technique. From this perspective, it was the transformation of puritanism—we might even overstate the case by contending that it was the slow liberalization of puritanism and rise of rational Protestantism—not puritanism itself, that explains the congruence between religion and the market in early New England. Religion had everything to do with the development of a market culture in early New England, but it was not necessarily old-time religion, if by that we mean the ideals of the founders.

While retracing the great distance from puritan origins to eighteenth-century provincial culture, *Heavenly Merchandize* does not map the terrain in contemporary terms such as secularization or modernization. Echoing Weber, who regarded the Protestant ethos to have hardened into the "iron cage" of capitalist bureaucracy, many historians have pondered an idealistic and communal puritanism descending into Yankee cleverness and ambition through the course of the seventeenth and early eighteenth centuries.[19] New Englanders, as this account goes, capitulated to individualism, materialism, and fractious social values.

This book considers transitions in formal religious discourse, yet also detects variation and contestation in daily pieties, church practices, and political agendas in each generation. It maintains that puritan ideas about providence, an especially salient aspect of puritan religiosity, developed in response to the different social conditions through which God was assumed to work. As those conditions changed, so too did the framing of providence. Change did not evidence capitulation in such a malleable religious culture.

More important, the following chapters show that New Englanders did not jettison communal values for mere individualism. New understandings of providence reoriented their perceptions of community and thus of moral good. The systems of exchange in the transatlantic market appeared to be means of society and instruments of divine rule in the world. If we merely contrast a biblical, communal, and pristine puritanism of the 1630s to a putatively rational, individualistic, and secular religious style of the 1720s, then we fail to comprehend the moral imagination of the creators of a market culture in early New England. Convictions about God and the good ran through every turn in the story.

Until we appreciate the significance of the transition from puritan to postpuritan Protestantism in early New England, we will not grasp the beginning of the vexed history of religion and the market in America.[20] In this regard, *Heavenly Merchandize* may serve as a contribution to a lively and robust debate about cultural values and the current economy.[21] That discussion has been confused by summary historical judgments, misleading generalizations, and caricatures. We are better served by a history that gives attention to the constant interplay of religious ideas and exchange practices, personal dilemmas and corporate loyalties, devotional aspirations and economic technique, over a long period of negotiation and modification. The remarkable alliance between Protestantism and commerce in America has its origins in the moral decisions of the ministers and merchants accounted for in the following narrative.

Chapter One

ROBERT KEAYNE'S GIFT

In 1653 Robert Keayne bequeathed a generous gift to the town of Boston: £300 for the construction of a public market building, or exchange, with a water conduit. His last will and testament also provided £100 to stock a granary at the marketplace and £40 to feed clergymen attending annual synods at the exchange. Keayne also donated an unspecified number of books—including his own three, handwritten volumes of commentary on the prophetic books of Daniel, Ezekiel, and Hosea—to establish a public library in the building. There was more. He bequeathed £70 to the poor fund of the town's church, £50 to a school for indigent children, £10 and two cows to the local artillery company (a volunteer militia), and, to be dispensed at the death of his wife, £300 to Harvard College. In sum, Keayne devoted over £800 of his total estate of £2,700 to civic and religious causes.[1]

Keayne estimated the market building as the most important of his bequests; he intended it to "be a great ornament to the town as well as useful and profitable," and gave detailed instructions for its construction. He thought it should be prominently located in the Cornhill district, at a key intersection overlooking the harbor and wharves, near his house. He designed it as an imposing, rectangular structure. The ground floor was to be open-air. Protected from rain and snow in the winter and refreshed by breezes in the summer, merchants, shipmasters, and shopkeepers could gather in this semiprotected space, store their goods, and market their wares. Keayne wanted the second floor to have several rooms for civic and religious purposes, including a library (furnished with his works on divinity and military affairs) and a room for church meetings. Other uses came to Keayne's mind: courtrooms, a granary, and an armory.[2]

Such a structure had first been proposed in town meetings in 1649, but Keayne was the first to step forward with a plan and the money for its construction. Less than a year after his death in March 1656, 163 residents of the town contributed a total of about £100 to complete the building. Subscribers to the project included the most prominent merchants in Boston—seventeen long-distance traders and seven local traders and shopkeepers. Among the more generous donors were Edward Tyng, who along with fellow merchant Robert Hull and minister John Wilson, was a witness to Keayne's will, and other worthies of Boston's mercantile community:

Richard Bellingham, Peter Oliver, Hezekiah Usher, Thomas Clark, Jacob
Sheafe, Thomas Brattle, and Joshua Scottow.[3]

Boston's Town House, as it came to be known, was completed in 1658.
The building committee followed many of Keayne's instructions while expanding the general purpose of the structure. The ground floor was open
as Keayne suggested. The second floor consisted of one large room. It
could be used for merchants to meet, rest, or negotiate, but its formal
purpose was to hold town meetings. The third floor housed the library,
two courtrooms, a council chamber, and meeting rooms for ministers and
selectmen. The town rented space on the ground floor to shopkeepers. It
became a favorite location for booksellers. A railed walkway and turrets
graced the roof. The committee unfortunately omitted the water conduit
that its benefactor had proposed as a safeguard against fire. The whole
edifice burned to the ground one day in 1711.[4]

As a public moral gesture, Keayne's gift conveyed mixed concepts of
social exchange. The very plan of the structure evoked the humanist ideal
that commerce should be an instrument for social cohesion. Its unenclosed
first floor, rectangular shape, and central location expressed Renaissance
conventions for civic-mindedness (figure 1.1). Open to all residents of Boston, the exchange encouraged merchants to view their activities as public
duties, carried out on behalf of the town and commonwealth. It was a hub
of social networks, where members of various trades and social classes gathered as neighbors. As if to certify this communal ideal, the small contributions of apothecaries and innkeepers, farmers, fishermen, bakers, and artisans such as tanners, shoemakers, coopers, and masons made up the bulk
of the funding beyond Keayne's gift. The building symbolized business in
the service of social integration. In this space merchants acted as citizens
and plied their trade as a civic office. As Keayne put it, the Town House
"is a work of charity and mercy"; its advantages would "redound to the
whole town in general."[5]

Keayne's design also reflected a puritan worldview in which religious
discipline defined the proper bounds of commerce. The placement of the
Town House allowed for supervision by the church. It was located in sight
of wharves yet also across the street from the First Church meetinghouse
and one of its pastors. Visiting merchants and ministers were to meet in
the building, bringing material and spiritual exchange into the same space.
We might surmise that the library, which Keayne thought more crucial
than the courtroom, contained gazettes and almanacs that merchants found
useful, but he wanted traders to read biblical prophecy as well as advice on
foreign currencies.[6]

Humanist and puritan convictions flowed together in Boston's Town
House, symbolizing the possibilities of both integration and conflict. Humanists and puritans equally infused economic exchange with moral pur-

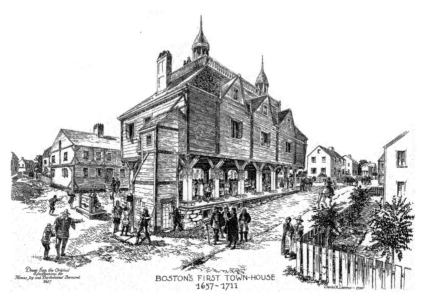

BOSTON'S FIRST TOWN-HOUSE
1657-1711

Figure 1.1. Charles Lawrence's 1930 engraving of Boston's Town House, based on architectural drawings, reflects Keayne's plans for the building: a rectangular structure with an open ground floor for merchants to gather, two additional floors for meetings, and a turreted roof. Courtesy of The Bostonian Society/ Boston Historical.

pose directed to the common good. From this perspective, Keayne's building promised the coalescence of civil and religious criteria for economic exchange. Yet, as he learned throughout his career, many puritan leaders thought that these two conventions were fundamentally incompatible. Humanists prized trade as a means to national prosperity and happiness. Puritans prized it as a means of service to one's immediate neighbor and God. The civil order and the society of the godly were interrelated, but not identical. From this perspective, humanists and puritans held different understandings of the community to which merchants were ultimately accountable: the commonwealth or the church. The story behind Keayne's exchange, then, offers a particularly revealing account of a first-generation New England merchant compelled to negotiate between overlapping and sometimes conflicting moral discourses.

Keayne cannot stand for all New Englanders, but he does represent a dilemma common to many of them. Like many other Bay Colony merchants, he learned his trade and was converted long before he immigrated to New England. The following discussion of his encounters in the Old World probes the deep sources of an uneasy, even strained relationship between the mandates of commerce and the prescriptions of godliness in puritan America.

KEAYNE, THE MERCHANT TAYLORS' COMPANY,
AND CIVIC HUMANISM

A survey of Keayne's life on both sides of the Atlantic sets the context for probing his early career in England. He was born in 1595 in Windsor, Berkshire County, England, the son of the butcher John Keayne. We know little of his early life. In 1605 his father apprenticed him to the London merchant-tailor John Heyfield. He worked eight years in the Cornhill District of London, secured admission to the freedom of the Merchant Taylors' Company, a prominent guild, in 1615, and married Anne Mansfield in 1617. While in London, the young merchant also joined the puritan movement and established connections with dissenting leaders. Anne Mansfield was the sister-in-law of John Wilson, of later fame as one of the first ministers of Boston's First Church.

Keayne thereafter devoted himself to godly teaching. He collected books, regularly attended preaching events in London, and often took notes on sermons when he traveled for business. As his business prospered, he also assumed civic responsibilities. He joined the Honourable Artillery Company of London in 1623 and subscribed as an adventurer behind the Plymouth Colony. Eventually he became acquainted with John Winthrop, whose uncle was a leading vestryman in the parish church of Keayne's Cornhill residence. He advised Winthrop on procuring armaments for the Massachusetts Bay Company. In 1634 he invested £100 in the company. On July 17, 1635, when he was forty years old, he, his wife, and one surviving son out of four, Benjamin, departed England for Boston.[7]

By the time that Keayne left for New England, he had established himself. He expanded his business until he had become a freeman and accumulated between £2,000 and £3,000 in estate. He saw himself as an adherent of Winthrop, Wilson, and Cotton, future mainstays of the governing party within Massachusetts puritanism. He also was the cousin of Edward Rawson, who would become secretary of the General Court. Keayne came to New England as one of the wealthier passengers on the ship *Defence*, a vessel loaded with the colony's future luminaries.[8]

In Boston, Keayne's investment in the company netted him a choice town plot, once removed from the First Church, facing the market square. He built a house there and immediately made a donation to the town's defenses, a battlement on Fort Hill. He and Anne joined as full members of the church during his first year of residence, an act that testified to his conversion. During the next two years he was appointed to a committee on town lands and elected selectman. He held many public offices during the rest of his life; he was reelected selectman four times, elected deputy to the General Court seven times, and appointed to several minor positions such as surveyor of the highways. In 1638 he helped found the colony's militia, the Ancient and Honourable Artillery Company, and thereafter sat on several committees of military affairs. During his first three years in Massachusetts, the General Court awarded him two large land grants: 314 acres on Rumney Marsh and 400 outside the Boston area.[9]

In November 1639, however, Keayne suffered the first of three public humiliations—small scandals, really—that marred his reputation and shaped his self-presentation throughout the rest of his life. A fellow merchant accused Keayne of selling six-penny nails for ten pence a pound. Other charges of overpricing followed. When profit margins on common goods were limited by custom, and frequently by law, to between 10 and 30 percent, Keayne was said to have taken 50, 75, and even 100 percent. In a split decision, the General Court ruled against Keayne and fined him the astonishing amount of £200, which it later reduced to £80. In parallel proceedings, the First Church formally admonished Keayne and placed him under disciplinary censure until the following May, when the merchant's penitence satisfied church elders. In 1642 the suit of one Goody Sherman brought Keayne into court again. She accused him of stealing and slaughtering her prized sow. Keayne successfully defended himself on the evidence that he had killed his own sow and she had merely misplaced hers.[10]

When the dust settled from the nails and sow cases, Keayne's business and even public stature recovered until the third scandal a decade later. From 1643 through 1649 he engaged in lucrative trade with Bermuda and the West Indies. He was a prominent investor in New England's first sustained manufacturing venture, the Saugus Iron Works. In 1649 the General Court awarded him yet another land grant: more than a thousand acres at Pocusset Hill. In 1651 he was appointed judge in the Suffolk County Court. In 1652, alas, Keayne was again brought up to face embarrassing charges. Two former employees and two debtors accused him of habitual drunkenness. The General Court found him guilty, fined him, and removed him from his office as judge. Only a year after this scandal, he began to write his last will and testament, with its elaborate prescriptions for Boston's Town House. Also known as his apologia, this document contained Keayne's reflections on his controversial career.[11]

We have few details about Keayne's business during his formative years in England, but we can infer that he closely identified with the Merchant Taylors' Company of London. The very first line of his apologia pointed to his civic responsibility as a member of the guild: "I, Robert Keayne, citizen and merchant tailor of London." To be sure, he immediately declared the other matrix of his self-understanding: "by freedom and by the good providence of God now dwelling in Boston." Yet he obviously took pride in his professional ascendance, from his move to London in 1605 and his apprenticeship under John Heyfield through his entrance to the guild as a freeman in 1615.[12]

Master merchants such as Heyfield introduced apprentices to different aspects of merchant culture. Most fundamentally, they taught the techniques of exchanging credit, such as keeping books, maintaining accounts, and using bills of exchange (signed promissory notes that could be transferred from one merchant to another). They exposed apprentices to a repetitive, formulaic, mathematical, and contractual language. Merchants intended their accounts to quantify, and thereby certify or reinforce, relationships between creditor and debtor. Calculation protected the moral trust between buyers and sellers. Merchant Taylors required all members annually to present their ledgers to the guild, to be examined by senior members for accuracy and fairness.[13]

Masters also exposed their apprentices to published advice manuals of the period, which instructed would-be merchants on accounts and, perhaps more important, protocols for trade. During Keayne's life in London the most popular of these manuals were Thomas Tusser's *Five Hundred Points of Good Husbandry* (London, 1573), John Browne's *The Marchants Avizo* (London, 1589), and Gerard Malynes' *Consuetudo: Vel, Lex Mercatoria* (London, 1622). The manuals circulating in Keayne's London were quite different from an earlier generation of publications such as Antoine Marcourt's *Boke of Merchauntes* (London, 1539). Marcourt cast a critical glance at merchants. From his advice it appeared that they were prone to avarice and dishonesty. Writers such as Brown and Malynes portrayed merchants as mutual fellows, a true society, bound by codes of honor and trust that spanned oceans. While different kingdoms held to different "civil laws," Malynes argued, merchants followed the international and timeless "Law of nations," and in so doing they provided "the sole peaceable instrument to inrich Kingdomes and Commonweales, by the means of *Equality* and *Equity*."[14]

Laced with this sort of self-assurance, advice manuals taught merchants to deploy their own rhetoric of honor and sociability. Browne's *Avizo* was the most widely used of these manuals among merchant apprentices at the turn of the sixteenth century; by 1640 it had gone through six editions. Keayne might well have looked on Browne as a model; like him, Browne worked his way up through the merchant ranks, professed to be something of a soldier and expert on military affairs, and expressed a deep religious devotion. Browne provided inexperienced traders with a lexicon of manners, even the exact words to use when conducting business. The *Avizo* included rules for keeping different ledgers, the proper terminology for bills of exchange or bills of attorney, and examples of letters to port keepers, friends, and fellow merchants. Every letter to another merchant, Browne suggested, should begin with "I pray for your good health and prosperitie," provide some interesting but not terribly valuable news about local market conditions, and end with expressions of piety that were oblique enough to avoid offending someone of a different religious tradition. The wise merchant not only stayed abreast of the commercial news but also voiced concern for honesty, courtesy, and the honor of fellow merchants. "Shewe yourselfe lowly, curteous, and serviceable unto every person," Browne advised.[15]

Just as these advice manuals introduced aspiring traders to the rhetoric of merchant honor, so the Merchant Taylors provided a local community to enact codes of valor. The company in fact promoted a nearly religious devotion to its work. It demanded a high level of loyalty from its members. To become a freeman in the guild, Keayne took an oath to "be a good and true Brother unto the Merchant Taylors of the fraternitie." He joined in prayers—also prescribed by the company's regulations—to "keepe this noble citty of London" from plague so that "wee may often in brotherly love and trewe love assemble and meete together." The rhetoric of brotherly love and devotion reinforced submission to the guild as an organ of corporate discipline. Keayne agreed to heed all summonses issued by the company's wardens, who held responsibility for oversight of apprentice-master relationships and the conduct of members. He promised to bring disputes with a fellow merchant before the assistants—elder merchants who judged cases in a special court—rather than a civil magistrate. He swore to expose all unlicensed, foreign merchants in the city. Should he ever take on apprentices, he promised, he would provide them with food, lodging, instruction, and wages according to the company's rates. He consented to learn the "concils," or rules, and "mystery," or ceremonies, of the association and to attend all its feasts and festivals. He vowed to avoid all unseemly public behavior—gambling, rioting, late-night drinking—and speech that "might" bring "great infamy, slander, and rebuke" upon fellow merchants. Finally, he consented to contribute to the charitable work of the guild. This last was a large enterprise. The guild maintained a regular fund to assist disabled or underemployed workers. From 1605 to 1635 the Merchant Taylors established fifteen additional benevolences, chiefly pensions for orphans and widows of members but also funds for local poor relief and repair of neighborhood church buildings. Here were all the formal elements of a Christian church, absent Christian theology: fellowship, pedagogy, moral discipline, ritual, and poor relief.[16]

The Merchant Taylors also labored to establish a public reputation for civic-mindedness. Keayne became an upper-level apprentice and member of the company at a turning point in its history. Deprived of its traditional rights of monopoly and statutory preferment in the late sixteenth century, the Merchant Taylors had begun to lobby municipal and royal officials. They also conducted something of a propaganda campaign to influence opinion at large. They wrote about their contributions to the Crown, including outright gifts of money, in times of military crisis. They highlighted their expertise in the patriotic skills of military technology, marching, and parade. They offered their building as a site to train soldiers. They stressed the national value of their investment in the East India Company and assistance to members who settled in Virginia and Bermuda. They patronized historians and poets who portrayed the merchants as civic benefactors on a heroic scale. They boasted that their members were well disciplined and reliable. All of these efforts paid well. By 1615, the year Keayne joined, the Merchant Taylors' Company was the wealthiest guild in London, composed of men well connected to municipal and royal government. It had reached its zenith of civic prominence.[17]

Two elaborate public festivals marked the high points in this campaign. In 1607 the guild hosted a dinner for James I, at which he was made an honorary member. Preparations for this event, of which Keayne must have heard, were unprecedented in company records. The Merchant Taylors' Hall, where festivals and dinners were often held, underwent several renovations. Workers installed a new garden wall and a window for the king's view at the table. The company commissioned new paintings and restored its old tapestries, in which it took great pride. Members spent more than £1,000 on the banquet. Recorded by company clerks in admiring detail, the menu described a meal of excessive variety and proportion.[18]

In 1613 the Merchant Taylors sponsored a second event, a public festival and pageant in honor of one of its regular members, John Swynnerton, who was elected lord mayor of London in 1612. Members assembled in the streets, arrayed in traditional costume. They presented a huge float: a chariot drawn by sea horses and driven by Neptune, a favorite of merchants. The tableau announced the performance of a play written by Thomas Decker. Frequently patronized by the company, Decker provided a script that commended Swynnerton and London's commercial prospects. Several smaller dramatic presentations and orations swirled around the play. All of these works used tropes from the classical canon: virtue personified, the gods as patrons of civic life, the drama of republican Rome. They celebrated the civic value of merchants, predicted the prosperity of the metropolis, and extolled the virtues of Swynnerton—a man qualified to care for the city, provide for the poor, and rule with justice.[19]

The Merchant Taylors relied on humanist writers such as Decker in other venues as well. One of their members, John Stowe, made a career as a propagandist for the company. His 1598 *The Survey of London*, a huge, meandering history of the city, gave dozens of examples of merchants who, from the founding of the Roman Londinium to the reign of Elizabeth, made donations to civic projects such as hospitals, religious lectureships, and poor relief. As patrons of the church and city, merchants were exemplary citizens. Like political writers who promoted republican government as an ancient custom, Stowe appealed to tradition. His civic-minded merchants built London through their patronage of church and city.[20]

Inspired by humanism, the merchants turned to a Renaissance curriculum when they founded a school to train the children of members. The Merchant Taylors' School educated John Heyfield's two sons. If Keayne had overheard their conversation about their studies, he would have learned the names of humanist educators such as Richard Mulcaster, a student of the famous John Colet, who built the curriculum on Greek and Roman moralists. Keayne also would have known of literary and dramatic productions by students. Many of the school's graduates, such as Edmund Spenser, Thomas Lodge, Thomas Kyd, and James Shirley, became well-known writers. Their verse and prose reiterated typically humanist themes such as the power of civic virtue to withstand fate and compel fortune.[21]

When Keayne became a Merchant Taylor, he entered a culture thick with symbols, rituals, and moral rhetoric. The account books, language of honor and politeness, oaths to honor fellow merchants, guildhall with its tapestries and paintings, costly feasts, pageants, military exercises, appeals to Greek and Roman texts and images, evocation of civic virtue, and the merchants' duty to London all amounted to a distinct ethos.

The discourse of humanism provided the moral template for these disparate expressions, a rationale for the various activities of Merchant Taylors. There are several ways to consider the term "humanism" in this context. It bears close affinities with the culture of the Renaissance: the production of art, patronage of scientific, technological, and geographic discovery, commerce, an exuberant consumption of worldly goods, and the profession of civic virtue. It also evokes northern European humanists of the period, who proposed that social virtue be grounded on useful, benevolent work in behalf of the commonwealth. Hostile to religious sectarianism, northern humanists wrote in pragmatic terms about the need for European states to mitigate poverty and political oppression without degenerating into chaos, and they often turned to the new middle class, including its merchants, as agents of social reform. This ideology informed the civic leaders of the seventeenth-century Netherlands. Patriotic, nationalistic, and pragmatic, Dutch magistrates favored commerce, approved of increased personal consumption of luxury goods, and ignored Calvinist clergy who complained of secularism, materialism, and selfishness.[22]

Finally, we should consider what has been called the tradition of civic humanism. This ideology combined reverence for tradition and antiquity, classical teachings on political virtue, and contemporary yearnings for a nonabsolutist frame of government. It focused especially on the notion of the nonaristocratic citizen as the strength of a republic: the private individual who regarded the commonwealth as the highest duty. During the first decades of the seventeenth century, many civic humanists also elucidated the purpose of English expansion overseas in terms of national grandeur. Jacobean humanists thus promoted colonization for the sake of profits and the kingdom's glory rather than for any explicit religious rationale. Indeed, civic humanism held no consistent metaphysical, theological, or philosophical doctrine. Although Keayne's fellow merchants did not personify the latent political radicalism of civic humanism (nor, for that matter, would they have been the heroes in its narrative), they too defined virtue as service to the civic commonwealth. They embodied an early modern form of Cicero's merchant-cum-citizen, the material provisioners for the *res publica*.[23]

The Merchant Taylors, then, reflected what we might think of as a variant of civic humanism: a discourse that legitimated commercial pursuits in civic terms. Civic-humanist merchants relayed to Keayne an enthusiasm for the production and consumption of worldly goods, tapestries and feasts included. They showed themselves as a learned profession, dependent on mathematical and scientific discoveries as well as expert in technological and military arts. They claimed to represent an ancient tradition of civic virtue that was alien to aristocratic privilege. They offered themselves as antidotes to the kingdom's contemporary social and economic ills. In England they eventually associated themselves with a statist, Arminian Anglicanism. Yet, instituting their own protocols for politeness and social exchange, they fostered a quasi-religious devotion among its members without claiming any theological creed. They defended commerce as a noble profession—the circulation of goods through society. They maintained that traders thus promoted the public weal by undertaking personal gain. Merchants were the benefactors of kings, patrons of the nation, and heroes of the city.

Civic-humanist merchants grounded their claims on a pragmatic, flexible approach to contemporary problems. From the 1580s through the 1620s, commentators noted momentous developments in the kingdom's economy: a growing population, a turn to the production of market goods such as wool and iron, an increase in the distance between sites of production and exchange, an intensified reliance on bonds, bills, and other forms of paper credit, and a sharp rise in commercial litigation. Each of these sparked moral questions. Preachers, essayists, and political advisers argued especially about the implications of new exchange practices that fell outside the bounds of customary, local prohibitions. What was usurious lending, given increasingly complicated credit networks? Was usury, indeed, illicit at all? Merchants who bought grain where plentiful, transported it to locations suffering from a dearth, and sold it at high prices did not necessarily violate local prohibitions against engrossing. Were they yet guilty of engrossing by other standards? Did enclosure fall under the category of oppression of the poor, given that new patterns of husbandry often employed the indigent? Was increasing social stratification inherently fractious and vicious, or an acceptable cost of the nation's prosperity? What *was* the commonweal, after all?[24]

Usury in particular roused heated debate and became, to some extent, *the* early modern ordeal to try one's economic morals. It represented the quintessential conflict between economic opportunity and moral custom. Observers linked it to nearly every disputable social development from enclosure (because landowners found it more profitable to sell their lands and lend cash to merchants than to receive rents) and widespread price inflation (the result of increasing the cost of investment in goods) to self-interested meanness in general (because creditors often made profits from social and economic inferiors). Critics noted usury as the bane of London, where loan brokers routinely charged as much as 30 to 50 percent on loans. Decker, the Merchant Taylors' poet laureate and dramatist, bemoaned the damage that uncontrolled usury did to merchants' reputations: "upon *Usury* hast thou," London, produced "common Theeves." Merchant Taylors' School graduate and dramatist Thomas Lodge, along with essayist Thomas Lupton, argued similarly that the traffic in usurious credit had corroded interpersonal trust between merchants.[25]

Concerns for social trust aside, most humanists judged usury on more practical criteria: its effects on the kingdom's economy. The authors of Holinshed's *Chronicles*, for example, argued during the 1570s and 1580s that the legalization of rising interest rates in combination with wage controls spelled disaster for cash-poor laborers, exacerbating poverty. Jurist Thomas Wilson and mercantile expert Gerard Malynes advised the courts of Elizabeth and James I to restrict usury for the sake of national productivity. They maintained that high interest rates encouraged landowners to invest in trade rather than agriculture, discouraged aspiring merchants from seeking loans for internal trade, and frustrated established overseas merchants, whose Dutch competitors could obtain credit at costs far below those available in England.[26]

Wilson and Malynes quoted theologians such as John Calvin and ancients such as Tacitus to charge their rhetoric, but they frankly grounded their appeals on national economic interest. They and other merchant-minded humanists from Thomas Smith in the 1560s to Thomas Mun in the 1620s defined the commonwealth in terms of economic productivity and appraised the moral problems of exchange accordingly. Malynes blunted his declamations against usury with technical analyses of different varieties of it, some less egregious than others depending on intention. In the end, he minimized the issue by contending that increased currency supplies would abate the practice quite naturally. These writers urged solutions through legal measures that could change from decade to decade depending on real economic conditions: demographic shifts, monetary supply, balance of trade, current prices. It was not a contradiction for them to urge a relaxation of usury statutes in the 1620s, indeed, to suggest that England's merchants be allowed to govern their activities by their own interests to the extent that they benefited the kingdom. Such was the pragmatism and economic realism of the merchant humanists.[27]

Robert Keayne came to New England deeply affected by his identity as a Merchant Taylor. He cherished the techniques of bookkeeping. He held separate account books for the poor fund, his shop transactions, debts owed to him (three volumes), credits paid to him, debts he owed others, an inventory of his whole estate, his dependents' money, and charges and profits from his farm. He kept, in addition, separate papers for debts due from his farmlands and from the ironworks, a book of receipts for money he had paid out, a book—"to be preserved and perused"—of his weekly expenses for food, clothing, and house maintenance, annual reviews of his personal finances, old debt books from London, several collections of paper bonds and bills, and various papers relating to his landholdings. It was not uncommon for merchants to value their books. Accounts of credit and debt were their bread and butter. Keayne nonetheless appeared to pay an unusual amount of attention to his ledgers. "As a good help hereunto," he advised his executors, "I advise that my shop books, debt books, and all my books of account may carefully be looked up, kept together and diligently perused, seeing that almost everything which belongs to my estate is by myself committed to writing in one book or another." Keayne's account books allowed him to control, through numbers, a complex set of social exchanges. No wonder they were precious to him, and a source of self-congratulation.[28]

Like other Merchant Taylors, Keayne exhibited a Renaissance admiration for worldly goods. He expressed his tastes by wearing silver lace, a gold cap, and other expensive clothes. In New England he came to hold three African slaves and to accumulate fine consumer goods such as silver plate, fancy jewelry, a library, and a watch. Had we a portrait of Keayne, it might well have presented him in fashionable and expensive dress. We do have a portrait of someone very much like Keayne, his contemporary in Boston Thomas Savage. Savage too had been a Merchant Taylor in London and had risen in the guild even higher than Keayne. Thomas Smith's painting of Savage portrays him in exquisite finery, including the accoutrements of the merchant as a military and civic leader: lace collar, elaborate sash, dress sword, and gilded cane pointing toward a background of soldiers assembled on a drill field (figure 1.2). Keayne aspired to similar prestige.[29]

Just as London's merchants advertised themselves as patriotic defenders of their city, so did Keayne. He was interested in technological advances that enhanced overseas exchange and colonial conquest: navigation, engineering, and military arts such as artillery and fortification. He and merchant colleagues such as Savage learned military skills and employed them

Figure 1.2. *Major Thomas Savage*. Oil on canvas, attributed to Thomas Smith, 1679. In the distant background, ships enter the harbor while the Massachusetts militia drills on a field. Smith portrayed Savage as a civic leader, military captain, and wealthy man of commerce. Photograph © 2010 Museum of Fine Arts, Boston.

for the colony. Keayne possessed an extraordinary amount of military equipment, including armor, two swords, and four guns. He wished in his will "to declare" his "affections" to "the society of soldiers," that is, Boston's Artillery Company, and "to be buried as a soldier in a military way." He advised Boston on armaments, training in their use ("the art of gunnery"), and the construction of battlements.[30]

Keayne also mastered the latest techniques for success in the market— the culture of calculation turned to making profits. He even displayed these

skills when discussing his bequests to the town. He provided details of
market transactions and made long-range forecasts of certain prices. He
argued, for instance, that his executors invest his donation for the education
of poor children in grain, store the grain in a magazine, sell it when prices
were high—at benchmark prices such as four hundred bushels of Indian
corn for £50—and restock the magazine when prices sank. Even small additions to the stock, he informed the executors, could add up and quickly
double its value. Keayne's further instructions also revealed the Merchant
Taylors' penchant for contracts and legal safeguards. He insisted that the
administrators of the poor fund, even if church deacons, provide some security such as a bond in case they mismanaged the account. They were to
augment its worth through prudent handling, mindful that Keayne himself
had made a more than 17 percent increase on the poor stock over the
previous two years.[31]

Many of these traits rubbed Keayne's neighbors the wrong way. Winthrop noted that Keayne carried to America a reputation for hard bargaining. In England it was rumored, certainly by fellow puritans, that he
had engaged in the "covetous practice" of charging higher prices for his
goods than did others around him. That image was not softened by the
fact that Keayne displayed a fussy, vindictive, and self-justifying temperament. He used provisions in his will to control those around him. He
hedged his gifts to Harvard College with numerous restrictions and conditions. He bound family members to a precise code of behavior lest they
forfeit their inheritance. He somewhat gleefully disinherited an ingrate
brother-in-law. He also voided a gift he had directed toward work with
Indians because one missionary, John Eliot, had contested part of the land
grant that Keayne had received in 1649.[32]

In all of this we might see a near caricature of the early modern merchant: driven by a rational and calculating approach to life and nearly autonomous in the conduct of his business. From another perspective, however, Keayne merely offered himself as a man of practical intelligence and
patriotism. John Stowe had valorized the Merchant Taylors in these very
terms. Keayne had the genius to keep accounts, work the market, and make
money. He had the generosity to give it to Boston, and the town's leaders
had the obligation to use it prudently. Keayne's beneficence spoke of the
necessity of trade, the promise of commerce, and the value of merchants
to the commonwealth.

Keayne took pride in these roles. He presented his last will and testament, alongside his building, as a monument to his worth. How else, at a
time when bequests ran to five thousand words at most, can we account
for a document of some fifty thousand words, many of which pointed to
the virtue of "me, Robert Keayne," as he identified himself at the start of
his apologia? He hoped that it would be printed so that "everyone that is

concerned in the will may have a copy of the whole by him." This omitted very few Bostonians.[33]

Boston's Town House, to return to it once again, symbolized Keayne's calling as a merchant citizen. Its central location testified to his importance to the civic community. If the town could not offer the spectacle of a Merchant Taylors pageant, then its residents could at least behold the prominently placed exchange and admire the civic-mindedness of its patron.

A cynic might read the building as a monument to profits plain and simple, but one further piece of evidence hints at the deeper cultural significance of Keayne's gift: its humanist-merchant ethos. During his first year in London, there appeared a play that might have given him the very idea for his bequest to Boston. We do not know that he saw it, but he must have heard of it. It was immensely popular, made its first appearance when Keayne had just moved to the city, and its author, Thomas Heywood, was a favorite within London's merchant community.

Heywood's play, *The Second Part of, If you know me not you know nobodie*, is a comedy about commerce, religion, and morality. Heywood modeled and named the hero of the play after Sir Thomas Gresham, who founded London's Royal Exchange in 1565 and provided the endowment for London's Gresham College. Heywood's fictional Thomas Gresham is an unusually conscientious merchant. Avaricious and ambitious businessmen, ever ready to pursue litigation in service of profits, appear at every turn. Gresham has a rather lighthearted indifference to personal gain, dislikes law courts and lawyers, freely cancels the accounts of his poorer debtors, gives alms generously, and dismisses his mercantile losses with admirable equanimity. Yet at the start of the play he is engaged in a nasty lawsuit with another merchant. Through the intervention of a local "preacher" with the title "doctor" (the appellation sounds puritan) and a merchant friend named Hobson, the suit is settled amicably. Hobson shows Gresham that one can be happy while achieving only modest means and devoting money to charitable causes. Gresham concludes that it is better to be a loser by "a thousand pound" than to tarnish a friendship; he dismisses his lawyer and concedes his claim against his former rival.[34]

All of this conversation and negotiation takes place in the open market of the Cornhill District of London. It ends with a sudden rainstorm. Prodded by the preacher, Gresham proposes then and there to fund a public building—an exchange—for merchants "and their friends." At such a building they can conduct business in a cordial atmosphere, protected from the elements and removed from the litigious ethos of the courts. When the expense of the project causes Gresham's intentions to falter, the preacher impresses on him his civic duty. He reminds him of London merchants who served the city by building churches, almshouses, and water conduits. Gresham then muses on how, in contrast, contemporary merchants neglect the poor and pursue profits without regard for the commonweal. In the end, Gresham promises to endow a city university and does indeed build an exchange, or Bourse, at Cornhill. It has a large open space underneath ("this space that hides not heaven from us," Gresham remarks), meeting rooms upstairs, and a water conduit nearby.[35]

The parallels between the Town House in Boston and Heywood's fictional exchange are striking, from the plan of the building and its meeting rooms to the mention of water conduits, gifts to a local university, almsgiving, and even the Cornhill name. Whether or not Heywood's comedy directly influenced Keayne, it reflects how Keayne might well have embraced a humanist understanding of trade and philanthropy. The virtuous merchant views business as a morally freighted exchange. He honors fellow merchants and treats them as friends rather than suing them in civil court. He does not grasp for profits with undue passion. He offers his wealth to civic causes. These codes and rules legitimated commerce as a social good and justified the businessman who pursued his material ambitions as a public servant.

It was fitting that Keayne entitled his manuscript bequest "the last will and testament of *me*, Robert Keayne" (italics added). This otherwise curious, self-referential heading—unusual for early modern bequests—recalled the title of the play, *If you know me not.* . . . The first line of Keayne's will prolonged the evocation of Gresham's world. It was as though Keayne, once "merchant tailor of London," named himself as the New England antitype of the fictional, and perhaps historical, hero. He was Boston's patron, a well-trained humanist merchant full of business acumen, piety, civic loyalty, and plans for an exchange.[36]

KEAYNE AND THE GODLY COMMUNITY IN ENGLAND

We might surmise that the Merchant Taylors' Company, with its humanistic discourse, shaped much of Keayne's moral world, especially during the last few years of his apprenticeship and entry into the company in 1615. There is evidence, however, that soon thereafter he encountered an equally influential culture. Among other clues, we know that he married the godly Anne Mansfield in 1617. From that point on, Keayne increasingly became involved in a tight-knit religious community that offered a steady dose of preaching and spiritual advice for young merchants in London. The radical Protestants, or puritans, to whom Keayne attached himself shared many of the reformist platforms of humanists, but they interpreted the market through a different conceptual frame. Unlike the Merchant Taylors and their humanist advocates, they did not define the goal of commerce as the national welfare. Nor did they legitimate a distinct language of mer-

chant decorum and honor. Fixed on biblical conventions and religious discipline, they set godliness against mundane rationales for merchant success.
They stressed obligations to the local congregation and its immediate
social context—neighbor-to neighbor-relationships—as the criteria for
economic virtue.

There were varieties of cultures that we might label puritan, from the
spiritually intense, individualist, and volatile style that came to be known
as antinomianism to the theologically eclectic or even indifferent, practical,
and family-oriented religiosity of less doctrinaire adherents. A different
version of puritanism influenced Keayne. Sometimes labeled puritan orthodoxy, it found expression in a well-defined network of like-minded English dissenters: divines such as William Perkins and William Ames, devotional writers such as Arthur Dent and Richard Rogers, influential
preachers who made the Atlantic crossing, such as John Cotton and
Thomas Hooker, and lay leaders such as John Winthrop. These sorts of
puritans, like other Protestants, believed that true Christianity involved a
deep sense of human sinfulness, the need for redemption, and the importance of personal faith in Christ. Moreover, they stressed the Bible as the
only reliable source of divine revelation, the overwhelming sovereignty of
God and his providential guidance over worldly events, and the necessity
for corporate moral discipline over individuals. They often took their cue
from the staid, socially responsible, and rigorous teaching of classical Reformers such as John Calvin and Heinrich Bullinger. In sum, they were
deeply Calvinist. They stressed collective discipline not only within the
church but also within civil society and, as a result, took responsibility for
wider political and economic affairs.[37]

The puritanism that shaped Keayne's worldview (hereafter called simply
puritanism) rivaled the culture of merchant humanism. To be sure, puritans
and humanists alike compelled merchants to view commerce within the
bounds of communal loyalty, eschew gross usury and profiteering, resist
civil litigation, and provide poor relief. Keayne's religious mentors were
much more likely than his commercial cohorts, however, to distance themselves from the business of trade, propound a distinct set of moral conventions, and issue critiques of merchants as nearly inescapably prone to avarice. They often argued that civic virtue and the national interest were
inadequate criteria for genuine moral behavior. Puritanism admittedly had
no necessary or inevitable connection to any social or economic ideology.
Yet puritan convictions encumbered the moral consciences of merchants
who otherwise might have pursued a more profitable mode of exchange
that enriched the commonwealth. Calvinist discourse produced tension in
the moral world of Keayne and his associates.

Keayne was exposed to the puritan teaching and parochial discipline that
formed an alternative to Anglican religious life. To be sure, in some areas

of the kingdom for short periods—particularly in the county of Essex and in certain London parishes—the godly settled into established patterns as Church of England clergy and laity. For the most part in London, however, they did not find permanent positions in formally recognized ecclesiastical organizations. They formed covert networks, tied together by religious conviction and kinship, geographic origin, or trade. They often met in underground conventicles to hear sermons and practice corporate disciplinary measures such as censuring wayward followers. Their most influential ministry in the city, however, took place through preaching: sermons delivered in public spaces, lectures delivered by visiting ministers, and publication of theological treatises by Cambridge divines or of devotional tracts by distinguished pastors.[38]

While moving up the economic ladder in London during the 1620s, Keayne witnessed these performances with notable enthusiasm. One of his three surviving notebooks on sermons covers a fifteen-month period from 1627 through 1628. During that time he took copious notes on seventy-eight sermons or lectures, most of them delivered in London. He heard fifty different preachers. Thirty-eight of the sermons were delivered in his London neighborhood of Cornhill. Keayne identified many of the preachers simply as "a stranger" and never mentioned his parish church, St. Michael Cornhill, which may indicate that he favored irregular preaching events. He heard godly ministers, including William Jackson and George Webbe, who made their names at high-profile venues such as the outdoor pulpit at Paul's Cross, well-published divines such as Richard Sibbes, and future elites among New England's clergy such as John Cotton, John Wilson, John Davenport, and Hugh Peter.[39]

These sermons, as Keayne summarized them, followed scriptural narrative and reiterated biblical regulation, rather than pursued a humanist, or what the godly deemed a profane, moral logic. Mainstream puritans from Perkins to Thomas Hooker contended that the Word itself, plainly explained, had the power to convey divine rules for society, convict individual consciences, and promote obedience. Keayne's notes, sometimes little more than a series of textual references with brief summaries of points, tracked preachers as they exposited the Bible. He marked off sections of each performance with citations and quotations from numerous verses. He focused on ministers' interpretation of individual texts as commands for particular social situations. By his record, New Testament precepts to care for the poor meant giving money to the needy within one's congregation. Christ's cleansing of the Temple contained a prohibition against usury or any other form of oppressive lending. Biblical injunctions against pride could be read to condemn fashionable clothing. Keayne heard exhortations from a plain exposition of the text. In this sense, his note taking inscribed an alternative to the civic humanism of merchants. As he recorded preachers' words, he participated in a different mode of social reflection.[40]

Even as Keayne took notes on sermons that became the basis for sophisticated theological works—he heard, for example, the great Cotton preach sections of what would later be printed as *The Way of Life* (London, 1641)—he focused on the interdependence between right belief and moral discipline. Many preachers in fact told him that the purpose of understanding the Bible was practice. In London he made a nearly verbatim transcription of Richard Sibbes's "Art of Contentment." Sibbes argued that bad theology, such as Arminianism, led to confused behavior. Anglicans and secular-minded humanists made poor civil rulers because they trusted only in "civill" standards for justice; they lacked the divine wisdom to do anything "well." Conversely, good theology issued in practical wisdom. "Religion" is not "speculative," Sibbes explained, "but it tends to practice"; it was "a busie trade" that issued in the daily "duties" of obedience, pity, and almsgiving.[41]

By defining "religion" as "a busie trade," Sibbes brought economic rhetoric into the scope of religious teaching. He, and the other preachers Keayne heard in London, used such tropes not to sanction new modes of exchange but to chasten them. Dissenting sermons amounted to a piece-by-piece critique of commercial practices. Puritans condemned merchants who attempted to circumvent local price regulations by buying goods where plentiful, transporting them, and selling them at a markup where there was a dearth. They criticized financiers who purchased and sold bonds or foreign notes in the emergent money market—a tactic to circumvent antiusury laws. They opposed traders who bought goods or farmers who hoarded their stores, kept them, and waited until prices rose to sell them. They scorned the use of notaries, lawyers, and brokers, whose "monstrous customes," in the words of William Jackson from Paul's Cross, made them "vermin of the earth." Just as many businessmen were turning to common-law courts to adjudicate commercial disputes, Keayne listened to Sibbes disparage civil litigation and lawyers. At a time when merchants increasingly made profits from moneylending, Keayne heard William Borough condemn the "usury" that infected the Cornhill District and tempted the well-to-do to forgo almsgiving in favor of profitable investment.[42]

Many of these critiques mirrored contemporary humanist rhetoric, but the street preachers who filled the air of Keayne's London did not display the subtlety or economic pragmatism of mercantilist thinkers. Puritan orators did not put a fine point on their critiques. They did not tolerate the theoretical justifications coming from humanist counselors to the Crown such as Francis Bacon. Nor, for that matter, did they have patience for the technical distinctions debated among learned moralists of the period. They blasted usury plain and simple, any part of it as bad as the worst, any version of it a sin.[43]

Puritans outside London made the same arguments. Dissenters as varied as Thomas Hooker, Thomas Shepard, and Richard Greenham were of one mind on this subject: wicked Dutch financiers, shifty Italian merchants, and inhumane London credit brokers tried to make a profit from credit. The godly merchant, in contrast, never made loans for a guaranteed profit, despite what humanists sometimes allowed. He might legitimately invest in trading ventures, which could be seen as putting out his credit, but that was a form of buying into the venture and risking failure along with it. Greenham, a country parson outside Cambridge, put the issue most starkly. No godly businessman could rightly conceive of making a profit from giving loans in any sense. Revered as a folk hero for his agitation on behalf of distressed farmers, Greenham even went so far as to replicate the medieval contention that usury was an alchemical ruse, the pretension that money in itself could beget more money.[44]

City preachers, however, produced the most vehement critiques. Puritan speakers at Paul's Cross, several of whom Keayne noted, linked usury to extortion (taking fees, pawns, or surety for loans), oppression (charging uncustomarily high prices), avarice, deceit, and mammonism. Usury served as a synecdoche for the abuse of nearly any form of credit. Preachers made it synonymous with oppression when goods were sold on credit at unfair prices, with rent racking when lodging was provided on credit at inflated rates, or with unfair labor practices when debtors worked off their loans at low wages. "Let biting *usurers*," William Pemberton pleaded, "become free lenders. Let blood-sucking *extortioners* become ready restorers. Let poore-murthering oppressors become comfortable helpers. Let pincing *misers* become bountifull benefactors." Such language allowed little nuance, and less ambiguity, in its condemnation of contemporary credit practices.[45]

Associating usury especially with falsehood, lying, and deceit, godly orators often described it as a complete reversal of the true meaning of commerce: communication and union within the body social. Premised on dissimulation, usury broke social bonds. Miles Mosse claimed in 1595 that "to cover their sinne, and to upholde their credite," usurers "have devised faire cloakes to shroude their ragged garments, and have begotten a more cunning, and subtile kinde of traffique in the world," so that there were "thirteine thousand devises, which men of evill conscience have invented" to practice their wicked art. It was "now one thing now another," inflated prices or unfairly low wages, high rents, or the taking of pawns, "alwaies being *usurie*, and yet never plainely appearing to be *usurie*."[46]

Some puritans raised the rhetoric even higher. Usurers so disgusted Nathanael Homes that he called them "anthropophagos," or cannibals. From distant Norwich, William Burton portrayed usury as a demonic specter, which "walketh up and down the streets" of London "like a marchantman," ready to "possess" men "in buying and selling," always "the devils huntsman." In 1627 John Grent used the Paul's Cross pulpit to summarize half a century of puritan apprehension about usury in London: "amids your great dealing, and traffique," there are "Merchants, most odious among you," that is "merchants" of *"Time,* Usurers," who personified the "deceit and misrepresentation" that threatened to undo the commonwealth. Such was "the chiefe *Symptome* of a Cities sicknesse."[47]

Puritans did not merely condemn usury per se, a position they would find increasingly difficult to maintain throughout the seventeenth century. More important, they linked an essential component of commerce—the sale of credit—inextricably to a chain of further economic vices: price gouging, rent racking, and refusal to give alms. No wonder that Keayne later reeled from the thought that he might be both "usurer" and "oppressor." Usury was the paradigmatic temptation of merchants, standing for nearly all of their crimes of greed, inhumaneness, and self-interestedness. Influenced by John Calvin, who laced his sermons with images of the vileness of usury and seductiveness of money, puritan polemicists decried fellow Protestants who fell into avarice by saying that they were as covetous as Catholics. They equally insulted Catholics by describing them as being as usurious, materialistic, and dishonest as merchants. Keayne never heard such a diagnosis from the Merchant Taylors or civic humanists, whose moderate, patriotic, pragmatic, and self-congratulatory rhetoric treated usury as a fiscal problem to be solved by monetary policy.[48]

Time and again, dissenting ministers warned that merchants were tempted to take advantage of their neighbors, forget their duty to the poor, and become self-interested. Humanist manuals described strict account keeping as a virtue; puritan preachers recast it as a disguise for inhumaneness. Puritan John Field complained in 1583 that while London's market had once been a place to exchange "earthly commodities" such as meat, grain, and metals according to God's law, it had become a place where people dealt in sheer calculation: the arithmetic world of "profit." As a result, "worldly affaires and businesse" had fallen to mere idolatry, which prompted Field to growl, "O *London* repent." The Wiltshire preacher George Webb declaimed in 1609 from the Paul's Cross pulpit that "truth has been set to sale" in the commercial precincts of "this city *London.*" Puritans often critiqued the market as being as false, disingenuous, fabricated, and socially ruinous as its cultural twin, the theater.[49]

In sum, puritan moralists gathered the chain of abuses— usury, oppression, and extortion—into a single mass of moral degeneracy: deception, hard-heartedness, and meanness. They made few allowances for the new credit measures and market strategies making their way into the merchant's manuals and humanist tracts. They drew stark dichotomies between commercial profits and Christian piety. This made it exceedingly difficult for merchants such as Keayne to move between the cultures of mercantile associations and the church. It compelled them to decipher the relative merits of prosperity and godly devotion and to negotiate, sometimes anxiously, between conflicting moral orders.

In other terms, the puritan preachers whom Keayne followed contrasted the calculating ethos of merchants with the evangelical dispositions of saints. Cotton, Wilson, and Sibbes linked self-sacrifice and a providential mind-set to proper economic behavior. Cotton warned Keayne that believers ought to trust in God's care and obey divine commands no matter how unprofitable, lest their desire for "marchandize, and profites choke" their "harts." Wilson, who delivered the sermon at the funeral of Keayne's father in England, contrasted those who trusted in divine purposes to those always on the alert to enhance their own estates. Only humble, self-effacing merchants could enter the hustle and bustle of London's commercial society and be protected from undue grief and worldly temptation. True contentment, Sibbes preached, resided in the knowledge that economic misfortunes were divine reproofs to strengthen the soul and wean it from material affections. They were not arbitrary disasters to be avoided at all costs and resented when inescapable. These preachers stressed humility, trust, self-denial, charity, and contentment as the prime economic virtues. Their catalog of antithetical vices—pride, calculation, self-assertion, selfishness, and ambition—recommended neither the elaborate display of the Merchant Taylors nor the more subtle ethos of self-promotion among England's humanist merchants.[50]

Keayne first encountered godly sermons through his association with a network of dissenters who would become the core of New England's early leadership. Besides Cotton, his most influential spiritual mentors were Wilson and Winthrop. They learned the meaning of godliness through their acquaintance with a remarkable cluster of puritans in East Anglia, particularly Essex County, England: Arthur Dent, Richard Rogers, George Gifford, Stephen Marshall, John Knewstub, and Thomas Carew. These pastors shared a vast correspondence, preached in each other's parishes, and published lectures and devotional tracts long favored by puritans in Old and New England. Noted for their intense efforts to reform society on a local level, they relentlessly critiqued new economic practices. Nearly to a man, they preached against rising interest rates, inflated prices, enclosure, and the investment of excess capital in distant trade rather than local almsgiving. They expelled profiteers from their congregations, hounded usurers out of their parishes, turned common fields to poor relief, authored town covenants that set limits to prices on common goods and services, and insisted that their well-to-do parishioners provide easy, even free, credit to the needy. Theirs was a conservative economic program with a vengeance.[51]

Beneath their specific recommendations, puritan ministers modeled for their lay followers the importance of turning to the Bible for moral guidance. Whereas merchant-minded humanists drew on Stoic moralists, Roman historians, and contemporary iterations of civic virtue, preachers propounded a scriptural discourse peculiar to the saints. They instructed the laity to read the Bible daily; it would be difficult to identify a more "popular" form of literature in this sense. East Anglian puritans favored the Geneva Bible, a translation with copious marginal notes made by dissenters under Calvin's sway. The Geneva Bible provided a running commentary on social issues. Like puritan sermons and lectures, it decoded ancient commandments to reveal a critique of new exchange methods. The editors expanded on Old Testament prohibitions against usury, for example, by noting that the slight allowance for the practice in Deuteronomy 23:20, when Israelites made loans to foreigners, "was permitted for a time for the hardness of their heart" but was not proper for contemporary society. Psalm 15:5 promised, in their rather innovative reading, that the one who "giveth not his money unto usurie" would be spared excommunication from "the Church."[52]

The Bible was one subject for pious reading; other forms of popular devotional literature also circulated among Keayne's coreligionists. Spiritual writers urged a daily discipline of self-denial and economic moderation. Keayne read frequently in such literature, cherishing in particular a pamphlet on the Lord's Supper, upon which he meditated in his prayer "closet." John Dod's *Plaine and Familiar Exposition of the Ten Commandments* (London, 1603) set the model for other spiritual writers. Dod contrasted godly walkers—who trusted providence to such an extent that they were nearly indifferent to worldly gain and were joyful as a result—with worldly people made anxious and despairing by an unremitting search for riches. Merchants who endlessly strove to enhance their business, lived for their books, or continually calculated the future of their trade fell under Dod's censure. His saints cared more for joy, love, humility, and charity toward neighbor than for their accounts.[53]

The most frequently published and widely read manuals emphasized the moral importance of the believer's confidence in divine control over temporal events. Lewis Bayly's *Practice of Piety* (London, 1612?), which went through sixty editions in the seventeenth century, Arthur Dent's *Plaine Man's Path-way to Heaven* (London, 1601), and the immensely popular work authored by John Wilson's teacher Richard Rogers, *Seven Treatises* (London, 1603): they all applied the doctrine of providence to daily practice. According to these works, reliance on economic calculation and trust in providence were morally incompatible dispositions. Rather than invest their excess capital in ventures as a matter of course or, worse, spend it on unnecessary consumer goods, providentially minded merchants provided alms on the spot to neighbors in need. As Bayly put it, the one who relied on divine provision performed acts of charity that cut against mere calculation: "*forgiving Wrongs, remitting Debts* to" those "unable to pay . . . *giving Alms* to the Poor." Bayly also urged merchants to examine their conscience, lest "under pretence of" their "Calling and Office" they had "robbed and purloined" their neighbors by "*Oppression, Extortion,*" and "other *indirect dealings.*"[54]

The rhetoric of spiritual manuals and catechisms, as well as of sermons, reinforced puritan suspicions that merchants often disregarded scriptural rules for commerce. In his *Godly Prayers and Meditations* (London, 1583), John Field taught families to pray together using the Ten Commandments. When he came to the eighth commandment, against stealing, he composed petitions that God would keep them from commercial deceit, engrossing, forestalling, and general selfishness. Edward Dering's numerous catechisms for puritan families (1575–1583) issued nearly identical warnings against the temptations of the market. John Mayer's *English Catechisme* (London, 1621) instructed puritan families on the social ills of the day: usury, rent racking, oppression, enclosure, inflated prices, and merciless creditors. It advised its young readers against financial ambition. They were to "be content with a moderate gain." Should any of them become merchants, Mayer continued, they were to set their prices to yield a minimal profit: they were, against natural instinct and professional training, to "sell for an indifferent gaine." *The English Catechisme*, in sum, promoted neighborly affection in contrast to "this world," where "love . . . is waxen cold all over."[55]

Similar social critiques came through an even cheaper and more widely diffused form of literature: religious chapbooks, broadsides, martyrologies, and news ballads. Widely consumed by the godly, they shaped common perceptions of providence, morality, and commerce. Works such as Thomas Beard's *Theatre of Gods judgements* (London, 1597; with several editions through 1631) and John Reynolds's *Triumph of Gods revenge* (London, 1621, with more editions through 1635) promised their readers that God would punish economic oppression and injustice. They related often gruesome tales of divine revenge. Disfiguring and painful diseases, suicidal melancholy, violent accidents, and stunning financial calamities fell on profiteering shopkeepers, merciless employers, rich misers, grain hoarders, common-field enclosers, rent-racking landlords, and ambitious merchants. Few of the standards in this genre failed to include self-interested traders, usurers, oppressors, and engrossers in their catalog of sinners who were to suffer the most excruciating judgments in the afterlife as well.[56]

When Robert Keayne joined the circle of puritans who produced and consumed these works, he was exposed to vivid imagery that contrasted godly humility with commercial aspiration: a near antithesis to the humanist celebration of the virtue and honor of merchants. Had his favorite preachers and spiritual counselors witnessed Thomas Heywood's play de-

scribed earlier, they would have disapproved because they would have detected a confusion of moral priorities. In the comedy, Gresham finally deserves admiration because he serves London. His pastor-adviser functions
in the end as a prop to lead the merchant to civil obligations. As much as
puritans would have joined in Heywood's critique of self-serving, litigious,
and usurious modes of exchange, they would have denied the implication
that civic virtue or the national interest eclipsed more transcendent criteria
for economic behavior. They understood commerce to be merely a vehicle
for a form of godliness that sacrificed financial success—even if profits
prospered the civil order—for the sake of obedience to God's word and
charity to one's neighbor.

Puritan devotional language helped to produce a culture in competition
with the pragmatic humanism of the Merchant Taylors' Company. Renaissance humanists and Reformed moralists, to be sure, shared many agendas,
particularly in the sixteenth century. Early Cambridge dissenters such as
Lawrence Chaderton, the mentor of a generation of divines and devotional
writers, adopted the eclectic, practical, and reformist ethics of Erasmus. By
the early seventeenth century, however, this alliance had become strained.
In the Netherlands civic-minded magistrates viewed commerce as a means
of national prosperity. They dismissed the moral exhortations of Calvinist
clergy, which they deemed worrisome, ascetic, and uncivil. In England humanist writers and political advisers likewise became impatient with the
biblical literalism and moral absolutism of godly preachers. Playwrights
such as Thomas Kyd, a graduate of the Merchant Taylors' School, often
portrayed puritans as unrealistic fuss budgets, while they implored merchants to assume their duties as the new patrons of honor, civility, and
prosperity.[57]

Keayne's contemporaries did not use the terms "puritan" and "humanist" precisely in the way employed here, but they nonetheless recognized
that these two conceptual frameworks, although overlapping, often implied
incompatible moral perspectives. The Merchant Taylors of London came
to view godly teaching as a burden on their affairs. During the late sixteenth
century many of the leaders of the company were religious radicals. They
had close connections to the city's puritan leadership, banned plays in the
company's grammar school, displayed a Geneva Bible in the guildhall, and
nearly severed relations with St. John's College, which was founded with
Merchant Taylors' money and had become a den of crypto-Catholicism.
During the 1620s the company reversed its orientation. Seeking royal preferment, trustees of the grammar school appointed nonpuritan headmas-
ters, and the company reestablished friendly ties with St. John's. The Merchant Taylors became known not only as patrons of the Crown but also as
strong supporters of the archenemy of puritans, Archbishop William Laud.

Economic pragmatism, implicit in humanist perspectives of the period, trumped previous religious affiliations.[58]

We might speculate that these developments in the Merchant Taylors disaffected Keayne and provoked in part his immigration to New England. He had, by John Winthrop's account, "come over" to Boston "for conscience sake," and the antipuritan turn of the Merchant Taylors may have contributed to his uneasy "conscience."[59] This is not to say that Keayne rejected his merchant training and the humanist social ethos. He continued to believe that in New England they could be integrated into a godly worldview—that he could work for profits, the common good, and piety together. The Town House, to return to our opening, embodied the possibility that merchant culture might coexist with godly sensibilities under the rubric of a puritan order.

Yet Keayne's Town House might also be read as an architectural apologia in the face of persistent critique—an attempt to overcome other puritans' ambivalence and even anxiety about the conjunction of profits and piety. Keayne discovered in New England that many religious leaders never thought merchant culture was anything but a rival to godliness. Like their English predecessors such as Sibbes and Bayly, they suspected that merchants all too easily jettisoned biblical rules in favor of a merely civil wisdom. Keayne's closest spiritual mentors in Boston—including John Cotton and John Winthrop—determined to institute corporate moral discipline over commerce. The form and content of their disciplinary measures occupy the next chapter in the study of godliness and commerce in early New England.

Chapter Two

ROBERT KEAYNE'S TRIALS

Soon after Robert Keayne appeared before the General Court of Massachusetts in November 1639, Governor John Winthrop wrote a lengthy journal entry about him. He pondered the charges of oppression, Keayne's self-defense, and the guilty verdict. Why had the court judged the merchant's practices not merely illegal but also "very evil"? Why had it assessed such a large fine? Keayne, Winthrop explained, was reputed to be "an ancient professor of the gospel" with high social standing. He could claim neither ignorance nor low social status as an excuse. Furthermore, "private friends," civil "magistrates," and church "elders" previously had "admonished" him against profiteering. Being "wealthy," he had no pressing need. Despite all of this, he had disgraced New England before the "curious observation of all churches and civil states in the world."[1]

How had such a man fallen? Winthrop suggested that Keayne had been "misled by some false principles." Keayne rationalized his behavior by claiming that merchants in London and Boston commonly raised the prices of one set of commodities beyond their going rate in order to recoup losses from disasters at sea, miscalculations in the worth of goods, or bad deals. It was "the common practice in all countries," Winthrop observed, for merchants to reach for any possible "excuse" to inflate "the prices of their commodities." Keayne ought to have held to a different rule.[2]

Shortly after his civil trial, Keayne appeared before a disciplinary proceeding at Boston's First Church. Facing severe scrutiny, he mourned his covetousness yet defended himself. He repeated his previous claim: the best merchants now priced their wares by the same technique that he used. The next day Pastor John Cotton confronted Keayne's "false principles" head on by preaching a primer on commerce. He argued that Scripture condemned merchants who set their rates merely to maximize profits, "that a man might sell as dear as he can, and buy as cheap as he can." The Bible also censured the practice of raising prices to offset the costs of other ventures. Bad business deals or accidental losses ought to occasion trust, submission, and humility, not entrepreneurial innovations roused by anxiety, because they were "cast upon" traders "by providence." Merchants should set their prices according to local custom and the intrinsic value of their goods, regardless of temporary market conditions. Cotton also took the opportunity to blast usury, contending that merchants always sinned by charging interest or fees on any loans.[3]

Following Cotton's analysis, the First Church formally censured Keayne, a punishment falling just short of excommunication. The task was so somber that the government called for a public fast that day. It lamented the merchant's "excessive Rates" as a "Dishonor of Gods Name," an "Offence of the Generall Court," and the "Publique Scandall of the Cuntry."[4] Still agitated by the affair some three weeks later, Cotton continued to preach on trade. In one biting sermon, he discoursed on Judas Iscariot, who sold out Jesus for the lucre of "oppression . . . unlawfully gotten." According to Cotton, Judas feigned remorse and died a self-justifying, hypocritical "reprobate." As was his habit, Keayne took detailed notes on Cotton's sermon. He hardly could have missed the implication. Cotton's references to oppression and unlawful gain, vain gestures of remorse, self-justifications, and avarice fingered Keayne as Boston's Judas.[5]

Keayne had come to New England as a Merchant Taylor and a professor of godliness. He thought that he could pursue his profits according to the protocols of his merchant associations, obey his puritan conscience as much as possible, work out a pragmatic compromise day to day between business and piety, and serve the commonweal. He could belong to two moral communities at once —defined by the civic humanism of merchants and orthodox puritan piety—and be subject to both. His apologia consisted of one long argument to that effect.

Winthrop and Cotton disapproved. By their lights, a fundamental error explained the merchant's accounting procedures, credit rates, and price margins. He had confused his loyalties and betrayed—again, Cotton's evocation of Judas—his commitment to Christ's church. He subjected himself to the codes of fellow merchants when godly elders and pastors had taught him different rules. Scripture prompted trust in providence, concern for neighbor in the most immediate sense, and deference to the local church. The ethos of merchant communities, with their calculations of long-range profits and losses, nationalist agendas, and indifference to the daily needs of neighbors, contradicted puritan teaching and challenged the authority of the First Church of Boston.[6]

This was no clash in absolute terms between religion and commerce, piety and prosperity, spiritual devotion and material ambition. Like other leaders of the Great Migration, Winthrop and Cotton hardly opposed merchants and profits per se. Winthrop especially realized their importance to New England. The issue between Keayne and his critics concerned the ultimate authority over trade and a contest between communities that claimed to regulate merchants' activities. In London this rivalry pitted professional associations such as the Merchant Taylors' Company, commercial networks, and royal advisers on economic policy against puritan preachers, authors of devotional tracts, and ministers who waged the occasional, localized campaign against usury and oppression. In Boston it pitted aspiring entrepreneurs and import traders with ties to London against pastors, their congregations, and many of the colony's civil rulers and magistrates.

Unlike their fellow reformers at home, however, puritans in New England grasped the opportunity to institute and normalize their claims over merchants. From the 1630s through the 1650s, they attempted, through the preaching and oversight of a regular ministry, formal and public church trials, church synods, and even civil law, to hold businessmen accountable to Christian teaching. They hoped to accomplish what the Church of England had failed to do in the Old World: promote religious discipline over commerce. Robert Keayne's trials were certainly remarkable but not unique. They exemplified a long-standing puritan campaign to compel merchants to practice trade by the rules of godliness.

Boston's First Merchants

The following discussion of that campaign returns frequently to Keayne, an important figure and touch point, but the contest between merchant communities and religious discipline played itself out far beyond him. He joined a prominent group of immigrant traders who maintained their collective identity and loyalties even apart from the guilds and companies prevalent in England. They formed a community in and around Boston, bound together by a nexus of cultural styles, common interests, professional associations, and commercial agendas. New England, to be sure, included other commercial types. Fish exporters from the West Country in England established isolated outposts in Maine; fur traders often moved upriver (north and west) in search of pelts; small shopkeepers operated in every town; and a variety of inland traders did business in villages and bare settlements.

Keayne belonged to yet another group: import merchants who maintained regular ties with London and exchanged an expansive array of goods with customers and suppliers in England, the Canary Islands, and the West Indies. Within the scope of English trade as a whole, they comprised a middling sort. They did not rise to the level of London's Merchant Adventurers, who dominated trade in the metropolis through the early seventeenth century. Early Bostonians never built the far-flung trading empires and massive wealth of England's new overseas merchants such as shipowning partners in the East India Company. Yet they achieved far more success than the peddlers, shopkeepers, and artisans who sold their wares in market stalls. In England, Keayne and his associates would have settled in the in-between company of well-to-do retailers, urban merchants, and provincial magnates.[7]

Boston's importers were the most visible, successful, and politically prominent merchants in New England, and they quickly established themselves as a like-minded coterie in the 1630s. A well-defined cadre of about twenty in the early years, they included Keayne, Thomas Savage, John Coggeshall, Edward Tyng, Richard Bellingham, Peter Oliver, Henry Shrimpton, Edward Hutchinson, and William Alford. They built Boston's most fashionable houses and did so in the same neighborhood. Keayne, Tyng, Hutchinson, and Coggeshall lived next to each other. They named streets after the lanes in London where they had begun their trade. They opened shops in the same vicinity, funded the wharves and storehouses that shaped the topography of Boston's waterfront, congregated in the market square, and eventually built Keayne's Town House.[8]

As they established their businesses during the 1630s and expanded them during the 1640s, these merchants operated in a social sphere defined by their commercial partners: the collection of contacts, agents, correspondents, factors, friends, and family members engaged in trade. Although they briefly considered the formation of a guildlike company, their English creditors and suppliers obliged them to deal through previously established ties and company associations. Shrimpton and Hutchinson, among others, used cousins and brothers as agents, creditors, and suppliers in London. Keayne eventually used his son Benjamin, who set up a trading house in London's Birchin Lane. In addition, Keayne drew on his contacts in the Merchant Taylors' Company, as did Savage. Tyng and Alford also relied on acquaintances from merchant companies in England. Keayne and his associates lived in the interlocking networks defined by overseas commerce.[9]

Overseas traders quickly assumed leading positions in Boston's public affairs. In 1638 twelve merchants, led by Keayne, organized the first regular militia in Massachusetts. Nearly all of Boston's import merchants joined this Ancient and Honorable Artillery Company; membership signaled good standing in the trading community. As an organization devoted to soldierly discipline, public defense, and municipal duty, the Artillery Company allowed them to express their common identity as virtuous citizens. So too did the local government. Merchants used frequent election to local and colony-wide office to create or improve avenues for commerce. They promoted the construction of roads and bridges, legalized trading arrangements with Indians and European clients, and sponsored military defenses. This all amounted to a New England version of what Keayne had found in the Merchant Taylors' Company of London: a community of merchants who promoted themselves, in civic-humanist fashion, as the economic and military patrons of the commonweal.[10]

Colonial politics reinforced their common ethos. They aspired to compete in the Atlantic market, which thrust them into legal debates about price and wage controls, interest rates, monopolies, litigation, and trading with New England's putative enemies. In England many puritan merchants of the 1630s advocated what they called "free trade," by which they meant the elimination of royal and parliamentary policies that favored the Merchant Adventurers and sanctioned monopolies. In New England men such as Keayne wanted free trade in the sense of the liberty to use the innovative means employed by their English and Dutch rivals: new forms of negotiable paper such as bills of exchange and bonds, accounting measures that factored changing interest rates and currency values, rapid communication through the best-placed brokers and agents, speedy resolution of commercial disputes in specialized courts, and constant adjustment of prices according to market conditions.[11]

These agendas often set Boston's importers at odds with religious leaders and yeoman farmers who valued local restraints on exchange. Fluctuations in the economy called for constant legislation, especially during the first two decades of settlement in the Bay Colony. During the 1630s a rapid influx of new settlers increased demands for goods and pushed prices and wages upward. The General Court enacted colony-wide price and wage limits in 1634, rescinded them a year later, then compelled the towns to enact their own limits. Decreased immigration and scarcity of capital (cash and bills of exchange carried over from England) sank consumer demand in the early 1640s.[12] Farmer debtors, unable to market their goods and often in arrears to merchants, defaulted on loans. This economic depression provoked a remarkable series of legislative acts. From 1640 to 1642 the court protected debtors from foreclosure by demanding that creditors accept goods in kind as payment for debts and by restricting interest rates. It also passed several laws that limited the movement of foreign traders within the colony.[13]

Import merchants protested and sometimes skirted these policies at nearly every step. Gaining political strength after 1642, they persuaded the General Court to lift an 8 percent ceiling on interest rates for bills of exchange. They agitated for an open policy on trade, arguing that Boston's port ought to receive all potential business partners. They eventually prodded the government to create a separate inferior court in Boston to deal with credit and trade litigation. Keayne and Tyng joined five other merchants as the only judges when the court first met in 1651.[14]

Boston's merchants gradually pulled themselves out of the doldrums of the early 1640s by supplying London importers with fish and timber and establishing ties with English and Spanish dealers in the Canary Islands, who sold wine and sugar. In 1645 Bostonians began to export beef to Barbados. In the 1650s they shipped immense quantities of naval stores, such as

pitch, tar, and wood, to the parliamentary navy. By the early 1650s, men
such as Robert Keayne had established regular lines of business to different
regions in the British Atlantic. They built or bought into ships, sold cattle
and horses to the West Indies, received cotton and sugar in return, and
sent those commodities directly to London for credit. They purchased
cloth and utensils from London agents, which they imported and sold to
shopkeepers and inland traders at the Boston exchange.[15]

Many merchants set themselves apart from other New Englanders not
only by their social and political agendas but also by a distinct religious
ethos. They shared an affinity for radical versions of puritan teaching on
grace and spiritual experience: what their opponents derided as antinomian
deviations. English critics branded them with names such as Antinomians,
Familists, Seekers, and Anabaptists. New England critics also referred to
separatists, spiritists, and millenarians. The term "antinomian" covered a
broad, even diffuse range of ideas and practices.[16]

Despite such variety, antinomians shared this common impulse: dissent
from the moral authority of established puritan congregations and customary Christian instruction on social duties. During the so-called antinomian
controversy of 1636 through 1638, several pastors in Massachusetts, led by
Thomas Shepard of Cambridge, charged lay teacher Anne Hutchinson and
her brother-in-law, the Reverend John Wheelwright, with promulgating
false doctrine and sedition. In the course of the crisis, many merchant sym-
pathizers with Hutchinson signed a petition urging the General Court to
leniency, a tactic that affronted several of its members. The court named
some fifty-eight adult males in Boston, or about one-sixth of all adult males
in the town, to be admonished and disarmed for holding antinomian views.
It expelled Wheelwright from the colony and mandated a strict review of
all strangers admitted into the colony. Notwithstanding the popular resentment of some merchants against these measures, and the fact that Cotton's
teaching initially had inspired Hutchinson, the orthodox party refused to
tolerate dissent. The court banished her. Cotton distanced himself from
all antinomian ideas.[17]

Winthrop's account of a 1637 synod in Cambridge, listing some ninety
antinomian "errors," captured the orthodox critique. According to the official record, the radicals denigrated the worth of the Old Testament law.
They refused to admit that God's moral commands prepared people for
faith. They denied that lived holiness—what Reformers called sanctification—evidenced regeneration. They furthermore disregarded the orthodox claim that individuals should manifest faith by good behavior and submission to corporate discipline. Hutchinson's followers relied on the
immediate witness of the Holy Spirit and personal, private revelations,
rather than on obedience to scriptural rules, to assure themselves of salvation. They renounced any congregation where disciplinary practices vio-

lated their private consciences and accused pastors such as John Wilson with godless moralism. They claimed, as individuals, to possess spiritual knowledge, including insight into Scripture, apart from and even in contrast to customary social teaching and church oversight. Antinomian perceptions of grace trumped the standards of the community.[18]

Members of the synod and other critics often noted a powerful confluence of antinomian dissent and mercantile interests. More than half of Boston's merchants associated themselves with Hutchinson's cause, and nearly every import trader in the first generation, except for Keayne, tended to antinomian sympathies. Hutchinson's husband (Edward), son, and brother-in-law were overseas importers. Oliver, Coggeshall, William Coddington, William Aspinwall, and William Brenton—all prominent in the Boston exchange—gathered in the Hutchinson home to hear Anne teach. They all left the Bay Colony as antinomian exiles. Authorities disarmed Savage for his connections—he was Hutchinson's son-in-law—and he departed for Rhode Island. The merchant-antinomian network extended beyond Boston too, including William Jennison of Watertown, Edward Gibbons of Charlestown, and Thomas Hawkins of Dorchester.[19]

Broadly conceived, deviations from the puritan order reinforced the cohesion of merchants in the Artillery Company, where military prowess, commercial aspirations, civic humanism, and dissent from puritanism flowed together. Nearly half of the company's founders were outright antinomians, Anabaptists, or advocates for toleration of radical views in Massachusetts. John Underhill, perhaps the most extravagant of the lot, pursued commercial schemes in northern New England, proposed military campaigns to defend and extend New England's borders, boasted of civic honor and English patriotism, and repeatedly denied the right of New England's churches to censure him or his subordinates. Winthrop and his associates took a conservative stance toward commercial and military ventures, nearly isolationist in some cases. Many erstwhile overseas merchants and aspiring traders in the Artillery Company envisioned instead a dynamic offensive against Catholic trade and territory. Among others, John Leverett, Robert Sedgwick, and Nehemiah Bourne campaigned for the northward expansion of New England's borders and for the colonization of Long Island and Elutheria in the West Indies.[20]

Antinomianism appeared at least congruent with, if not a justification for, quite unlocal loyalties, a rejection of the puritan congregation in favor of a geographically expansive community bound together by trade and designs for the English empire. The orthodox lumped the Boston radicals and other dissenters together into a single religious style: heretical, deviant, immoral, and commercial. Winthrop believed that Hutchinson's followers sought nothing more than free rein for their spiritual pride and material greed. He contrasted those who succumbed to doctrinal error and grew "suddenly riche" to faithful businessmen who avoided antinomian errors and refused to deal with dissenters and other "profane scoffers." He viewed the West Indies and the northern New England frontier as coverts for free-spirited traders to luxuriate in antinomian ideas. Winthrop and Shepard also contemplated the fearsome parallels between New England dissenters and the followers of Roger Brierly from Yorkshire, or Grindeltonians, who eschewed all forms of moral discipline, and Dutch Anabaptists, who appeared capable of justifying the most excessive mercantile practices with the weirdest theologies. The General Court of Massachusetts encoded this perspective in a 1639 law that forbade "oppression, atheisme, excesse, superfluity, idleness, [and] contempt of authority" in one sweeping clause.[21]

Critics' elision between merchants and antinomianism developed into a rhetorical reflex. In his introduction to Winthrop's history of the antinomian controversy, Thomas Weld pictured the Hutchinsonians as merchants who sought to market "their Commodities" and "freely vent their" heretical "wares" to unsuspecting customers. Peter Bulkeley followed suit, inscribing new commercial, cosmopolitan, and consumer sensibilities into his narrative of the crisis: antinomians were "itching to be fed with, and to be venting novelties," a people "always new-fangled, running after new fashions, taking up with the fashions of every Nation." John Wheelwright's fulminations against puritan teaching warranted his banishment, Winthrop wrote, because his ideas tore at the fabric of common morality, justified a "corrupt conscience," and endangered proper, charitable modes of "trade" in the local community and overseas. Thomas Shepard, the most vehement opponent of Hutchinson, critiqued the radicals of the 1630s for subjecting truth to the going "market" price for ideas and promoting the telltale vices of merchants: "cheating" and "oppression."[22]

New England's leaders had come face to face not only with the persistence of civic-humanist assumptions in Boston's commercial community but also with dissent from within puritanism itself—a spiritual dissent that sharpened the rivalry between commercial groups and the church. Merchants confirmed their disrepute among conservatives when they petitioned Parliament for religious toleration and proposed a relaxation of the strict residency requirements enacted during the antinomian controversy. Puritan opponents read the protoleration arguments as a repudiation of godly doctrine in favor of merely civil logic: appeals to English rights, civil liberties, and the pragmatic benefits of trade for the commonwealth.

Lesser puritan lights made that judgment as well. In his 1654 *Wonder-working Providence*, Edward Johnson—a companion of Winthrop, a surveyor, and the founder of Woburn—condemned merchants, antinomians, toleration, and secular political reasoning all at once.[23] According to his rambling and fanciful retrospective, Boston had epitomized an awe-inspiring transformation from isolation and poverty to human concourse and economic productivity. He celebrated the town, "the very Mart of the Land," as an entrepôt for goods flowing from New England to Virginia and the West Indies. Yet he observed that "traffique" in New England had fallen on hard times after a successful start. Decreased immigration, scarcity of money, depressed prices, shipwrecks, piracy, and Indian wars had made "Merchants and traders themselves sensible of the hand of the Lord against them." Johnson recounted how Boston's traders had invited antinomians, Anglicans, and other enemies of the puritan way to reside in New England in order to increase opportunities for trade. They "would willingly have had the Commonwealth tolerate divers kinds of sinful opinions" for the worst of reasons, "that their purses might be filled with coyn." No wonder, he concluded, that "the Lord was pleased" to "let in the King of Terrors among his newplanted Churches." Antinomian and humanist merchants had provoked divine punishment.[24]

Nathaniel Ward, friend and distant relative of Winthrop, lawyer in England, sometime chaplain to the English mercantile community in Prussia, and pastor in Agawam (Ipswich), denigrated the ideology of toleration as mere civic humanism. In his 1641 election sermon for Massachusetts, Ward pitted the civic principles of "the old Roman and Grecian government," the "rules of government" held by "heathen commonwealths" and in vogue among English humanists, "which sure is an error," against "religion and the word of God," by which "we may better frame rules of government to ourselves." In his popular, widely printed, and scatological critique of toleration, *The Simple Cobler of Aggawam*, Ward blasted the antinomian-mercantile-tolerationist-humanist nexus. Civic values centered on the commonwealth and economic pragmatism—what he called "State-pretences and planting necessities"—rather than good old New England piety bred demands for "lax Toleration." Ward would have all "Antinomians, Anabaptists, and other Enthusiasts" know that they had "free Liberty" only "to keep away from us." Their settlement, he claimed, subjected New England to the same immorality that ruined the mercantile-humanist states of Venice and the Netherlands. More pointedly, religious toleration for the sake of commercial opportunity made a bad bargain: a devaluation of the "Truth of God at such a rate." Like Winthrop, Shepard, and Bulkeley, Ward conjured an antinomian-commercial alliance founded on purely pragmatic justifications.[25]

From the perspective of Winthrop and Cotton, Johnson and Ward, antinomianism attracted merchants because it sanctioned independence from the church. Although it implied no single economic ideology, it reinforced or, worse, condoned merchants' proclivities to follow their own regulations and rules. It provided a presumption of moral community, even purpose, among men who did business apart from godly discipline—who identified more readily with an extended society of long-distance traders, military adventurers, and geographically mobile men than with the local Christian community. It allowed merchants to neglect customary puritan restrictions on commerce while claiming grace and spiritual insight.[26]

Antinomianism, to view it another way, resonated with civic humanism. Hutchinsonians claimed to have a secret knowledge that superseded orthodox doctrine. They elevated interior claims to grace above the demands of church discipline. Without sharing radical doctrine, humanist writers on commerce likewise divorced their peculiar insights from religious supervision. They maintained that colonial merchants could pursue their vocation as an act of virtue apart from clerical and particularly Calvinist regulation. They promoted colonization in the New World as a state venture legitimated by classical, civic values and performed according to specialized knowledge. The pronouncements of divines, the humanist Malynes emphasized, "can give but little satisfaction to instruct Merchants" because commercial exchange depended on technical expertise: forecasting market prices, anticipating fluctuations in currency values, accounting for long-term debts and credits. Commercial competition did not warrant, in Malynes' opinion, gross avarice, fraud, or other illegal dealings, but it did compel merchants to conduct themselves according to their own professional standards. There was no rationale for merchants to subject themselves to interference by ministers who naively denounced usury and large profit margins wholesale. When antinomians resisted orthodox intrusion into their affairs, they tacitly promoted Malynes' line of thinking. In this respect, antinomianism and humanism together reinforced an ethos among Boston's merchants of dissent from corporate religious discipline.[27]

Other deviations from puritanism, combined with civic-humanist impulses, also hardened the resistance of merchants such as William Pynchon. A major investor and luminary in the Massachusetts Bay Company, Pynchon immigrated to the colony with Winthrop in 1630. After brief stays in Dorchester and Roxbury, where he became a magistrate and treasurer for the colony, he emerged as the region's most prolific fur trader, making contacts with English trappers and Indian suppliers to the north and west and selling pelts through his agents in England. He eventually established himself as local overlord in Agawam (Springfield), in the Connecticut River Valley. He owned cattle and vast tracts of land; employed fur traders, agents, transporters, and other laborers in the family business; and served as sole magistrate, head of the militia, and moderator of town meetings. Like other rich merchants, he viewed himself as a civic leader. Besides occupying the most important public and military offices, he patronized the town's public projects and paid for its church.[28]

Despite his beneficence, Pynchon ran afoul of civil and ecclesiastical authorities. They accused him of paying low wages, charging high prices, and monopolizing trade. In 1638 the General Court of Connecticut, which at the time claimed jurisdiction over Agawam, charged him with another crime. The colony had deputized him to procure corn from local Indian tribes for downriver towns and fined him for malfeasance when he failed to do so. In a lengthy trial that foreshadowed Keayne's ordeal the following year in Boston, the court called the ministers of the church in Hartford, Samuel Stone and the eminent Thomas Hooker, as witnesses. Hooker claimed that Pynchon foiled the deal so that he could buy corn for himself, hoard it, sell it during times of scarcity at inflated prices, and so "rack the country at his pleasure," sins otherwise known as engrossing, regrating, or forestalling.[29]

Like Keayne, Pynchon wrote an "Apology," a self-defense of his conduct that portrayed his critics as ignorant in the techniques of trade. Pynchon argued that negotiations with the Indians fell through because the court offered too low a price for the corn. He used the occasion, moreover, to accuse puritan leaders of violating his rights as an English merchant. Portraying himself in humanist fashion as upholder of the conjoined virtues of what he called "the public good and the liberty of a free man," he appealed to English freedoms, commercial custom, and the prosperity of the commonweal. After repeated harassment by Hartford ministers, he oversaw the incorporation of Agawam into Massachusetts under the new name of Springfield.[30]

Springfield soon developed a reputation as an unruly place where settlers with nonpuritan sensibilities could make a quick killing in trade.[31] For his part, Pynchon began to denounce openly the puritan order in the Bay Colony. In 1646 he signed the Remonstrance of Robert Childe and Thomas Fowle, a petition against the colony's requirement of full church membership for freeman status and the disciplinary regimes of puritan churches. In a related letter to Winthrop, Pynchon defended the Remonstrance in antinomian-sounding terms. The "certaine fourme of discipline" currently in effect, he wrote, not only contravened English rights but also allowed "a could [cold] spirit"—moralism and legalism—to "rule in ministers."[32]

In the details of his theology, Pynchon did not embrace the spiritual intensity, primacy of supernatural grace, and immediate revelations of the Boston antinomians. He leaned toward latitudinarian, semirationalist ideas. In *The Meritorious Price of Our Redemption* (London, 1650), he jettisoned orthodox essentials such as the divinity of Christ and the substitutionary theory of the atonement, which held that Christ suffered as a payment for the sins of humanity. Yet, established pastors such as Cotton and Wilson detected a similarity between his ideas and Hutchinson's. They described his book in the same terms as they had her teachings: an "Innovation," full of "Errours and Heresies" and "Exorbitant Abberations." They had some reason to assert this otherwise odd association between Pynchon and antinomians. He too rejected puritan claims to regulate social behavior and justified his dissent with unorthodox arguments about the superiority of private religious knowledge to clerical doctrine. Pynchon authored his "errors" along with arguments for toleration and the independence of commercial men from the church. As if to certify this convergence between heresy and economic autonomy, he voiced his ideas through a fictional merchant confuting an orthodox minister. Alert to the connection between religious and commercial dissent, the General Court replied with a potent gesture. They had Pynchon's book burned in Boston's Market Place. He retreated to England in 1652.[33]

Robert Keayne subscribed to neither antinomian nor latitudinarian doctrine. He professed to abhor what he called "all anabaptistical enthusiasms" and displayed his orthodox understanding of the importance of the sanctified life; his attempts to obey God's will, however flawed, gave crucial "evidences of justification," and to neglect them would be a "great sin." He equally rejected Catholicism and the putatively Arminian error of looking on good deeds as spiritually meritorious. He renounced "all confidence or expectation of merit or desert" in his services to Boston and the bequests of the will. All of this conformed to puritan orthodoxy. Against the proponents of toleration, he also affirmed the prerogative of New England's churches and magistracy to wield strict discipline in religious and social matters; he claimed to "unfeignedly approve of the way of the churches" and "the civil government" of Massachusetts.[34]

Keayne even attempted to distance himself from New England's wealthiest magnates—Shrimpton, Hutchinson, and Pynchon might have come to mind—and from London overseas traders who amassed great fortunes. He prided himself on his relative modesty. By the time of his death, he claimed to have accumulated £1,730 in house and lands and £700 in goods. This reached the level of a well-to-do merchant but did not amount to a mercantile dynasty. As he put it, he had "traded for myself about 40 or 50 years" and had gained less than £100 a year, "which we account to be no great matter in driving but a small trade by an industrious and provident man." He could not have made even 5 "per cent clear gains" for his whole career in Boston. Keayne's modest level of wealth demonstrated that he conducted his trade "honestly and lawfully," unlike autonomous traders and antinomian radicals. It stood all the more to his credit, he concluded, that he gave so much to the town out of pure "desire" for the "public good" and "not at any private advantage of me or mine."[35]

The General Court in effect recognized Keayne's doctrinal correctness. It cleared him of any heresy by appointing him to secure and keep watch over the weapons of accused radicals. As a member of the church in good standing, Keayne attended the trial of Anne Hutchinson and made a transcription of the proceedings. He also recorded the report given at a meeting of the First Church by three of its representatives who followed Hutchinsun, Savage, Oliver, and Coggeshall to Rhode Island to provide disciplinary oversight: to remind the outcasts and any local pastors that the church had put them, as Keayne put it, "under admonition and some under excommunication."[36]

Even before his trial for oppression, however, Keayne may have had some intimation that he too, though untainted by antinomianism, might be caught in the same net that captured his radical associates and neighbors. The prospect of fellow merchants' being hauled before disciplinary trials so fascinated him that he took detailed notes on their examinations and censure. He had good reason to fear: the General Court tried him for oppression just after the peak of the antinomian crisis. Hypersensitive to the prospect of sedition, Winthrop and Cotton were poised to rein in wayward New Englanders, especially those with mercantile associations. Keayne's orthodox loyalties—his desire to be a member of the First Church—ironically placed him at their disposal. They made an example of him.

Keayne, however, suffered from more than bad timing. He had displayed the very tendencies that gave antinomians and dissenters like Pynchon such a bad reputation among the orthodox: independence of moral judgment, self-justification, and commercial ambition. Indeed, in his apologia, he echoed some of the very arguments used by the Hutchinsonians. The church censure, he admitted, recalled his culpability before God, but mere "men," he argued—and he meant the pastors and officers of the First Church—had no business judging his motives and commercial tactics. The disciplinary action was presumptuous and wrong, anything but "just and righteous," coming as it did "from men" rather than "from God." If that sounded antinomian, then Keayne's other line of argument reflected civic humanist assumptions. Self-assertiveness, even hard-won profits, by his reading, perfectly comported with social virtue because they enhanced the commonwealth. Defending himself against the charge of price gouging and advising his executors on the poor fund, he claimed that he, unlike his clerical judges, knew the secrets of the economy, including market prices and book accounts. His bequests to Boston advertised him as a successful merchant and man of civic virtue, who had turned his practical genius to public gain.[37]

Keayne contended that he could act as a member of two moral communities—his merchant networks and the church—without contradiction. His prosecutors and spiritual advisers scorned such double-mindedness. To Cotton, Winthrop, and Wilson, Keayne's attitude smacked of antinomianism and his economics of pure humanism. It was a shame, Cotton declared in 1641, that so "many men can tell how to keepe their purses, their credits, and estates," but know not "how to keepe" their "hearts."[38] Boston's officials thought that Keayne's profession of piety masked his duplicity. His resistance to the authority of the church evidenced "evil," as Winthrop had put it, because corporate discipline defined the very reason for the settlement of New England.

The puritans of Massachusetts Bay formulated their ideals for discipline long before they departed England. Godly divines and pastors proffered religious supervision as a remedy for the usury and oppression, the inflation of prices and rents, and the neglect of almsgiving that, as the devotional writer George Gifford put it, obliterated "love" and "good neighborhood" in English society.[39] Like their Reformed counterparts in France and the Netherlands, puritans sometimes defined discipline as church governance or polity. Yet they also used the term to mean corporate measures to inculcate piety, promote social solidarity, and rebuff what they thought was a nearly violent selfishness. They understood discipline to be the instrument by which the church regulated the behavior of parish residents through three measures: instruction about the godly life and criticism of vice; censure and excommunication by the local congregation; and reform of unjust laws and courts. Puritan discipline implied social control, including restrictions on new modes of exchange that endangered the community.[40]

Puritan preachers attempted to conform disciplinary practices, whether teaching, church censures, or legal reform, to the plain and practical meaning of Scripture for their communities. They avoided abstract, philosophical reasoning on moral principles and instead attended to Old Testament rules and New Testament exhortations that obliged the faithful to particular deeds in the community. The great Cambridge teacher William Perkins and his associate William Ames, high authorities for New Englanders, and John Cotton each demonstrated the potency of this method. In their cases-of-conscience treatises, Perkins and Ames raised specific moral dilemmas— how to choose a vocation, the use of secular litigation, conditions for almsgiving, the status of usury—explained biblical rules on such matters, and instructed their readers to make application according to the needs of neighbors. Philosophical and political idioms—notions of "our civill right," as Cotton put it at the end of a lengthy treatise on Christian vocation—served discipline less than did simple obedience to God's law.[41]

Godly moralists thus set the grammar of the Bible over other moral discourses, such as civic humanism, grounded on what they deemed to be merely economic expedience and the nation's glory. Perkins insisted that merchants who claimed to increase England's wealth, yet impoverished their neighbor by profiteering, rationalized their misdeeds with deceptive language. Arthur Dent and Richard Greenham issued similar warnings:

too many people conversed in a vernacular of diligence, thrift, and social duty to validate practices that the Bible denounced under the rubric of covetousness. A preacher at South Shoobery in Essex, Dent mastered the technique of contrasting divine command—refrain from riches, love your neighbor, give charity to the poor—with patriotic and secular excuses for self-interest and commercial technique. Detecting cruelty in usury, price inflation, credit contracts, and rising rents, Dent bludgeoned civic reason with biblical rhetoric. He bemoaned "oppression of the Church, the Ministry, the poore, widows, Orphans": how everything "swarmes with Oppressions, Oppressions, and nothing but Oppressions, Oppressions. In truth this is a most cruell and oppressive age wherein we live: yea a very Iron age."[42]

Puritan leaders taught their people, time and again, to reject common conventions that valorized the accumulation of wealth as a national program. Preachers such as Dorchester's John White, who encouraged and advised settlement in New England, weighty divines such as Hooker, and nearly every devotional writer popular among puritans, including Dent, Gifford, and Richard Rogers, made the same case: if English businessmen really aspired to alleviate poverty, then they should follow the Word. They should slow their pursuit of profits, reduce their consumption, refrain from acquisitive habits, limit investments in commercial ventures, forgo usury, and instead use their money to provide interest-free loans or, even better, alms on the spot to needy neighbors. Their rhetoric often outpaced their logic; taken to an extreme, their advice might also leave godly men with few profits and therefore little money for charity. It nonetheless revealed puritans' confidence that biblical instruction pierced the conscience of otherwise self-regulated businessmen.[43]

Godly teachers accordingly denounced merchants who raised their prices to meet market demand or cover their losses in other deals and in the process exacerbated the plight of the poor—"a common sinne," according to Ames. The anonymous author of *A Godlie Treatice Concerning the Lawful Use of Riches* (London 1578), like other moralists, condemned traders who set their rates by the latest trends in the exchange when they ought to have followed customary and stable valuations according to communal needs. Along with Ames, the author of *A Godlie Treatice* urged local officials to set and enforce strict price ceilings. John Knewstub, a friend of the Winthrop family, lectured Suffolk businessmen in 1579 on "buying and selling." He told them to eschew mere profit making and look upon exchange as a means "to witness our love towards our neighbor by our well dealing." Greenham organized his parishioners into a cooperative to circumvent local markets and sell grain at low rates.[44]

Just as puritans combated price inflation, they delivered hundreds of sermons and wrote dozens of pamphlets against usury. In formal treatises,

several divines did consider possible reasons for charging fees or interest
on credit. Given the dependence of trade on credit, the fast-changing circumstances of the market, and the development of new exchange measures,
Perkins, Ames, and Cotton admitted that merchants might legitimately
make loans to commercial ventures, as a form of investment, and reap
profits. They nonetheless concluded that typical loan practices, which
committed borrowers to fixed fees or interest rates, nearly always violated
Scripture. Usury depended on brokers or other agents who issued contracts
based on inflexible accounting rather than face-to-face negotiation. It required the enforcement of such contracts in secular courts. It thereby op-
pressed the poor, took advantage of economic inferiors, or bankrupted and
destroyed debtors whom the lender had never known personally. Even
when given to a fellow merchant, a usurious contract broke moral solidarity: it replaced moral consideration with impersonal legal obligation. Perkins contended that "usurers and oppressours," as well as "ingrossers,"
should be barred from the Lord's Supper. He suggested that merchants or
financiers consult with Christian neighbors about the effects of their loan
practices on the community before joining Communion.[45]

Ames and Cotton also stressed the importance of evaluating credit in
the local context. While in the Netherlands, Ames wrote in defense of the
regents of Zeeland, who had banned lombards, or bankers who lent money
at contracted interest rates, from the Lord's Supper. He concluded that
"usury," as "commonly practiced," was "deservedly condemned of all: because it is a catching art, and no regard of charity or equity being had, layes
in wait for other mens goods." While in England, Cotton took a similar
position. He urged Christian lenders to submit their conscience to the local
community—what he called "the advise of wise and unpartiall friends"—
rather than follow legal and commercial convention.[46]

In less formal utterances, puritan teachers simply decried all forms of
usury. Thomas Shepard frequently evoked the cold-hearted merchant-
creditor and inflexible usurer who impoverished the godly debtor who naively trusted in older, personal modes of exchange. "Usury" and "oppression" went hand in hand, Richard Rogers preached, and like "witchcraft
and idolatry have no place among God's people." The Dorchester pastor
John Blaxton drew on Calvin to assert the same likeness between usury and
demonic power (figure 2.1). Bezaleel Carter, a fervent preacher in rural
Cavenham, denounced well-to-do parishioners who were "gripers, grinders
of the poor, extortioners, usurers," and in many other ways "merciless."
Puritans in Dorchester seethed at their local usurer, Matthew Chubb, an
Anglican, for demanding interest on a loan to the town and impoverishing
one of his debtors. This sort of cruelty so angered Hooker that he condemned all creditors as hypocritical, mendacious, and covetous. The notion
of a rich Christian, he claimed in equal excess, was a contradiction in terms.[47]

The pronouncements of learned divines and exhortations of country parsons claimed isolated successes for godliness. Gifford supposedly preached the town of Maldon toward communal solidarity and care for the poor. Thomas Hooker's 1626 lectures in Chelmsford managed, by reputation, a brief reformation of market manners. Thomas Shepard's parishioners in Essex shared interest-free loans with each other so frequently that they invested relatively little in commercial ventures. In London pious individuals such as Nehemiah Wallington—a wood maker who once attended nineteen lectures and sermons in one week, read Perkins and Ames, and meditated on the spiritual counsel of Greenham and Dent—shaped his small business to religious doctrine. Praying to "see God in my buying and selling," he snubbed the "lying, deceit, oppression, bribery," and "usury" that filled his fellow artisans' stalls. He also abated the accounts of poor borrowers and never sued for unpaid debts. He refused to raise the prices of his wares beyond customary rates, more fearful of overcharging than of losing a profit. He contented himself with a modest income.[48]

Reformed social teaching restrained the economic ambitions of other citizens as well. After reading Calvin and several puritans, the physician Richard Napier charged no interest on hundreds of loans during the 1620s. Joyce Jeffries, a puritan widow of means, made some five hundred loans during a ten-year period starting in 1638, lending chiefly to neighbors and kin at lower rates, abating the accounts of those who died in arrears, frequently forgiving the debts of widows, and only once pursuing a debtor in court. Many of the godly wrote antiusury stipulations in their wills, directing trustees to provide loans from bequests without charging interest even when allowed by law.[49]

Where embraced by such devout individuals, or taken as polity by the occasional town overcome with godliness, puritan teaching retarded commercial aspirations, but English puritans found few opportunities to use more coercive means of discipline: church censures and civil punishment. Godly reformers judged that neither the Crown, Parliament, and the secular courts nor the church, its bishops, and local ecclesiastical tribunals did much, despite all their protests, to prohibit market vices such as usury. Winthrop kept his own copy of grievances made to Parliament in 1623, which bemoaned judicial corruption in favor of rich merchants, monopolies, lax discipline against usurers, and ineffective poor relief. While royal advisers such as Francis Bacon defended usury as politically and economically expedient, and the House of Commons raised legal limits on interest, civil courts failed to enforce the remaining economic statutes. They brought few usury, engrossing, and price-gouging cases to trial. Such laxity alienated puritan moralists from the state as an organ of economic discipline.[50]

Figure 2.1. The frontispiece from John Blaxton's *English Usurer* (London, 1634). A merchant sitting before his scales, coins, and account books is inspired by a demon to charge interest on his loans. Pigs typify the moral character of usurers. The quote below the image reflects the common understanding of Reformed teaching. It is taken from John Calvin's letter "De Usuris," which was translated and reprinted in James Spottiswood's *Execution of Neshech* (London, 1616). This item, RB96503, is reproduced by permission of The Huntington Library, San Marino, California.

Reformers also complained that the Church of England rarely resolved to punish engrossing, price gouging, and usury. In fact, they perceived the flaws of hierarchical, episcopal discipline quite clearly in its neglect of the sins of the market, despite the fact that some bishops had preached sternly, even fervently, against usury. The effectiveness of Elizabethan ecclesiastical courts depended on the energy and personal predilections of episcopal officials. While often zealous in enforcing regulations requiring conformity of their clergy, bishops were notorious for their failure to supervise the laity. The number of presentments for usury, oppression, or engrossing rose above the minuscule only in areas with strong puritan influence. Archdiaconate courts often commuted penances for small fines rather than enforce injunctions against such sins, provoking dissenters to petition Canterbury for stricter supervision. Walter Travers gave a dire diagnosis in 1588. Thirty years of Reformation had not purified the economy, he asserted, because prelates themselves practiced those telltale vices of the market: "oppressions and extortions" and "covering and cloakinge."[51]

Church courts fared no better under James and Charles. Pressed for money, episcopal administrations increasingly turned to monetary fines as a means of discipline. The resulting ease of commutation of penance, the inability of courts to compel defendants to appear, and the desire to keep citizens within the church, rather than push them toward dissent, led to leniency, especially an unwillingness to use excommunication. Episcopal injunctions from 1603 to 1630 focused on conformity and the maintenance of the established ministry rather than on commercial matters. Some bishops inveighed against oppressive merchants but did nothing to punish them. As Cotton later put it in defense of the New England diaspora, bishops were "removed from the people," incapable and unwilling to "attend to every offence of every private brother." The Church of England, he continued, turned a blind eye to the "oppression" of the marketplace, the various ways in which profit mongering and "lying" pitted neighbor against neighbor. In other words, Anglican discipline was far too unwieldy, distant, hierarchical, and apathetic—if not downright complicit in avarice, deceit, and usury—to attend to commerce on a local level.[52]

Beginning with Thomas Wilcox and John Field's 1571 *Admonition to Parliament*, dissenters produced a flood of pamphlets that demanded an alternative form of discipline, what William Fulke called "a Consistory or segnorye of Elders or governors" that supervised the everyday activities of parishioners on a local, congregational level.[53] Fulke's language evoked the polity of John Calvin, who tutored many dissenters in exile and whose Genevan church served as a model for many puritans. Calvin's English admirers translated and printed his works, especially on morals, in astounding numbers in the 1570s and 1580s, and his critics complained of his popularity among preachers and other disciplinarians. Before Winthrop delivered his great address, "A Model of Christian Charity," many of the godly believed that the city on a hill was the fabled Swiss republic where the church punished conspicuous consumers, crafty usurers, and price-gouging merchants. After admonishing, censuring, and excommunicating them, the consistory remanded them to city councils, which fined or expelled them. Geneva exemplified the personal, localized, and immediate application of church discipline.[54]

The godly in England did institute Calvinist discipline whenever possible. Late Elizabethan and early Stuart reformers created underground conventicles and disciplinary bodies that circumvented established courts. In Northampton and Norwich, for example, they organized classes (associations that practiced discipline on a parish or regional level), gathered neighbors to discuss immoral behavior, heard sermons that highlighted the sins of commerce, and punished usurers. Members of the Dedham Classis, one of the few Elizabethan presbyteries, studied Genevan polity and thereafter established committees to supervise economic activity in its jurisdiction. Dissenters made efforts in this direction even in London. John Winthrop's uncle, churchwarden at St. Michael's Cornhill—Keayne's parish—exposed the congregation to discipline by presenting it with a copy of Calvin's *Institutes* and establishing ties with a neighboring French Reformed church.[55]

When radical Protestants gained control over local politics, in such places as Norwich during the 1580s or the Suffolk towns of Bildeston and Bury Saint Edmunds during the 1620s, they also enacted severe statutes and used them against reputed usurers, engrossers, and profiteers. In 1608 the inhabitants of Boxford agreed to a town covenant that restricted rents and prices and set aside common lands for poor relief. John White turned the prosperous community of Dorchester into a model of discipline. His congregation adopted a covenant that obliged members to repudiate "all ways of gain which shall be adjudged scandalous by the godly wise," a vow that subjected business to the church and wayward merchants to public shame. Abetted by a disastrous fire that signaled divine judgment, White and his friends ousted usurers, created employment projects, and enhanced poor relief.[56]

Such examples admittedly were few and far between. After 1580 the royal court brooked little campaigning for elders, consistories, or presbyteries. Conformist bishops eventually put an end to disciplinary experiments in places such as Norwich. The pronouncements of the godly about Genevan-style coercion faded into wishful thinking after the 1620s. Yet puritans did not abandon the platform held neatly intact from Calvin, through the Marian exiles and later reformers such as Travers and Cartwright, to the generation of John White and John Winthrop. Prevented from the pursuit of moral discipline in England, they looked to New England to institute their ideals. There, they imagined, mutual affection and care for one's neighbors would define one's economic obligations, and the church-state order would compel their performance.

DISCIPLINE AND TRADE IN EARLY BOSTON

Puritan leaders aspired to much more than economic reform in the settlement of New England, but they often returned to that issue. Winthrop's "Modell of Christian Charity," delivered to his companions about to embark the *Arbella* for Massachusetts, was one long manifesto for a godly economy. Other tracts, such as John White's *Planter's Plea*, urged the faithful to flee to nowhere else but New England, where they could avoid the oppression of England, the dissolution of Virginia, and the sheer materialism of the Netherlands. William Bradford's *Of Plymouth Plantation* reiterated the critique: English dissenters who initially immigrated to the Netherlands found little but avarice in the dense, urban order of Amsterdam. The Reformed churches of Leiden, which allowed its members to trade on Sunday, host lavish parties, and otherwise conduct business without religious oversight, dumbfounded English dissenters.[57]

By White's account, the settlement of New England offered the latest and best opportunity for English Calvinists to fulfill the divine mandate for the economy. In England, "idlenesse, riot, wantonnesse, fraud, and violence" ruled. New England would compel settlers to "labour, frugality, simplicity, and justice." Farmers, fishermen, merchants, and artisans could find in Massachusetts a good living, which was to say could produce, sell, trade, and make a profit within the bounds of Christian discipline. Such would be the case, White argued, only if leaders—"good Governours, able Ministers"—defined and enforced the moral obligations of exchange. Using Calvin's metaphors, White described discipline as the ligaments in the body social: "when the frame of the body is thus formed and furnished with vitall parts, and knit together with firme bands and sinews," then common folk and even poor people would benefit from the prosperity of the whole.[58]

Shepard and Winthrop defended the Great Migration against its English critics in similar terms: economic corruption in England, economic discipline in New England. In 1630 Winthrop argued that monopolies and unjust courts constricted economic circulation at home. In 1645 he observed that New England afforded an opportunity for virtuous and prospering trade as long as residents rejected a civic morality based on "naturall corrupt libertyes." A godly polity did not include license for merchants guided only by civic standards; it meant exchange in "subiection to Authoritye," and enjoyment of the "ordinances" of preaching and church discipline, "the main end (professed) of our coming hither." True "liberty,"

Winthrop warned some settlers in 1642 who wished to return to England,
did not allow them to desert "the commonwealth" because of their individual needs. God's Word obliged them to solidarity with their neighbors,
even if this meant "to suffer affliction" with them.[59]

The authors of the first comprehensive statement of church polity in
Massachusetts placed these sentiments at the center of their 1648 Cambridge Platform. "Subiection to the order and ordinances of the Gospel,"
as it decreed, bound individuals into a common life; and disciplinary measures such as admonition, censure, and excommunication strengthened
these bonds. As Hooker put it in a different context, godly people esteemed
the exchange of the "ordinances of God," preaching and discipline, "grace
and love," as a much more valuable "commodity" than mere foodstuffs
and market wares. Moral communion ought to subsume commerce and
citizenship. So too Winthrop: the settlers of Massachusetts Bay ought to
be "knitt together" into a body (again, Calvin's sinews of discipline) in
which the proper administration of the Word of God stitched member to
member. "Wee must uphold a familiar Commerce together," Winthrop
wrote, referring to the transfer not only of goods but, more important, of
affections and teaching, in a spirit of mutuality and "liberallity."[60]

Puritan agendas thus obliged merchants to give their allegiance primar-
ily to the religious community, which guided them on social practice. Commercial associations served only as secondary instruments: never objects of
loyalty in themselves, always subject to spiritual correction. Hooker contended that the believer ought "to sever himselfe" as much as possible from
"publicke" societies, such as business institutions, that legitimated ungodly
habits. Market exchange often fostered "Deceitfulnesse"; prices fluctuated,
the value of truth fell, and "theeverie and couzenagae [swindling]" flourished. In this culture, sinners all too easily disguised, even denied, their
guilt. Church discipline, in contrast, demanded honesty, truth, and candor.
It required confession by the troubled conscience, "publick pennance," or
open acknowledgment of culpability. It also fostered self-denial, the sinner's willingness to be "cast . . . out of [the] Congregation" for the sake of
personal and collective reform. Hooker and his colleagues urged merchants
to ponder the probability that commercial dictates and the norms of merchant communities—even when directed to the national interest—would
sometimes contradict godly teaching. In such cases, businessmen ought to
defer to the local church, whose rules included the power to censure usurers and other sinners. Puritan economic discipline enforced a Christian
moral identity over but not necessarily against commercial groups.[61]

As in England, puritan leaders in Massachusetts Bay inculcated their
discipline partly through teaching and preaching. Not even the most strin-
gent preachers, to repeat, gainsaid prosperity as a worthy goal and industriousness as the means to it. Puritan investors in the Bay Company, yeoman

farmers who immigrated to Massachusetts, civic leaders such as Winthrop, and pastors such as Cotton envisioned a harmonious economic order in which citizens reached at least a modest level of economic competence and maintained a comfortable, even comely, household. Godly preachers criticized unproductivity as much as they did ambition. Just as they chastised aristocrats in England who made money from rents without improving their lands, they condemned New Englanders who aspired to riches but wasted their capital on social frivolities and gambling. They lampooned merchants who speculated in risky ventures instead of making sound investments. They warned settlers against laziness, idleness, and imprudence. In a 1630 sermon occasioned by Winthrop's departure for Massachusetts, Cotton exhorted the company to find a lawful calling, submit to religious discipline, repay their debts if possible, and "use [their] talents fruitfully," which was to say "with a publicke spirit, looking not" to their "owne things" but "on the things of others." New England gave settlers a chance to pursue their vocations rightly.[62]

The same preachers, however, also asserted a contest between economic mind-sets and biblical charity. The leaders of the Great Migration assumed that they had left behind the freewheeling and brutal world of London's loan brokers, scriveners, and usurers, but they nonetheless fretted about exchange, particularly the abuse of lending practices, in New England. "The Lawe of nature," as Winthrop argued in his *Arbella* speech, taught people in England to relate to each other coldly as "one man to another," with inflexible obligations that usurers embedded in their contracts. The "Law of the Gospel," in contrast, compelled New Englanders to regard each other "as a brother in Christ," united "in the Communion of the same spirit." The needs of neighbors thus overrode rights conceived in a merely civic and impersonal manner. In a godly society, disparities of wealth called for mutuality. The Bible called on Christians to set aside private property when certain "seasons and occasions," such as the "perills" of the settlement of New England, demanded "extraordinary liberallity." Service to "the community" of "the church" in exile implied, in this instance, that Christians "must sell all and give to the poor as they did in the Apostles times." Winthrop invoked a moral dictum developed by English dissenters over the course of half a century: God designed credit as a means of social union, not merely as a commercial instrument, and certainly not as a means of profit only. The wealthy ought to give away their money as an act of pure kindness. From this perspective, common commercial practices such as usury appeared to be gross immoralities.[63]

To put Winthrop's argument in different terms, excess capital ought to be directed first to the needy, as long as their plight was involuntary, and only secondarily to commercial investment and private consumption. Robert Keayne's collection of lace, gold, and other luxury goods may have enhanced his status among fellow merchants in the Artillery Company, but it signaled moral temptation. Shepard and Cotton lauded laymen such as Plymouth's Robert Cushman and Winthrop himself, who refrained from conspicuous consumption and provided alms on the spot to indigent neighbors. Christians "exercised" the "duty of mercy," as Winthop condensed all of this into a single sentence, in "Giveing" one's money to poor neighbors and in "forgiveing" their debts.[64]

New England preachers taught church members to read the economy not only through programmatic statements about colonization but also through their regular preaching and special lectures. Robert Keayne took extensive notes on dozens of sermons in which Cotton dwelled on the potential contradictions between deference to the church and commercial success. He listened to Cotton's discourses on the economy delivered during his trial for oppression, including the unsettling claim that when "marchandize, and profites choke" their "harts," New Englanders begin to appear like mere papists.[65]

Keayne also recorded Cotton's use of economic types and metaphors, asides, anecdotes, and illustrations that deflated the civic-humanist pretensions of merchants. Alluding to commercial vice rather than making lengthy arguments, preachers often simply assumed that a self-regulating merchant caste tended to corruption. Keayne heard Cotton say that good ministers were, like Jesus, fishers of men, and fish naturally were as bloodthirsty as merchants: "as one fish prayes upon another, soe the great opresse, and dewower the poor." Before meeting Jesus, many of the disciples "wear accownted notorius opressors, and extortioners." "Christ promiseth Crosses" in place of "pleasure," "Credit," or "profitt." Besides sheer unbelief, according to Cotton, no sins were as vile as those of the market; they were of a piece with sexual deviation and violent crime. "Blasphemy, whordome, drunkenes, Gluttony, opression, Covetiowsnes, wanton beastly filthiness," belonged together in Cotton's lexicon of sins, as did "Extortion, Opression, Sodomy, Gluttony, whordome, or any Iniquitie." When Keayne dutifully attended, listened to, and recorded such sermons, he received a steady critique of new commercial techniques—which preachers made all the more potent by tacit assumption.[66]

Keayne fastened hard on Cotton's economic motifs, an avid consumer and recorder of a form of verbal discipline that must have bordered on the painful for an import trader. In 1640, for instance, Keayne wrote a detailed summary of Cotton's rambling exposition of Mark 6. In one section, according to Keayne, Cotton examined Jesus' choice of vocation, carpentry. Jesus could "have lived profitably and done good in privat," but he chose instead to "Learne a Callinge of his father and to live as him, and helpe him." Cotton elaborated this difference between the self-interest of those who were "rich" and the honest, charitable, and modest aspirations of commoners who worked for the sake of family and neighbor. Jesus lived "not Idely" and did not count it a "disgrace or shame" to "Labor in calling." His example reproved "all the prowd Gallants in the world, and all their high flowen thoughts," their pretensions to be "greate" and "rich." In the second section, Cotton mentioned merchants' temptations to make money an end in itself. He drew an unflattering and far-fetched parallel between King Herod (who, under the influence of Salomé's dance, unwittingly promised to execute John the Baptist) and men of commerce. No less than Herod, merchants often enjoyed a high social life, shared the company of foreigners, entered into contracts with impious men, and engaged in worldly practices such as dancing, "dalliance of wantone behavior," keeping "Evell Company," and making "unlawfull oathes and Covenants." Even if they did not commit fraud or broke the law, even if they paid all their debts, acted frugally, and conducted themselves honorably in the best civic-humanist fashion, they were damned if they lived from a worldly rationale rather than from self-sacrifice and trust in Christ.[67]

Winthrop boasted that such teaching and preaching showed some signs of success, especially before the eruption of antinomianism. He noted that godly counsel and "practice of Discipline" of the church in Boston re-formed many "profane and notorious evill persons." In 1632, to cite one instance, Winthrop and others in the General Court confronted Thomas Dudley, then deputy governor, about his business dealings. By Winthrop's account, Dudley had sold seven bushels of corn to fellow members of the church congregation—"poore men" at that—for a future payment of ten bushels. Although technically legal because it never mentioned interest rates or prices in monetary units, the "bargin" amounted to a more than 40 percent increase on a loan. Dudley's colleagues convinced him that such "oppressinge usury," especially inflicted on a fellow Christian, was uncon-scionable. He confessed his sin and submitted his resignation to the court, which forgave him and allowed him to stay in office.[68]

Winthrop might also have referred to the reformation of commoners such as John Dane, James Cudworth, and Dennis Geere. Dane and Cud-worth claimed that they had come to New England to join a community that would strengthen them against the temptations of a dishonest life. Geere, an otherwise unknown layman who immigrated in 1635, gave a more detailed testimony in his 1637 will, as recorded by its executors, Win-throp and Wilson. Geere confessed to having practiced usury without re-morse in England. Under the tutelage of the church in Massachusetts, God "hath discovered" to him "all usury to be unlawful." As an act of repentance he offered to "restore all such moneys" he had received from his English debtors "by way of usury, whether it were 6 or 8 per cent." The details are telling. Under a godly regime, Geere rejected even a nominal profit margin on loans—one that had long been legalized in England. He was "laboring hereby," he continued, to "manifest my distaste against every evil way." Furthermore, he gave the residue of his estate, beyond provision for his family, to the colony. Geere had learned by discipline, that is, to work hard, provide a comfortable home for his family, eschew usury, and give his surplus to the social body of which he was a dutiful member.[69]

Godly teaching alone, however, did not tame the economic impulses of every New Englander; so the churches of Massachusetts and Connecticut also relied on coercive measures such as church censures and the civil law. They especially favored discipline in the church congregation. Cotton's *Keys of the Kingdom of Heaven* (London, 1644), Hooker's *Survey of the Summe of Church-Discipline* (London, 1648), and Richard Mather's *Church-Government and Church-Covenant Discussed* (London, 1643) defined punitive discipline in ways that set the churches of New England apart from Anglican, episcopal polity. According to these writers, discipline consisted of lay elders exercising the power of spiritual judgment and, in the words of Cotton, "sitting in the presence of the Congregation, and hearing and judging cases before them."[70]

Elected elders and deacons, along with their pastors, confronted parishioners accused of sins such as lying, heresy, outbursts against public authorities, Sabbath breaking, absence from public worship, drunkenness, fornication, and economic vices such as oppression and usury. Concerned laymen visited the wayward, sometimes over the course of a year or more. They met in private gatherings to examine the accused and discuss the relationship between scriptural rules and suspect behaviors. After closed interviews, church officers admonished the guilty. If the sinner remained unrepentant, they brought the case before the whole congregation for disclosure and comment: what Hooker called "the publicke Congregation" gathered in "an open meeting." The church then censured, administered public rebuke, temporarily suspended from Communion, or, as a last resort, excommunicated obdurate sinners until they repented and made public confession. As Cotton instructed church members poised to try one dishonest tailor, their judgment carried eternal consequences: the people together "rightly binde and upon good growndes any man under wroth[,] god bindes that person."[71]

The actions of the ruling elder, deacons, and pastors of Boston's First Church revealed a relentless confrontation between disciplinary ideals and commercial autonomy. We can recall Keayne's case, but his was not unique. From 1630 to 1654, the congregation passed some forty sentences of excommunication. Most of them concerned Sabbath breaking, heresy, drinking, and fornication. Eight cases, however, dealt directly with economic vices. This amounted to a significant portion of the church's concerns, even more than the six cases of libel and violence. The first excommunication ever recorded, in fact, concerned one Robert Parker, who was found guilty of oppression, or overpricing his wares.[72]

In their deliberations, moreover, church officers connected the sins of the market to other forms of social disintegration: as deviant as heresy, disorderly as drunkenness, violent as fisticuffs, and factious as adultery. Elders often linked economic and verbal corruption, oppression and slander. When the church excommunicated William Franklin in 1646 for overcharging another resident for some tools, they noted the interconnections between his "extortion, deceipt, and lying." Tanner William Harvey fell "into Scandall" by ignoring his business—sloth too was a sin—and by compounding his "negligence in his Calling" with "lyes and forgeryes." The church admonished one woman named, ironically, Temperance Sweete for a train of abuses, culminating in the sale of wine with "some iniquity" in "the pryce thereof." Goody Sweete was "reconciled to the church" after she "penetentially made open acknowledgment" of her multiple failings. Tailor Thomas Marshall found the church so ready to censure him, to intervene in "his Dealing" on accusations of unfair prices and seemingly any other misbehaviors that they suspected, that he left the Bay Colony in 1644.[73]

By conflating unjust prices with clearly defined sins such as deceit, theft, and violence, puritan leaders rebuffed antinomian and civic-humanist attempts to distinguish economic behavior from spiritual and ecclesiastical life. They made market practices a central concern for church discipline. In the process, they strengthened their mandate to punish commercial misdeeds. Keayne knew the implications of such resolutions from his own near excommunication.

Ever the note taker, Keayne also recorded the disciplinary trials of others. He wrote a nearly verbatim, eight-page account of the trial of Anne Hibbens in 1640, bracketing his transcription with equally long recitations of two of Cotton's sermons on social obligation.[74] Hibbens ran afoul of the church after a dispute with local carpenters. She accused them of charging unjust fees and doing shoddy work on her house. Church elders called in another carpenter to review the work, invalidated her complaint, and privately told Hibbens to desist from her accusations. She nonetheless persisted and brought in carpenters from Salem to render a second opinion; by her account, they told her that the work was worth less than half of the forty shillings she was charged. One of the Boston carpenters, John Davis, then requested a church council. Sixteen people spoke, including Davis, Mistress Hibbens, her husband, the two pastors of First Church, and eleven laymen, including the merchants Oliver and Bellingham. The long and pointed proceedings, unbounded by any discernible rules of order, rested on common language and informal protocols: laced with scriptural allusions, questions about conscience and motives, professions of sincerity, and accusations of immorality. After exposing Hibbens to intense scrutiny, the church delivered a "censure of admonition" and warned her against further grievance.[75]

Two months later, several elders reported that the admonition had failed. Hibbens continued to complain about the carpenters and disparaged the church's decision. Elders called her to a second trial and confronted her with the heart of the matter: she presumed to "bring out the Trueth" of her business affairs by her own private conscience rather than submit her judgment to the religious community. She even had the temerity to claim to have assisted the ministers in their campaign against the "oppression" of high prices. They determined that a mean spirit drove her to disregard her husband, disobey the church, and lie. They linked her "Judgeing and Condemning" to attendant vices: "uncharitable Jealousies and Suspicion," "Irregular dealing," "obstinate Judgeing," and "sundry Untruethes." Keayne recorded Cotton's dreadful sentence: "[I] from this time forward pronounce you an excomunicatd pson. From god. And his people." Elder Leverett commanded Hibbens "to dep[ar]t the Congregation; as one deprived, wortheley, of all the holy thinges of god." Fifteen years later, she was convicted of witchcraft and executed.[76]

Keayne provided one other detailed account of the workings of church discipline. It concerned Richard Wayte and, like the cases of Keayne and Hibbens, came from the crucial period in the denouement of the antinomian crisis. Wayte, a tailor, had been disarmed in 1637 for his association with Hutchinson. The familiar conjunction—religious dissent and economic deviance—shadowed Wayte during the next three years. In 1639 the First Church censured him for cheating his customers, chiefly by charging high prices and purloining bits and pieces of leather from customers who provided material for gloves. Wayte refused to admit his guilt, and the church excommunicated him. The next year he repented and asked for readmission. During hearings on his request, according to Keayne's notes, Wayte recalled how he came to relent. Church members had given him "Cownsell" during lengthy conversations in his house. Cotton preached sermons that pricked his conscience. He sometimes awoke at night with Scripture verses running through his mind. So, he told the meeting, God "burthened my Spirit." His long and pitiful confession convinced Cotton, who informed Wayte that "yor Cowntenance shoes, you are greved."[77]

Cotton moved the vote to readmit Wayte, but several church members protested. They questioned him about other issues: overpricing a customer for some knives, lying about several conversations, keeping bad company. The church readmitted Wayte, but a few months later compelled him to appear again for omitting several sins from his previous confession and repentance. During four more meetings over the course of three months, Wayte faced intense examination. Again, various members asked him to admit every detail of his wicked dealings and display genuine repentance, including remorse and grief for dishonoring God. Wayte attempted to prove his sincerity, to no avail. He had lost all credibility. Wilson pronounced him to be "Cutt of from the Ordinances of the church Like a Heathen," cast away from "gods faythfull servants."[78]

Hibbens's and Wayte's trials, so intimately detailed by a merchant who had suffered through a similar ordeal, enacted a long-standing puritan ideal: local, personal, and corporate discipline that denied any separation between business and religion. In this moral arena, a merchant could not claim equal but separate fidelity to commercial and Christian community. The Boston church claimed the prerogative to intervene in exchange: limit Keayne's profit margins, determine for Hibbens the worth of carpentry work, criticize Wayte's prices, and judge his motives for renouncing oppression. The sentences of excommunication pronounced on Hibbens and Wayte amounted nearly to damnation—an eternal judgment usually reserved, in Reformed doctrine, for God's mysterious decree.

Spiritual censures brought fearsome consequences, but the puritan leaders of New England had longed from their days in England also to forge civil law into an instrument of discipline. They provided a substantial conceptual framework for this effort. Divines such as John Davenport drew technical distinctions between spiritual and temporal powers—pastors issued excommunications, magistrates issued fines and bodily punishments—yet argued that all public institutions were subject to the same rule: conformity to biblical regulation. Shepard regarded "laws and orders enacted in any place" by civil magistrates to be "good" to the extent that they followed the rules "expressly mentioned in the word [of God]." New England, Winthrop opined, had different rules for moral and political thinking than did humanist jurists and unbelieving magistrates: "if religion and the word of God makes men wiser than their neighbors," then New Englanders ought to "frame rules of government for ourselves" and reject the false wisdom and incomplete justice of "heathen commonwealths." The usefulness of Massachusetts's laws, furthermore, depended on their practical institution in local contexts. Shepard called this the "prudent collection and special application" of the "rules, recorded in Scripture, to such special and particular circumstances which may promote the public weal and good of persons" in particular "towns." Shepard's connection of scriptural "rules" to "particular circumstances" echoed puritan prescriptions for church discipline: the flexible application of biblical texts to local conditions.[79]

Civil legislation and enforcement, however, complicated puritan discipline. English law required Massachusetts's magistrates to conform their practices to political and administrative standards at home. The charter of the Massachusetts Bay Company created the General Court as a ruling body consisting of a governor, deputy governor, all stockholders or freemen, and assistants elected by the freemen. In fact, relatively few of the stockholders had immigrated to Massachusetts by 1630, making the General Court and the assistants nearly coterminous. In 1630 the court voted to give all legislative power to the assistants (to themselves) and named themselves justices of the peace. In 1634 several of the outlying towns issued protests against this rather closed polity. Each town thereafter sent two or three elected representatives, or deputies, to the annual meeting of the General Court to advise and vote on legislation. The assistants, however, maintained their powers as the only court in the colony until 1636.[80]

During the next eight years, the General Court established quarterly, or inferior, courts for the counties of Essex, Middlesex, and Suffolk.[81] These county courts, headed by their respective assistants (who, acting as judges, were called magistrates) served as the first courts of hearing in many cases. Assistants had the further power to appoint special temporary courts, called Commissioners' Courts, in towns where no magistrate lived. In 1644 the General Court specified that all debt cases should be tried first in the inferior court closest to where the creditor or debtor lived, in order to facilitate the judgment of neighbors in the community where disputes arose. Under pressure from import merchants, the General Court created another inferior court in Boston to deal with commercial litigation.

The administrative simplicity of Massachusetts's legal system belied the complexities of colonial jurisprudence. Its charter did not give the General Court leave to contravene English law. From 1630 to 1650 the court relied on a mélange of English common-law rulings, including contract law; the ad hoc decisions of assize courts in England, whose judgments sometimes differed according to local custom; and scriptural commands as interpreted by the clergy. The court recognized the need to incorporate English jurisprudence into its system when it commissioned Cotton and Ward—the divine and the lawyer—to produce models for a constitution. Cotton filled his proposed law code with scriptural allusion. Entitled "Moses his Judicialls," it was enlarged into *An Abstract of Laws and Government*. Sensitive to the potential for political interference from London should the colony's constitution flaunt customary rights and regulations, Ward drew from Cotton's *Abstract* but attended more to the common law. The General Court approved Ward's *Body of Liberties* (1646) as the colony's first law code and later expanded it into the *Laws and Liberties of Massachusetts* (1648).[82]

Despite these eventual concessions to English precedent, the General Court did attempt a reform of civil laws dealing with commerce. Several codes rested on scriptural, rather than common-law, decrees: specific provisions for debt relief, the annulment of contracts or deeds signed under economic duress, a limitation on servitude to seven years, the requirement that eldest sons receive twice the inheritance of other heirs, and severe restrictions on usury—a relatively low ceiling on interest rates and prohibitions against interest on loans outside of those intended for commercial investment. Legislators derived other statutes indirectly from biblical principles. The court, for instance, passed a series of sumptuary laws in the early 1630s, which proscribed aristocratic garb (the public display of sash, velvet, and sword) and restricted the amount of money to be spent on food and drink at social celebrations. These and other restraints encouraged the well-off to channel their wealth to the poor, who did not have the benefit of the institutionalized poor relief characteristic of later Protestant societies. The court also limited the franchise to church members, restricted the movement of strangers in the colony, forbade Massachusetts merchants to deal with profane traders to the north, and attempted to make submission to church discipline a requirement for new immigrants. All of these codes hampered merchants. Thomas Lechford, a critic of the Bay Colony's establishment, complained that New Englanders jettisoned English common law, and natural law, "upon pretense that the Word of God is sufficient to rule us."[83]

Many of these early regulations, following godly agendas originally formulated in England at the turn of the seventeenth century, defined limits on usury, prices, and wages. The court initially enacted the old Elizabethan law that set a 5 percent ceiling on loans to individuals and 8 percent on commercial investments. Citing Old Testament precedents, Cotton attempted to make antiusury statutes even stricter: he held that New England would never be pure without sanctions against all forms of usury. Although the court did allow a 10 percent return on bills of exchange sent overseas, it also required interest-free loans on short-term, private debts. The court did not intend its liberal limits on bills of exchange, as it explained, to "be a color or countenance to allow any usurie amongst us contrary to the Law of God"; it obliged magistrates to judge whether specific loans were usurious and unlawful according to personal and local considerations.[84]

The colony's leaders moved swiftly to make resistance to many of London's contemporary market ways a matter of flexible public policy. The Massachusetts economy flourished during the burst of migration from 1630 through 1638, producing inflationary pressure. Legal measures enacted during this period reflected local conditions. The court, for example, attempted to control prices and wages or authorize localities to do the same. In 1634 and 1635 Winthrop and Hugh Peter complained of "excessive rates," especially taken in the bustle of quayside bargaining in Boston, where "merchants and seamen" sometimes sold essential commodities to eager consumers at double the customary cost. The court legislated strict price limits on foodstuffs and a general 30 percent margin on all goods. Any exchange, Cotton remarked, was subject to regulation according to the needs of the local community; if colony-wide law did not cover specific cases in dispute, or if neighbors could not form a consensus on a fair price for certain goods, then the magistrate ought to set it for the community.

The court also set ceilings on wages for tradesmen and craftsmen, many of whom, according to Winthrop, were so well paid that they worked only half days.[85]

During the next decade, however, commerce suffered from a dearth of capital, intermittent disruptions of exchange with London, and a rapid decline of immigration. The relative lack of consumers led to periods of constriction and depression. Even as they aspired to a robust commerce, Boston merchants often depended on nearly barterlike conditions. In this context, the court repealed many of its restrictions on prices and wages. Fluctuations in supply, the needs of different groups of settlers—producers as well as consumers—and local variations called for constant adjustment. The court eventually passed the duty of price and wage control to towns. Yet even when it rescinded regulatory statutes, the court still empowered magistrates to fine and imprison "ill disposed persons" who took advantage of such "liberty to oppresse and wronge their neighbours" by demanding "excessive wages" or asking "unreasonable prizes" for goods. It gave the governor the right to decree price ceilings. It also continued to pass the occasional price regulation, often responding to clerical complaints, through the 1670s. Such flexibility conformed to puritan agendas for the personal and practical application of moral disciplines. The legal adjustments of the mid-seventeenth century, occasioned by temporary conditions, continued to evoke puritan regulatory regimes developed in England.[86]

Religious mandates for price regulation also shaped policy toward the most noted industrial experiment in the Bay Colony, the Saugus Iron Works. In 1641 John Winthrop Jr. proposed that the court support and subsidize a foundry to supply iron to the northern colonies and England, a long-standing objective for colonizers. During the 1640s, the government organized small foundries at Braintree and Lynn, on the Saugus River watershed. The ironworks required intensive labor, employing a manager, woodsmen, miners, smelters, colliers (who made the charcoal to fire furnaces), and transporters. After several years of small successes and large failures under Winthrop's management, the court opened the ironworks to private ownership by so-called undertakers. From 1645 to 1652, Keayne and several import-merchant colleagues—Hill, Scottow, Oliver, Bellingham, Savage, and Tyng—heavily invested in the enterprise. They hired a Scot, Jonathan Gifford, to be their agent and on-site manager.[87]

Despite this private ownership, the court required religious supervision over the ironworks; the Saugus project hardly amounted to an independent industry shaped by market considerations. The assistants demanded that employees, many of whom were hardscrabble Irish and Scottish laborers, attend a nearby church and pay taxes accordingly or, even more unlikely, form themselves into a local congregation. Unaccustomed to puritan sermons, to put it mildly, they resisted. Nearby pastors complained about drunkenness, disorderliness, violence, and assorted other profanities among workers. More important, the court set prices for Saugus iron. It refused the undertakers' repeated petitions—submitted by Keayne—to allow them to sell their iron overseas at high rates or raise domestic prices to ensure a profit. It also insisted that undertakers receive payment in kind, when cash served them much better. Social and spiritual duty, the court explained, obliged them to submit to strict price regulation, even at the expense of their personal gain. It had sanctioned the works to supply fellow Christians, not to enhance the profits of investors beyond a modest return. Addressing the investors in the language of Christian devotion ("our loving friends . . . as wee account yow to be"), it pressed on them their duty to sell only to New Englanders, at quite low prices, and trust God to provide the necessary income. Members of the court promised somehow to "find out so aequall a way whereby our occasions may be comfortably suplyed, and yourselves encouradged and inabled to proceed in yor undertakings by the blessing of the Lord, upon which our poore prayers are not wanting." Gifford, at least, was not so "encouradged." Apparently fed up with managing such a frustrating venture, he took to skimming some of the slim profits for his own comfort. This provoked Keayne to a most unpuritan action, a lawsuit against Gifford on behalf of the other undertakers. The court judged in favor of the plaintiffs, but bad record keeping and a good attorney released Gifford without recompense to Keayne and the others, whose substantial investments netted them little.[88]

Puritan discipline also concerned the day-to-day exchange of credit and commodities among farmers and merchants. As instruments of economic regulation, the courts established by the General Court meted out punishments for violation of economic statutes, adjudicated business disputes between colonists, and issued warnings against unseemly behavior such as speculation in land, trading with the French, and unfair loan practices. From 1628, when it met prior to Winthrop's departure for New England, through 1643, a period from which the records are fairly complete, the Court of Assistants handled more than 400 cases. It dealt with drunkenness (some 90 cases); followed by fraud or violations of wage and price statutes (50 cases); fornication (45 cases); seditious speech and contempt of authority (44 cases); libel, swearing, and other speech crimes (37 cases); theft (35 cases); neglect of civic duty—such as causing fires, cultivating lands outside proper boundaries, and neglecting the watch (32 cases); master-servant relations (29 cases); battery or murder (21 cases); scandalous comportment and sumptuary violations—such as improper clothing, gaming, or improper tobacco use (19 cases); and illegal trading with Indians (12 cases). Matters of commercial exchange, from price margins to trading partners, that is, occupied the assistants' docket more frequently than any other issue, save for alcohol consumption. Commercial crimes, in addition, often implicated the accused in other misbehaviors such as libel, mistreatment of servants, and sumptuary violations.[89]

The assistants most often leveled monetary penalties on the guilty. They fined John Chapman twenty shillings for selling lumber above the legal rate in 1633 and punished James Hawkins similarly in 1635 for demanding high wages. (As a rare and fitting exception, the court inflicted corporal punishment—the stocks—on Edward Palmer in 1639 for "extortion" because he had sold the wood for the stocks at exorbitant rates.) Serving as the place of first hearing for cases that involved small amounts of money, quarterly courts dealt with similar issues. In one year alone, starting in March 1658, the Essex County court fined one Mr. Wade "for excessive prices," punished Robert Payne and William Bartholomew "for selling dear," and dealt with one case of usury. Rigorous prosecution of oppression and usury distinguished civil discipline in Massachusetts from legal practice in England.[90]

In addition, the colony's civil courts, unlike their English counterparts, depended less on formalized legal procedure than on the collective judgment of neighbors: common opinion informed by religious teaching. This process of resolving disputes, often resulting in ad hoc solutions, rested on lay language, simplified pleading, and informal presentations; some judicatories disallowed lawyers, briefs, writs, and technical pleas altogether. Massachusetts courts typically probed private affairs and motives, urged plaintiffs and defendants to candor, and referred frequently to the Bible to illumine particularly vexing cases. By Winthrop's judgment, godly protocols prompted magistrates and juries to use their discretion and judge cases by spiritual principles that transcended legal technicalities and English rights. "The qualitye of the person and other circumstances" ought to be considered above mere law codes, he urged. Likewise, the use of personal discretion gave magistrates the freedom to administer "Admonition" and "Reproofe" as well as temporal punishment. Courts, like the church, ideally provided spiritual oversight.[91]

In such intimate settings, as Keayne well knew, religious counsel, neighborly adjudication, and scriptural admonishment counted for legal procedure. One final instance from his career serves as a case in point. In 1642 a woman of modest means named Goody Sherman accused Keayne of slaughtering her prized sow, which had escaped her property. She initially brought her case before the church, which heard detailed testimony about the physical appearance of pigs and the characters of the contestants. Witnesses cleared Keayne of butchering the stray sow, but Sherman nonetheless persisted. She hired a visiting English merchant, George Story, to prosecute her case in the inferior court. Keayne swiftly countersued for libel. He won his case, to a judgment of £20 against Goody Sherman.[92]

Records of the Sherman-Keayne trial mark the peculiarly religious coloration of puritan justice. Much of the testimony included close debate of Old Testament rules concerning lost animals, stray cattle, and neighbors' duties to each other. Moreover, encouraged by popular sympathy for Sherman and critiques of the court for rendering such a costly judgment in favor of a rich merchant against a poor housewife, Story asked the General Court to reconsider the issue. In such instances, the higher court, mirroring English courts of equity, considered appeals based on religious criteria such as mercy and fairness, which superseded common law. In Sherman's case, the court voided the £20 debt to Keayne and directed Sherman to pay him only his £3 court fees. Yielding to Christian sentiment, Keayne agreed to abate even this penalty.[93]

The use of discretionary powers by magistrates, the role of appeal, the importance of scriptural interpretation and informal procedure in the courtroom, and the ethos of public accountability and personal transparency in legal proceedings all conformed to puritan ideas of discipline over social and commercial exchange. Davenport spoke for the likes of Cotton, Shepard, and Winthrop when he argued that New England's disciplinary "theocratie," a social order under "the Laws of God," produced a uniquely godly polity.[94]

Davenport also argued, however, that civil law would conform to godliness only if electors, juries, legislators, and magistrates derived their judgments from Christian principles. Unbelievers' "unacquaintance with the Law of God," he maintained, blinded them to proper moral judgments because the precepts of natural law, presuppositions of civic humanism, and cumulative wisdom of common law did not lead to true justice. So Davenport insisted that only church members, who subjected themselves to scriptural teaching, should be empowered to elect deputies to the General Court and hold the office of magistrate. They were "fitter" than unbelievers "to judge and determine according to God" the outcome of particular cases. "All true Moral Justice," Davenport concluded, rested on the election of godly rulers by godly citizens. In economic terms, only the saints, guided by Scripture, could "be found civilly honest, and morally just" and fit to "have judgement" in matters of "Humane Contracts, mens Goods and Lives, and outward Liberties."[95]

Puritan leaders, that is, recognized that legal protocols posed challenges to religious discipline. To the extent that puritans relied on civil courts to correct and adjudicate exchange, they accepted at least some of the professional and secular standards of legal practice in England. Jurisprudence obliged the Bay Colony magistrates, for all of their reformist agendas, to contend with common-law and natural-law precedents. Even in Boston, courts eventually admitted a language of civil morality that sometimes rivaled godly discourse, leaving ministers and magistrates such as Winthrop dissatisfied. They expressed their reservations in several ways, including a steady critique of barratry. Winthrop had been trained as a lawyer, but he, like other puritans, denounced his profession more than endorsed it. Cotton spoke for most when he described "Advocates" as motivated by a drive for success rather than a love of truth. Lawyers, he claimed, "bolster out a bad case by quirks of wit, and tricks and quillets of Law," using "their tongues as weapons of unrighteousness" for "corrupt Causes." Following such critiques, the General Court and some towns restricted the role of lawyers in Massachusetts Bay. Not to be outdone, New Haven banned lawyers from the colony altogether.[96]

Many puritan divines implied that civil judicatories with their profane protocols could dispense half justice at best. Hooker complained to Shepard as early as 1640 that the General Courts of Connecticut and Massachusetts had succumbed to "politic respects . . . and attending to our own devices," by which he meant political necessity and legal precedent. As a result, Hooker asserted, magistrates refrained from strict regulation over the economy; they capitulated to "toleration and connivance at extortion and oppression" when they ought to have pursued "a real reformation" by "looking at the rule" of Scripture.[97] Admitting the impurity of courts even in New England, puritan spokesmen urged believers to refrain from civil litigation. Winthrop in fact came to disparage any legal adjudication of commercial disputes, credit relations, and other matters of exchange. He preferred "the counsel and persuasion of elders" in the church to negotiation or arbitration in the courtrooms of Massachusetts Bay.[98]

Given such a judgment, church leaders contemplated the need to exercise discipline over the very legal institutions that they had created as instruments of reform. In 1635 the town meeting in Boston prohibited anyone from lawsuits without receiving permission from church elders. Inhabitants of towns such as Lancaster covenanted with each other "to end all differenc[es] by arbitration" rather than "goe to lawe with another in actions of debts or damages." So too the First Church in Boston. In a 1649 meeting, the members voted to censure any of their number who "should goe to law one with another without the Consent of our brethern." This decision made explicit the contrast between brotherly discipline and civil law.[99]

By that time, Robert Keayne had come to rue too much interference by the church in the affairs of merchants, not the incursions of secular justice. He wanted greater freedom for merchants to negotiate commercial matters by civil precedent rather than by the demands of puritan disciplinarians. His many trials—his painful endurance of sermons that compared merchants to ravenous beasts, church censure and near excommunication for commonsense commercial tactics, irritations at pious meddling in the Saugus Iron Works, and even encounter with Goody Sherman—had confounded his economic expertise. The leaders of the First Church had been all too successful, from his perspective, in fulfilling their long-cherished goals of instituting godly regulation over trade.

Keayne might have wished for more civic humanism, not less: for a social ethos that legitimated merchants who claimed moral respectability, piety, professional independence, and commercial acumen all at once. Indisposed to make distinctions between religious mandate and social authority, his spiritual elders would not tolerate a community of independent traders. Rejecting his claims to civic virtue, even linking it to antinomian excesses, they insisted that he could not belong to two moral communities at once. The puritanism he encountered punished merchants who aspired to success in the market on their own terms.

Keayne, perhaps, had always suffered from bad timing. His successors in Boston fared much better in the hands of the church. They and their ministers did not separate religious ideals from commercial mandates, but they did redefine the meaning of corporate discipline. New ideas of providence, the civil order, and the very purpose of New England reshaped the relationship between the market and religion during the decades immediately after Robert Keayne's death.

Chapter Three

JOHN HULL'S ACCOUNTS

In March 1680 Boston merchant John Hull wrote a scathing letter to the Ipswich preacher William Hubbard. Hubbard owed him £347, perhaps five times the pastor's annual salary, which was long overdue. Hull recounted how he had accepted a bill of exchange from him as a matter of personal kindness. Sympathetic to his needs, Hull had offered to abate much of the interest due on the bill; yet Hubbard still had sent nothing. "I have patiently and a long time waited," Hull reminded him, "in hopes that you would have sent me some part of the money which I, in such a friendly manner, parted with to supply your necessities." Hull then turned to his accounts. He had lost some £100 in potential profits from the money that Hubbard owed. The debt rose with each passing week.[1]

A prominent citizen, militia officer, deputy to the General Court, and affluent merchant, Hull often cajoled, scolded, and shamed his many debtors, but never had he done what he now threatened to do to Hubbard: take him to court. "If you make no great matter of it," he warned the minister, then "I shall take myself bound to make use of that help which God and the country have provided for my just indemnity." It would have been neither unreasonable nor unusual for a man of Hull's standing to sue a delinquent debtor. Second-generation Boston merchants gave and received credit at nearly every turn in their business. An overdue account or unpaid bill encumbered a whole series of transactions. Hull was sued for unpaid bills at least once, even as he waited for payment from his debtors. In Boston the Suffolk County Court of Common Pleas, built on the precedent of English inferior courts, increasingly heard such cases after 1660. During the 1680s, in the midst of a great commercial expansion in Massachusetts, debtor-creditor disputes took up much of the court's docket.[2]

Hull had a legal prerogative, even a fiscal duty, to pursue his case, but the prospect of litigation troubled him nonetheless. "I have been very slow, hitherto, to sue you at the law," he wrote to Hubbard, "because of that dishonor that will thereby come to God by your failure." Practical considerations aside (he thought that lawsuits often wasted time and yielded unreliable judgments), Hull undoubtedly knew that the puritan founders of New England urged believers to bring economic grievances before church tribunals rather than secular courts. He had experienced conversion under John Cotton's teaching at Boston's First Church and owned a copy of Cotton's catechism, which stressed the moral discipline of the church. According to Cotton and lay leaders such as John Winthrop, godly counsel might override the dictates of civil justice and compel a well-to-do merchant to forgive the debts of a needy neighbor—and a pastor at that. By such standards, Hull's threats displaced religious duty with profane litigation.[3]

For his part, Hubbard may have recognized the irony of the whole affair. Four years prior to Hull's letter, he had argued in an Election Day sermon for Massachusetts that the commonweal depended on loyalty to the civil order and its legal institutions. He said nothing about church discipline. He even intimated that the colony's problems stemmed in part from church leaders themselves, who quarreled over sacramental practices, the economy, and politics. Hubbard announced that Massachusetts required "skilful and expert men"—the newly elected governor John Leverett and the merchant-magistrates of the colony—who understood "the times" better than did the ministers. Hubbard noted the problem of rising indebtedness—a further irony—but never urged almsgiving, the abatement of overdue accounts, or arbitration by the local congregation. He pleaded merely for the spread of a charitable spirit throughout society under the watchfulness of wise rulers. The "Church," Hubbard insisted, needed secular authorities with "Gloves of iron to handle the thorns and pricking Bryars" of religious and social controversy.[4]

According to Hubbard, providence guided New England through the mundane events of civil society: the leadership of civil magistrates and authority of public institutions. Unlike previous puritan ministers, he did not portray merchant groups as rivals to the church, who ought to submit their commercial transactions and legal rights to religious discipline. Even after Hull's angry letter, Hubbard extolled overseas traders and celebrated transatlantic commerce as providential gifts to New England. When agriculture, barter, and local trade "began to be stopped up," he preached in 1682, "God in his merciful providence opened another, by turning us into a way of Trade and Commerce, to further our more comfortable subsistence." Hubbard also authored a flattering funeral elegy for the merchant Daniel Dennison, one of his parishioners, and secured the publication of a treatise by Dennison that reiterated the theme of deference to civil government. Hubbard in effect had sanctified Hull's vocation, and with it his appeal to litigation. As it turned out, none of this brought satisfaction to Hull. He died, unpaid, before the case came to trial. Two years later, in 1685, his legal executors agreed to settle with Hubbard for £210.[5]

Although the issue between Hull and Hubbard came to an unremarkable end, it reveals the knotty relationships between religion and commerce from the mid-1650s through the mid-1680s, when Boston's economy rebounded from its depression and merchants established a vibrant regional economy with ties across the Atlantic. Many overseas merchants in New

England, like Hull, participated in England's system of expanding markets, complex credit relationships, and legal procedures that diverged from the disciplinary ideals of the founders. Once frowned upon by previous puritans such as John Cotton, debt litigation formed an important link in the network of exchange in the Bay Colony during the second half of the seventeenth century. Hull nonetheless devoted himself to puritan teaching and resisted a merely secular conduct of business. He belonged to a cadre of Boston merchants who were loyal to the local congregation and fluent, even loquacious, in the language of piety. Hull's pastors and spiritual advisers maintained a customary critique of market-driven exchange practices such as usurious lending, oppressive prices, conspicuous consumption, and neglect of almsgiving. Yet much like Hubbard, the ministers to whom he listened most intently taught him that the fate of New England depended on its public institutions. They discovered providence—God's rule in history—in the affairs of civil society: government, laws, and commerce. This made it easier for Hull, despite his hesitations, to conduct business apart from the oversight of a local congregation, even to threaten a neighboring pastor with litigation. Hull's story represents neither secularization and the decline of piety nor the mere unfolding of a commercial ethos essential to puritanism. Instead it represents the importance of theological and moral transformations from within puritanism—changes in conceptions of the church, providence, and the civic order.

Hull and the Expansion of New England's Market

Hull's career unfolded at the center of Boston during the 1650s and lasted through the mid-1680s. Born in the cloth-making town of Market Harborough, Leicestershire, in 1624, he attended, as befitted a future trader, a grammar school founded by a member of the Merchant Taylors' Company. He immigrated to Boston in 1635 with his father, Robert, a blacksmith; his mother; and his half-brother, a goldsmith. The colony gave Robert twenty-five acres at Muddy River (now Brookline) for a small farming plot, but he found his main employment among Boston's artisans and small traders. Robert joined the First Church soon after his arrival. Like many other urban tradesmen, he attached himself to Anne Hutchinson's teachings, for which he suffered disenfranchisement. The General Court reinstated him with little commotion after a few months. After two years in Boston's public school and seven years of apprenticeship, John entered the silversmith trade. He refashioned used objects and coins, imported silver from the West Indies, and made utensils sold chiefly for household use. He became one of Boston's most prominent silversmiths, the number of whom had reached twenty-four by 1680. His apprentices included future master silversmiths such as Jeremiah Dummer and John Coney.[6]

Hull's business, participation in the church, and civic responsibilities advanced quickly in concert. He settled himself in his father's modest house, several blocks south of the town center and docks, and began to attend the First Church. In 1647 Governor Winthrop performed Hull's marriage to Judith Quincy, which brought him into a distinguished clan. Judith's father cofounded the town of Braintree, and her brother achieved prominence as a magistrate, militia leader for Suffolk, and member of the General Court. The year after his marriage, Hull joined Cotton's First Church. Following a practice common among overseas traders, he soon after joined the Artillery Company. He understood church and militia memberships as intertwined privileges, linked fellowships, dual signs of communal favor. "Under the ministry of Mr. John Cotton" and "the breathings of [God's] own good Spirit," he wrote in his diary, "I was accepted to fellowship with his church." The militia, he continued in the next line, also "gave" him "acceptance and favor," making him "serviceable to his people" as an officer.[7] A record keeper for the regiment, Hull prided himself on his steady promotion through the ranks to sergeant major over the next eight years. In 1652 the General Court appointed him the first master of the mint for the colony, charged with fashioning Massachusetts shillings, sixpence, and threepence. In exchange for his service, the colony provided him with a new shop and tools and paid him a 5 percent stipend on the coins minted.[8]

Turning his income from the shop to trade, Hull steadily rose in the ranks of Boston's merchant community. In 1653 he recorded his first substantial commercial investment: £120 worth of pelts sent to London on two ships. The capture of those shipments by Dutch privateers did not deter him. His diary marks an increasing outlay in goods and transport. By 1680 he owned major shares in at least fourteen seagoing vessels and transported goods on another thirty. He corresponded with merchants throughout the North American colonies, the Caribbean, and England, tracking market trends, consumer tastes, and supplies. He used commercial agents in London, Jamaica, and Bilbao: his uncle Thomas Pariss, cousins Edward Hull and Thomas Buckham, and other factors such as John Ives, Thomas Papillon, and William Meade. He purchased New England fish, furs, and salted beef and sold them in the West Indies, Spain, and England. He bought New York whale oil and traded it for Virginia tobacco. He sent timber and wood products such as tar, resin, and turpentine to England. He imported hats, clothes, and textiles from London; salt, wine, and iron from Spain; and sugar from the islands. He also acted as military provisioner, selling European saltpeter and English armaments to the Massachusetts militia just before the horrendous conflict known as King Philip's War, a conflict between English settlers and native tribes in 1675 and 1676.[9]

Hull invested in land and commercial infrastructure as well as commodities. He purchased several parcels of pasture in Boston and added four hundred acres to the family holdings in Braintree; by the end of his career, he had accumulated twenty-two land deeds. He owned his shop, built warehouses in different sections of Boston, and bought shares in several wharves in town. He received a thousand-acre plot outside Boston as payment for commercial debts and purchased another of the same size. He invested heavily in the Pettasquamscutt Purchase in Rhode Island, using the land first for mining lead and then for raising horses to supply sugar plantations in the West Indies. He even dallied in horse breeding, combining a practical scientific bent with a talent for predicting demands for different breeds. He also owned a sawmill, which produced the timber and byproducts he exported. Like other overseas New England merchants, Hull commanded an astonishing array of products, services, and markets.[10]

He also mastered an equally complex set of skills: account keeping, long-distance negotiation, prediction of market demands and freight costs, communication with lawyers and magistrates, acquisition of insurance, and supervision of shipmasters. When he detected inflationary trends, he accelerated the purchase and delivery of goods and raised his prices. He learned to figure his ledgers in anticipation of future sales and receipts. As an account keeper, Hull often relied on older, relatively simple formats such as single-entry bookkeeping with personal notes to explain transactions. Yet he began to use more sophisticated methods and double entries in the 1670s. He kept a fantastic array of account books. At his death, his executors faced more than twelve thousand pages of business records.[11]

The General Court designated him treasurer for the colony from 1676 to 1680; thereafter he paid less attention to his imports and exports and more to the banking side of his business. As treasurer and mint master, he learned rates of exchange, annual forecasts of taxation and expenditure, inflation rates, and the impact of delinquent payments. He studied the effects of monetary policy on trade, once proposing that Massachusetts overvalue its currency to stem inflation and encourage overseas investment in New England. He also knew something of larger economic patterns. He commented several times on technical issues such as the balance of trade for the colony and the home country.[12]

By the time of his death from illness in 1683, Hull had amassed a substantial estate, worth some £6,000. He belonged to the upper ranks of Boston's traders, but not among the very elite. Other merchants, such as James Oliver, Elisha Hutchinson, and Samuel Shrimpton, accumulated far more wealth—on the scale of twice his estate. Building on the trade and contacts established by their fathers (Peter Oliver, Edward Hutchinson, and Henry Shrimpton), they assembled merchant dynasties that dwarfed and long outlasted Hull's business. Several of Hull's colleagues, such as Wait Winthrop,

Edward Tyng, Joseph Dudley, and Thomas Lake, claimed vast tracts of land in northern New England. At the other end of the spectrum, Boston accommodated a variety of humble shopkeepers, and small towns and villages to the north and west supported peddlers, chapmen, and modest entrepreneurs who bartered, exchanged goods for services, and otherwise operated in a local nexus of personal acquaintance and reciprocity.[13]

Hull, then, can stand for the successful but not fantastically wealthy overseas merchant whose career thrust him into England's transatlantic system. During the English Civil War, which ruptured partnerships with London and royalist colonies such as Bermuda, Barbados, and Virginia, many newer traders established a fresh set of contacts in England, financed new ventures, explored different overseas networks, diversified business, and traded more aggressively in capital and credit. The spread of settlements north and west of New England's seacoast after the mid-1650s, enhanced by a return to robust immigration numbers, offered opportunities for investment in vast tracts of land, providing rents and mortgages for capital. Domestic consumption rose. Other merchants besides Hull gained control of inland transport and the various sectors of maritime industry: ownership and maintenance of wharves and docks, shipbuilding, employment of masters and crew, provision and lading, and insurance.[14]

All of this indicated a high degree of economic consolidation in the hands of large-scale traders. A single merchant like Hull, to imagine one probable scenario, owned land for timber, hired a manager to supervise the production of barrel staves, employed laborers to transport the staves to Boston, and paid workers to load them on a ship that he had built and owned. He insured the voyage, employed the captain, arranged through local agents the sale of the staves in London, exchanged credit with an English merchant, saw to the purchase of English cloth in return, and financed the return voyage. He then sold the cloth in a shop that he owned, to a peddler who bought on credit. Hull controlled, and took profits from, nearly all components of a complex transaction.[15]

London's administrative powers increasingly impinged on New England's commerce with the Restoration in 1660, when authority for colonial policy gravitated from parliamentary committees to privy councilors, the Lords of Trade, and royal advisers. Parliament passed or renewed several of the Navigation Acts intended to funnel New England's commerce through English hands. The laws required New Englanders to use English crews and ships for long-distance routes, restricted imports directly from Europe, and placed tariffs on imports to New England. Although troublesome to many New Englanders, the Navigation Acts eliminated competition from Dutch ships in colonial harbors and spurred further trade with other English colonies. The acts also established a bureaucracy—records, inspectors, agents—that linked regional markets to Boston and speeded communication across the Atlantic.[16]

Colonists' participation in this imperial system depended almost entirely on credit. Because Hull's mint never produced enough currency for large-scale trade, cash-strapped New Englanders scrambled to control transferable, which is to say paper, wealth. They kept an increasingly sophisticated tabulation of debts and credits in ever-expanding "book" formats: diaries (copies of business correspondence, bills, and notations on goods ordered, bought, or sold), accounts or ledgers (tables of credits, debits, and sums by the names of customers), daybooks (records of the day's business), waste books (short notations on individual transactions), and assorted notebooks for other business (such as rents, mills, mines, and wharves). They wrote and received bills of exchange: signed promissory notes that pledged payment in goods or cash by an inscribed date. Recipients of bills of exchange often transferred them as payment to other creditors. In June 1679, to give a relatively simple but common example, Hull sent to his agent in London, John Ive, three bills of exchange along with sixteen barrels of sugar and some beaver pelts, all to be credited to Hull's account. One of the bills, worth £50, was made out to one Spencer Pigott from Sarah Smith. Pigott had paid Hull with this bill; now Hull was paying Ive, who probably would have credited it to Hull's account and sent it back to another merchant in New England in payment for goods shipped to London. Smith eventually paid someone other than Pigott or Hull for the note. Like other staples of his trade, Hull's dependence on bills of exchange reflected widespread practices.[17]

Merchants in Hull's day used other forms of credit as well. They circulated negotiable instruments such as bonds (typically a note from a well-to-do creditor backing someone's large-scale commercial debts—a form of countersigning), deeds, contracts, mortgages, and even insurance policies. Shifting interest rates, legal restrictions, and contested repayment dates often confused the valuation of such notes. As a result, their signers and holders frequently brought each other into court. Informed by commercially oriented versions of common law, civil litigation expanded accordingly. Traders such as Hull fretted not only about their accounts but also about the latest round of lawsuits.[18]

The technicalities of exchange rates, calculation of the cost of deferred payments, protocols for debt litigation, and variety of investment schemes demanded expertise. Some modest traders, such as John Baily, failed to master the requisite skills and resigned themselves to small-time business at best; "it's enough to make a man mad," Baily complained, "to take notice" of the confounding layers of accounts. More successful merchants consulted the latest commercial manuals, offered by some twenty publishers and booksellers clustered around the Town House in Boston. In 1685

alone Hezekiah and John Usher sold fifty titles concerning overseas navigation, thirty-six that dealt with the law, and several English gazettes that
tracked market values in and out of London. Bostonians owned copies of
Lewis Roberts's *Merchants Mappe of Commerce* (London, 1638; 4th ed.,
London, 1700) and *Act of Tonnage and Poundage and Book of Rates* (London,
1675). Roberts provided keys to the value of coins, prescribed the composi-
tion of bills of exchange, and described the bills' currency in different
cities and states. He gave details on trade regulations and rules in international ports. He stressed throughout how English merchants ought to increase exports over imports and return specie to England. The General
Court provided the Boston Town House with books on jurisprudence
for merchants to consult: Edward Coke's *First Part of the Institutes of the
Laws of England* (London, 1628) and Michael Dalton's *Countrey Justice*
(London, 1618).[19]

Dozens of other such manuals circulated in and around Boston, including secretary's guides, layman's manuals on the law, international rules
for commerce, and tables of values for specie, notes, and bills used throughout the Atlantic. Samuel Tompson from Braintree, for example, copied
extensively in 1678 from Edward Cocker's *Magnum in Parvo, or The Pen's
Perfection* ([London], 1675). He recorded the proper form for dozens
of legal instruments, including a bond, bill of exchange, release from
debt, arbitration agreement, indenture, receipt, loading of inventory, will,
power of attorney, bill of sale, and bill of obligation. The formal language
of such documents required merchants to master a grammar of law and
commerce; fluency in this language certified traders as a like-minded
cohort of experts.[20]

A new genre of social commentary published in London provided a similar, albeit more theoretical and indirect, assertion of the professional status
of Anglo-American merchants. Advisers to Parliament, royal counselors,
and advocates for England's overseas trading companies gradually assembled a body of literature that derived economic principles from technical
analyses of market exchange and the overall, long-term production of
wealth. The most influential of these economic writers had practiced overseas trade: Director of the East India Company Sir Josiah Child, Thomas
Culpeper, Thomas Mun, Edward Misselden, and Sir William Petty. They
addressed the nation's economic problems—shortage of coin, depression
in the cloth trade, scarcity of goods, unemployment, and rising poverty—
with proposals to enhance exports and the overall exchange of goods in
and out of England. Sometimes offering contradictory tactics to achieve
this aim, especially in regard to interest rates and tariffs, they nonetheless
all rested their arguments on fiscal statistics, trade data, and comparisons
especially with Dutch and French commerce.[21]

In their advice to the government, these protoeconomists subordinated customary moral teaching about commerce to empirical analyses. Misselden, for example, criticized civic-humanist commentators such as Malynes, who urged external restraints over fiscal supply and interest rates. Malynes assumed that prices ought to be stable, specie had an absolute value in itself, and usury corrupted credit transactions. The new economic writers decried these presumptions. Specie, they argued, was merely a form of money, and money had no absolute value; it only had exchange value, its worth on the market in terms of consumable goods. Analysts such as Misselden and Sir William Petty suggested that the sooner English policy makers learned that lesson, the sooner they would encourage English merchants to raise their prices as the market determined, adapt to rather than resist currency fluctuations, compete in the exchange of credit, and—here was the payoff—enhance England's balance of trade.[22]

England's economists essayed the moral implication of this line of thinking: commercial men who sought profit as best they could—who bested the Dutch and French using the latest strategies to maximize returns on credit—enhanced the overall economic condition of England and properly fulfilled their vocation. The merchant who boldly played the market sustained the commonweal. "Is not gaine the end of trade?" Misselden asked. If so, then merchants ought to seek their private welfare as an "exercise of their calling." In such cases, "the private" interests of merchants served "the publique": "what else makes a Common-wealth, but the private-wealth . . . of the members thereof in the exercise of *Commerce*?" Regardless of previous moral reservations about self-interested merchants, he claimed that the successful trader spread civilization, knowledge, and civic piety. Merchants enlightened the whole nation with their "frugality, industry," and "policy, all working together for the publicke." For Misselden, these values were not particularly Protestant, certainly not Calvinistic dispositions, but professional and patriotic habits derived from no particular creed.[23]

In London, where Boston's traders occasionally traveled to arrange their affairs, more popular forms of literature—essays and poems, histories, and plays—also portrayed the merchant as a national hero. Writers during the second half of the seventeenth century acclaimed merchants in different terms than did their humanist predecessors: not as pious almsgivers and patrons of local institutions but as specialists in wealth who enriched England's empire with every commercial success abroad. Edmund Waller, a popular poet, applauded overseas merchants in Misselden's terms of empire and civilization. In his *History of the Royal Society* (London, 1667), Thomas Sprat boasted of the confluence of scientific discovery, new banking practices, technological advances, political freedom, and mercantile sagacity in London. James Howel claimed that the city's merchants had built an incomparable metropolis, "a *Hive of Bees*," that outpaced Amsterdam for "large Warehouses, and spacious fair Shops" with "all mercantile Commodities." John Dryden's plays invariably featured merchant adventurers who outwitted Dutch competitors with skill, inquisitiveness, sagacity, and expertise.[24]

The cosmopolitan networks that tied New England's merchants into England's market system, along with the increasingly complicated traffic in credit, outpouring of technical handbooks, balance-of-trade arguments, and popularization of the merchant as champion of the nation, identified overseas traders as economic specialists, public leaders, and cultural brokers at the same time. Boston's merchants did not celebrate all the cultural effusions of the metropolis, but they nonetheless embraced their role as civic patrons. They enacted public virtue—and religious callings—as they navigated commercial waters with skills and strategies that previous moralists condemned.

The very landscape of Boston, through which credit and goods flowed to the rest of New England, symbolized the civic prominence of Hull and his colleagues. They erected and maintained forty wharves through the early eighteenth century, promoted the construction of two waterfront batteries and a seawall, owned twelve shipyards, and employed more than one thousand vessels. Boston's maritime infrastructure, and the number of ships entering and leaving, dwarfed those of competing New England ports. Merchants' shops dominated certain districts of the town. Constables rang bells to open and close markets at the Town House and other venues, ordering civic time by commercial opportunity. Merchants built the town's most elaborate houses, clustered in their own neighborhoods. They lobbied for and oversaw the construction of roads, bridges, and ferries linking the town to inland villages. Topographical markers signified cultural influence. Political and intellectual news from abroad circulated through the booksellers, libraries, and printers founded by merchant clans. Overseas traders patronized Boston's nascent community of artists, who gave visual representation to high English taste. Men of commerce formed the core of Boston's civic, public order. Success in the commercial system amounted to public leadership. It brought power to Hull and his colleagues.[25]

HULL'S PIETY AND CHANGES IN CHURCH DISCIPLINE

Despite a common sense of professional expertise, Boston's merchants shared no monolithic ethos or religious identity. Religious variations among merchants multiplied especially after London began to pressure colonial governments to ease restrictions on religious dissent in the Bay

Colony. During the 1650s, many of the radicals exiled during the antinomian crisis of the 1630s returned to Boston from England or Rhode Island
and reestablished their businesses. Among them, Robert Sedgwick, Valentine Hill, and Thomas Broughton achieved some success; Thomas Savage
and Edward Hutchinson (son of Anne and father of Elisha) built great
trading houses. Many of these former dissenters made commercial and
familial connections outside the tight coterie of orthodox traders who first
gathered in Boston's Town House.[26]

After 1660 royal policy protected previously ostracized or recently arrived traders with neither puritan nor antinomian affiliations; some had
few or shifting religious sentiments, others resolutely conformed to the
Church of England. Samuel Maverick and other independent-minded men
worked in Nova Scotia with no religious oversight and arranged deals with
French customers. Thomas Deane, Richard Wharton, Thomas Breeden,
and Thomas Temple came to Boston in this period primed to benefit from
contested land claims in northern New England. A confirmed Anglican
and royalist, Wharton used a combination of new territorial entitlements,
a ready clientele among London's elite, and contacts at the royal court
to create a mercantile empire. Merchants such as Shrimpton, Wharton,
Temple, and Hutchinson all embraced Anglicanism to one degree or another. Temple fervently attached himself to the Church of England;
Shrimpton and Hutchinson attended Anglican services because they offered a friendly alternative to the puritan order and strengthened ties with
London. Wharton and his fellow Anglicans favored the restored monarchy
and attempted to build their trade with royal patronage. When resistance
to the Navigation Acts prompted a royal investigation beginning in 1664,
many of them signed a petition professing fealty to the king and abhorrence
of Boston's reputation for resistance. They petitioned for religious toleration and welcomed other challenges by the Committee of Trade and Plantations to the laws of Massachusetts Bay.[27]

What we might call, then, Boston's imperial merchants, like its ex-
antinomians, formed cohesive communities not through the puritan
church but through interrelated commercial, familial, and social alliances.
Wharton, to give one example, was related to the merchant Joseph Dudley
and married into the commercial families of William Tyng and Thomas
Brattle. Shrimpton too had familial ties to Tyng and to one of Boston's
older trading houses founded by Thomas Usher. This formed something
like an extended clan of elite merchants in Boston: Wharton-Tyng-Brattle-
Usher-Dudley-Shrimpton. Some of the Tyng and Usher traders aside, they
had little sympathy for the New England of John Winthrop, with its peculiar charter, puritan discipline, congregational way, and restrictions on
commerce. Devoted to the nation, obedient to its uppermost authorities
in church and state, attuned to the economic agendas of empire, and ambi-

tious to display the cultural signs of wealth and position—from tastes in reading to the latest fashions in clothing and architecture—they inherited and transformed the political and moral ethos of a previous generation of civic-humanist merchants. They were England's merchants of state residing in Massachusetts—the very sort of traders, however provincial, Misselden applauded.[28]

Hull had dealings with some of these men, but he represented what we may call, in contrast, a puritan merchant. The term reflects a political sensibility no less than a religious one. He chafed against the restored monarchy and its Navigation Acts (among other reasons, his mint violated royal prerogatives to issue coins), cherished the charter of the colony, and protested incursions on the powers of the colonial government. Hull, moreover, valued New England's social customs. He complained about English manners and social mores during frequent trips to London. A fervent member of the congregational order, he disapproved of the settlement of Quakers and Anglicans in Boston. He engaged in transatlantic trade but expressed little enthusiasm for cosmopolitan cultural styles. As much as he aspired to commercial success, he prided himself on his modesty, even his reluctance to amass a great fortune. For all of his technical skill and civic energies, Hull operated with puritan convictions that distanced him from many of his fellow traders by hedging his competitive drive.[29]

Hull was not alone. Joshua Scottow, another puritan merchant active in this period, authored two essays that bemoaned the popularity of commercial fashions and religious laxity in New England. Hull's son-in-law Samuel Sewall followed in the same pattern. He too accumulated a sizable but not grandiose estate, embraced orthodox puritanism, became a lay leader in the town's religious affairs, supported the General Court and the political prerogatives of the colonial government, and donated much of his wealth to local civic institutions. George Curwin at Salem also fit the puritan mold, as did Ipswich's Daniel Dennison. There were differences among these puritan merchants. Scottow, for example, displayed more willingness than did Hull to deal with the French in Acadia, form alliances with free-spirited land speculators, and use litigation. Somewhat of a scoundrel, Scottow in fact garnered a reputation for being unscrupulous despite his orthodox credentials. Hull, Scottow, and Sewall nonetheless viewed themselves alike as patrons of the puritan establishment and the defenders of Massachusetts Bay against imperial interests.[30]

Hull's affiliation with a new church in Boston further shaped his social sensibilities. Individual congregations within the puritan establishment promoted different protocols for church discipline, many of them centered on the meaning of baptism. During the late 1650s and 1660s, an increasing number of second-generation New Englanders, although baptized and mindful of Reformed beliefs, did not attest to the conversion experience that qualified their children for baptism. Fearing that these children would distance themselves from the covenant symbolized by the sacrament, many religious leaders began a campaign to allow baptism to the children of dutiful parents who had not become full communicant members. They argued their case through the Cambridge synod of Massachusetts churches and published their recommendations of the practice in 1657 and 1662. Later critics derided their innovation by calling it the Halfway Covenant.[31]

Debates about the Halfway Covenant turned to questions of church discipline, the demarcation between the regenerate church and unregenerate parishioners, and obligations to the civic order. Advocates for the new measure claimed responsibility for the spiritual and moral well-being of New England at large: the continued promotion of Christian identity in all sectors of society, regenerate or not. John Davenport and James Allen, the pastors of First Church, decried the new baptismal piety as moral compromise and a hindrance to true conversion. The majority of lay members in Boston's First Church likewise rebuffed Halfway proposals through the 1670s.[32]

In contrast to the conservatives at First Church, Hull and other merchants embraced the new practice because it appeared to them to reinforce Christian identity as a familial and civic duty in the midst of an increasingly diverse society. They determined to form a new congregation as early as 1666. After three years of disagreements and negotiations among the synod, the town's pastors, various committees, and the upper and lower houses of the government, they gained approval from the General Court to establish a church committed to the Halfway Covenant, identified by traditional standards for admission to the Lord's Supper but a more generous access to baptism. Eleven of the congregation's twenty-eight original members were overseas traders. They constituted a pantheon of successful puritan merchants in Boston, including Hull, Scottow, Brattle, Hezekiah Usher, Peter Oliver, Thomas Savage, Joseph Belknap, Benjamin Gibbs, Benjamin Gerrish, and Thomas Hubbard. The creation of Third Church in 1669, later known as the Old South Church, amounted to an exodus of merchants from First Church.

Hull operated at the center of things at Third Church; Davenport publicly rebuked him for leading the separation. When the new congregation finally received approval, it elected Hull and Edward Rainsford the first ruling elders. Hull's shop furnished the church with silver Communion vessels—a conjunction of commercial largesse and ritual piety befitting a congregation founded on wider accessibility to the sacraments. Hull also acted as the broker of the property for the meetinghouse. The site perfectly suited its merchant members. It was located two hundred yards from the marketplace, on the corner of Milk Street, which ran down to the harbor, and Cornhill Street, the main road from the center of town to Roxbury.

Hull oversaw the erection of an expensive building, traditional in design but more spacious and well appointed than First's meetinghouse, with a second-floor gallery and a steeple. It cost nearly £2,000, a hefty price borne by its founding families. It signified the ascendance of the new church and commercial-friendly puritanism over the old disciplinary order.[33]

Personal relationships cemented ministerial-merchant cooperation at Old South. Hull had a hand in the selection of Thomas Thacher as the first pastor and procured Thacher's first associate, Leonard Hoar. The congregation called Samuel Willard from Groton as Thacher's successor in 1678. Samuel was the son of Simon Willard, a military man and merchant with heavy investments in westward lands. Other such ties bound the congregation. Hull's only surviving child, Hannah, married Sewall, a future magistrate and sometime merchant who eventually served as a lay leader at Third Church. Sewall and other merchant members, such as Brattle and Anthony Stoddard, sent their sons into the ministry. Samuel Willard married Eunice Tyng, daughter of a merchant with expansive familial connections to other traders. In such a religious community, merchants could practice their trade and piety at once, surrounded by fellow church members who knew firsthand the demands and customs of commercial life.[34]

Boston's three puritan churches drew members from different areas of the town—there were no parish boundaries—but neighborhood settings and clerical leadership still shaped the social ethos of congregations. (Four other churches had been established in Boston by the end of 1686: a Quaker meeting, a Baptist congregation, a French Huguenot society, and the Anglican King's Chapel.) First Church, at the center of the town, retained a few well-established merchants—including Richard Bellingham, Edward and William Tyng, and Jeremiah Dummer—but had a large number of artisans, laborers, and small-business men. The majority of lay leaders claimed to sustain local interests, invested themselves heavily in municipal politics, and frequently criticized the General Court. Its pastors suspected that purely secular agendas had corrupted the colony's magistrates and overseas traders.[35]

Boston's Second (afterward Old North) Church was more hospitable to merchants than First, yet not as dominated by overseas traders as Third. Founded in 1650 in the newly populated North End, Second Church drew from a mixed population. Boston's northern precincts included its poorest inhabitants—propertyless immigrants and unemployed laborers—and some of its newer, wealthier merchants, including Sir Thomas Lake, Samuel Balche, Thomas Temple, Thomas Cushing, and Samuel Greenwood.[36] The congregation grew to be Boston's largest, especially under the pastorate of Increase Mather. A cosmopolitan by New England standards, Mather studied at Trinity College Dublin, served as an army chaplain in England, accepted the call to Second in 1664, and acted as a negotiator in London between the Crown and Massachusetts in consort with merchants such as Sewall. An avid consumer of English imprints, he displayed an entrepreneurial flair, authoring the first two works printed on a Boston press and assuring for them sensational appeal: one sermon addressed the execution of two murderers, and the other memorialized two merchants killed in a shipboard explosion in Boston Harbor. He formed close associations with two merchant patrons of the congregation, the wealthy Balche and Temple. In 1674 his preaching converted the future treasure hunter, financier, and governor William Phipps, who later married John Hull's widow.[37]

Second Church, however, did not especially attract Hull and his colleagues. Mather initially opposed the Halfway Covenant despite the support of his father, Richard. He maintained traditional disciplinary standards and viewed restrictions on the sacraments as an important measure to promote conversion. Concerned especially with the large number of impoverished parishioners in his part of town, he groused about new commercial practices: too much usury and profit taking, too little abatement of debts and almsgiving. He expressed more interest in converting merchants to a godly lifestyle than in baptizing their children.[38]

Hull's Old South, again, was a different matter. Situated in Boston's well-to-do southern precincts, it maintained its mercantile character through the 1680s. Membership records listed some tradesmen and small producers such as bakers, but few laborers and dozens of traders. From 1669 through 1710, First Church had seven merchants in the preferred civic association for overseas traders, the town's artillery company; Second Church had ten; and Third had the most by far, twenty-eight. Third's congregation, the most commercially oriented in Boston, also had the wealthiest profile of the three by a substantial amount, measured by the number of members in the highest tax brackets. It offered merchants such as Hull a new congregation in which to reconsider the relationship between religious conviction and commercial mandate.[39]

Sacramental debates and the establishment of Old South, different requirements for membership, varied social groupings, and political squabbles all unsettled the practice of corporate discipline in Boston. They confounded the notion of a concerted regime over social domains such as commerce. They thereby diminished the coercive power of congregations over merchants, intensifying a trend during Hull's lifetime for churches to refrain from interference in individuals' business affairs. Even First Church, the least progressive of Boston's congregations, relaxed its grasp on trade. From 1655 through 1689, the congregation conducted 35 disciplinary trials: 17 for drunkenness, 6 for fornication, 3 for speech crimes, 3 for violations of the Sabbath, 1 for heresy, 1 for violence, and 4 for economic practices such as oppression. It devoted few cases to commerce, compared with the years from 1630 to 1654, and addressed no commercial cases after 1669. The existing records at Second Church mirrored those at First. The church brought only 12 people to trial from 1674 (when the extant records begin) through 1685: 6 for drunkenness; 5 for assorted speech crimes such as slander, swearing, and lying in civil court; and 1 for embezzlement. At Hull's Third Church, only a handful of admonitions and censures appear in the records from 1670 to 1705, and these concerned drunkenness, fornication, verbal contempt of the pastor's authority, and nonattendance at public worship. Thacher and Willard certainly called aside wayward parishioners for spiritual and moral admonition, but the only economic issues discussed in congregational meetings involved the proper use of funds donated to the church by overseas traders: for building projects, poor relief, missions, and pastoral salaries. Church records from nearby Roxbury and Charleston, even distant Plymouth, indicate the same pattern. Throughout the Boston area, pastors and church officials focused their discipline on public decorum, sexual probity, civil orderliness, sobriety, and institutional responsibility. Unlike their predecessors in England and Boston, Hull and his contemporaries never faced the prospect of ecclesiastical censure for their price margins, credit fees, interest rates, and treatment of debtors.[40]

Despite their reticence to punish merchants, none of Hull's favorite pastors or fellow church officers offered an easy accommodation with contemporary market practices. Most second-generation ministers in Massachusetts, including Thacher and Willard, inherited a mandate to teach against entrepreneurial excess. They all decried iniquities associated with overseas commerce, from neglect of the Sabbath and religious toleration to fashionable consumer tastes and gambling. A succession of preachers, many of whom knew Hull, bemoaned the endless assault on godliness by imported tastes soon after the commercial expansion of the 1660s. John Higginson decried toleration of Anglicans and other imperial traders ascending the social ladder in Boston. Samuel Whiting deplored merchants who valued profits over prayer. Urian Oakes attributed the competitive drive of merchants to the spirit of Machiavelli, a sideswipe at England's new economists. He diagnosed transatlantic trade as a vector for innumerable moral infections: worldliness, greed, contention, faction, selfishness, usury, and indebtedness, not to mention prostitution, drunkenness, and frippery. Such bile had a long shelf life in Massachusetts. Eleven years after Oakes's tirade, Hubbard lashed out yet again against nonpuritan traders, stretching the rhetoric to extremes: cosmopolitan merchants, with their high fashion and immoral habits such as dancing, sated themselves with "Commodities to make fuel for Lust," forsaking the true church for their "private recesses," where they offered "sacrifices to Bacchus and Venus." Similar critiques

through the mid-1680s, evoking the neighborly modes of exchange promoted by the first generation, conveyed residual fears of social contention,
neglect of the poor, widespread inhumanity, and degrading materialism.[41]

These criticisms, however pungent, touched chiefly on cultural and social styles, and particularly the loyalties of imperial merchants, rather than
on the new exchange practices that puritan and imperial merchants employed alike. Second-generation puritan leaders never became as technical
as John Cotton, who analyzed Robert Keayne's business in detail. They
knew by tradition that usury, oppression, and pure market pricing were
wrong, but they lost the specific meaning of such terms in the swirl of
contemporary techniques: multilayered and indirect exchanges, the necessary treatment of credit as a commodity, new accounting measures, fiscal
rationalizations for market prices, complex debt litigation, and competition
with London's and Amsterdam's merchants. Yet they still recalled deep-
seated puritan antipathy to abusive credit practices, price inflation, and
aggressive litigation.[42]

Hull, like Keayne, avidly consumed even the most censorious preaching.
He attended lectures and sermons in different churches in and around Boston, frequently two or three times a week. He befriended Thacher and
Willard and associated frequently with other clerical lights in Boston, especially Mather. He took extensive notes on the Election Day, artillery, fast-
day, and Sunday performances of various pastors (figure 3.1). He suffered
the criticism of Oakes, Mather, Hubbard, Higginson, and Samuel Danforth of Roxbury, as well as the weekly exhortations by his pastors at the
Third Church. He recorded Thacher's 1672 warning to the merchants at
Old South against the sins of commercial Boston: "oppression" of the poor
(price gouging), "corruption" in the courts (lax enforcement of moral laws),
the uprooting of "Civillity" and "morality" (scandalous speech and disre-
spectful comportment), and "a mind to other waies and worship" (toleration of nonpuritan religious groups). Echoing early seventeeth-century
moralists who blasted London, Thacher denounced "this bloody Cyty" of
Boston with its "blood acts" throughout and forecasted divine judgment.
Hull also heard Thacher and Oakes discourse on the duty of Christian
merchants to avoid the social habits—and habitats—of cosmopolitan associates. "Communication with corrupt" men, "the meer civil person" with
"good maners," Thacher preached, "makes the name, offerings, and religion of God to stink in the world." Willard likewise admonished merchants
against addiction to high style.[43]

Hull also noted how preachers urged merchants to rely on the sovereignty and goodness of providence throughout their business affairs. Confidence in God's purposes offset the pull of economic ambition and yielded
equanimity. "True happiness," as Oakes put it in a sermon that Hull summarized in detail, resided in "escaping worldliness" and "attending" the

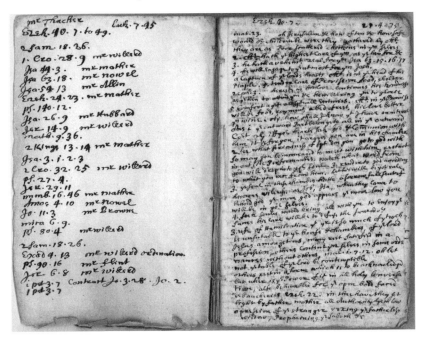

Figure 3.1. Sermon notes by John Hull, volume 46, April 1675. Original manuscript from Notes on Sermons. On the left page, Hull recorded sermon texts and preachers, including Thacher, Increase Mather, Hubbard, and Willard. On the right, he took detailed notes on Thacher's jeremiad-like sermon from Ezekiel 40, beginning with a quotation from Jesus' lament for Jerusalem in Matthew 23. Courtesy of the Massachusetts Historical Society.

"ordinances" of the gospel. Seen through the doctrine of providence, the vicissitudes of mundane successes and failures drew souls away from material attachments, toward Christ. Thacher put it this way: while the world's goats complain "upon every little cross," Christ's "sheep are quiet in suffering" and therefore promote "the practice of charity, meekness of wisdom, self-denying love," and care for the poor. These puritan preachers evoked the personal, neighborly, and morally laden modes of exchange promoted by the first generation.[44]

Hull, who took enough interest in theology to join a 1668 committee that debated doctrine with the town's Baptists, filled his diary with similar providential reflections.[45] The first part of it, "Some Passages of God's Providence about Myself and in Relation to Myself," uncovered supernatural interventions at nearly every turn in his autobiography: a miraculous "deliverance" from a wild horse in the streets of Boston at the age of twelve ("God," he marveled, "held up [the horse's] foot over my body"), the safe delivery of his children, provision of an apprentice, all sorts of storms,

piracies, and safe passages at sea, and his various appointments in the militia
and colony's government. In a typical entry, he reflected on the meaning
of a huge loss, nearly £600 worth of goods captured on three ships by the
Dutch: "God mixeth his mercies and chastisements, that we may neither
be tempted to faint or to despise." On the occasion of another Dutch disaster, he comforted himself with a twofold reflection: "the Lord" used his
loss "to join my soul nearer to himself, and loose it more from creature
comforts"; and providence soon thereafter repaired the fiscal damage, making "up my loss in outward estate." These readings reflected the teaching
of ministers who attempted to dissuade merchants from fretfulness and
preoccupation with money in purely rational, mathematical, terms. God,
Hull surmised, used misfortunes to teach him to be content with a modest
income and rely on supernatural protection.[46]

In one sense, the idea of providence encouraged Hull with the prospect
of future reward for patience and diligence—an analogue to long-term calculations of present costs and anticipated profits. It sometimes overcame
his fears and spurred commercial risk taking. Unlike more empirical ap-
proaches to trade, however, it also retarded a purely mathematical account
of social causes and effects. He privately pondered eclipses and droughts
as prodigies and tokens of the proximity of Christ's return, as much a part
of his affairs as were price fluctuations, trade statistics, and negotiations
with imperial officials.[47]

Hull integrated providential schemes and puritan moral teaching also
into his everyday business practice. He blended news of prices with admonitions to worship, commentary on the state of trade with meditations on
the Second Coming, and financial details with spiritual introspection. Imperial traders employed impersonal politeness and gave exclusive attention
to financial accounts in their business correspondence; Hull injected the
rhetoric of intimacy and moral accountability into his correspondence.[48]
Letters that dealt with apparently mundane matters—accounts and the status of goods—contain godly exhortations, prayers, and lamentations over
the state of the world. In several letters to his shipmasters, he placed
thoughts on providence (typically acknowledgments of divine mercy for
speedy transatlantic voyages) next to instructions on buying and selling.
He wanted others, as he informed Daniel Allin in 1672, to judge him by
the extent to which he circumscribed his trade with piety. His "reputation"
stood not merely on his fiscal reliability but also on "the mercy of god" by
which he had "done nothing in all my transactions but that as I am able to
give a good and Satisfying Accot of."[49]

Hull demanded that his associates operate under the same principles.
He commanded his ship captains to resist their occupational temptations:
mistreating common sailors, swearing, dealing on the Sabbath, neglecting
worship on board, making a fast bargain, unloading damaged goods on

unsuspecting buyers, or trading in slaves. As he summarized his instructions to captain Richard Rook, "we solemnly advise you to take heed and carefully avoid all and every sinful way which evil will bring sorrow and suffering to poor mortals, and especially the sorrowing of religion."[50] In 1673 Hull wrote a series of letters to the managers of one of his timber mills, George and John Broughton. Furious because the Broughton brothers had mismanaged the mill, quarreled with each other, and delayed a shipment of logs to one of his more valued customers, Hull lectured them on the relationship between public moral credit, religious duty, and economic virtue:

> I cannot tell what to thinke of you; some say you are for nothing but your own interest, that you are not frugall but will loose twenty shillings for want of a seasonable layeing out of one shilling, that you are haughtey and hy flowne. . . . [I]t is noe wonder iff all goeth backward with you and [I] advize you to bee yourselves very delegent frugalle humble. . . . Confute all that may bee said against you and lett your intire Love to one another and honner to your aged parents and honnest punctualyty to your Creditores give a cleare testimony. . . . [God] will take care of your name Creddit and reputation.

Hull's advice to the Broughtons illuminated his own sense of the inseparability of piety, virtue, and commercial practice: trust in providence prompted humility and frugality, which enhanced public reputation and thereby secured a good credit rating among one's associates.[51]

Frugality and social reputation brought practical benefits, but Hull's reading of these and other market virtues sometimes interfered with fiscal prudence. He often abated the accounts of widows, wrote off bad debts as the cost of Christian charity, and balked at trading paper credit rather than specie with impious, or at least unfamiliar, agents and suppliers. He also pestered debtors with moral lessons when he might have turned more effectively to legal pressure. His 1674 correspondence with fellow merchant Robert Marshall was typical in this regard. Marshall had taken a loan from Hull, gone to England, lost the money in bad investments, and displayed no inclination to repay his creditor. Hull professed to be morally wounded because he had yielded his business interests to personal consideration: he had "denyed soe much my owne reason and profitt to pitty you in your Extreamyty." As usual in such cases, Hull delayed in bringing his case to court. He pressed the moral issue, ending his letter with a string of biblical references on providential rewards and punishments "to reade and thinke on." In this and other cases Hull admitted that he had sacrificed his commercial sense to religious sensibilities.[52]

Even with his astuteness as an economic technician, Hull remained somewhat aloof from cosmopolitan market culture. He echoed the stan-

dard laments for Boston's decline into self-interested materialism. He discerned economic venality in imported habits and tastes: "pride in longhair,
new fashions in Apparell, drinking, gaming, idleness, worldlyness." Tuned
to modesty and humility as Christian virtues, he maintained a relatively
small house, refrained from luxury goods (with the exceptions of wine and
silk stockings), and never (that we know) had his portrait painted. He refused to join other Boston merchants whose homes were closer to the
newer docks and wharves, where news and goods arrived first and shipments could be examined and purchased before lesser traders claimed
them. At times, Hull appeared to despair over the hustle and bustle of the
trading life. "All employments," he wrote with a sigh, "a smite upon them;
at least, in general, all men are rather going backward than increasing
their estates." He attempted to quit the trade several times during his career and declined potentially profitable ventures out of spiritual conviction.
At one such moment he mused on his retirement by drawing nicely on the
trope of seagoing vessels: he wanted "to be more thoughtfull of Launching
into that vast ocion of Eternity" than of sending forth yet another shipment
of exports. Hull saved his admiration for puritan leaders such as the former
governor John Endicott, who "died poor," having spent his "pious and
zealous" life persecuting Quakers and attending more to the "public" than
to "his own private interests." In such terms, the closer Hull drew to
puritanism—the more he scribbled his sermon notes, conversed with
Boston's pastors, and meditated on devotional tracts—the more he
bounded his financial ambition. Puritanism sometimes betrayed the emergent market personality.[53]

Yet again, Hull was no relic from the days of John Winthrop. He pursued
profits aggressively, sometimes inflexibly. Pious resolves to quit business
aside, he fastened on his accounts fiercely. He provided expensive silver
pieces to satisfy the ostentatious tastes of such elites as Elisha Hutchinson
and John Pynchon. He traded with New England's enemies. He followed
market trends for luxuries quite closely, attuned to the latest styles in
fans, hats, ribbons, and lace—and critical of his suppliers when they sent
him unfashionable goods. He sometimes pushed his timber managers to
relentless work schedules and advised his tenants to a preoccupation with
profits that appeared incongruous with puritan devotion; "follow your Bui-
synes Closs and give mee an accot" as "your duty to god and mee," he
wrote to William Heifernan with a stunning lack of modesty. He even
made hard bargains with the colony, refusing to lower his allowance as
mint master despite several pleas from a government committee. He spent
the last few months of his life frantically calling in debts from the government and fellow merchants, as though unpaid accounts glared at Hull as
his memento mori.[54]

The complex credit measures upon which Hull relied involved him in the very sort of impersonal and oppressive transactions that puritans of the 1620s and 1630s damned. He dealt with London credit brokers who, because of unfavorable exchange rates, charged New Englanders as much as 25 percent interest, compelling him to raise prices and credit fees to unprecedented levels. He speculated in insurance and mortgages, profiting rather perversely from shipwrecks and foreclosure. Hull transformed credit into an everyday commodity—in violation of nearly every dictate against usury uttered by godly moralists of an earlier period. He also menaced his debtors with litigation, even prison, in ways that would have affronted first-generation religious leaders. He could be considered as the very sort of hard-driving merchant who provoked country traders and customers from other American colonies to complain about New Englanders' high mark-ups on bills of exchange, excessive prices, and monopolies. English visitor John Josselyn decried the hypocrisy of puritan merchants in Boston who denounced well-meaning Quakers while smuggling goods, monopolizing commodities, charging "excessive prices," enslaving farmers and fishermen through oppressive credit schemes, and scooping up mortgages and repossessed vessels like so many fallen apples. "If they do not gain *Cent per Cent,*" Josselyn observed, "they cry out that they are losers." Hull might have prided himself on his piety and civic prominence, but Josselyn colored Boston's merchants as a "damnable rich" cabal flattered by preachers whom they patronized.[55]

Josselyn's critique rang true in at least this respect: Hull navigated between religious teaching and commercial acumen without a precise discipline enforced by the church congregation. Hull's pastors certainly preached to him, but they did not interfere with his professional competence and mercantile expertise. Neither Hull nor his pastors ever presumed that they ought to direct his accounts: his credits and debts, the commodities he exchanged and customers with whom he dealt, his interest rates and legal pursuit of debtors, prices and fiscal decisions. Hull fretted about worldliness, but he bore the burden of determining his business practices as a matter of private conscience, only dimly informed by preachers who condemned illicit byproducts of the transatlantic economy such as imported fashions, and personal dispositions such as avarice, without specifying proper profit margins or credit transactions. His story signaled a turning point in the relationship between puritanism and commerce in early New England.

Institutional changes in the church help to explain this shift in the short term. Boston merchants moved into the transatlantic market during the 1650s and 1660s, when fractures in the puritan order and the complexities of overseas trade belied pretensions of a common set of rules and procedures to reform commerce. Yet that is to speak only of temporary hindrances to ecclesiastical coercion over merchants. In the long run, puritan preachers in Massachusetts developed profound legitimizations for new conceptions of discipline that explicitly allowed merchants to operate outside the control of congregations: ideas about the means by which providence dispensed justice and judgment in New England's social affairs. Their pronouncements from the late 1660s through the early 1680s prompted merchants such as Hull to ground their moral responsibility in the civic order itself, the public institutions of Massachusetts.

Jeremiads, Providence, and New England's Civic Order

Not all of the established clergy in Boston regarded discipline and the civic order in the same way. Although most of them shared a distaste for imported cultural styles and the apparently bottomless ambitions of a new class of commercial men, they promoted different forms of moral oversight as antidotes. At First Church, Davenport and his successors—James Allen and John Oxbridge—insisted on the necessity for the regenerate church to reassert its rule over society and warned New Englanders against the subordination of the congregation to the power of civil government. "The Danger to be feared in reference to the Civil State," Davenport asserted in 1663, concerned "a perverting of *Justice*" and abandonment of scriptural norms in favor of secular, pragmatic notions of the good. In his 1669 Election Day sermon, an infamous assault against the Halfway Covenant and Old South, he reiterated his argument for the primacy of the gathered congregation as a community of discipline and the unreliability of civil magistrates and law courts. In his 1679 election sermon, Allen pleaded for a recovery of the practices of the previous generation.[56]

The pastors at Old North and Old South, in contrast, appealed to civil authorities to remake society. They never explicitly discarded church censures in the old pattern, yet they did configure strategies for reform that invested public institutions with divine purpose. Slowly, from the Halfway Covenant through the mid-1680s, they set the burden of a moral economy on the shoulders of civic men: magistrates, legislators, and merchants such as Hull. In the process, they marginalized the original puritan agenda for religious discipline over commerce.[57]

A series of public crises in the mid-1670s especially sparked the pastors at Second and Third Church to reconsider the relationship between providence and public institutions. The Restoration and threat of imperial intervention in the colony's affairs hung over the whole period, from an increasing number of trade inspectors and the presence of dissenting religious groups protected by royal mandate to periodic rumors of a revocation of Massachusetts's charter. In 1675 and 1676 King Philip's War unleashed unprecedented violence and destruction throughout southern New England. In 1676 a fire devastated the North End of Boston, including the Old North meetinghouse. Increase Mather ticked off one calamity after another in his private journal: political "designs against New England," the near death of "trade," unusually dry summers and frigid winters, Indian raids, and a governor who quarreled with the representatives. "'Tis the saddest time with N. E. that ever was known," Mather observed. Voicing alarm, the General Court called thirty colony-wide fast days during 1675–1676, some six times the annual average for the rest of the seventeenth century.[58]

Desperation drove Mather and other ministers to providential interpretations of public events. Mather privately began to puzzle over the reason for—that is, the intelligibility of— every misfortune that befell Massachusetts. "Providence doth now [set] me upon Humiliation extraordinary," he wrote as King Philip's War began, and it was his job to discern the precise "cause for it." His perceptions hinted at a regularity to moral cause and providential effect. He asserted that the "special hand of God" delivered an outbreak of smallpox in Boston Harbor because the governor had licensed too many drinking establishments. God sent a cold front during the 1675–1676 winter to hamper the militia because troops had murdered an innocent Indian. He allowed Indian raids to terrorize the people because officers violated the Sabbath. The Lord confounded "the English forces" in an important battle at the very moment that the upper house of the General Court voted down reforming measures promoted by pastors. "It seems to be an observable providence" that Indians killed militia officer Edward Hutchinson, Mather surmised, because Hutchinson had rebuffed his church's admonishment for drunkenness. (Where church censure failed, providence administered a more direct and severe punishment.) Mather began to seek religious meaning in mundane events, read ordinary history alongside Scripture as a means of divine revelation, and decode providence in visible, temporal events as well as in the atemporal progress of the gospel.[59]

These private ruminations reflected a trend among Massachusetts Bay ministers who made sense of corporate strains by drawing on puritan notions of providence and covenant. Many of their fast-day and election sermons in particular, sometimes called jeremiads, probed for patterns and predictability: a nearly causal paradigm to the sequence of events. Recollecting Reformed tenets, they asserted that providence called select nations through a covenant that threatened judgments for sin and promised blessings for reform. From William Stoughton of Dorchester to Oakes and Willard, ministers often concluded that civil authorities, who represented the social order, secured the commonweal by enforcing the covenant as a social obligation.[60]

Mather had precedents for his jeremiads, but he was the master of the genre. Frequently published and an intimate of Hull and other puritan merchants, he took partial associations and formed them into a full-blown identification between the public order of New England and divine rule. He did so most spectacularly in two 1673 sermons delivered on a December day of humiliation in his church (a day of corporate confession designed to avert divine punishment) and published together. Their titles voiced Mather's ambiguity: *The Day of Trouble is Near . . . wherein is shewed . . . what reason there is for New England to expect a Day of Trouble. And what is to be done, that we may escape these things which shall come to pass.* Preached on the verge of King Philip's War, *The Day of Trouble* envisioned widespread calamity—"things which shall come"—yet pleaded for measures to avert such calamity—"what is to be done, that we may escape." In the first sermon, Mather maintained that Israel and the New Testament church suffered troubles as means of divine correction for idolatry, spiritual torpor, and oppression of the poor.[61]

In the second sermon, Mather correlated biblical precedents with events in New England in rich detail. New England's Christians, he charged, lacked spiritual vitality; they appeared, "as to their discourses, or their spirits, or their walking, or their garb," like unbelievers. Commercial success had so become their idol that they donned worldly garments and turned away from the poor in their midst, taking profits at the expense of their neighbors. Even "Professors of Religion *fashion themselves according to the world.*" Mather resorted to the same language that English reformers had used to condemn London in the days of James I and Charles I. "Is there not Oppression amongst us?" he asked. "Are there no biting Usurers in *New England?* Are there not those that grinde the faces of the poor?" Signs of providential chastisement inevitably followed. Vice flooded New England and eroded the political order. The great first generation—godly rulers all, according to Mather—had nearly died off. Present misfortunes portended further judgments.[62]

Nothing in Mather's puritanism expressed an affinity with high-flown economic ambition and impersonal techniques to exchange credit and accrue profits. Here and elsewhere, he fingered commercial vice as the chief occasion for chastisement. Three years after *The Day of Trouble* performances, he attributed further misfortunes, including warfare and economic depression, to the venality of merchants. They had set "excessive" prices by the laws of the market rather than by "the just value." He professed shock at the widespread acceptance of "that odious sin of Usury," which transformed debtors into means of profit. He excoriated land-grabbing speculators who provoked Indian ire toward English settlers. New England's calamities predictably had followed the sins of its most prominent citizens.[63]

Mathei issued customary social criticism, but he also offered an uncustomary reading of New England's history. He developed his interpretation further in *The Day of Trouble* and other writings. Reviewing the history of Massachusetts in 1676, he marveled at how the virtuous "Fathers of New England" suffered no crushing disasters. Moral degeneration during the 1660s and early 1670s had, by the law of God working its way out in the flow of events, provoked severe punishment throughout society. Such was the action of providence. The events, Mather astonishingly claimed, "spake no less" than Scripture itself. He modified New England's narrative into a divine drama in which, to quote him again, "the events spake," which is to say that history became scripture. He did not abandon the Bible, but it was the history of Israel that fascinated him, and the correlation between Israel and New England. He made his case against the Halfway Covenant with a biography of his father. Other ministers looked to New England's history for indications of divine purpose. Hubbard composed lengthy narratives of New England's settlement and Indian wars; Oakes meditated on the latest historical works from London; and Samuel Danforth of Roxbury published almanacs featuring historical vignettes. These historian-divines drew moral and theological conclusions from the patterns they discerned in public events, sometimes dispensing with traditional methods of disputation based on the Bible and its refraction through creeds and magisterial authorities such as Calvin.[64]

Previous puritans of various stripes also read God's hand in history. For over a century, Reformed pamphleteers and divines in England had portrayed a cosmos driven by providential judgment. Calvinists in England, the Netherlands, and Scotland furthermore asserted a political dimension to providence in terms of a national covenant, with mandates of social reform dictated by magistrates. Parliamentary leaders made the association between the nation and biblical Israel long before the Boston preachers, and the migration to New England appeared to its founders as one miracle after another. Yet first-generation puritans, trained in England under erratic political circumstances, did not presume that providence shaped temporal affairs in logical, predictable patterns. God allowed whatever came their way—prosperity, disaster, complexity—to call forth faith. Public events were mere tokens of deeper and elusive spiritual realities.[65]

Taking their cues from Calvin, their Cambridge teachers, and Continental divines, puritans such as Cotton, Winthrop, and Hooker understood providence to be essentially mysterious to human intelligence. When they attempted to decipher momentous events with scriptural lenses or discerned special providences—extraordinary events that enacted divine judgments—their interpretations confounded the notion of a consistent pattern in history. They made few stable predictions about the future of New England or any other political state. From this perspective, Winthrop's earlier sketches of New England's history serve as a contrast to Mather's assertions of the 1670s. Winthrop maintained that the Lord guided the settlement of Massachusetts, but he did not describe a precise correlation between contemporary affairs and divine purpose, acts and consequences, moral practices and historical outcomes. The collective workings of providence remained inexplicable to him. Lacking clarity in such matters, he resorted to Scripture as a guide that transcended national agendas or provincial ambitions. He thought that the murkiness of history obliged New Englanders to subordinate civil reasoning, humanist ethics, republican theories, and other political claims to the wisdom of the Bible, delivered and administered through the church.[66]

The palpable determination of preachers such as Mather and Willard to uncover divine purpose and moral order in the calamities around them marked a shift from this tradition. They extended and modified their predecessors' interpretation of history, gathering interpretive precedents and making an unprecedented elision between New England and Israel. Mather identified the civil body (of Massachusetts) as a special object of providential oversight in ways that perhaps only William Bradford did (for Plymouth Colony) in the previous generation. He eventually likened the colony's public institutions with the people of God. "This is Immanuels Land," he asserted at the end of "The Day of Trouble." "Christ by a wonderful Providence" had "caused as it were *New Jerusalem* to come down from Heaven." Thus "the dealings of God with our Nation" were "different than with other" nations and colonies. The real church, by Mather's reading, was New England.[67]

The more Mather wrote and spoke in this vein, the more he invested New England's civil leaders, members of his Boston audience such as Hull, with responsibility for moral reform. They represented the godly nation. Shaken by the outbreak of war, the General Court asked him for an address at its October meeting in 1675. He elaborated the meaning of his previous sermons: the future of Massachusetts lay in the hands of its legislators and magistrates. Taking its cue from Mather, the court designated a committee to draft a series of reform measures, the "Provoking Evils" legislation. Paraphrasing Mather's list of sins, the court ordered county judicatories and town constables to proceed against immodest clothing, Sabbath violations, periwigs, swearing, tavern haunting, and unlicensed public houses. The laws gestured toward religious discipline by urging the churches to attend to the training of youth. Yet they affirmed the civil magistracy's complete authority over economic practice, empowering county courts or grand juries to make presentments and set fines for excessive prices and other oppressions. Two months later, when Mather delivered a widely attended lecture on the state of the colony, published as *An Earnest Exhortation*, he admonished the magistrates to be zealous in the execution of the laws and prodded them to consider further measures. Such civil measures, he surmised, would protect the commonweal and secure the country's prosperity.[68]

Widely influential, Mather's *Earnest Exhortation* provided an interpretive template for Thacher and Willard and set the tone for his own further preaching.[69] In his 1677 election sermon, *A Discourse Concerning the Danger of Apostasy*, he jettisoned previous puritan claims that true moral discipline came through the churches to the wider society. Instead, he asserted what he admitted was a "controversial" proposal that "the Magistrates" assume "power in matters of Religion" and reform the churches as well as society. This, he argued, enacted the biblical pattern and replicated the precedent set by the founders of New England: a political-religious order led by civil rulers whom "Scripture compared to Corner stones" because they "lay such Foundations as shall make Posterity either happy or miserable."[70] He urged the General Court to produce and publish a history of New England, as if it were the court's duty not merely to enforce divine law but also to detect its iterations in recent events. He insisted that the magistrates take heed to monitor the churches, supervise candidates for ministry, promote orthodoxy, and compel congregations to reconciliation after the divisions created by the Halfway Covenant and foundation of Old South. In effect, the magistrates ought to exercise discipline over the churches.[71]

Departing from older patterns of church discipline, Mather also demanded that ministers refrain from debates about politics, economics, and other civil matters (ironically, he was lecturing the magistrates on their duties). "For a Minister of Christ" to pretend to "be a Merchant" or for preachers "to be Gospel Lawyers, to handle the *Code* instead of the Bible," was "very uncomely," he tartly explained. He specifically referred here to pastors who engaged in commerce and argued cases in civil courts, but in the process he excluded them from interference in economic and legal practice. Civil matters called for civil expertise, in which the lay leaders of the colony, not its preachers, specialized. Willard signaled his agreement with Mather in his 1679 sermon on the death of Governor John Leverett. He apologized for the appearance of being a "busie body in matters of State" but allowed himself at least this one political observation: rulers ought to know "how to deal in the very change of a peoples manners . . . as the times vary." That is, the good ruler read the times, interpreted history and social change, and therefore knew what justice and the common good meant in particular circumstances. Only "Skillfull, discerning" rulers could "understand the times and seasons, and what Israel ought to do." Willard implied that civil rulers rather than pastors had the practical experience to supervise life in society.[72]

Mather's interpretations engaged most of the Boston-area clergy, who convened a special synod to discuss reform in 1679. Attended by the pastors of Old South, along with Hull and Savage as lay representatives, the synod published its recommendations as *The Necessity for Reformation*. It reiterated Mather's previous analyses: factions, slander, contentious litigation, land speculation, aggressive settlement on the frontier, defrauding the Indians, oppression, high prices, excessive profits, and inflated wage demands all signified the eclipse of godliness by worldly spirits. Avarice seethed everywhere. Merchants suffered this much rebuke. *The Necessity for Reformation*, however, did not demand their submission to church authorities. The synod allowed that it was "impossible" for individual congregations to exercise discipline over such a large and diverse population, so it solicited magistrates to model moral virtue, support the Cambridge Platform, enforce previous moral legislation, and promote covenant renewals in the churches. After the convocation, Mather and Willard privately pestered the governor, deputies, and other public officials to enforce statutory limits on wages and prices.[73]

The General Court responded to the synod with legislation that excluded congregational discipline from civic and economic matters; it omitted mention of the church (except for a brief reference to religious education) and empowered county courts yet again to deal with oppression, profiteering, and idleness. It also mandated a committee of lay magistrates to review all previous moral statutes.[74]

Despite some reservations about the legislation, Mather, Willard, and other principals in the synod supported the court by promoting a new covenant-renewal ceremony in their congregations. Intending the ritual to be a means of moral and spiritual dedication, Mather and Willard held ceremonies at the Old North Church on the same day. In his sermon on the occasion, Mather recapitulated his argument that the government had a mandate to enforce obedience to the "external" covenant by which God promised corporate, temporal prosperity for social virtue. The church, on the other hand, engaged its members in a spiritual covenant of grace: the hope of eternal felicity premised on faith. He urged his members to renew their vows to both iterations of New England's covenant. They were related obligations, because the spiritual covenant led believers to promote the civic good, which the external covenant secured. Mather mentioned nothing of the congregation's responsibility to oversee the civic conduct of its individual members. The church ought to offer the means of grace, especially the sacraments, while public officials saw to such matters as commercial exchange.[75]

Preaching for his congregation after Mather, Willard said nothing about corporate religious discipline in the old style. He endorsed the covenant renewal as "a judicious and voluntary act" of individuals who, in the interiority of their "own heart[s]," detected sin, repented, and recommitted themselves to God. Willard hinted at the problem of covetousness and pride but listed no specific misdeeds to bring the point home. Without saying as much, he celebrated a ritual that promoted spiritual renewal and left economic details to the government. Two years later, in his 1682 election sermon, he yet again claimed that magistrates carried responsibility for civic behavior, from economic exchange to proper speech. By this time New England's crises appeared to have abated, and Willard was downright sanguine about the state of the colony, with its separate "ecclesiastical and civil constitutions."[76]

The covenant renewals culminated a long period of theological adjustment, when leading lights of the New England clergy, especially the pastors of Second and Third Churches in Boston, constructed an interpretation of New England's history that overturned the scenario of the founders. Leaders such as Cotton and Winthrop envisioned moral discipline as the authority of the believing congregation, which wielded the peculiar mandates of Scripture over the social activities of its members. Tracking civic occurrences as providential history, Mather and Willard located divine rule in public institutions. The church functioned as one of many corporate associations, with its own sphere of activity. Congregations served the commonwealth by promoting moral sincerity and a godly conscience. Merchants conducted their trade to enhance prosperity. Magistrates enforced the law. Preachers infused the whole system with providential purpose and direction while minimizing interference by the church in technical matters of exchange and civil justice. The jeremiads, to put it in the strongest terms, thereby justified the displacement of congregational discipline from social exchange. Economic reform rested not in the imposition of ancient and immutable laws—custom and Scripture—through the church, but in the responsibility of civil leaders to rule according to their social expertise.[77]

More specifically, puritan preaching gave merchants a mandate to rely on legal authorities for moral supervision and to depend on civic laws, as administered by the courts, to arbitrate disputes over credit, prices, and contracts. Devout traders such as Hull hesitated to pursue debt litigation too readily—charity often decreed forgiveness rather than legal harshness—but the erratic supply of money compelled them to rely on book debts and negotiable instruments and accordingly pressured them to raise interest rates and bring debtors to court. They accepted litigation as a necessary cost of economic competence and an instrument of providence.

The number of debt cases in the Massachusetts Superior Court of Judicature accordingly soared during the 1670s and 1680s and rose markedly in the county courts. In the Suffolk County Court of Common Pleas, the percentage of the docket devoted to causes for debt (unpaid debts and defaulted bonds) doubled from 1670 to 1680, taking up more than a quarter of the total cases. The court became the preferred forum for economic adjudication in the Boston area, spending more than three-quarters of its time on debt and other matters of commerce such as contested bills of exchange, failure to deliver goods, and disagreements over contracts, bonds, rents, probate, and land boundaries. Similarly, the percentage of debt cases in the Essex County Quarterly Courts rose from 2 percent of the docket in 1662 to more than 50 percent by 1683. Comparable figures emerge from the records of the Middlesex County Courts in a slightly later period. Many of the cases, moreover, revealed the spread of debt litigation from contests between merchants over bonds and unpaid bills to a host of issues involving artisans, farmers, and unemployed citizens as well.[78]

Nearly all puritan traders in Boston—including Tyng, Scottow, Savage, Oliver, Brattle, and Usher—filed causes for debt in the Suffolk court, and their readiness to use civil justice reflected new attitudes toward social discipline. Occupied with commercial suits, Massachusetts courts adopted formal procedures, demanded specialized legal argumentation, and relied on the economic expertise of merchants themselves, aided by legal experts such as Richard Cooke.[79] Court records included dozens of pages of accounts and a flurry of papers for a single case. In 1672, to mention only one example, Cooke represented several creditors who sued Hull's timber-mill manager, Thomas Broughton, for outstanding debts. Broughton had paid his creditors, including Hull, Usher, and Shrimpton, with mortgages and bills of exchange on partial shipments of goods long-since sold. Differences in interest rates, accrued interest, multiple ownerships of bills, contested land claims, and even unknown signatories required so much scrutiny that one creditor (unnamed in the records, no doubt to preserve his reputation) admitted that it appeared that he "hath been payd: but he best knoweth" not "how" or by whom. The need for economic proficiency, added to professional standards of legal protocol, with their peculiar language, mixtures of common law and shifting precedent, and impersonal decorum, marked a departure from the personal, flexible, and informal agendas of the first generation, who argued that the church ought to reform the courts according to scriptural norms and language.[80]

The jeremiads did more than invest new legal measures with legitimacy. Even when they hammered against self-serving merchants, ministers observed the growth of civil society as a didactic exercise. They provided a religious rationale for the increasingly specialized legal protocols and credit practices that helped merchants to expand New England's market—indeed, to recover it from the stagnation of the 1640s and link it to vital overseas networks. Puritan pronouncements on civic affairs paralleled the moral observations made by England's mercantilist thinkers, such as Misselden and Petty, who also derived the laws of commerce from observations of history: the effects of policies on nations' balance of trade. Preachers in Boston's Second and Third Churches, no less than the economists, suggested that service to the public good amounted to a moral rule. Merchants who refrained from the gross excesses of imperial culture and downright avarice, then, might well pursue their profits and litigation apart from customary strictures against new modes of exchange, as long as they contributed to the commonweal.

New conceptions of providence helped Hull and his merchant colleagues to negotiate between pious resolve and commercial demand. Hull inscribed providential interpretations onto his own reflections about his calling as a merchant and civic leader and the state of New England. Along with his pastors, he anxiously noted imperial threats to the charter of the colony in the mid-1660s, rising contention, the death of first-generation leaders, and toleration of Quakers. Charting an increase in supernatural prodigies and portents, the frequency of fast and thanksgiving days, renewed war with the Dutch, unusually cold winters in 1665, a fire among Boston's warehouses in 1672, and the proximity of Dutch privateers at Long Island in 1673, he detected a divine storm on the horizon. Like Mather, he felt "a general sense of the anger of God appearing in such threatening, and the issue unknown." In 1675 he noted the demise of several fellow merchants and magistrates, including Hezekiah Usher, Peter Lidget, and Richard Russell. In 1676 the fiery destruction of Old North Church stunned him. After King Philip's War ended, he remarked on the continuing calamities: smallpox, the death of Leverett, and a conflagration that destroyed several docks and warehouses, including his own. Throughout all of this, Hull listened intently to the jeremiads coming from the pulpits of Second and Third Churches and expressed hope that the 1679 Reforming Synod would provide remedies. His reading followed closely on the interpretation of men such as Mather and Willard, who taught him to infuse his civic duties and mercantile objectives with religious principle.[81]

Joshua Scottow, Hull's fellow merchant at Old South, explicitly acknowledged Mather and Willard as inspirations for his two jeremiad-like histories published in 1691 and 1694, *Old Mens Tears for their Own Declensions* and *A Narrative of the Planting of Massachusetts*. Providential cause and effect in history filled his narratives as much as it had Mather's. Like Mather, Scottow idealized the founders of New England as spiritual giants. The Lord rewarded their civic "skill," excellence in the arts of war, and deeds of "Gallantry and Bravery" with uncommon success. He recounted the people's recent decline into frippery and pale religiosity, their loss of energy and diligence, and their worldliness and unbelief. The calamities of war and political abasement before the Crown came as predictable judgments. Recalling the agendas of the Reforming Synod, Scottow pleaded with civic leaders to take command. He urged merchants to exercise discipline along with commercial prowess: to rebuild New England in emulation of the first settlers who passed "over the largest Ocean in the Universe" in ships "all Laden with Jewels of Invaluable Value." Scottow replicated and condensed in one treatise twenty years of change in puritan teaching: the distancing of New England's past from the present, reading of public events as the unfolding of predictable moral laws, attribution of covenantal identity to the civil order, and, finally, the importance of secular leaders— magistrates and merchants—to the future of New England.[82]

Hull certainly conducted his affairs as if his contributions to civil society were providential mandates. One of many merchants who increasingly bore the cost of poor relief in Boston, he donated much of his hard-won profits to charitable projects such as the construction of an almshouse.[83] Hull assumed other posts of civic leadership. He was elected to the office of selectman in 1658 and frequently thereafter. He sat on special courts devoted to commercial disputes and on a committee that recommended the creation of a bicameral legislature for the colony. Beginning in 1671, five towns voted him their deputy to the General Court at different times (the law did not require residency). He traveled to London to advise a delegation commissioned to negotiate matters of trade and corresponded with the colony's agents in London. As treasurer, he oversaw and under-wrote the government's purchase of arms and munitions for the militia. After King Philip's War, he paid for several diplomatic missions to London. He arranged for, and financially backed, Massachusetts's purchase of lands in Maine. Royal officials thought him important enough to include him among the defendants in proceedings against the Massachusetts charter when imperial-colonial frictions over commercial law mounted to a crisis in the early 1680s.[84]

Boston's clergy had urged Hull and his fellow merchants to enact piety through public leadership, valorizing their business skill and administrative expertise. Hull thought of himself in these very terms. His success, even though not as formidable as that of some of his competitors, brought him into a circle of men unequaled in Boston for their knowledge of the empire that increasingly impinged on life in the colonies. With his transatlantic ties, administrative experience, business acumen, and loyalties to New England, he and his associates viewed themselves as civic patrons. Drawing a parallel between himself and the heroes of the Great Migration, Hull recounted how God had "moved the hearts" of merchants to supply "fitt matterialls for a Commonwealth" in New England. He cherished that "choicest" company of "military men, seamen Tradesmen" with "Larg Estates and free spirits" who "spent" themselves "for the Advancmt of this worke . . . to make this wilderness as Babilon was once to Israell," to plant "a Jerusalem" in the New World. As Hull explained to the General Court when petitioning for repayment of the "seven hundred pounds at Interest" he had paid the Crown for the colony's land claims in Maine, "my encouragement was that God had called me to the place and had given me what I had for such a time,—that it was for a good people." He had acted like the valiant founders of New England; he counted it his "duty to spend and to be spent for the Public welfare." Yet the practical wisdom that earned him the money to lend for the public now compelled him to demand repayment, to display his commercial drive by laying out the interest rates and various factors now deepening the colony's indebtedness to him, and to plead "not to suffer" him "to lose more than needeth." Dependent on civil leadership and economic prosperity, New England would have to follow the fiscal rules and market principles that drove merchants such as Hull.[85]

Puritan preaching in the 1660s and 1670s provided the template for Hull to make his own image as a civic patron, public benefactor, and devout believer all at once. He did not find it excessive to claim for himself a role in the providential history of Massachusetts. Nearly twenty years after his death, Increase Mather's son and successor at Old North, Cotton Mather, further validated Hull's perspective with a memorial to his wealth and political sagacity. Mather claimed that Hull's success fulfilled a prediction by pastor John Wilson during Hull's youth: "it came to pass accordingly that this exemplary person became a very *rich*, as well as emphatically a *good* man, and afterwards died a *magistrate* of the colony."[86]

Willard and other pastors extolled men like Hull, regardless of how merchants accumulated their estates, in the belief that they used their profits for public and religious purposes. When Hull died in 1683, Willard eulogized him as a true saint, confirming Hull's self-image as an expert in making and giving away money. As an exemplar of the godly merchant, Hull, by Willard's reading, tempered economic aspiration with inward devotion and prayer, his "constant and close secret Communion with God." He was not like the imperial merchants, making idols of money, flaunting their wealth, and neglecting the covenantal duties of family worship. He openly confessed his faith in Christ, sometimes provoking his merchant competitors to scoff at him. He expressed loyalty to his pastors and nurtured pious practices in his home. He "strove to grow better as the times grew worse." Yet Willard also discerned the work of "Providence" in Hull's "prosperous and Flourishing Portion of the Worlds Goods." Hull did not neglect the "outward occasions and urgency of Business." He exhibited proficiency and diligence in his trade. A public-minded man, he invested his wealth in a variety of civic associations, from municipal commissions and the colonial Assembly to the artillery company and, as only one among other public institutions, the church. By the time of his death, "this Government," Willard preached, "hath lost a Magistrate; this Town hath lost a good Benefactor; this Church hath lost an honourable Member"; and Boston's militia "Company hath lost a worthy Captain." His conscience fortified by piety, Hull had "a sweet and affable Disposition" that led him to make several donations to the indigent of Boston: "the Poor have lost a Liberal and Merciful Friend." Hull merited "the love and respect of the People," who "had lifted him up to places of honour and preferment." Such combination of economic expertise, civic-mindedness, and personal piety, Willard claimed, pleased God.[87]

Other Boston traders did not measure up to Hull in Willard's ledger, but they also earned his plaudits as civic men. Speaking at the funeral of his parishioner Thomas Savage in 1682, Willard reiterated a theme from the jeremiads, that the death of luminaries bespoke coming judgment. "God hath now for a long time been pleading with N-E in this kind," as he put it. Massachusetts had lost in Savage a skillful, pragmatic, and patriotic merchant. "His long service in publick imployment" and "his skillfulness in that service," Willard claimed, marked him as one of great "personal worth." Willard's close friend and colleague William Hubbard, whom Hull had threatened with a lawsuit, eulogized merchant Daniel Dennison in similar terms: a boon to the commonwealth because his financial prudence and practical genius expressed his piety.[88]

Just as London had its literary valorizations of merchants to parallel the formal tracts of economic writers, so Boston had an anonymous fable entitled *A Rich Treasure at an Easy Rate* as a corollary to the jeremiads and merchant eulogies. First published in London in 1657, Boston printers produced their own version in 1683 with several reprints thereafter. It provided a popularized version of the merchant as a civic patron and subject of providence. Reading like a condensed *Pilgrim's Progress* for the devout trader, the fable featured a figure named Godliness who settled in a populous town. Godliness found no comfort among extremely wealthy residents, whose pride, prodigality, covetousness, maliciousness, and laziness affronted him as much as the imperial merchants offended men such as Hull. Among the poor, Godliness observed idleness, lying, begging, stealing, and drunkenness. Only among the solid, modest, yet successful merchants did Godliness find himself happy. He finally settled in the company of his neighbor Labor, a merchant who "had travaelled all Countries" and "thence brought and Transported" their "Commodities, and Traded with them into all other Countries." Diligent and cheerful, Labor undertook "the most Pious and Beneficial Acts" to uphold "the Commonwealth." He was a civic-minded man. Working together, Godliness and Labor inspired the townspeople, "set many poor People to Work, and paid them duly, and by that means enabled many, poor before, to pay their Debts." Godliness taught Labor to season industry with inner piety, to "flee Lying, Swearing, Profaneness," and to support the church with generous donations. This was the moral ideal of merchants such as Hull: to trade well, exercise their vocation energetically, nurture religious devotion, provide for the poor, and assume the role of a patron of the social order. *A Rich Treasure* gave, in effect, Mather's and Willard's teaching without the theology—and without even the slightest hint that the local church should constrain merchants by coercive measures that impeded their success in the market.[89]

If *A Rich Treasure at an Easy Rate* achieved a favorable reading among the likes of Mather and Willard, Hull and Scottow and Sewall, it did so because it stressed the interdependence of religious devotion and economic competence. These men had helped to create a robust market economy, but they had not succumbed to secularism. They resisted what they perceived as the excesses of imperial culture and the venalities of market exchange. Puritan preaching continued to inform the conscience of traders such as Hull. Yet even as ministers urged merchants to purify their motives and check their private affections, they valorized New England's public order. They minimized the coercive regimes of church discipline. Placing divine purpose and the weight of reform on civic rulers, they fell silent on the new credit mechanisms, and technicalities of overseas trade, that merchants deployed.

The most remarkable development in the relationship between religion and commerce in this period concerns this shift: puritan legitimizations of civil law and economic expertise as providential mandates in place of the corporate discipline of the congregation. Orthodox puritan leaders of the first generation wielded church censures and suspected civil law of being unjust; Mather and Willard marginalized censures, offered the sacramental privileges of the church to an increasingly broad spectrum of their parishioners, and called on civil leaders to guide the church. They sacralized technique, sanctified expertise, and separated economic competence from the responsibility of the gathered church.

The most widely read piece of literature about John Hull, perhaps, was written by Nathaniel Hawthorne in 1840. In a legend entitled "The Pine-Tree Shillings," one chapter of his sardonic tales about colonial Massachuestts, *The Whole History of Grandfather's Chair*, Hawthorne imagined Hull as an amiable, portly, and wily businessman who made buckets of money from his mint. The story, brightened by a jocular account of Sewall's marriage to Hannah Hull, centers on a dowry of newly minted shillings. In celebration of the wedding at his house, Hull had Hannah, who was quite "plump," sit on one side of his huge merchant scale; on the other side, his servants heaped handfuls of coins until his daughter was lifted from the floor. " 'There, son Sewall!' cried the honest mintmaster . . . take these shillings for my daughter's portion. Use her kindly, and thank Heaven for her. It is not every wife that's worth her weight in silver!' "[90]

Hawthorne's story conveys an odd conjunction of joviality and moral earnestness, material contentment and puritan decorum. It casts Hull in the role of the affable but hard-driving Yankee who brought New England out of the doldrums of overly scrupulous founders into middle-class, provincial comfort. Hawthorne's tale is pleasant but misleading. It does not suggest the real source of Hull's wealth: multilayered credit exchanges, strict account keeping, and financial legalities that eclipsed more personal modes of exchange. Hull in fact had made a contract with Sewall to pay him £500 as a dowry, and Sewall kept a precise record of Hull's payments long after the wedding day. Hull himself had taught Sewall to keep his accounts close.[91]

Nor did Hawthorne probe the moral complexities at play in Hull's career. The endurance of the old critique of oppression and usury, and the persistence of the ideal of the modest and self-effacing businessman, alongside the emergence of a commercial order in Massachusetts, undoubtedly made puritan merchants such as Hull at least a bit anxious. His autobiography and reflections on New England are not all that cheerful. As much as the conceptual framework of providence might allow merchants to bridge moral traditions and newer economic practices, to live coherently in the midst of the possibility of contradiction between Christian and commercial identities, it did not mark the full legitimization of New England's expanding market. It amounted to a halfway measure, to borrow a phrase from later characterizations of the sacramental practices of the period. Protestant religiosity and economic modernization moved toward congruence slowly, generation by generation, in the specific dilemmas and local cultures of merchants and their ministers. The next step in this move necessitated a change in the moral rhetoric itself and the sacralization not only of New England's civic order but also of the British Empire: its Protestant monarchy, commercial power, and science of economic exchange.

Chapter Four

SAMUEL SEWALL'S WINDOWS

On a late April day in 1695, Boston's Samuel Sewall, merchant, magistrate, and member of the Council of the Province, awoke to "warm and Sunshiny" weather, as he put it in his diary. The light must have pleased him; he was to host Old South's minister Samuel Willard and Old North's Cotton Mather at his newly built house for the midday dinner. An inveterate observer of Boston's social affairs, Sewall knew about public reputations and gestures. Houses were, by common perception, metaphorical bodies, reflecting the spiritual and moral states of their owners. Yet until now he had lived in his father-in-law's crowded dwelling, a drafty wooden structure ("very bleake," as his friends described it) unequal to his station. He nonetheless had hesitated to construct his own home, fearing the expense during a time of political transition and economic duress in Massachusetts—not to mention the risks of building in the aftermath of the Salem witchcraft crisis, when devils attacked people and houses alike. He had consulted Willard on the matter. Willard dismissed his qualms as overly scrupulous. It was time to build.[1]

"The new House," as Sewall called it, had taken three years to construct, and he hardly suppressed his enthusiasm. He noted the laying of the kitchen floor, his ritual driving of one nail into the bottom floor, the time he visited the site and nearly fell through the second-story floor. Sewall employed John Cunnable as the chief carpenter. Trained in London, Cunnable knew the latest architectural fashions and most likely built the house in the style then popular among London's merchants: a combination of Renaissance, classical forms with Netherlandish accents. The house consisted of a brick exterior built on a wood frame. Sewall imported from London sixty small blocks of stone for quoins (interspersed between bricks at the corners to reinforce the appearance of strength), another Renaissance marker. The size and style befitted Sewall's stature. As a crowning touch, he had the builders include a large number of windows on the front, facing Marlborough Street, near the Hull house. The glass panes alone, which Sewall numbered 480, were a costly luxury. Windows—the eyes of the house-as-body and important fashion statements in themselves—gave all the more reason to be grateful for a bright day that would illuminate the blessings of trade and civic prominence in the sight of Boston's two most eminent pastors.[2]

A reader of Calvinist theology, Sewall might have known better than to take pride in his possessions. At the height of dinner—two o'clock, as Sewall recorded—God sent an "awfull Providence." Dark clouds rolled in with thunder, lightning, and "a very extraordinary Storm of Hail." Pellets "as bigg as pistoll and Musquet Bulletts" flew at the building. The sound of hail tinking against glass must have turned heads. Scores of windowpanes shattered. "Hail-Stones" that "broke throw the Glass and flew to the middle of the Room, or farther," pelted Mather, Willard, and Sewall. "People afterward Gazed upon the House to see its Ruins."[3]

Sewall turned to Mather on the spot and asked him to pray. Mather's prayer, as Sewall remembered it, contained moral sermonizing rather than pleas for divine intervention. Drawing on the house-body metaphor, he "told God" (it was not unlike Mather to instruct the Almighty) that "He had broken the brittle part of our house that we might be ready for the time when our Clay-Tabernacles should be broken." The hailstorm conveyed a spiritual message: Sewall ought to temper his material and social aspirations with thoughts of mortality.[4]

Mather gave two public lectures, entitled *Durable Riches*, later that year on natural disasters, providence, and economic virtue. He admitted that it had been a bad year for Boston, punctuated by fires, shipwrecks, piracy, and an unusually harsh winter followed by an equally damaging drought. He mourned "those *Losses* which attend us in our Estates." Remarkably, however, he did not deliver a jeremiad, tracking the sins of New England that provoked judgment or ascribing recent misfortunes to direct divine intervention. Instead, he discoursed on the reasons that providence allowed temporal afflictions that were in themselves explicable in scientific terms. They were "but *Instruments*" that God used to teach universal moral lessons to individuals. As he had prayed that April afternoon in Sewall's ruined house, he maintained that material losses weaned people from an excessive dependence on wealth. He quoted at length from folk proverbs and classical maxims to the effect that the prudent man held riches loosely. Such moralizing about providence marked Mather's counsel as compatible with a wide array of Anglo-American Protestant teaching, promoted by liberal Anglican bishops and dissenting divines alike.[5]

In the second lecture, Mather recalibrated his message. The right use of wealth benefited the rich person even as it served the common good. Merchants ought to make as much money as they could, provide for their families, and donate their profits to the church, the poor, and civic projects such as schools and the military. Mather claimed that the honest, charitable, and public-minded businessman garnered an enhanced reputation, made prudent decisions, enjoyed prosperity, and placed himself in a position to benefit the Protestant political order. It was a moral law: "there is

a *Recompense* in *This Life*, which the Liberal man is made a partaker of."
Mather in fact promised that "God will bless him a *Success* of his *Business*."[6]

Sewall did not record his immediate response to Mather's ad hoc prayer
or later lectures, but he must have taken Mather to heart. He later prayed
and fasted with other pastors in his new house, asking God to purify his
affections, and he continued to conduct daily business in his usual manner.
He recorded the arrival of ships from other colonies, reflected on provincial elections, marked the passing of previous governors, and noted political
controversies at home and abroad. He especially turned to the momentous
news arching across the Atlantic: the death of Queen Mary and mourning
especially of fellow merchants, reports of French privateers in the Caribbean and other turns in the war with France, and the appointment of a
new archbishop of Canterbury. Sewall did just as his pastors told him. He
contributed his share to commercial prosperity in the Bay Colony and enhanced New England's trade in the British Atlantic. He served the commonweal as a civic leader and citizen of the English Crown.[7]

Assorted moral sensibilities collided in Sewall's house, from conspicuous
consumption and commercial prowess to ruminations on providence and
pious resolve. The story of his windows serves to illustrate the endurance
of religious convictions among New England's puritan merchants from the
mid-1680s through the early 1720s. Yet it also signals a further transformation in the relationship between religion and commerce in provincial Boston. Mather's opinions about the providential lessons of hailstones offered
merchants a moral law that chastened their inner affections without compelling conformity to previous puritan rules for economic exchange.

Mather and Sewall considered the economy as they observed England's
contest for empire in the Atlantic world. Conflicts between Catholic and
Protestant dynasties appeared to them to presage apocalyptic battles and
to illumine the importance of commercial power as an instrument of Protestant hegemony. These convictions gave reason for New Englanders to
bestow high moral purpose, even religious sanction, on the dictates of economic thinkers who offered clues to England's success in its colonial wars.
Imported in various forms to New England, the ideas of England's political
economists redefined the very terms of exchange and reshaped the grammar of moral teaching on commerce in provincial New England.

Boston's merchant community was diverse enough that a single businessman such as Sewall cannot capture the whole of this story; nor can a
single religious leader such as Mather. Contemporaries such as merchant
Thomas Fitch, and pastors Samuel Willard and Benjamin Wadsworth, represent other lines along this imperial trajectory. In the context of a series
of political and social upheavals, they each reconfigured puritan ideas
about providence, political loyalties, and the meaning of the nation. They
all jettisoned jeremiads against the most salient market behaviors and

envisioned the exchange of credit in the transatlantic market—and much of what that exchange represented—in ways never imagined by their predecessors.

Sewall's and Fitch's Problems with Money

Sewall and Fitch cannot stand for all overseas traders of this period in New England, but they well represent prominent merchants who remained loyal to the congregational establishment in Massachusetts.[8] Born in Hampshire, England, in 1652, Sewall moved to Massachusetts in 1661. He attended school in Newbury and matriculated at Harvard in 1667. He seemed to be headed to the ministry, remaining in Cambridge until 1674, where he received an MA, became a tutor, supervised the college library, and preached occasionally. After his marriage to Hannah Hull in 1676, however, he assumed much of his father-in-law's business. He joined the Old South Church in 1677 and followed Hull into the Artillery Company in 1679, where he advanced through the ranks to become captain in 1701. The General Court appointed him the supervisor of the printing press in 1681. He moderated town meetings on and off for years and was elected assistant several times, in which capacity he served as a magistrate and an overseer of Harvard. He was made a member of the newly configured provincial Council in 1691 and reappointed annually until 1725. Reputed for his civic-mindedness, sobriety, and learning, he presided as the probate judge for Suffolk County from 1715 to 1728 and chief justice of the Superior Court of Judicature from 1718 to 1728, two years before his death (figure 4.1).[9]

Sewall's trading activities peaked in the 1690s, declining thereafter as judicial and administrative responsibilities occupied him. Like other merchants, he built his business on family connections: the inheritance of contacts and capital from Hull and relationships to other mercantile families such as Gerrish, Dummer, Tyng, and Usher.[10] He traded in the most common commodities, exporting codfish, mackerel, whale oil, pork, tar, molasses, and cranberries to London, Barbados, and Jamaica and importing a variety of fabrics, sugar, tools, salt, and chocolate. He often exchanged books along with other goods. He imported (and, by all accounts, read) the latest biblical commentaries by English dissenters, Calvin's treatises, world histories, Latin classics, even au courant works in natural theology; and he just as frequently sent tomes of divinity and commentaries to his customers as far south as New Jersey.[11]

He also consumed some luxuries as eagerly as did his mercantile colleagues, an indication of his appreciation of the value of exchange in both

Figure 4.1. *Samuel Sewall*. Oil on canvas by Nathaniel Emmons, 1723. Sewall wears a judicial robe and conservatively styled cap. Courtesy of the Massachusetts Historical Society.

directions across the Atlantic. During a 1689 trip to London, he marveled at the abundance of goods available in warehouses and marketplaces. He kept a strict account of his purchases: a saddle, gloves, and, as always, books. Although he, like Mather, feared that cosmopolitan style often rested on social pretension, he furnished his house with new furniture and fabrics, from fine curtains to elegant tableware and "a True Looking Glass of black Walnut Frame of the newest Fashion." He pondered the spiritual meaning of refined objects such as silver Communion vessels, which represented to him a material form of pious aspiration, even desire. Sewall participated in a market that conveyed religious ideas and tasteful products as convergent lines of Protestant hegemony.[12]

Real estate offered Sewall another stake in England's commercial-political empire. He purchased territory in Maine, where he had distant family connections. Sewall's private interests and Anglo-French competition for land in North America met in his holdings on the frontier. He was among six of the seven judges of the Court of Oyer and Terminer who presided over the Essex County witchcraft trials, speculated in northern territories, and discerned a dangerous collaboration between the French, Indians, and supernatural evil arrayed against English settlers. In 1698 he invested in the Company of Scotland Trading to Africa and the Indies, an ill-fated venture to establish a colony in Panama; it too freighted his business with the politics of colonial empire. He found sounder investments closer to home. He owned a large plot on Block Island, receiving rent from local tenants. He bought and sold dozens of properties there, including wharves, houses, and pastures.[13]

An adviser on the province's fiscal policies, Sewall recognized the importance of monetary credit. London creditors readily devalued the worth of provincial bills, securities, and notes of exchange, which made business difficult for men such as Sewall. He relied less on bills of exchange than did Hull and pleaded with his agents and ship captains to secure what he called "ready Money," that is, London banknotes and European specie, such as pieces of eight, that found ready acceptance among his English counterparts. Determined to maintain his creditworthiness overseas, Sewall reprimanded debtors whose unpaid bonds and bills or outstanding mortgages left him shorthanded. He frequently haggled with delinquent debtors and expressed his frustrations at negotiations over the interest due to him on bonds and mortgages.[14]

Like his merchant colleagues, Sewall conducted his affairs with ruthless determination. In 1706 a particularly difficult case compelled him to explain his hard-nosed posture to his admirer Mather. One of Mather's parishioners had complained that Sewall had sold one of his Boston properties, which she rented as her home, to another bidder for £340, when the first right of sale belonged to her. In a lengthy and pained letter, Sewall maintained that her family already owed him some back rent and interest on another loan, and that her son had offered him a paltry £210 for the house. Sewall cared about Mather's opinion of him but nonetheless played fiscal rationality off of moral naïveté. He told Mather that he was more than willing to fulfill his neighborly duty to charity but not ready to play the fool. He followed his ledgers, measured interest accrued and abated, and demanded that his tenants exercise the same diligence and honesty in their affairs. Good money was scarce in Sewall's time, and he meant to secure it as the very lifeblood of his vocation.[15]

Fitch, one of Sewall's closest associates, encountered similar problems and conducted his affairs with similar resolve. He was born in 1669 in Boston, the son of a cordwainer and clothier, also named Thomas, who immigrated to New England around 1650.[16] Thomas the elder joined the First Church and assumed a position of modest respectability, frequently

acting as a legal overseer and auditor of several estates. We have no record
of young Thomas's life until he joined Old South Church in 1691. Three
years later, Willard performed his wedding to Abiel Danforth, the daughter
of Roxbury pastor Samuel Danforth. Having established himself in overseas trade, Fitch thereafter circulated chiefly in Boston's commercial community. He lived a rather unspectacular life, quietly accumulating thirteen
pieces of prime real estate, including part of the Boston Common, and
buying seven thousand acres of land in Lunenburg and Dunstable. Of his
and Abiel's six children, three lived to adulthood: Martha, Mary, and John.
In 1725 Fitch provided a lavish wedding for the marriage of Martha to
merchant James Allen, attended by Council members and other merchant
worthies. Mary married the merchant Andrew Oliver. John attended
Harvard and exhibited some leanings to the ministry but eventually carried
on the family business. He also extended the Fitch commercial network
by marrying Mary Stoddard, the daughter of yet another merchant.
Thomas Fitch died in 1736, leaving an estate of £6,000 to his wife (about
half of the total, excluding lands) and substantial bequests to Harvard and
poor relief.[17]

Fitch outpaced Sewall in the pursuit of profits and made the exchange
of credit integral to his business. He traded in the usual commodities—fish
and wood products—but also dealt with an array of suppliers far more
diverse that the small collection of London merchants who worked with
Hull and Sewall. During the 1710s and 1720s, he corresponded with hundreds of agents and clients, including Huguenot, Dutch, Scottish, and
Flemish merchants, many of them unknown to him personally. Fitch also
developed a more expansive business inland than did his predecessors. He
bought wheat, pork, and turpentine from country traders from Maine to
Connecticut. He sold luxury imports, such as lace, silk, fine furniture (including leather chairs made in Russia), and decorated ivory combs, to other
merchants, counting Sewall, David Jeffries, Edward Bromfield, Andrew
Belcher, and Edward Hutchinson among his customers (figure 4.2). Most
profitably, he came to specialize in trading money and credit instruments.
He took payment in English currency, Massachusetts bills of credit, or
bonds and mortgages and made much of his profits from the interest on
them or from exchanging them for yet another round of paper securities.[18]

Boston's mercantile infrastructure, from roads and bridges to wharves
and docks, provided him with another set of ventures. He and other merchants, including James Pitts, Oliver Noyes, Daniel Oliver, and Anthony
Stoddard, established the Long Wharf as a private corporation in 1710.
Constructed from 1711 to 1713, the wharf dominated Boston's waterfront.
Beginning at the end of King Street, it jutted fifteen hundred feet into
the harbor and could moor up to fifty vessels at a time. Fifty feet wide, it
was lined with brick warehouses on one side and shops on the other. Fitch

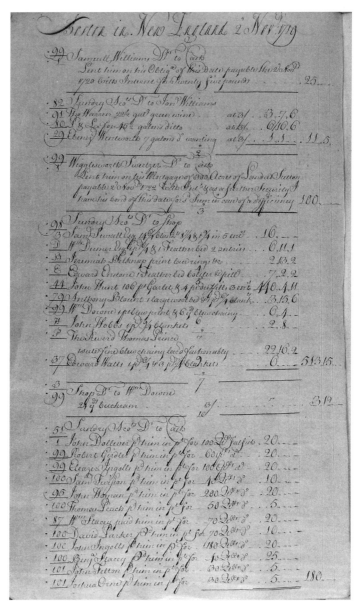

Figure 4.2. Account book of Thomas Fitch, November 1719. Original manuscript from Thomas Fitch Account Books and Letterbook. The numbers in the left column are keys to the index of accounts. The transaction is described in the central column. The right column calculates the debt owed to Fitch. Sewall's name appears on the thirteenth line from the top. Courtesy of the Massachusetts Historical Society.

and his fellow proprietors met frequently to tend to its affairs: leasing warehouses, collecting rents, assessing moorage dues, making repairs, hiring dockworkers, negotiating taxes and regulations with municipal committees, suing ship captains and renters for overdue debts, and paying carpenters for maintenance. They also used the wharf as a venue for exchanging credit and auctioned outstanding debts from the wharf's users as speculative investments.[19]

Fitch labored to master the variables of the market, from consumer tastes and price fluctuations to monetary depreciation. He expressed anxiety about his choice of goods—whether they would sell and at what price— the status of cargo, and how his ships fared in bad weather. In 1703 he urged a London agent to ship wine while it was scarce in Massachusetts and to inform him whether English buyers would accept his price for turpentine. In 1710 he inquired about the current taste for furs in London and the going rate for whale oil. More important, he constantly fretted about his creditors and debtors: how they valued the bills of credit, specie, bills of exchange, bonds, and mortgages that passed between him and them. He exchanged information about the relative worth of provincial bills, English banknotes, and silver. He advised his agents on how best to pay him and how to handle the various pieces of paper that he sent as payment, suggesting, as he wrote to one London agent, that "many don't apprehend" the "current price of exchange here."[20]

Very few of Fitch's hundreds of letters omitted the problem of money. The lack of a stable currency brought Massachusetts to the brink of fiscal crisis several times during his career. London suppliers sometimes balked at dealing with him because he could not offer speedy repayment in sound notes. In 1703 he apologized to an English supplier for not clearing his debts. "money is extreame scarce with us." He wrote a lengthy letter to another London merchant, reviewing the bundle of papers he enclosed, including clumps of various bills with different redemption dates. In 1705 he explained monetary affairs to his chief agents in London. The latest exchange and discount rates led him to prefer payment first in "ready money," by which he meant specie and Bank of England notes. Second, he valued recent bills of exchange with short terms, to avoid depreciation. Third, he was willing, grudgingly, to take long-term bills of exchange. Fourth, and least useful to him, were bills issued by the provincial government, the values of which plummeted quickly. When in 1723 a London merchant paid Fitch with a bill of exchange originating in Annapolis, Fitch warned the merchant that he would charge 9 percent interest if he could redeem it immediately and 40 percent if he had to wait. On the other hand, he implored a Philadelphia merchant to accept his payment in provincial bills of credit, arguing that the merchant could readily send them back to Boston, where New Englanders would accept them at face value despite depreciation overseas; "our money here is shamefully cutt," yet "by so many countenanced that" they "do pass in payments and no body in town refuses them," so that "to draw for Boston money is safest." Yet again, always maneuvering for an advantage, Fitch asked one his New York customers who paid him in New York bills to discount their value by 10 percent, given the going rate for them in London.[21]

The more Fitch accounted interest rates and discounts, negotiated various means of payments, accepted mortgages for payments, and traded in bonds, the more he turned to the civil courts to adjudicate his affairs. He prided himself on his facility with legal matters. In 1708 one James Appleton, a modest and aspiring merchant, threatened to sue Fitch for unpaid interest on one of his bills of exchange. Fitch mocked Appleton in a letter to John Crouch in London. Appleton, he wrote, "don't understand much of the law" and had hired a poor attorney. Because Fitch had indeed—"as appears by my books, his accounts, and his own pocket book"—paid off the note, he in fact relished a courtroom encounter, where, he predicted, he would crush Appleton. In 1724 Fitch wrote to David Jeffries, his fellow merchant and parishioner at Old South, demanding payment on an outstanding bond issued in 1717 for £950. With accrued interest and a declining value of the bond in London, Jeffries owed more than £1,100, and Fitch meant to sue.[22]

Whereas John Hull approached litigation hesitantly, Fitch embraced it. He advised Jeffries that good exchange required the "gentlemen of law" to protect honest dealing. Fitch employed lawyers to examine the mortgages he received and provide "counsel in the law" about land titles and bonds. He warned a young man with various debts to him, including outstanding bills and a contested mortgage, that he would use the best lawyers and "shall no ways be a sufferer." Fitch frequently sued debtors in the Suffolk County Court of Common Pleas, adding to the explosion of the number of legal causes for debt in the courts. In contrast to what many previous puritans had decreed, Fitch turned to litigation rather than to arbitration in the church.[23]

In the process of using the courts, Fitch participated in a legal culture attuned to English standards of practice. Teaching themselves from English law books, New England's attorneys proposed to organize a bar association. They adopted professional fee schedules, relied on formal jurisprudence, and deployed the latest protocols for litigation. By the 1730s attorneys, rather than laymen, argued nearly every commercial case in New England courts. Lawyers hired by Boston merchants confronted lawyers hired by their English counterparts, contesting the worth of bills of exchange traded from London, through the Caribbean, to Boston. Given the indirect, distant, and multilayered transfer and contestation over credit, contractual obligation eclipsed appeals to personal moral duties; lawyers in the 1710s and 1720s rarely relied on traditional religious idioms for their arguments. The special language of law reflected a system of justice suited to a mathematical analysis of interest rates, currency values, and contracts. Royal decrees on currency, economic mandates, and transatlantic standards of justice flowed together in litigation. Traders such as Fitch confronted them at every turn in their business and asserted their professional status when they deployed them in the Suffolk County courtroom.[24]

Fitch conveyed many of these assumptions in his correspondence. As handbooks for merchants, such as Thomas Hill's *Secretary's Guide* of 1703, suggested, he relied on formal and impersonal rhetoric.[25] Businesslike and dispassionate language expressed the ideals of an emergent economic science in everyday exchange: calculation, precision, and technique. It also evinced action: quick, efficient, diligent. In a typical letter from 1723, to David Foxcroft, he brushed past a greeting, then quickly attended to matters of business:

> Yours of the 19th March and 10 Sept. I received and agreeable to your desire shall pay off the 39 lb to Madm Phillips. Mr. John Lloyd has not ever sent me the 20 lb, wherefore I wrote him the third instant to do it at the first opportunity, and also to dispatch to me the sixty or eighty pounds or whatsoever sum you shall order into his hands to be remitted, which you may do free as well without my drawing for it . . . and avoid all manner of inconveniences as to time of payment; and therefore I desire you to order the payment to him.

In the rare instances when Fitch used moral terminology (he mentioned Foxcroft's "justice and honour"), he referred to financial creditworthiness. The bulk of Fitch's letter consisted of pure transactions: two other mentions of debts owed to Fitch, reference to three lawyers at work for him, and a discussion of price changes and shifting currency rates. The letter closed just as formally: "your humble servant, Tho Fitch."[26]

Previous puritan merchants such as Hull, or older contemporaries such as Sewall, also attended to pure business in their correspondence, but they often injected moral and pious digressions. Fitch never did. Commercial exchange called for a measure of politeness—delicately phrased requests, proper titles, deferential phrasing—yet also for a reasoned, calculating tone. Fitch ended his letter to Foxcroft, as he did all of his business letters, without one reference to providence, Scripture, or Christian sentiment. As he conducted his affairs, he emphasized the fiscal, prudential virtues of punctuality, accuracy, and industry.[27]

Fitch's formalized rhetoric, like his trade in bills and mortgages, sale of credit, and reliance on civil litigation, signified a further transition in the sensibilities of puritan merchants. For all of their accounts and expertise, predecessors such as John Hull eschewed exchange with unknown and distant customers and regarded litigation as often oppressive. Fixed on a civil order defined by New England's special covenant, Hull chastened his exchange with jeremiads and other religious utterances that conveyed customary strictures. Even if his pastors no longer summoned congregational discipline over specific prices and credit practices, they reminded him that Reformed teaching held usury to be a sin and oppression a shame. Fitch, in contrast, made usury, market pricing, and civil litigation the very core of exchange. He never pondered them as the unfortunate, even lamentable, costs of doing business well. They *were* his business.

Sewall and Fitch thus differed from John Hull and other predecessors at Old South: more sanguine about commerce, less encumbered by puritan restrictions against impersonal exchange. How could such merchants, leaders in the puritan church order and devoted believers, practice their trade in a manner so unlike their forebears? Nothing suggests that their pastors viewed them with anything but esteem. What moral ideas informed economic choices that many New Englanders previously condemned as impious and avaricious? To answer these questions, we must turn to transitions within puritan teaching: new notions of providence and its relation to the political order in New England and across the Atlantic.

The Politics of Empire

England and her New England colonies underwent decisive changes in government during the 1680s and 1690s, bringing merchants and ministers into public affairs dominated by political disputes, the monarchy, and the language of civil liberty. The most remarkable of those changes in Massachusetts, by all accounts, occurred in 1685. Inspired by an ideology of colonial empire, incited by competition with France for American territory, and provoked by reports of New Englanders' noncompliance with the Navigation Acts (not to mention their reputation for hostility to the Anglican monarchy), the Lords of Trade and advisers to James II annulled the charter of Massachusetts Bay. They empowered a temporary council to rule the colony. In 1686 the Crown installed a new administration, called the Dominion of New England, which stretched from Maine to New Jersey, under the royalist, Anglican governor Sir Edmund Andros. The Crown suppressed the Massachusetts General Court, muzzled the Boston town meeting, installed Edward Randolph as secretary and surveyor of the customs, and appointed Joseph Dudley as chief justice. Imperial merchants such as Wharton, Shrimpton, Dudley, and Wait Winthrop received positions on the Council and entitlements to contested lands in the north in return for their support of Andros. They formed short-lived speculative land ventures such as the Million Purchase in northern Massachusetts and the Pejepscot Company in Maine and New Hampshire. Members of the puritan establishment, including Sewall, resented the loss of political power, a new system of patronage, what they deemed to be corruption in the courts, and the Anglican pretensions of an increasing number of royal officials. Horrified by the Dominion, many merchants and ministers spread rumors of a Stuart-Catholic plot to reduce New England's political and religious liberties.[28]

Opposition to Andros and the Dominion mounted in Boston during the next two years, headed by municipal political leaders such as the physician Elisha Cooke and an increasing number of overseas traders, including some Council members, frustrated by the tariffs, territorial boundaries, and trade restrictions enforced by Andros and Randolph. In 1688 Increase Mather surreptitiously left for London to plead with the Crown for a restoration of the old charter. News of the so-called Glorious Revolution—the overthrow of the Stuarts and assumption of William of Orange—reached Boston during the following months. Long-standing antipathies to Andros erupted into popular mutiny in July 1689, after which Andros escaped Boston. While Mather continued to negotiate with the representatives of William and Mary, the government of Massachusetts reverted to the previous Council, the governorship of Simon Bradstreet, and the legislative authority of the General Court.[29]

Public affairs subsequently took peculiar turns. Boston preachers welcomed the reign of William and Mary as a godsend: the accession of true Protestants, friends of the Reformed party, protectors of religious liberties, and foes of Catholicism. Yet the outbreak of hostilities between English and French dynasties in 1689 with King William's War and their continuation with Queen Anne's War proved costly for Massachusetts. French-allied Indians attacked English settlements in New Hampshire and New York in late 1689. Many English settlers who survived left the frontier; land values in Maine plummeted during this period. Massachusetts responded by funding an expedition against Quebec in 1690, led by Old North member William Phips. The campaign failed dismally, costing hundreds of lives and £50,000 to an already-strapped public treasury. Military adventures in Queen Anne's War were even worse: disease-ridden, lethal, ghastly debacles.[30]

More troubles followed Phips's misadventure in Quebec. In 1691 Increase Mather returned from London with a new charter that omitted many of the colony's original rights. The Crown's insistence on toleration for established Protestant churches, including Presbyterian and Anglican, appeared to critics to interfere with a standing order premised on congregational polity and the covenantal status of puritan churches. The new charter allowed elections to the lower house of the General Court but replaced church membership with property ownership as the qualifi-

cation for voting. It asserted the Crown's prerogative to select the governor, who named the Council, had the power of veto over legislation, and
appointed all county officeholders, including justices. The town still
elected selectmen to issue proclamations on local affairs, but the charter
delegated many of their previous powers to minor officials such as inspectors and constables.[31]

The charter of 1691 provoked outrage, and the first royal governor, none
other than Phips, precipitated controversy. The Mathers lionized him. He
filled the Council with North End parishioners. Samuel Willard of Old
South and James Allen of First Church sniped at the Mathers and engaged
themselves with anti-Phips, anticharter political factions led by Old South
merchants and Cooke. To top it off, the witchcraft crisis—exacerbated by
widespread social anxieties and fears of war—erupted in Salem in the
winter of 1692.[32]

Boston's merchants aligned themselves with different platforms in the
ensuing contests for municipal and provincial power, which often set the
Council and governor against the town meeting and lower house of the
General Court. After London recalled Phips in 1694 for misconduct, a new
group of merchants, headed by Andrew Belcher and Nathaniel Oliver, rose
to prominence. Currying favor with Governor William Stoughton, they
nearly monopolized the grain trade in the town and pushed through a series
of laws to regulate competition from small-time traders. During the governorship of Joseph Dudley (1702–1715), Belcher and the coterie of elite
merchants with whom Dudley collaborated, and to whom he doled out
patronage, faced widespread opposition. It was so widespread, in fact, that
it brought Old North and Cotton Mather back into solidarity with the rest
of the town, a majority of ministers and merchants allied against the Dudley regime. United opposition to Dudley, however, did not spell civil or
economic unanimity. Political divisions within the colony and especially
the town, including debates about monetary policy, marked social affairs
through the mid-eighteenth century. They belied a monolithic commercial
type. Various merchants had different political interests.[33]

With its large fleet and well-protected harbor, Boston nonetheless maintained its dominance over colonial commerce through the 1720s. Imperial
policies facilitated greater exchange of commodities throughout the British
Atlantic, much of it passing through the hands of Boston traders. The
Crown supplied greater protection against piracy. Huguenot immigrants,
arriving in Boston from France via London, the West Indies, and South
Carolina, established new mercantile houses and contacts with the Continent. Increased population along the New England seaboard, enhanced by
immigration, and the spread of settlements north and west expanded the
market for imported goods such as cloth, furniture, and tools. Wartime

provisioning stimulated orders for ships and naval supplies. Per-capita income rose during this period, as did real economic output. Yet there were
periods of frightening downturns and a rise in genuine poverty. King William's War episodically blocked trade in and out of Boston, halted timber
production on the frontier, and bankrupted land speculators. The end of
Queen Anne's War dampened demand for naval supplies and left many
dockworkers and shipbuilders unemployed. Economic and social stratification attended the developing market in New England.[34]

Political quarrels and competing interests among merchants also exposed moral disunity among puritan churches and sometimes divided individual congregations. Changes at Old South were particularly revealing.
Through the 1690s, the congregation maintained many commercial families, such as the Sewalls, Davises, Clarks, Gibbses, and Olivers, who resisted
the Andros regime. Angered especially by Andros's commandeering of
their meetinghouse for Anglican services, lay leaders at Old South led a
popular agitation against the governor and Dudley. Along with Sewall, rising merchants such as Edward Bromfield, who joined the church in 1698,
hewed close to traditional puritan moral sensibilities. Bromfield was well
versed in Reformed devotional language, attuned to the preaching of divines such as Willard, suspicious of cosmopolitan cultural styles, and antag-
onistic to Anglicanism. Old South, however, also included the leading
printers and booksellers in Boston—Bartholomew Green, Samuel Gerrish,
Daniel Henchman—whose social and political opinions defied definition.
Several young merchants joined the church, such as Wait Winthrop in
1689, Fitch in 1691, Oliver Noyes in 1693, and David Jeffries in 1711, who
displayed a pronounced taste for new cultural fashions and little affinity
for the dense devotion of an older generation. Yet again, Old South accommodated elite merchants who made their fortunes by accepting the patronage of Andros and Dudley and conducting business in ways that offended
the old guard: Thomas Savage the second, his son Ephraim, and Andrew
Belcher. Faced with such diversity at Old South, even lay elders such as
Sewall looked less to the individual congregation to shape their religious
identity than they did to a host of Boston ministers, including Mather, who
represented a moral and religious ethos dispersed throughout the town and
monopolizing no particular church.[35]

To religious authorities such as Mather and Willard, the accumulated
changes—the loss of old charter privileges, the need for provincial rulers
to negotiate with royal appointees, quarrels among municipal leaders and
churches, and even divided sensibilities within congregations—raised
questions about New England and its common loyalties. What was, after
all, the community that encompassed and gave meaning to social discipline
in Massachusetts? What, in effect, replaced the fading assertions of the

jeremiad: the vision of a civil order defined by the covenant, identified as New England, and ruled by pious merchant-magistrates according to scriptural norms?

In the process of formulating answers, Increase and Cotton Mather, along with Willard and other ministers, turned their attention to transatlantic political affairs, especially the struggle between what they understood to be England, Protestantism, and liberty on one side and France, Catholicism, and tyranny on the other. Discovering their civic identity in the empire, they also accepted the emergent ideology—the political economy—that promoted trade as an instrument of English hegemony. At the turn of the eighteenth century, Boston's preachers and pious merchants adopted a social discourse that muted covenantal idioms, including strictures against high-flown economic ambition, cosmopolitan styles, and commercial tactics previously denounced under the rubrics of usury and oppression. They began to speak of market mechanisms as integral to the political and moral commonwealth.

A collective sense of urgency among colonists, to put this differently, prompted collaboration between Boston's merchants and ministers. While in London to negotiate the new charter—where he hosted Sewall and escorted him through the metropolis in 1689—Increase Mather relied on New England merchants and their partners in England for funds and introductions into circles of influence. He received money from Boston traders, found benefactors among sympathetic English merchants such as the East India Company's Robert Thompson, and made contacts in the New England Coffee House, a favorite gathering place for Boston's businessmen. Mather also allied himself with Philip Lord Wharton and Sir Henry Ashurst, the son of a rich dissenting merchant. Granted audiences with James II and William (a breathtaking accomplishment for a provincial preacher), Mather witnessed firsthand the triumph of Whig politics and the power of the language of liberty, property, and constitutional rights.[36]

Mather's negotiations with Whitehall brought mixed results, but his exposure to emergent political and economic idioms had important consequences. Throughout his stay in England, his merchant patrons advised him to defend Massachusetts as a faithful partner in a constitutional regime buttressed by commercial strength. In several 1689 essays directed to English critics, he accordingly retraced the history of New England in thoroughly Whiggish terms. He contended that Andros had violated the property rights of English citizens in Massachusetts and, more important, that the revocation of the charter was an unconstitutional act. New England's citizens extended the range and prosperity of the English empire, he explained, on the assumption of charter privileges. He maintained that New England's commerce with the West Indies enhanced the nation's overall economic prosperity. Massachusetts's merchants paid more in duties than any other colonists, their trade enriched partners in London, and their shipbuilders supplied the English fleet. New Englanders formed a military and economic bulwark against the French in Canada. If "his Majesty" would "restore his Subjects in New-England to their ancient Priviledges" encoded in the charter, Mather pleaded, then they would fight the French in Canada and "be worth Millions to the English Crown and nation" in the form of "Bever-Trade," cod-fishery, and "encreasing of English Seamen." Moreover, Massachusetts had granted religious toleration as the Crown decreed, accepting the presence of Anglicans and Presbyterians without rancor. Mather's contentions may not have been candid in all regards. Yet they signified an important development in his conception of the civic order. He replaced the jeremiad with constitutional history and covenantal obligations with imperial loyalties. All of this indicated a shifting sense of communal identity. Later agents from Massachusetts to the Crown, such as Jeremiah Dummer, asserted that imperial identity as a political axiom.[37]

When prominent Bostonians blasted the 1691 charter, Mather implored New Englanders to accept its terms not only as politically expedient—no better could be negotiated—but also as a protection of English rights and liberties. He insisted that "great Priviledges are granted to the People in *New-England*" and "all English liberties are restored to them: No Persons shall have a Penny of their Estates taken from them; nor any Laws imposed on them, without their own Consent by Representatives chosen by themselves." He also gave assurances that "Religion is secured" in the charter, by which he meant that New England's churches had a constitutional defense of their platforms. Mather maintained that the presence of Anglicanism, also secured by the charter, was a small price to pay for legal recognition by an empire that offered Massachusetts protection against the French and commercial opportunities throughout the English Atlantic.[38]

While Increase Mather formulated in London the political rationale for the new charter, Cotton Mather articulated in Boston a providential rationale for celebrating the accession of William and Mary.[39] Three years of the Dominion—an offensive administration appointed by a king with Catholic religious sensibilities—had vexed New Englanders, who nonetheless recognized their increasing dependence on London for military protection and commercial concourse. The new monarchy appeared to Mather to be a providential remedy, as it did to other Boston-area ministers such as Cambridge's William Brattle. Mather dedicated a December 1689 Thanksgiving sermon to Ashurst, assuring him that Massachusetts Bay had always been a loyal colony of England. "Their Majesties have not in all their Dominions," he professed, "more Loyal Subjects, than the People of New England." Mather strained the logic here, contending that New England's Reformed churches conformed to pristine English Protestantism and thereby manifested their patriotism. Logic and historical memory aside, he located the royal accession in a providential narrative stretching back to creation, through Jesus Christ, to the "continual *providence* of God" ruling affairs of state. Providence worked in the midst of a vast war between Catholic powers and Protestant princes, Jacobites and Whigs, and "we now see upon the British Throne, A KING, whose unparallel'd zeal for the Church of the Lord Jesus at the Lowest Ebb," that is, during Jacobite opposition, "hath made Him the Phenix of this Age." As for New England, Mather predicted the reclamation of land deeds stolen by Andros and his minions, the restoration of political rights, protection against Indians, and enhanced trade in the north at the expense of French Catholics.[40]

During the next three decades, Mather and other Boston ministers framed civic duties by imperial designs, represented in the reigns of William and Mary, Queen Anne (1702 to 1714), and the first of the Hanoverian monarchs, George I (1714 to 1727). This turn was remarkable in itself—previous puritans hardly revered the monarchy—and it signified more widespread changes in public and religious discourse. Boston's ministers transposed an older puritan and republican language of constitutional legitimacy, property rights, commercial growth, and civil liberties to Whig ideologies and the political economy of the late seventeenth century.[41] They assured the citizens of Massachusetts that commercial competition, war against Catholicism, and devotion to the empire formed the platform of God's rule in the world.

For Mather, Phips embodied such political virtues along with customary New England pieties. Born into a farming family in Maine in 1651, Phips moved to Boston as a youth, where he ascended from ships carpenter to captain and merchant with interests in Acadia. Along the way, he developed a reputation for being ambitious, contentious, and irregular in his business. He also pursued sunken treasure in the Caribbean, an activity that established merchants associated with piracy and diplomatic misconduct. Phips, however, scored a stunning victory for England in 1687. After scouring the Bahamas' seas for weeks on end, using the latest charts and diving techniques, he discovered more than £200,000 of silver on a sunken Spanish vessel. He presented the treasure to the royal court and was knighted for his service.[42]

Celebrated on his return to Boston in 1689, Phips soon thereafter sparked controversy. Critics such as Sewall and William Hubbard complained about his aristocratic airs and his penchant for risky ventures, including dubious trading alliances in Acadia and the calamitous assault on Quebec. Many Bostonians perceived a Mather-Phips-North End cabal dominating local politics. Yet to the Mathers, Phips stood as an icon of patriotism. He had assisted Increase Mather in negotiations for the charter while in London, exhibited his faith by being baptized and joining Old

North Church, and served the Crown. He was, as Cotton Mather described him in the 1690 election sermon, a latter-day Nehemiah who pleaded with the king for his people and protected the poor.[43] Mather continued to defend his most prominent parishioner in terms shaped by post-Dominion politics. In two 1692 sermons dedicated to Phips and printed under the title *Optanda*, he delivered a general meditation on the nature of good government. Virtuous rulers, he contended, displayed an *"Active* and an *Useful* Spirit," a *"Public Spirit,"* and put their skills and riches to use for the common good. The good ruler deployed his *"Talents,* which God bestow'd upon him" and his *"Riches,* if God have sent him any," for the nation. Phips was such a man: "a Good Commonwealths Man." He had risked his life and fortune for "the English Nation" and had brought £200,000—the riches "sent" upon him by providence—to the Crown's coffers. The citizens ought therefore to support Phips and pay taxes to relieve the debt from the Quebec campaign. They also ought to embrace the new charter that brought him into office, with its promise of prosperity and obligations of the monarchy to defend New England.[44] Preaching the 1693 election sermon, Increase Mather made the same arguments. The charter, with Phips as its executor, confirmed the right of representatives to determine taxes, encoded natural laws of contract, right, and popular sovereignty, and provided for civil courts and judges to moderate civil disputes.[45]

Mather's promotion of Phips took its fullest form in his biography of what he called New England's "famous Knight," first published in London in 1697 as *Pietas in Patriam*. Phips had died in England by the time Mather's book appeared, but he still symbolized the practice of godliness through "heroick virtue." According to Mather, Phips combined commercial ambition with "enterprising genius." Early puritans like Perkins and Cotton disparaged such entrepreneurial energies; Mather applauded them as talents fit for divine service. As courageous as the conquistador Pizarro, who furnished Spain with Peruvian silver, Phips also matched the prudence of Dutch merchants, whose wit, cleverness, and resoluteness made their "disposition for business." Phips acted as England's most valuable commercial warrior, relentlessly driven to risk and adventure. His pragmatism, skill, and determination, abetted by natural scientific intelligence and a knack for invention, led him to his great recovery of sunken treasure. The treasure hunter gave Mather a Spanish piece of eight as a souvenir, which hung on a wall in the pastor's house for thirty years—a shining token of economic patriotism.[46]

In Mather's narrative, Phips also drew pious lessons from his adventures. He confessed, by Mather's recollection, that "the various *providences*" that "attended me in my travels, were sanctified unto me." Mather explained: providence taught Phips to serve God by serving "the country." When Phips realized the "interests of the Lord Jesus Christ," he delivered his treasure to England, lobbied for the charter in London, led the expedition to Quebec, subdued Indians in other campaigns, joined the Old North congregation, and, as governor, minded "the welfare of the province" and "the preservation of the King's right" as "a good steward for the crown." Mather extolled him as the paragon of public service. Citing Horace, Mather exclaimed that "the old heathen vertue of PIETAS IN PATRIUM, or, Love to one's country, he turned into Christian." Phips demonstrated how providence sanctified economic and military action.[47]

Phips did not receive plaudits from Samuel Willard and his Old South parishioners; yet Willard also framed discussion of civil matters in post-1688 political terms rather than the covenant and jeremiad. In what might be taken as a response to Mather, his 1694 *The Character of the Good Ruler*, Willard warned against the system of preferment, favoritism, bribery, and patronage associated with imperial governors, Phips included. Yet Willard, as much as Mather, defined godly rule and moral justice as the pursuit of "Civil felicity" with a "Civil Polity" that safeguarded the powers of elected representatives, property, and English liberties. The good ruler allowed his subjects to "injoy their Liberties and Rights without molestation or oppression" from arbitrary government. Ministers outside Boston voiced similar ideas. John Wise of Ipswich contested the Andros regime by re-hearsing English liberties iterated from the Magna Carta to the Glorious Revolution.[48]

Boston ministers added pan-Protestant ecumenical loyalties to the mix of Whig politics, older republican notions of commonwealth and virtue, imperial agendas, and notions of economic proficiency. Addressing the Council, Assembly, and governor in 1700, Mather asserted the interdependence between Protestantism and national prosperity. When God delivered England from Catholicism and James's plots, economic prosperity ensued—and did so in ways that Mather calculated quite explicitly. "The Abolishing of *Popery* in the *English Nation*," he estimated, "is worth at least Eight Millions of Pounds Sterling, yearly profit." Protestantism had made England "*Rich*," and Massachusetts was definitely Protestant. Jettisoning the language of New England's special covenant, Mather spoke of "*America*," which of all colonial territories most resembled England for economic productivity, commercial energy, and abundance of consumer goods. The administration of then-governor Bellomont had every reason to support the charter privileges of Massachusetts because Protestant principles had shaped New Englanders into industrious and prudent contributors to the empire.[49]

Likewise, Mather urged the Assembly to loyalty to the Crown and continued investment in military ventures against England's Catholic enemies in Canada: reasonable costs to pay for the economic benefits and political freedoms of being English. "It is no little Blessing of God, that we are part of the *English Nation*," he argued, because "there is no *English man* but what has for his *Birthright* those *Liberties*, which are a rich *Inheritance*." Brushing aside the oppressions of the Dominion as the clutches of James's dying regime, he raved about the accession of William, "A KING" whose assent to parliamentary rule had "advanced the *English Nation*" and New England along with it.[50]

During the first decades of the eighteenth century, Boston's ministers intensified claims that the British Empire embodied providential designs for New England. They observed what they deemed to be a series of remarkable events: the 1707 Act of Union, the 1714 accession of George I, the suppression of the 1715 Jacobite Rebellion, George's military intervention on behalf of Protestants on the Continent, and the rising power of a Whig Parliament. New Englanders marveled at the transformation of the Crown. William and Mary, Anne, and George promoted, by common recognition, the Protestant interest, constitutional rights, and commerce across the empire. In England newspapers and serials publicized the empire as the means of peace and prosperity throughout the Atlantic world and the Continent. "The Sovereign of Merchandize," as one observer described Britain, made trade a tool for diplomacy, offered principles of political liberty, and relieved persecuted Protestants in Europe. Whig religious policy tolerated most Protestant sects in the kingdom. Enlightened commentators in Britain concluded that the current monarchy enacted moral good. Their counterparts among Boston's clergy, accepting the same terms of moral discourse, drew the same conclusion: God used the empire to shape world affairs.[51]

Mather's younger colleagues in other churches fused various conventions to link the imperial regime to providence. Benjamin Wadsworth of First Church offered a new formulation in 1702, lamenting the death of William III with claims that the king, like Israel's Josiah, served as a divine instrument to further political liberties against ungodly oppressions. Benjamin Colman, pastor of the new Brattle Street Church, went further. In a 1708 sermon to the governor and Council, he celebrated the union of the Scottish and English parliaments by drawing parallels between biblical Jerusalem and London. As the city of David, which Colman described in contemporary terms as "the *Imperial Seat* and Metropolis of the Kingdom of *Israel*," represented the reign of peace and happiness, so too the capital of the new British Empire. Colman exhorted provincial officials to pray for the "*External Prosperity*" of London because the success of the metropolis vindicated true religion.[52]

Colman made a two-pronged argument. First, commercial success, enhanced by the Act of Union, funded the military defense of Protestant hegemony. Using a trope from political economists, he asserted that "the Flourishing of *Trade*, and the Increase of Riches" strengthened "the Sinews

of War." Second, wealth supplied the social institutions that sustained republican political principles and Protestant cultural production. A polity
that supported enlightened ideas and philosophic virtue—London's literary societies and publications, its architecture, the Royal Society, and moral
reform societies—earned "a Reputation to Goodness," and that reputation
drew people to true religion. London's political, economic, and intellectual
superiority gave visible expression to divine goodness: it "ravishes away the
Souls of Men with the most pleasing Force." In sum, "Divine Providence"
had made Britain the vanguard of Protestantism, displaying God's design
for the world in the glories of the capital city. In a later thanksgiving sermon, occasioned by the defeat of the Jacobites in 1715 (a blessing of "the
same Providence that blasted the *former* Attempts"), Colman told his people that they owed allegiance to the monarchy because it had secured for
Massachusetts the "Tranquility" necessary for "Vertue and Religion,
Learning and Arts, Trade and Commerce."[53]

Other preachers also endorsed Britain's cosmopolitan empire. In 1717
Ebenezer Pemberton, at Old South, fancied New England's history as an
unbroken line of loyalty to England, culminating in the present "Duty,
Zeal and Affection to the Succession of the Crown in the Illustrious Protestant House of HANOVER." By his reading, Winthrop and his contemporaries
received the original charter as a gift of political liberty; subsequent colonists recognized the gift by adding to the Crown's treasury through commercial exchange.[54] Thomas Prince, Pemberton's successor, maintained
clerical encomiums to the house of Hanover in 1727, lauding George I for
his service on behalf of New England: building the royal navy, suppressing
Jacobites at home, subduing Catholic foes on the Continent, and making
"industrious Applications and wise Treaties" that benefited Boston's merchants. Having done so much for English Protestants throughout the Atlantic world, George appeared to Prince as "the Darling and Protection of
his People." Ministers such as Pemberton and Colman, and their colleagues such as Mather and Foxcroft, agreed that the Hanoverian government ruled Massachusetts well and deserved submission because it protected a Protestant polity.[55]

New England's clergy thought that providence transcended the current
dynasty even as it worked through it at present. Their language might have
sounded like pure veneration, but they did not fix their "Zeal and Affection" so much on the person of the king or the nation itself as on the
common benefits, to metropolis and colony, of a system that distributed
political liberties, religious freedoms, and mercantile benefits throughout
the empire.[56] Ministers vaunted reciprocity and cultural exchange with
London. Overseas traders were crucial to this exchange because they
formed legal, bureaucratic, and commercial ties across the British Atlantic.
Their pastors in Boston thought that merchants contributed to a vast re-

gime of civility set against Spanish and French competitors—a regime funded by the exchange of goods and blessings of prosperity.[57]

Given their identification of the civic order with the empire, puritan ministers placed the major burden of economic discipline—public policies and legal supervision—not on the churches but on the provincial government and its obligations to promote transatlantic commerce. In 1710 Pemberton revised and enlarged an election sermon into a hundred-page treatise on the nature of government, the most extensive discourse dedicated to that theme since Willard's 1694 *The Character of the Good Ruler*. By this time, Boston's ministers had made loyalty to the Crown a near commonplace in their preaching. Pemberton reinforced the place of Massachusetts in the metropolitan sphere. The imperial government stood at the apex of godly rule in the world, the defender of "the Common Rights of Mankind," so that the electors were "Instructed by GOD with a great Opportunity to serve HIM, your QUEEN, and *Country*" at once. This obliged Governor Dudley to justice and care for his subjects, and it obliged the Assembly to eschew partisan defiance of the executive.[58]

Pemberton gave Dudley, London's colonial agents, the Crown, and the Assembly, working in concert, nearly complete authority to configure economic policy. He made no specific recommendations, except for stricter enforcement of laws against forgery and against misuse of public bills of credit. As he argued, civil rulers exercised the necessary knowledge and skill to unravel the complexities of the market system: their "Prudence" enabled them to administer "the affairs of the Publick to the best advantage," as they used "*Dexterity* and *Skill*" in analyzing contemporary political and economic conditions. The "requisite . . . Penetrating *Sagacity* to foresee Publick dangers," he explained, derived less from religious doctrine than from political experience, familiarity with international affairs, and acquaintance with the histories of different polities, from ancient Rome to contemporary China.[59]

Colman reiterated such confidence in his 1716 election sermon, published as *Rulers Feeding and Guiding Their People*." Good representatives and magistrates, he argued, knew the latest statutes, reasoned from the constitution of the province, and obeyed imperial decrees. Moreover, their economic sophistication qualified them above the common, nontrading citizen to make judgments on commercial policy: "they should be well acquainted with various sorts of *Trade, Business, Imployment* to be followed by the People; that so the same may be the better *Directed, Protected, Encouraged*." Civil leaders ought to be experts in overseas exchange and international politics, because Massachusetts depended on Britain's transatlantic empire of trade. "The more they know of the *Scituation, Strength, Trade, Designs of Neighbouring Nations or People*," he preached in reference to civil rulers, "so much the better able they'll be to care for and promote, the good and welfare of their own People." Prince, again, followed suit some twelve years later, contending that political skill, military experience, and economic knowledge—their "thorough Intelligence of the State of their People"—qualified royal officials and their provincial counterparts to determine laws and regulations on trade.[60]

Boston's preachers presented an interpretive loop on a large historical scale: Protestantism led to wealth; wealth funded the empire; the empire combated Catholicism; the end of Catholicism brought civil liberties; and civil liberties allowed citizens to practice Protestant and market principles. Mather and his colleagues articulated a religious rationale for New Englanders to embrace a national identity that had momentous implications for commerce. As they did so, they engaged a new generation of social commentators and advisers to the state—England's political economists— who explained the economic import of empire in a remarkable series of statements on the nation, its money, and the very nature of exchange.

POLITICAL ECONOMY, MONETARY POLICY, AND THE JUSTIFICATION OF USURY

The English economic thinkers whom New Englanders encountered at the turn of the eighteenth century drew on the work of predecessors such as Misselden and Mun, who addressed the nation's policies on tariffs, currency, monopolies, and interest rates from the 1620s through the 1660s. The heirs to Misselden and Mun developed their ideas in the context of a crisis in the late Stuart administration, the accession of William and Mary, and subsequent dynastic wars. William Petty was perhaps the best known in New England of these second-generation economists. Erstwhile surveyor for Cromwell in Ireland, clothing merchant, member of Parliament, member of the inner circle that established the Royal Society, and naval architect, he specialized in taxation and public expenditure. Petty exhibited the power of mathematical analysis to inform policy, naming his method "political arithmetic." He built his arguments—for fewer restrictions on money, free-floating rents and interest rates, public employments and works projects for the poor, and more incentives to trade—on massive amounts of data summarized in a relentless stream of prose. He tracked the value of imports and exports, grain production and shipbuilding, prices, and wages for various occupations.[61]

Petty served as an authority for other economic commentators who defined commerce as a central program in the affairs of state rather than a merely domestic or private matter. They crafted a science to suit England's agenda in its commercial competition with France and Spain from the 1690s through the 1720s. Lawyer Charles Davenant, whose publications were frequently imported to Boston, served as commissioner of the excise under James, fell out of office during the first blush of Whig hegemony under William, and acted as inspector general of the imports and exports under Anne. Nicholas Barbon, the unlikely son of the Anabaptist preacher Praise-God Barebones, studied medicine and accumulated a vast fortune as a business projector, real-estate mogul, financier, and insurance provider in London. Dudley North, the outspoken Tory in the conversation, prospered in the Levant trade, doing business in Turkey before becoming commissioner of the customs under James. John Locke and Josiah Child, governor of the East India Company with connections in Massachusetts, identified themselves most fervently with the Whig faction.[62]

These political economists addressed an array of fiscal matters, and their writings amounted less to a single, sustained argument than to a mélange of specific proposals. They often have been associated with mercantilism—a regime of centralized regulation over commerce to abet the nation in competition with other European powers—but mercantilism itself was not so much an ideology as is was an accretion of various, and sometimes ad hoc, commercial policies. Although the term "mercantilism" is misleading (later thinkers such as Adam Smith caricatured it as shortsighted state intervention for the purpose of accumulating specie and enriching a small class of elite merchants), it nonetheless retains its usefulness. "Mercantilist" may stand as shorthand for thinkers in this period who stressed empirical and analytical methods, the productive value of overseas trade, linkages between domestic consumption and trade, and the political utility and moral worthiness of merchants.[63]

Differences in policy recommendations aside—they debated with each other about statutory limits on interest, tariffs and taxes, poor relief, luxury spending, international commercial treaties, and monetary supply—all mercantilists traced a cycle of interconnecting claims about the foundations of the commonwealth. England's freedoms, which promoted the virtue on which the commonwealth rested, depended on security against other, especially Catholic, nations. Empire enforced that security. International trade and colonization enlarged empire by extending English rule and funding the kingdom's navy and armies. Freedom of commerce and astute participation in the European and Atlantic markets enhanced trade. Free and expanding trade, in turn, depended on political liberties, the exercise of which, to return to the beginning of the cycle, promoted public virtue. The ideology of empire—England's Atlantic empire—thus circled through assertions that connected older republican mores to new commercial imperatives and, especially, the interests of the nation. Political economists assembled a social discourse that justified ambitious overseas commerce as a national, religious, and moral good.[64]

England's economists, to reiterate, suggested different particular solutions to the kingdom's financial problems: debasement of the currency, decline in exports to Europe, the dislocations of wartime spending, rising unemployment, and the Crown's inability to fund its military.[65] Locke and Child, for example, supported Parliament when it created the Bank of England in 1694 as a means to secure credit for the monarchy, passed a recoinage act, and reconfigured the Board of Trade to oversee colonial exchange. They argued that Parliament ought to regulate the amount of paper money in circulation according to the nation's supply of silver, which would cut inflation, raise the value of English currency overseas, rectify the imbalance in trade, and improve the overall economy. Concerned with protecting domestic industries, Locke also urged restraints on imported luxuries. Barbon and North rejected Locke's arguments. They maintained that parliamentary restrictions dampened trade, a position aligning them with overseas merchants against domestic manufacturers. Relying on statistics provided by Petty and elucidated by Davenant, they maintained that increased consumption even of imported luxuries, rising interest rates, and an abundance of money—whether pegged to silver or not—rectified trade imbalances in the long term, enriched the kingdom, and sped wealth throughout the economy. The answer to England's economic ills, they insisted, consisted of more money, fewer regulations, and a reliance on the natural dynamics of commerce to stimulate appetites, trade, and prosperity throughout the kingdom.[66]

In making these arguments, Locke, Davenant, North, and Barbon elaborated technical analyses that unsettled moral conventions about the nature of money. They reasoned that money did not function as a stable instrument of exchange with permanent values. Its worth changed as it flowed through the channels of commerce, according to its availability. The state might attempt, as a pragmatic and temporary expedient, to prevent a precipitous devaluation by limiting the amount of money in circulation, but the market—which is to say the collection of individual tastes and needs—eventually determined the price of money as readily as the prices of goods. Economic writers of the 1640s allowed that money might be treated as a commodity. The economists of the 1690s concluded that money *was* a mere commodity. Locke accordingly admitted that statutory limits on interest rates amounted to fictions. "The Price of the Hire of Money," he wrote in his major fiscal treatise, is a "*natural*" affair because no "Law" can "hinder Men, skill'd in the Power they have over their own Goods . . . to purchase Money to be Lent at any Rate soever" serves them. Locke and his interlocutors all affirmed an inviolable law: prices and the value of money rose and fell with the market. As North put it, "No Laws can set Prizes in Trade, the Rates of which, must and will make themselves," because "Money is a Merchandize." All attempts to combat usury or set a limit to prices beyond ad hoc, local prohibitions against price gouging rested on nonsensical "Theological Arguments," in North's telling dismissal. He, along with Child and Davenant, contended that any stimulation to overseas trade, inflationary and usurious or not, rose to a moral dictate. They struck at imposed limits on interest as vehemently as previous essays attacked high interest rates, even inverting the definition of usury to mean the discouragement of creditors by restrictions on their profits.[67]

Many political economists voiced a corollary to their conclusions about money and prices: the nation's wealth depended less on legal coercion than on the natural dynamics of international and domestic markets. Instinctive desires for consumer goods, abetted by social aspirations for approval and status, compelled citizens to produce and exchange in order to make profits and buy commodities. "There can be no Trade unprofitable to the Publick," North asserted, and "the main spur to Trade, or rather to industry and ingenuity, is the exorbitant Appetites of Men." Barbon and Davenant especially set these putatively natural dynamics within a collective purpose: unimpeded trade and consumption funded England's contest against competing empires. In a complete reversal of puritan and humanist teaching, Davenant went so far as to argue that although profligate spending ruined some individuals, it nonetheless strengthened the commonwealth, promoted its independence, and therefore amounted to a social virtue. Barbon and North's validation of natural appetites indicated a growing conviction among political economists that individual interests determined economic value, even the worth of money, and that the market ordered the pursuit of such interests into a social system.[68]

Even when given in piecemeal fashion, mercantilist arguments about the source of economic value and importance of commercial expansion to the kingdom entered into a widespread social discourse. Dissenting clergy in England such as Thomas Delaune, who was known in New England, replicated many of their contentions, from the nature of money to the necessity of banks and usury for England's prosperity. The popular press in London, which produced newspaper editorials, broadsides, pamphlets, and gazettes, paraphrased or recorded parliamentary deliberations that referred to Davenant and Petty. Economic theory served mud-slinging politics when disputants argued about the effects of monopolies granted by the Board of Trade, tariffs, protection of home manufactures, navigation acts, monetary supply, and the relative merits of the Bank of England and private banks. All drew on technical data and made their cases by appealing to assumptions common to political economists: the need to uphold political liberties, expand commerce, and enhance the nation's overall wealth.[69]

Political and economic debates entered the popular press in other forms. A burst of advice manuals for merchants in the period replicated the ideas of Child, Petty, and Davenant, among others. Several new periodicals, many of which appeared in Boston, reviewed contemporary controversies and provided extracts from political economists: John Houghton's *Collection for Improvement of Husbandry and Trade*, Edward Hatton's *Merchants Magazine*, Charles King's *British Merchant, or Commerce Preserved*, and Daniel Defoe's *General History of Trade* and *Mercator, or Commerce Retriev'd*. A sometime merchant, Defoe attracted readers less for his consistency on policy—he shifted his views and attitudes toward overseas merchants as political parties changed—than for his wit and familiarity with the regimens of commerce. The serial publications of Richard Steele and Joseph Addison referred frequently to mercantilist arguments, as did nontechnical treatises such as James Puckle's *England's Way to Wealth and Honour* (London, 1699). The popularity of literary-commercial periodicals rose with the heat of debates between writers.[70]

Literary purveyors of political economy also popularized their theories through criticism of the misuse of the public debt and London's stock market. Essayists such as Defoe and playwrights such as Steele and Susanna Centlivre drew thick lines between hardworking merchants who served the nation and shifty financiers who abused the Bank of England. The bank issued long-term annuities and bonds to private investors. It used those shares to provide relatively inexpensive credit for public expenditures, which energized the economy and funded the military. The whole system, however, gave rise to uncontrolled speculation and political corruption. According to detractors, stockjobbers and brokers who sold shares in the bank bribed politicians, misled investors, spread rumors, and sold insider information about the government's affairs. They traded thousands of pounds on the slightest bits of knowledge about diplomatic, military, and commercial policies, often buying and selling fantastic amounts of stock in short periods of time. By the 1710s a series of legislative measures, such as prohibitions against short-term speculation, remedied many of the bank's affairs, but the corruptions of stockjobbers and concerns about the public debt still troubled critics.[71]

Practices in London's stock market far exceeded the bounds of humanist and early puritan moralizing, which emphasized the interpersonal obligations of exchange. The appearance of regularly published listings of stock and commodity prices, starting in 1698, abetted impersonal, profit-taking calculation. Huge ventures such as the Bank of England, the Royal African Company, the East India Company, and the South Sea Company dominated the exchange in London. Speculators placed nearly 40 percent of all commercial investments in the bank: a powerful example to merchants such as Fitch that credit itself offered a profitable investment. Traders arranged complicated contracts that shifted shares in the bank back and forth as bets on their future worth, sometimes buying them on a mere promise and selling them without ever having paid for them—an early form of futures trading. Contemporary critics observed in such cases the nearly total abstraction of commerce: trading in stocks and bank shares that only indirectly contributed to the transfer of tangible commodities.[72]

For English and American commentators, the South Sea Company exemplified the cupidity of the exchange. Parliament approved its foundation in 1711 and gave it a near monopoly over future trading with Spanish colonies. Its directors accepted government bonds or securities in exchange for shares in the company, whose worth rested on the possibilities of ventures, particularly slave trading, in South America and the Spanish West Indies. Promoted by members of Parliament, some of whom had taken bribes in the form of stock, the company attracted thousands of investors and in effect became a leading creditor to the government. Jonathan Swift and Defoe defended the scheme as a means of investment in the government and English trade, whereas Addison and Steele critiqued it as an incentive to bribery, corruption, and deceit. The early successes of the company, which had nothing to do with actual returns on overseas trade, prompted imitations. Prospectuses for ventures in the Greenland fishery and Virginia agriculture promised fantastic returns on stock bought on credit; investors provided a £2 deposit for £100 worth of shares that supposedly could be redeemed within a year for a 100 percent increase. Stock bubbles inflated at alarming rates. During a frenzied period in 1720, stock in the South Sea Company rose from £175 to £1,000 a share. It crashed with a massive sell-off in the summer of 1720, provoking widespread bankruptcy and government intervention. Parliamentary investigations into the South Sea bubble, as it was called, made the weekly news. Commentators issued a barrage of criticisms, filled with denunciations of brokers and gamesters, quick profits and short sells, political venality, knavery, rumormongering, and the unpatriotic diversion of money from productive exchange.[73]

Controversies about the Bank of England and wild investment schemes channeled the latest political economy into the public sphere, where stockjobbers served as a ready foil for popular representations of the good merchant. London's commercial manuals and literary essays featured the productive trader who eschewed speculative manias and served Britain's interests with skills and strategies informed by the latest economic science. Writers such as Defoe heaped praise on young, courageous businessmen who met the risks of long-distance trade with mathematical mastery, diligent bookkeeping, and hard-won reputations. Such optimism testified to the power and prevalence of the new political economy. The laudable merchant did not speculate in bad ventures, but neither did he harbor traditional qualms against rising interest rates, aggressive pursuit of profits, usury, and slave trading. In 1711 Addison asserted that patriotic service marked merchants as the epitome of social virtue. "There are not more useful members in a Commonwealth than merchants," he wrote in *The Spectator.* Steele's encomiums reached higher. Merchants were, in his opinion, "the greatest Benefactor[s] of the *English* nation," serving as "so many Centinels placed in all the Nations of the World to watch over and defend" Britain's empire; the English trader appeared to be "a sort of miracle-worker" who "turns all the Disadvantages of our Situation into our Profit and Honour." Steele infused the commercial and imperial nexus with a religious status: merchants were the redeemers of England.[74]

Many of the debates rehashed in London's press did not offer ready prescriptions for Boston's merchants, who, as colonials, figured as competitors with London and mere suppliers of wealth and goods to the metropolis, but mercantilist methods of analyses and definitions of money and credit resonated across the Atlantic.[75] Boston's puritan merchants and pastors turned to the discourse of political economy as a science of success in the market. Some of their information came through letters from London partners, who shared accounts of the East India Company, the state of England's cloth industries, and rumors of war. Bostonians, including Fitch, also read excerpts from London newspapers and gazettes reprinted in Boston's first newspapers: John Campbell's *Boston News Letter* (founded in 1704) and William Brooker's *Boston Gazette* (1719). Boston papers reported on parliamentary hearings, fiscal policy, commercial treaties, the latest scandals in the stock market, diplomatic intrigues, and bits of news from Europe: the state of trade in Venice, French encroachments on Dutch sea-lanes, and commercial activity in Hamburg. Such stories scripted commercial competition in the transatlantic political theater.[76]

Occasional news indirectly illuminated mercantilist ideas for residents of Boston; more direct presentations came through the importation of English books by a growing collection of booksellers. Sixteen new bookshops appeared between 1700 and 1711, adding to the twenty operating around the Town House at the end of the seventeenth century. They sold London gazettes and papers, the works of Defoe, merchants' handbooks, and law books, many of which communicated the agendas of England's political economists. Merchant Edward Bromfield frequented the shop of his fellow Old South member Daniel Henchman, purchasing statistical and legal handbooks along with Reformed devotional treatises and sermons—a consumer's consent to the compatibility between piety and imperial commerce. Another Old South bookseller and publisher, Samuel Gerrish, imported dozens of volumes on English trade and the royal navy, annual histories of the monarchy, reprints of the records of parliamentary debates, political tracts on paper money and bills of credit, discourses on the nature of money and the Recoinage Act, advice manuals and essays for merchants, and the major treatises of most of the relevant political economists, including Davenant, Petty, and Locke. He sold hundreds of books on English law, banking, and litigation.[77]

Boston printers and publishers also marketed their own versions of almanacs and editions of commercial handbooks that relayed the chief dictate of political economists such as Petty and Davenant: the best conduct of commerce relied on mathematical analyses of long-term profits and national productivity. The first book of mathematics published in America, James Hodder's *Arithmetick* (1719), illustrated every mathematical, statistical, and tabular task with commercial problems (from multilayered contracts to the calculation of interest on foreign currencies) and reduced every economic transaction to numbers. Almanacs included patriotic maxims, anniversary and other notable days for the Crown, and demographic data. Printers also produced several commercial manuals for New Englanders at the turn of the eighteenth century. Thomas Goodman's 1702 *Experience'd Secretary* introduced aspiring traders to the legal protocols, cosmopolitan diction, and formalized communication that displaced the morally laden, personal rhetoric recommended by John Brown's *Marchants Avizo* and used by John Hull. Goodman advised traders to write simple, clear, yet legally precise letters that stuck to business, even between family relations. Thomas Hill's *Young Secretary's Guide* of 1703 modeled equally formal, polite, and impersonal language, bereft of religious or moral rhetoric, adding to Goodman a legal lexicon and dictionary of aristocratic titles and addresses (figure 4.3). It was the language Fitch used almost exclusively in his business correspondence, and if he learned his style from Goodman or Hill, then he encountered political economy in the process. Boston's printers did not publish a New England Petty or Davenant, but they did make books that instructed merchants in the calculating skills and scientific worldview promoted by the great economists in London.[78]

Boston clergymen accumulated a small collection of books on political economy, including Davenant's *Discourses on the Public Revenues, and on Trade in England* (London, 1698) and *An Essay upon the Probable Methods of making a People Gainers in the Ballance of Trade* (London, 1699) and Child's *New Discourse on Trade*, (London, 1694). Old South ministers established a church library with treatises also by Defoe and Locke. At Old North, the Mather family library held merchant's manuals and occasional tracts on trade policy, from issues of Steele's *Guardian* to essays on public credit, the Whig government, and the politics of overseas investment schemes. One of the advice books in the Mather collection, *The Compleat Tradesman*, made explicit the connection between mathematical proficiency and mercantilist ideology. Advising young merchants on tabulating prices, making ledgers, keeping accounts, and pursuing debt litigation, it urged cunning and diligence as a national duty and free trade as a political necessity: England "is properly a Nation of Trade," and its rulers ought to heed the advice of

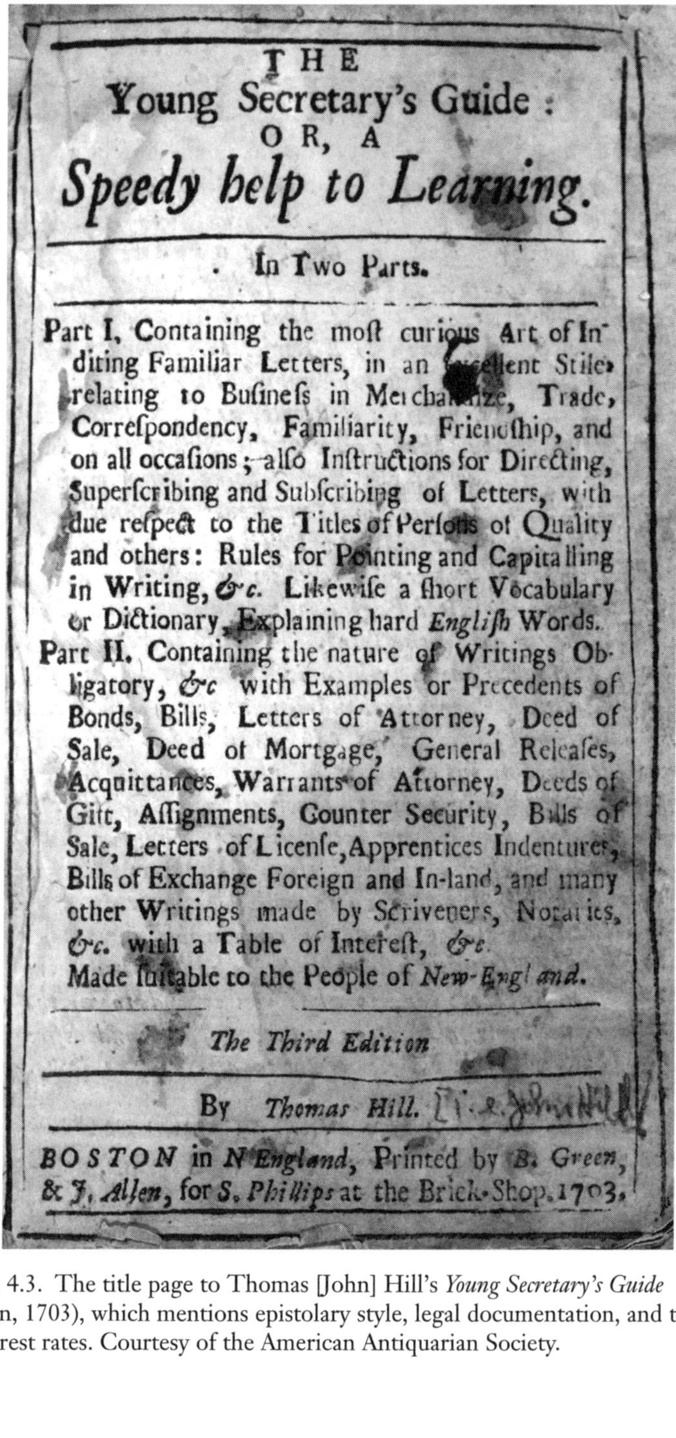

THE
Young Secretary's Guide :
O R, A
Speedy help to Learning.

In Two Parts.

Part I, Containing the moft curious Art of In-
diting Familiar Letters, in an Excellent Stile,
relating to Bufinefs in Merchandize, Trade,
Correfpondency, Familiarity, Friendfhip, and
on all occafions; alfo Inftructions for Directing,
Superfcribing and Subfcribing of Letters, with
due refpect to the Titles of Perfons of Quality
and others: Rules for Pointing and Capitalling
in Writing, &c. Likewife a fhort Vocabulary
or Dictionary, Explaining hard *Englifh* Words.
Part II. Containing the nature of Writings Ob-
ligatory, &c with Examples or Precedents of
Bonds, Bills, Letters of Attorney, Deed of
Sale, Deed of Mortgage, General Releafes,
Acquittances, Warrants of Attorney, Deeds of
Gift, Affignments, Counter Security, Bills of
Sale, Letters of Licenfe, Apprentices Indentures,
Bills of Exchange Foreign and In-land, and many
other Writings made by Scriveners, Notaries,
&c. with a Table of Intereft, &c.
Made fuitable to the People of *New-England.*

The Third Edition

By *Thomas Hill.*

BOSTON in N England, Printed by B. Green,
& J. Allen, for S. Phillips at the Brick-Shop. 1703.

Figure 4.3. The title page to Thomas [John] Hill's *Young Secretary's Guide*
(Boston, 1703), which mentions epistolary style, legal documentation, and tables
of interest rates. Courtesy of the American Antiquarian Society.

merchant advisers. All laws should promote the "conveniency and advantages for a Trading People," that is, the availability of credit and ease of international exchange. As for merchants, they should pursue profits according to their own best economic intelligence: "our business is to keep unity with our selves, and enjoy a free Trade" in "profitable Places, whereby we become Masters of Trade." One of its Boston readers, most likely Mather, made marginal notes on its discussion of the valuation and use of money in London.[79]

Mather also relied on popular literary commentary about the economy. He favored Addison and Steele's *Spectator*, for which he wrote (but never published) several essays "to the best interests," as he put it in fashionable diction, "of the Nation." Defoe held Mather's, and other New Englanders', interest as well. Known as a dissenter, Whig, and strong supporter of William and Mary, Defoe belonged to a group of London merchants who invested in New England ventures. He wrote in behalf of the Massachusetts charter in 1690 and, later, lobbied for the protection of the congregational order against the encroachments of the national church. He applauded New Englanders' patriotric struggle against French forces and urged the home government to increase England's military presence on the border with Canada. He also patronized the London dissenters' Society for the Reformation of Manners, spoke at the London Merchants' Lectures about civic virtue, and promoted works projects to remedy urban poverty. Despite his elusive, fairly unorthodox religious opinions, Defoe must have appeared to Mather and his colleagues as an ideal associate on the other side of the Atlantic: a merchant with a large literary audience who justified dissent, legitimated robust overseas trade, sounded the note of social reform, and supported Protestant empire against Catholic challenge throughout the Atlantic world. Mather corresponded with Defoe about reform societies and adopted some of his literary devices, from satirical fables to titles. Just one year after the appearance of Defoe's *Robinson Crusoe*, Boston publishers printed *News from Robinson Cruso's Island* (Boston, 1720), Mather's satire against the critics of Governor Samuel Shute (1716–1723). When Mather, despite his own warnings against excessive consumption and social pretensions, began wearing a periwig, he identified with the metropolitan sensibilities and economic ideals that Defoe reflected (figure 4.4). Succeeding writers in New England emulated England's poets who venerated the nation's naval might and commercial supremacy. When America's poets celebrated colonial participation in England's empire of Protestant civility, they at least tacitly recognized the legitimacy of mercantilist theory. They consented to economic policy made scientific by Petty and Davenant, turned political by North and Barbon, and popularized by Steele and Defoe. For New Englanders, the dictates of England's political economists served as more than

Figure 4.4. *Cotton Mather*. Mezzotint engraving by Peter Pelham, 1727. The Latin caption and Mather's periwig advertise him as a cosmopolitan intellectual. Courtesy of the American Antiquarian Society.

a literary link to the metropolis; they expressed the genius of a Protestant empire that furthered the cause of religion.[80]

It was no contradiction, then, for latter-day puritans to claim a religious purpose for the discourse of political economy. Taking bits and pieces of a large and diverse literature, they applied mercantilist logic to their local conditions quite deliberately. They did so most clearly in technical debates about credit, money, banks, and economic policy in Massachusetts from the 1690s through the 1740s.[81] These deliberations harkened back to the 1680s, when Boston merchants complained about the colony's lack of currency and overreliance on bills of exchange, the value of which suffered depreciation overseas. In 1681 several of them proposed to organize a company, called the Fund. They planned to exchange among themselves paper notes, issued to borrowers who used mortgages as collateral. John Woodbridge, the pastor in Newbury and a relative of high-placed merchants and Council members, described the project in his *Severals Relating to the Fund* (Boston, 1682). Woodbridge claimed to have consulted with several merchants in London, "well Read in the nature of *Banks*," who explained that "most civilized Nations"—most likely a reference to Italian and Dutch precedents—adopted similar measures to speed exchange, lower interest rates, decrease debt litigation, increase manufactures, and enhance the balance of trade.[82]

The Fund never succeeded, but five years later its backers raised another proposal and promoted it by circulating in Boston a London treatise entitled *A Model for Erecting a Bank of Credit*. Like Woodbridge's *Severals Relating to the Fund*, *A Model* urged readers to rely on the hard-won wisdom of merchants, who determined to employ fiat money (paper money rather than specie) secured by private property such as land. Its arguments resembled those of Petty and Child about the importance of making money available as a means to stimulate consumer appetites, which encouraged production; money "quickens Merchandizing and Trade," "promotes Shipping and Navigation," and "helps the Consumption" of domestic products and imports—all of which "helps to civilize the Ruder sort of People" and "incourages others to follow their Example in Industry and Civility." As "the Trade and Wealth of any Country" rose, it provided greater taxes to the government and encouraged even further domestic production. *A Model*, like mercantilist essays, treated money not as the representation of absolute or intrinsic standards, but as a mere instrument for commerce, the value of which changed with its power to facilitate trade: the "high or low Value of the Money" was less important than "the Value of Goods" imported and exported from nation to nation.[83]

Prodded by further monetary problems and increased oversight from London and the new royal governor in Boston, the provincial Council and the General Court established a public bank in 1690. They authorized the

province to issue bills of credit—paper notes printed by the government—
to pay especially for military defense and the campaign against Quebec
that year. The court iterated imperial agendas in its act: it intended to
remedy the fiscal "calamities of the country," all "for the maintaining and
defending of their Majesties interest against hostile invasions." The resulting legislation empowered a committee to emit £7,000 in notes, rang-
ing from five shillings to five pounds, with which the province would pay
its militia, military provisioners, and overseas creditors. The notes, to be
redeemed with 5 percent interest in five years, were to be retired when
private holders (technically creditors to the government) submitted them
as taxes. Bank of England notes rested on a permanent national debt backed
by landholding creditors and functioned as paper securities that could be
transferred in international trade. Massachusetts bills, in contrast, represented a temporary debt. They were to be used only within the colony and
quickly retired—regulations readily violated by most merchants. Further
military expenditures, exports of money to England, and the resulting scarcity of bills prevented the government from retiring the original notes and,
instead, prompted further emissions: £30,000 in 1691, £3,000 in 1702, and
£30,000 in 1709. In 1712 the court mandated that bills of credit be accepted
as legal tender in ordinary business transactions (figure 4.5).[84]

By 1714 depreciation of these bills (some merchants lowered their value
by as much as 30 percent), price inflation, rising interest rates, and an increase in debt litigation prompted demands for further government emissions as one solution and the allowance for private banks modeled after the
Fund as another. Elisha Cooke Jr., along with John Colman, the merchant
brother of Benjamin, led the campaign for a so-called land bank: a privately
owned company designed to issue the extraordinary sum of £300,000.
Other private-banking proponents planned to raise funds through investments in building projects such as a bridge over the Charles River. Opponents eventually suppressed private banks in favor of continued monetary
control by the Council and General Court. In 1716 the province issued
£100,000 of notes, this time backed by mortgages; in 1721 it emitted
£50,000. These efforts did not solve Massachusetts's currency problems.
The province's bills of credit continued to depreciate, falling to such low
values overseas that the whole currency system came under attack from
London during the late 1730s.[85]

During three crucial periods in this history—1690–1691, 1714–1716,
and 1719–1722—Boston publishers produced a rash of pamphlets on
money and trade, set against the background of parallel controversies in
London about the Bank of England and the stock market.[86] Arguments
clustered around three positions. Land speculators, landed but cash-poor
householders, many debtors, and a group of merchants who traded especially within New England, such as Noyes and Colman, favored the free

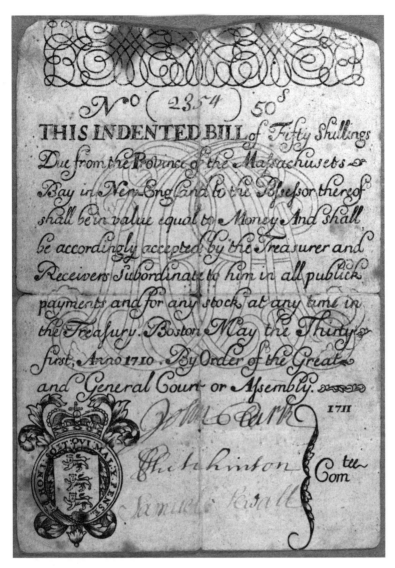

Figure 4.5. A fifty-shilling Massachusetts bill of credit issued in 1711, stamped with the royal insignia and signed for the province by John Clark, E. Hutchinson, and Samuel Sewall. Courtesy of the American Antiquarian Society.

production and flow of paper money, which is to say private land banks, schemes such as the Charles River bridge, and high levels of currency emissions. Debtors, they argued, benefited from an increased supply of money, lower interest rates, and even monetary depreciation, which in effect decreased debts with the mere passage of time. Speculators profited from a rise in land values.

Colman and the Chebacco (Ipswich) preacher John Wise wrote most forcefully for this position. As they did, they echoed Davenant's and North's assertions of the importance of internal trade and high levels of domestic consumption, and the relative unimportance of stable currency values tied to tangible wealth. Citing parallel discussions in London and using the Bank of England as a prime example, Colman contended that private banks would flush the economy with money. They would lower interest rates, end decades of wasteful and oppressive litigation over credit, and power economic activity throughout. "The Medium of Exchange, the only thing that gives life to Business," he pleaded, "Employs the Poor, Feeds the Hungry, and Cloaths the Naked." The lack of currency led tightfisted creditors to raise interest rates, hound debtors into court, and foreclose on unpaid mortgages; in this environment, "the whole Land are turned Usurers." Money, Colman insisted, was a mere instrument that incited and capacitated people's natural instincts to consume and therefore to produce: "Every Body almost would be Improving his Talent if Money were stirring." Colman deployed old moral rhetoric with a new, mercantilist logic.[87]

Wise produced the fullest apology for this position in his 1721 *Word of Comfort to a Melancholy Country.* He filled his treatise with Petty, Davenant, Barbon, and North: imperial jealousies and patriotic duties, new theories of money, statistical surveys of prices and values, comparisons with other European states, assertions about natural appetites, and, throughout, the scientific expertise of merchants as the preeminent guide to economic practice. Money, he argued, was a commodity and best managed by merchants who knew about interest rates, imports and exports, and the balance of trade. Because overall economic prosperity maintained merchants' interests, they would conduct the business of private banks, or use an expanded supply of bills of credit, to the benefit of the whole commonwealth. Drawing on statistical studies, he maintained that a ready supply of bills of credit decreased import prices and increased exports. Good rulers designed fiscal policy to inspire economic production and exchange. An abundance of paper money did just that, so that "our Outward wellbeing, is under GOD, involved in a Bank of Credit, as being the best Method in business." Binding progressive credit measures and religious claims even tighter, he described monetary abundance as a providential instrument. Money advanced New Englanders from barbarism to civility, provincial obscurity to cosmopolitan prominence, bills of credit were in his account "the means of our Salvation!" This being the case, Wise deemed mercantile specialists, "these Men" who "belong to our Metropolis," not as scoundrels and threats to a godly order, but as "Publick Benefactors, and Common Fathers to their Country; as being Men of Noble and Great minds." They can "Regulate the Price of all Things Yearly in the common course of Trade, and Commerce . . . as tho' Controllers and absolute Masters of the Market."[88]

As a final appeal, Wise returned to imperial themes. He quoted a mercantilist maxim, to the effect that "Money is the Sinews of War," and recalled how Massachusetts bills had carried the province through King William's War and Queen Anne's War. As powerful as the monarchy itself, money ruled as "the king of business, for increasing the Wealth, the civil Strength, and Temporal glory of a People." It supplied transatlantic merchants and spread civility along with their wares. Wise evoked Holland— once reviled by William Bradford as a cesspool of avarice and materialism—and Venice as happy and successful states supplied by private banks. English citizens should by implication do no less. "Let the Merchandize be accommodated, which will be for the Interest of the Crown; and fill our Country with Joyful Songs and Praises to God for His Goodness." Wise magnified Barbon and North by religious rhetoric.[89]

Highly placed and elite overseas merchants such as Hutchinson, royal officials such as Governors Joseph Dudley and Shute, large-scale creditors, and a few outspoken pastors opposed the very notion of private banks. They insisted on fiscal conservatism. Conceding the necessity for public bills, they demanded policies to stabilize their value: strict limits to the amount of emissions to prevent depreciation, sinking or redemption of bills according to a firm timetable, and ready conversion to specie. In theory, these policies abetted colonial creditors, whose loan contracts did not devalue over time, overseas merchants who had access to bills of credit and depended on their stable worth, which is to say reputation, in England, and political appointees compelled to appease London's demands for fiscal restraint. As readily as Wise extolled merchants and their natural instincts, Dudley raised the specter of stockjobbing and other mercantile mischief, clearly taken from reports out of London's exchange, along with the observation that it was an outright contradiction to offer private banks as a matter of patriotic duty when the Crown had never approved them. Another polemicist consigned the dearth of currency to merchants who imported foreign luxuries and exported specie and bills, all to the detriment of the public good.[90]

Opponents of private banks also warned of merchant cabals and the concentration of political and economic power in Boston. In 1720 Edward Wigglesworth, then a supply preacher in Barnstable and future professor at Harvard, decried an ever-deepening public debt as a political disaster and an ever-rising taste for extravagance in Boston as an economic calamity. He argued that the latest rates given in London on silver and Massachusetts bills had inflated prices, imbalanced New England's trade, and inhibited economic growth. Rather than print more bills, the government ought to shorten credit—as Parliament had done with the Bank of England—which would dampen consumption and speculation. The court also ought to promote increased interest rates on book debts, which would compel debtors to remit payments in bills at hand, shoring up the province's supply of money. Like Locke and Child abroad, Wigglesworth took a conservative position on currency but nonetheless made his arguments from the latest dictates of economic science, current trade data, and prevalent assumptions about the public good. He too eschewed outdated arguments about the intrinsic value of money or dangers of usury.[91]

Wise's *Word of Comfort* incited other indictments and counterindictments in the Boston press, which increasingly referenced affairs in England. New England polemicists adopted the rhetorical styles of Londoners such as Defoe, relying on satire, puns, and sharp wit rather than formal moral argument.[92] John Higginson clearly had the Exchange Alley in mind when he titled his contribution *The Second Part of the South-Sea Stock* (Boston, 1721). Attempting to refute Wise, Higginson evidenced New Englander's familiarity with economic news from London. He satirized the South Sea stock and the Mississippi Company (a similar project in France) as speculative foolishness. He linked fraudulent stock schemes and stock-jobbing to a promoney faction in the General Court that was motivated by "a selfish, contriving Spirit." The court spread "Confusion" with every currency emission. It produced bad bills that inflated the public debt and sent gold and silver overseas. Cheap credit tempted debtors to sign onto mortgages that they could ill afford. Real wealth consisted in fiscal solidity, not an abundance of consumer goods. As did Wigglesworth, Higginson reasoned from the assumptions of men such as Petty and Davenant—about the public good, monetary value, and the importance of empirical facts to economic policy—even as he contended for fiscal conservatism. He made no reference to biblical or puritan discourses about the means and ends of commerce.[93]

Many of Boston's puritan merchants, civic leaders, and influential pastors, Sewall and Mather among them, took a third, moderate position. Anxious to provide funds for the defense of New England against French Canada and sensitive to the needs for credit among poorer inhabitants, they supported interest-bearing government emissions. Yet fearful of depreciation and the temptation to export bills by the consumption of imported luxuries, they rebuffed private banks, recommended small issues under government control, and especially urged voluntary restraints on imports. The government in fact eventually followed their recommendations.

Mather demonstrated his familiarity with London's political economists in his 1691 tract, *Some Considerations on the Bills of Credit*. A supporter of paper emissions through 1715, he launched into a theoretical defense of fiat money, replete with quotations from London's specialists. He claimed to "have had some former Discourse about the *Nature of Money*," which taught him that money was "but a *Counter* or *Measure* of mens Properties and Instituted *means* of permutation." He accepted the political economists' argument that money was a mere contrivance to facilitate commerce. Criticisms of the public debt and paper emissions rested on the false premise that the value of money should be fixed to specie or other forms of tangible wealth. If economic conditions, such as the devaluation of bills of exchange and overall dearth of currency, required public bills, then the government ought to accede without concern for intrinsic monetary values. "If the Merchants cannot Buy as well as Sell for Credit," Mather asked, then "how shall they carry on their Trades?" Public bills, Mather astutely argued, had worked well enough for the French in Canada. Conversely, the lack of such a policy in Ireland had doomed its mortgaged lands to foreclosure by English creditors.[94]

In addition, Mather argued that ordinary citizens ought to trust the judgment of experts in such matters. Massachusetts's merchants had learned the best and latest methods in accounting, mathematics, and market pricing; they had studied the statistical and mercantilist manuals circulating through Boston. "It seems, possible now," he concluded in *Considerations*, "for *Boston* [merchants] to Correct the whole." Their commercial expertise and public spirit assured New Englanders that they would exchange the bills to enrich "Humane Traffick" in all spheres, increase the overall wealth of the province, and supply taxes to relieve the government's debts. Mather appended to his essay "Some Additional Considerations," which informed readers that bills of credit were widely used in the great cities of Amsterdam, Venice, and Paris. European successes made contemporary objections to public banks appear to be backwater foolishness.[95]

A magistrate and member of the Council, Sewall also wrote about provincial monetary policy. His reflections demonstrate the pragmatism of moderates, who supported public bills yet came to oppose the voluminous emissions proposed in the late 1710s and 1720s. In 1714 he supported a modest £5,000 issue because, as he figured by current fiscal data, it was "all for the Publick benefit." Two years later, he affirmed the idea of further emissions in principle but advised the Council to refrain from them until they retired older bills, collected outstanding taxes, and determined the real monetary needs of the province. He eventually accepted new legislation mandating a large £100,000 issue.[96]

By 1724, however, Sewall resisted the flood of emissions. In a speech to the court and Council, he decried the overabundance of bills. After warning against imported luxuries, for which Massachusetts traders paid by illicitly sending provincial bills abroad, he offered a strictly economic analysis. Some merchants had abandoned overseas business, using their capital to speculate in bills of credit rather than invest in trade: a perverse imitation of London speculators who traded shares in the Bank of England. Rapid depreciation of Massachusetts bills hampered deals overseas, decreasing profits and supplying less in taxes. Creditors, landowners, and salaried employees—including ministers such as Mather and public officials such as Sewall—suffered from depreciation as well; their contracts lost real value with every emission. "The Trade" of the country may have been increased with new money fueling consumption and speculation, "but not the wealth." Sewall's admonishment, that "the Emitting, as managed amongst us, we suppose is a Moral Evil," convinced the Council, which in this case resisted popular demands for more money.[97]

Fitch likewise engaged in the latest debates about currency and kept current on the legal and fiscal dynamics of trade. He often patronized Henchman's bookstore, where he procured almanacs, secretary's guides, and essays on the South Sea Company—all of which made easy reading of the latest economic science and informed his own affairs. He took part in two short-lived schemes, one in 1710 and the other in 1733, for Boston merchants to circulate private notes to be used among their workers and customers. As he explained to an English partner, "it's extream difficult to raise money here," and the merchants' notes speeded local exchange without depleting the supply of public money. Fitch took other positions on currency. During the monetary controversies of the early 1720s, he, like Sewall, warned against large emissions yet agreed to small ones with short-term dates of retirement to fund the government during a real crisis. He signed a public letter to this effect, which placed the issue in the context of imperial politics and the balance of trade between Boston and London. In 1735 he joined other Boston merchants who subscribed to an agreement not to receive or circulate Rhode Island or New Hampshire bills of credit, which, by their lights, worsened depreciation and added to the confusion in the province.[98]

The specific recommendations coming from Massachusetts's ministers and civic leaders revealed less about their economic mentality than did their dependence on England's mercantilists to provide the grammar of debate for monetary issues. No single policy in itself—for or against a large public debt, repeated emissions, or private banks—denoted a consistent outlook on the market. Individuals changed their counsel according to shifting economic and political conditions. Mather pleaded for bills of credit in 1691; after 1716 he complained about the futility of increasing emissions. He chastised agitators for expanding money supplies, such as Cooke, who failed to appreciate the government's obligations to appease powerful Londoners who lobbied for fiscal restraint in Boston. Sewall never promoted an abundant and free supply of paper money, but he accepted paper emissions as temporary expedients until they appeared to defeat the whole purpose of the bank. Like many traders, he also realized that personal bills of exchange sometimes served as a steadier link between American and British merchants than did provincial bills of credit.[99] Clerical denunciation of imported fashions seemed to imply an anticommercial morality, but critics of overconsumption portrayed it as a hindrance to free exchange rather than a concession to it. They contended that a larger volume of imports than exports ruined the competitive power of New England merchants in their trade with Britain. Confidence in, and anxiety about, the market system ran through almost every comment.

Throughout their disagreements, the leaders of Boston's puritan establishment adopted the discourse of political economy as a near science. As one Boston merchant observed, the pamphlet war on banks depended on some consensus about the very terms of debate; it spread mercantilist ideas as an economic orthodoxy throughout the town. "The minds of people were prepared for impressions," this writer claimed, "from pamphlets, courants, and other news papers, which were frequently published." The ideas of Child and Davenant, Petty and North, popularized through those "pamphlets," excerpted in "news papers," and given literary expression in various "courants," described how commerce in fact operated. Their analyses of the economic order were as indubitable as the descriptions of the solar system that astronomers in the Royal Society provided. Wise noted that "statesmen" such as economic counselors gave sounder advice than did moral treatises from the previous century. John Colman injected political arithmetic into his essays on money, discussing interest rates, mortgages, the London exchange, and the cumulative impact—in Petty-like terms—of his proposals. Clerical critics such as Wigglesworth, he claimed, could hardly refute such precision. He advised Wigglesworth "to stick to Divinity" and "have nothing to do with the Mysteries of Trade," which were "too Wonderful for him," "past his Comprehension," and "out of his Sphere." The minister of Old South in 1724, Sewall's son Joseph, advised ministers to heed the knowledge of political and economic specialists; he, at least, could not claim to be "versed on the Nicities and Mysteries of the Market Place." Mather admitted that he simply had to trust in the technical analyses provided by professional merchants who accumulated massive amounts of data.[100]

Mather and his colleagues attempted to elucidate the providential purpose for an economic order calibrated by others. Even as they warned individuals against sheer mammonism, they accepted the economists' fundamental terms—the power of empirical data. Unconcerned for fixed and absolute monetary value, they promoted nearly any measure to stimulate trade and secure Britain's hegemony over the Atlantic world. In the process, they treated money as a cultural sign, the value of which depended on its utility. As money mediated social exchange, influenced provincial politics, and served the church, its meaning changed over time.[101]

Ministers in Massachusetts recognized this impermanent, negotiated meaning of money as they reconsidered long-held religious proscriptions against usury and oppression. They challenged traditional teaching when they gathered at Harvard periodically from 1690 to 1699 to debate and resolve matters of polity for the churches in the aftermath of the Glorious Revolution. As secretary for these meetings, Mather recorded their deliberations and conclusions. Most of what he called the thirty "cases" discussed in Cambridge concerned synods, sacramental qualifications, ordination, the relative authority of pastors and congregations, and the errors of Anglican liturgical practices. Several, however, focused on economic issues. Ministers criticized private lotteries and games of chance as risky and wasteful: the very sort of vices that London moralists attached to the stock exchange. They also considered usury, what Mather described as "an Advance of any thing lent by contract." They meant an array of practices previously condemned as usurious: merchants or financiers who not only made profits from loans to needy debtors, but who also traded in money, mortgages, or other securities, determined interest rates according to the market for money, or made any other loan contracts that guaranteed them a profit.[102]

Mather informed New Englanders that the clergy no longer regarded usury as sinful. He and his colleagues jettisoned older puritan readings of Scripture for interpretations resting on scientific analyses, patriotic agendas, and practical necessity. Using the latest definitions of money, they contended that "there is no manner of reason, why the *Usury* of *Money* should be more faulty, than that of any *other thing*." Money, as political economists had shown, functioned as a mere commodity, "really as *Improvable* a thing as any other; and it is rather *more* than, *less productive* of advantage," so that "there can be no *reasonable pretence* that should bind me to lend my *Money* for nothing, rather than any other Commodity." The "Divine Law" of the Old Testament accordingly legitimated usury by disallowing it only in some cases. The New Testament gave "countenance" to it in Jesus' parable of the talents (Matt. 25:27). Furthermore, economic "Necessity and Utility" "justified" usury. The ethical principle of equity mandated it. Even the moral "Law of Charity" required it. "*Humane Society*, as now circumstanced, would sink, if all *Usury* were Impractible." Only Catholics soaked in canon law and papal superstition maintained old prohibitions against usury. "The several declamations of the *Ancients* against

Usury," the clergy concluded, "must be of no farther account with us." With this decree, Boston's ministers brushed aside a signal assertion of Reformed teaching on commerce from the days of Calvin.[103]

Five years later, Willard further encoded the new economic perspective in as full a systematic theology as ever produced in New England: a series of 250 lectures delivered from 1687 to 1707 and published as *A Compleat Body of Divinity*. Speaking to his merchant audience at Old South, he took many of the opinions of England's economic thinkers to be straightforward facts and correlated their advice on merchants' callings, trade, and credit with divine commands to engage in "Commerce or Exchange" for the "furthering of our own, and our Neighbour's Wealth." To be sure, Willard— who promoted, generally speaking, a more traditional theological outlook than did Mather and other prominent Boston ministers—offered customary exhortations to moral solidarity. Christian businessmen ought to care for the poor, give alms, treat customers and employers with equity, avoid ostentatious consumption, employ their "Scruple[s]" to avoid extortionate pricing, shun fraud, and "use Discretion and Piety" as general rules for business.[104]

Yet when Willard applied these vague exhortations to the techniques of exchange, he displaced older conventions with current economic axioms. Avoiding the term "usury," he ridiculed long-standing moral objections to "*Lending Money* upon *Interest*" as "*Noise* and *Railery*, without solid Reason, or Cogency of arguing," filled with "opprobrious Language" and "overheated Zeal" but void of real economic knowledge. Speculative investments, banking, trading in mortgages, and financing loans had been "found on Experience, to be as necessary and profitable for the common Benefit of Mankind" as any other trade. Old Testament prohibitions against usury applied to "the *Israelitish* Polity" and did not contain "*Universally* Moral" obligations. The Bible "no where absolutely" forbade usury. Medieval, Aristotelian arguments about the sterility of money, taken up into the Catholic teaching that money by its very nature was a fixed standard of measure and neither contained nor could increase value, "were insipid; and a Man of Reason, and Thought, would be ashamed so much as to take it into his Mouth; much more to leave it on Record." To the contrary, money "is become the most Fertile thing in the World; and most serves to promote Civil Commerce among a People, as Experience abundantly confirms."[105]

Willard furthermore dismissed the arguments of puritan divines such as Perkins, Ames, and Cotton. They disparaged loan contracts that guaranteed a profit to creditors who provided money for commercial ventures but shared none of the risks of failure. He trumped their qualms with "a point of Prudence" and, moreover, the doctrine of "God's Providence." Creditors and debtors ought to make contracts as a "rational Consideration," figuring the going rate of money and probability of commercial success.

Sometimes the venture would fail, and the debtor would suffer. Sometimes the venture would succeed and profit the debtor far above the contracted interest and fees. In each case, creditors and debtors ought to trust "the Ordinary Course of God's Providence" to work things out equitably. For Willard, Christian teaching mandated productive exchange for the common good. Mercantilist knowledge and commercial skill, gained through experience, provided realistic guidance to that exchange and reached the status of a moral imperative. After the ministers' 1699 declaration on usury and Willard's lectures, the selectmen of Boston began to lend the town's money at interest. They also began to sell public lands and use the proceeds from mortgages and sales to speculate in other real estate ventures. Municipal policy reflected changes in religious teaching.[106]

When it came to merchants who raised their prices as high as the market allowed, or what previous moralists called oppression, Willard also conflated pragmatic acumen with providential dynamics. He warned against profiteering from temporary shortages in necessary supplies but considered monopolies and collusion—the artificial inflation of prices by merchant cabals—even worse vices because they violated natural principles of exchange. Indeed, he encouraged traders to set their prices by the laws of the market. Commodities held no intrinsic value. Prices rose and fell with supply and demand "for good and just Reasons": changing tastes, variable demand, the cost of transport and insurance, and loss of products through storm or piracy. Willard sanctioned the very arguments for which John Cotton had censured Robert Keayne seventy years earlier in Boston. Again appealing to reason, science, and experience, Willard contended that merchants should be allowed to move their prices downward to gain new customers and upward on the very same items to make profits from steady customers, or to charge for sale by credit. Justifying practical wisdom with biblical authority, Willard claimed, in a fit of circularity, that "the Word of God indeed hath not fixed the stated Value of things, because these things are to vary according to Circumstances."[107]

In taking this position, Willard, like Mather, overturned the logic of his puritan predecessors. Previous divines took Scripture, with its strictures against usury and oppression, to convey absolute moral imperatives. They critiqued secular economics as the dispensable construct of a self-interested class of merchants. Willard and many of his contemporaries, in contrast, accepted mercantilist arguments as descriptions of fact. They treated the language of political economy as a universal certainty while discarding the original dictates of Reformed teaching. Mather thus conceded in 1727 that the churches no longer punished market practices, as they had in previous generations, because economic knowledge had made such rules obsolete.[108]

The end of usury as a prototypical economic vice signaled an ideological transition in Reformed teaching on the economy in early New England.

Boston ministers, to be sure, sometimes reiterated long-held anxieties about the corrosive effects of wealth, jeremiad-like warnings against luxury consumption, and rehearsals of moral obligations to neighbor. They some-times mixed the idioms of political economy, biblical exegesis, Reformed divinity, and local politics. Willard bracketed his technical discussions of credit and prices with repeated pleas for charity and equity. Many Massa-chusetts pastors in the countryside still regarded high profit margins, the foreclosure of mortgages, and debt litigation as usurious in the old sense. Mather warned merchants that justifications for paper money and innova-tions in credit did not relieve them of their Christian duties to charity; nothing in his economic advice legitimated harshness toward poor debtors or suing for the possession of the estates of indigent widows. In his 1716 *Fair Dealing*, he condemned "Hard Usages in the *Usury* . . . which the Law of Love will never justify." Willard, Mather, and their merchant parishio-ners stepped warily into the new economic arena.[109]

For all of that, however, Boston's puritan pastors had read enough politi-cal economy to realize that in the ordinary course of business—the daily transactions of merchants at home and abroad—the leading economic ad-vice fostered prosperity and furthered Britain's empire. They did not re-gard the emergent market system as a divine law in itself, but they thought of it at least as a providential instrument. In his election sermon of 1696, Mather announced that pious dedication would open exchange in New England and energize Boston's overseas commerce. Boston's ministers urged their parishioners to cherish participation in a system of trade that providence used to spread liberty and defeat England's enemies. One En-glish visitor to Boston satirized this conflation of moral zeal and commer-cial ambition. He denounced clerics who attacked private vices such as drunkenness while encouraging ruthless business practices. "[H]e that knows how to deal with their Traders," he scoffed, "may deal with the Devil and fear no Craft."[110] A bit harsh, perhaps. Mather and Willard did not sanction craftiness and deception. They nonetheless expressed more inter-est in the promotion of virtue within the market system than in a critique of that system itself.

MERCHANTS' CALLINGS AND THE CAMPAIGN FOR MORAL REFORM

Pastors in the post-1688 milieu had so infused imperial ideologies with transcendent purpose that they conformed nearly every utterance on the province, trade, and moral reform to commercial agendas. They even im-ported the language of the market into their most putatively spiritual coun-sel. Dedication to Christ, many ministers contended, amounted to a rea-sonable, prudent, and enriching investment, what Joshua Moodey of

Portsmouth calculated as a "rational" deal that yielded a 100 percent clear profit. As a master's student at Harvard, Pemberton learned to employ the idiom of economic self-interest and used it throughout his career. "The service of God," he preached, was "infinitely profitable [that is, preferable] to the service of Satan" and therefore a rational choice. Mather likened gospel promises to "a *Bill of Credit*" that, being "not inferiour to any Coin of *Silver or Gold*," merited complete confidence. In another context, he encouraged pious deeds as great "Transactions" that "will be Lying by us, like so many Good *Bills of Exchange*," which God "will be for ever Owning and Paying of[f]."[111]

Willard, however, set the standard for economically versed spirituality with his sermons published as *Heavenly Merchandize* (figure 4.6). He pleaded with unregenerate or lapsed believers to attend worship and believe the gospel as an investment in heavenly reward. Christian preachers had used contractual and financial tropes to express the meaning of the gospel for centuries, from explanations of the Crucifixion as a payment on behalf of indebted sinners to comparisons between spiritual and material recompense. Yet Willard's exposition of Proverbs 23:23, "Buy the truth, and sell it not," did more than employ commercial metaphors; it transposed the whole logic and language of the message into contemporary market idioms. In the process Willard reversed the linguistic direction set by first-generation puritans such as John Cotton. Cotton applied the language of faith to economic matters, chastening the ambitions or soothing the anxieties of merchants by telling them to trust God in their affairs. Willard brought the language of the economy to matters of faith, exciting the entrepreneurial instincts of merchants by exhorting them to invest in salvation.[112]

As he transposed evangelical appeal to market dynamics, Willard voiced the ordinariness and inevitability, and by implication the legitimacy, of the latest modes of exchange. Without a hint of critique, Willard probed the psyches of Old South merchants with reference to the most sophisticated transactions in credit and currency. He warned them against acting like impetuous speculators, who mortgaged their estates for flimsy projects or attempted to make huge profits from current fads in the stock exchange. Good merchants recognized such schemes as imprudent. He appealed to customers who had become believers—they had bought the truth—but who doubted the worth of their purchase. He knew that they often worried about their deals. Perhaps they had invested in "commodities" that had gone out of fashion or, on the other hand, flooded the market and lost value. Even sound ventures carried risks and brought anxieties: shipwreck, water damage, piracy, and devaluation by "a bad market." Mercantile insurers contested claims and paid shillings on the lost pound. So, Willard concluded, his people ought to rely on the solid commodity of "Divine Truth."

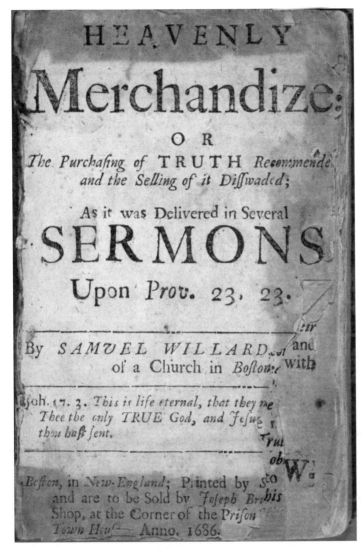

Figure 4.6. The title page of Samuel Willard's *Heavenly Merchandize* (Boston, 1686), torn at the lower right corner. Courtesy of the American Antiquarian Society.

It was worth "Millions" at the very "hour" of conversion and reliably backed by "heavens ensurance." The "end of buying and selling is to get gain," Willard conceded, and the gospel shone as "heavenly merchandize," which was to say, a great bargain.[113]

Boston's most prominent clerics returned to commercial tropes frequently, and they matched their rhetorical strategies with explicit recommendations of trade as a divine calling. Protestants always had justified commerce as a vocation, what they named a particular calling in distinction from the general calling to faith and love. They urged diligence and industriousness in its pursuit. Yet ministers at the turn of the eighteenth century exhorted their merchant flocks to profits in unprecedented ways. Devoting eight months of weekly lectures in 1705 to economic vocation, Willard asserted the importance of choosing a profitable trade and conducting it prudently. Merchants in particular ought to acquire the requisite training, intelligence, and "Skill" to pursue wealth beyond a merely competent living. "It is not enough to *get* an Estate, but there is Duty to endeavour that it may prosper," he wrote, because "*Riches* are consistent with *Godliness*, and the more a Man hath the more Advantage he hath to do Good with it." Public service transposed economic ambition into a means of holiness.[114]

Cotton Mather's most thorough statement on secular vocation, his 1701 *A Christian at his Calling*, correlated moral obligation, providential order, spiritual felicity, commercial knowledge, and market profits. John Cotton had counseled Christians to choose a mode of business that met the needs of the local community, even if such a trade produced slim profits. Mather, in contrast, set profitability as the chief standard for vocational choice because there was by definition "*no need for any such Business*" that was not "*profitable*." He advised the young merchant to understand that "he may Glorify God, by doing of *Good* for *others*, and getting *Good* for himself." Elizabethan puritans scorned as overly ambitious or anxious the merchant who incessantly labored. Mather urged unyielding, daily, relentless work. "How can you ordinarily Enjoy any Rest at Night," Mather asked, "if you have not been well at Work, in the Day? Let your business Engross the most of your time." The merchant ought to avoid gambling, tavern haunting, and smoking; he should "lay out" his "*Strength*" and "*Skill*" in buying, selling, and minding his books instead. Mather also called merchants to exercise prudence and acumen in the conduct of business. John Winthrop had demanded that leaders of the Great Migration lend money without question to those in genuine need. Mather gave nearly the opposite advice: to scrutinize would-be debtors carefully and refuse poor risks. In addition, merchants ought to be "well acquainted with all the Mysteries" of trade: making ledgers, tabulating balances, tracking costs and expenses, reading the latest data on exports and imports, knowing the market, and making business contacts. "'Tis ordinarily a *Sin*, and it will at length be a

Shame," Mather warned, to keep accounts badly. This was the sort of advice that economic pragmatists such as Defoe gave and disseminated in merchant handbooks.[115]

Unlike many commercial manuals, however, Mather's sermon on calling included a providential incentive for skillful, hard work. Led by prayer and Bible readings, the Christian merchant could "be assured," Mather asserted, that "the *Providence* of God" would bless all practical industry with riches. God confirmed the worth of merchants to society by rewarding their efforts with profits. To this extent, commerce and knowledge of God went hand in hand: "the Bible directs the *Merchant* unto this desire, *May I be a Wise Merchant, and find the Pearl of Great Price!*" Thirteen years after *A Christian at his Calling*, Mather strengthened his appeal. "Liberal Soul[s]" who made money and used it for the common good would "find the glorious Lord Wondrously at Work" for them, rewarding their "Restless" labors with plenty. By 1704 Increase Mather, who had looked on commerce as a mixed blessing at best in his jeremiad days, had acquired similar perspectives.[116]

The ministers of First Church, Old North, and Old South did not thoroughly conflate commercial success and moral or spiritual devotion. Traders may have been hard-pressed to know when they had crossed the line from diligence to anxiety, pursuit of profits to avarice, so pastors instructed them to test themselves by their intentions and practice: their attendance at worship, pious exercises, and service to the community. Cotton Mather periodically corrected his enthusiasm for economic success by reminding merchants that he had not meant to recommend diligence for the sake of mere riches, as though avarice had become a virtue; they ought to devote their hard-won profits to "*Pious Uses*," the common good. He also consoled parishioners with assertions that providence might bring misfortune— what he called "*Impoverishing* Dispensations"—to lure the soul to Christ. "*Poverty*," he claimed, could be accepted as "a Discipline, which the Wisdome and Goodness of our Eternal Father may Employ upon us, to Ripen us more effectually for the Blessings of Eternity." In two long lectures in 1700, Willard cautioned against work-induced fatigue and a preoccupation that distracted the believer from worship and daily devotion, the true means of securing providential blessing. Benjamin Wadsworth, the pastor of First Church from 1696 to 1725, imported commercial imagery into his sermons but often contrasted Christian humility with entrepreneurial ambition. Wadsworth, the most conservative of Boston's preachers, chastised the rich as nearly inescapably prone to scandal and wickedness.[117]

For all of their validation of the merchant's calling, ministers denounced a seemingly unending parade of sins in Boston's market, especially from the 1690s through the 1710s. They criticized Andros and the influx of English and Anglican merchants who displayed metropolitan impiety along with luxury fashions. Cotton Mather dedicated a whole sermon to the subject of the then-fashionable hooped petticoats, linking their popularity to impudence, vanity, and self-indulgence. Rumors of the establishment of a theater and a dancing school in Boston, which would have trained aspiring cosmopolitans in the manners of the metropolis, outraged Increase Mather. Most Boston ministers complained that debaucheries accompanied maritime commerce like so many seagulls swirling around the ships entering their harbor: gambling, swearing, looting, begging, drunkenness, and prostitution.[118]

The burning of the old Town House along with the First Church meetinghouse and several blocks of houses in 1711 gave the Mathers and Wadsworth a spectacular occasion on which to elucidate their criticisms. Increase Mather read the inferno as a natural event fraught with providential meaning, much like Sewall's windows in the hailstorm. Imported vices such as prideful apparel—"Silk, and Sattens, and Velvet, and Purple, and Silver and Gold"—periwigs, and costly houses displayed a godless materialism in the marketplace. The destruction of the Town House came from on high as a fitting punishment. Cotton Mather preached "a FUNERAL SERMON" for the buildings and exhorted those who lost their estates to pursue humility and reform. Wadsworth published five sermons about the fire, all centered on the destruction of the old meetinghouse and construction of a new brick building for First Church. He refrained from providential interpretations, careful to avoid the implication that his church especially deserved fiery judgment. Yet he admitted that the events could wean his parishioners from worldliness.[119]

Preachers also criticized the debasement of economic exchange in Boston's market quarters. Cotton Mather sounded the alarm in his 1696 election sermon, when he cited incivility of manners in the marketplace, tolerance for dishonest dealing, and indifference to the plight of the poor.[120] Economic recovery at the turn of the eighteenth century only made things worse. The influx of new merchants, expansion of trade from the countryside to the town, sophistication of accounting measures, addition of partners overseas, and surge of shops, stalls, and waterfront stores offering an increasing variety of products multiplied the temptation to defraud rich and poor alike. In his *Lex Mercatoria*, originally delivered as a lecture to the General Assembly in 1704, Mather enumerated what he perceived to be ten increasingly common scourges on trade in the Bay Colony. Many Bostonians committed common theft. Unscrupulous traders counterfeited goods and mislabeled their packages. Others packed barrels loosely and weighted them with rocks. Avaricious creditors practiced extortion by multiplying the cost of credit for desperate buyers, a form of loan-sharking. Some residents conducted illicit trades such as fortune-telling, prostitution, and gambling; others sold alcohol illegally to Indians or known drunkards. Dishonest debtors failed to settle their accounts by the contracted time. Merchants bribed magistrates. Citizens embezzled from the public treasury or municipal organizations, often by paying taxes with bad bills. Church members failed to pay tithes, using the money instead for business. Finally, overseas traders employed dishonest partners. Such sins shamed Massachusetts, Mather scolded, violated "the very Light of Nature," and sullied the reputations of even honest merchants.[121]

Puritan ministers detected more frauds over the next decade, from coin clipping to slander, libel, and false testimony in court. Mather also indicted the flood of unpaid debt that overwhelmed borrowers, sank creditors, and washed away Bostonians' credit rating in London. It was all too common, he charged, for merchant debtors to run up their accounts, go further into debt, and put off their creditors by lying or hiding. He lectured them to keep their accounts soundly. "Our *Books of Accounts*," he reminded them, "are a very Material part of our *Libraries*; and an Excellent Provision they are, to carry on a *Lucriserious Business*." He also urged them to anticipate their expenses and revenues, refrain from taking out loans when they knew of their inability to repay, and admit their insolvency to their creditors. Wadsworth condemned subtle deceits in contracts, the unfair administration of estates by trustees, bribery, and slippery practices that fell short of a legal definition of fraud but that were nonetheless mean-spirited. He decried merchants who delayed the delivery of goods beyond the contracted date, presumably a strategy to work the market for a higher rate. He condemned those who raised their prices on false pretenses, unreasonably profited from a monopoly or a customer's ignorance, engrossed goods, or took advantage of a laborer's need for tools. He likewise disapproved of artisans who did shoddy work (especially ships carpenters, whose mistakes endangered the lives of mariners), physicians who charged extra for visits to the extremely ill, lawyers who raised their fees for clients in dire circumstances, and sheriffs or constables who demanded higher salaries during crime waves. Wadsworth, to reiterate, preached the least commercial-friendly sermons of Boston's ministers, but even Mather, along with other Massachusetts pastors, expressed a gnawing sense that New Englanders had become accustomed to breaking promises, misrepresenting their wares, shading the truth, tricking customers, and manipulating contracts.[122]

Nothing in puritan theology suggested that the lusts elicited by market exchange should go unchecked, and religious leaders recognized the urgency of addressing social corruption.[123] Yet the day had long passed for them to call for local discipline in the form of congregational censures. Cotton Mather informed his colleagues in 1703 that the time had come to replace censures with pastoral counsel in all but the most egregious cases. At Old South, pastors began to hear relations of faith—confessional prerequisites for communicant membership—in private, a further indication of changes in disciplinary style. Willard and Wadsworth made the same observation: local congregations served ineffectually as disciplinary bodies in the new political and religious milieu. Nor, for that matter, could leaders call on a cadre of puritan magistrates empowered by the assumption that a particular covenant obliged them to legislate and enforce the peculiar rules of godliness. Given the various ruptures within the municipal and colonial governments, and the dependence of the provincial administration on the Crown, New England hardly appeared as a discrete moral corporation. In Boston the relative toleration encoded in the new charter, political factions, and the power of English officials enfeebled pretensions to a covenantal order embodied either in the local congregation or in a puritan magistracy. The assumptions of the jeremiad lapsed into anachronism.[124]

Seeking new modes of discipline, Mather, Willard, Wadsworth, Pemberton, and Colman formed themselves into a cohort of moralists speaking to and throughout the whole town. They portrayed commercial disorder as an affront not so much to the Christian congregation or to the New England covenant as to the commonwealth and king, who issued royal edicts against social vice. Economic misbehavior threatened individual souls, to be sure, and therefore merited exhortations to conversion, but fraud and avarice also endangered the civil order—an order increasingly sustained by trade and defined by imperial rather than narrowly provincial interests. Even Increase Mather conceded as much in 1700, when he prefaced Samuel Willard's *Peril of the Times Displayed* with a recommendation that New Englanders consider how Anglican, Baptist, Reformed, and Congregational churches in England pursued social reform as an ecumenical venture.[125]

Cotton Mather ultimately embraced the idea of an inter-Protestant ministry, in emulation of European initiatives to set aside differences in ecclesiastical polity for the sake of widespread reform. He suggested that the ministers publish and promote a common platform, "the Maxims of Piety," as their agenda. During the 1710s he settled on a set of ideas uncomplicated by doctrinal detail and infused with a spirit of pietism: the truth of the Trinity, the necessity of Christ for salvation, and the imperative for Christians to display public spirit and the virtues of charity and fair dealing. The maxims of piety, he hoped, would unite New England Protestants to their British and European allies, amend the moral affections of merchants, and cleanse the market of its impurities.[126]

Religious leaders also attempted to enlist private citizens in their campaign. Mather took the lead in the formation of societies for the suppression of disorders: small voluntary and ecumenical associations of lay and clerical leaders indirectly modeled on the Anglican Society for the Promotion of Christian Knowledge, which was founded in 1699 under the patronage of King William, and its offshoot, the Society for the Propagation of the Gospel in Foreign Parts (SPG). Boston printers republished William's 1690 letter on moral reform and printed several pamphlets for Mather and his group until the movement disbanded in 1714. Old South merchants such as Edward Bromfield, whose brother in England helped to found the SPG, worked with Mather to promote the societies and represented a strong lay leadership. In a 1702 lecture to would-be reformers, Mather set the agenda. Each "society" consisted of a pastor, a justice of the peace, a diligent record keeper (every religious as well as commercial enterprise required accounting skills), and from four to fourteen other laymen. These "Virtuous men of divers Qualities, and Perswasions," as Mather described them, helped enforce civil laws against immorality by scouring their neighborhoods for violations, going on night watches, reporting disorders, and administering personal admonition to offenders. These "watch societies" had little impact and short lives, yet they signified how Boston's ministers further relied on well-intentioned civic leaders, rather than the gathered congregation, to promote economic reform. Voluntary associations offered public-spirited individuals the opportunity to fulfill what Mather described as the calling of the good rich man: to spread moral exhortation, give counsel to neighbors, educate the poor, fund works projects, and provide alms. Mather identified his societies not by dogmatic distinctions such as Reformed creed, but by ecumenical loyalties to "the Nation," that is, to Britain, Protestantism, and commercial progress.[127]

Ministers often directed their reform efforts to the problems of poverty. Especially during the 1710s and 1720s, they contended that idleness, sloth, tavern haunting, and excessive consumption had depleted the moral and economic resources of Boston's lower orders. Mather, Wadsworth, and Colman produced a joint declaration against costly wedding parties, elaborate celebrations attending military training, harvest huskings, even fancy ordination exercises, as well as daily gatherings at the tavern. They complained that profane socializing consumed reserves of capital and credit and sometimes exhausted individuals' estates. Bostonians who overindulged in imported fashions channeled money from the province and endangered credit ratings overseas. Worse yet, the poor often followed the rich in their *Vicious Courses Procuring Poverty*, as Wadsworth titled one of his lectures from 1719. Poor people could ill afford to buy consumer luxuries. Universally prone to idleness—"the Mother of all Vices," in Wadsworth's lexicon—the poor aspired to high style while they either would not or could not find employment. Impoverished by their spending habits, many residents turned to alcohol or fraud and further damaged Boston's commerce by absorbing more capital in the form of poor relief.[128]

While pastors and watch societies exhorted the poor to industry and frugality, municipal and provincial governments raised relief funds and instituted works projects. From 1690 to 1715, Boston's selectmen used a

large tax increase to establish public schools, provide temporary financial
assistance, and transform the town's almshouse into a workhouse. Traders
such as Fitch, Oliver, Clark, and Hutchinson reinvigorated the work of the
town's Overseers of the Poor, which had languished since the committee's
inception in 1662. The new overseers proposed to address the growing
numbers of the indigent with solutions premised on administrative effi-
ciency and financial prudence. They mandated town-funded employment
projects such as linen and cloth manufactures to produce products for export, enhance the overall economy, extend the tax base, and provide capital
for further industries. Their charitable work reflected the advice of London's economists as much as their fiscal transactions did; Petty, Davenant,
and Defoe often recommended works projects.[129]

For Fitch and his fellow overseers, institutionalized poor relief offered
a strategy to strengthen Boston's economy and speed its incorporation into
the transatlantic system. Colman boasted that such efforts succeeded; in
1725 he informed a Scottish correspondent that programs to reform the
poor, abetted by more trade, more industry, and more money, had relieved
the worst sufferers, despite continued inflation. "With us everything is
dear," he admitted, "but the abundance of Trade gives every body money
to buy, so that we have not a beggar in our streets, and our poor [are] well
fed, and cloathed well." Colman's optimism marked a contrast with the
diagnosis of critics from the 1630s through the 1670s, who often complained that overseas commerce threatened the local community and
exacerbated poverty.[130]

Puritan congregations likewise oversaw the steady transformation of religious poor relief into an administrative affair, guided by legal protocol
and fiscal expertise. In 1720 the town's leading congregations formed an
association to pool charitable bequests, invest them at interest, distribute
the proceeds, and collect more contributions at quarterly lectures delivered
at Old North. Deacons, elected especially to care for the needy, worked
through standing committees. They relied on censuses of nearby neighborhoods and provided fiscal accounts to the rest of the congregation. In a
1719 meeting of Old South, for example, members elected three eminent
merchants—Fitch, Belcher, and Oliver—to audit "the Deacons Accounts
for the ensuing year" and submit detailed reports on gifts and donations.
As charitable officers for the church, merchants behaved nonetheless like
businessmen, systematizing their work to great effect. They provided a
rational and efficient form of charity to assist the town when civil measures
to relieve the poor fell short.[131]

Boston's puritan merchants and ministers undertook their campaigns
for social reform to purify and enhance commerce. They intended to conform the economy all the more to providential purpose: the ascension of
Protestant empire over Catholicism, prosperity throughout New England,

and social solidarity in Boston. Clerical moralizations echoed the jeremiads of the 1670s and 1680s, but the echo was faint and the sound transposed by their appreciation for the importance of the market to the transatlantic British interest. Oakes, Hubbard, and other pastors before the Dominion censured usury and oppression as telltale vices of the market, symptoms of the dangers of an impersonal and rationalized economic system. Cotton Mather, Willard, and Wadsworth aimed their denunciations at idleness and poverty, debauchery and drunkenness, fraud and corruption. They did not target the sale of credit, fluctuations in monetary value, or inflation, all of which, as London's economists had informed them, were natural and integral to the transatlantic system. They instead attacked social vices that clogged exchange and especially tempted the least successful inhabitants of Boston: peddlers, unemployed laborers, and small-time shopkeepers.

Mather and Willard signaled this purpose, in different but compatible ways, in two sermons that bracketed this period of intense reforming activity. In 1694 Willard delivered a humiliation sermon at Old South, published as *Reformation the Great Duty of an Afflicted People*. Muting the particular formulations of the jeremiad—direct divine punishment for New England's betrayals of the gospel—he argued that even unbelievers could discern the underlying causes of recent misfortunes such as the Dominion and commercial stagnation. Morally astute citizens could hear "a *Voice* in them, and it is intelligible; they say that God is angry," and "they serve to put men upon enquiry after the cause of them." The cause was moral injustice; "the light of nature" itself taught that nations could not flourish if shot through with vice and fraud. In order, then, to recover civil "felicity," or "a goodness in *Peace, Health, Prosperity, Credit, Liberty*," people had to repent. Social reform secured commercial prosperity and civil liberty.[132]

Fifteen years later, in a 1709 address to the General Assembly, Mather made a parallel argument with more vivid and politically direct imagery. Flushed with the notion of moral reform, in the midst of the campaign for honest trade and civic virtue, he rested his *Theopolis Americana* on a combination of apocalyptic and imperial assertions. Mather dedicated the printed version to Sewall, who had shown Mather his own notes on biblical prophecy. Mather took Sewall's suggestions as a cue to scriptural prediction: Protestant England would win the battle with Spain and France for the North American continent as a prelude to the millennium. "The Fall of the New Popish *Babylon*," Mather asserted, "will be accompanied with the Loss of her *American* Interest." New Englanders, then, should do all that they could for "the English" monarchy, confident that Protestants in America would share victory with those in Britain; the "wide Atlantick" should not "stand in the way as any Hindrance of those Communications" of loyalty between London and Boston.[133]

Mather interspersed the economy throughout his treatise. Just as profits sustained the worldwide struggle for Protestant empire, he claimed, so mercantile splendor marked the millennial culmination of that empire. The golden streets of the heavenly city in the book of Revelation (Revelation 21:21) referred to a literal city, with real gold "ten thousand times more glorious, than all that ever any Cortez pretended unto." Neither Spain nor France would enjoy economic hegemony. The Kingdom of God would be, in other words, a commercial and urban order, a "MARKET-PLACE; the Place where the Affairs of Trade bring together a Concourse of People." Scriptural gold, however, also represented moral qualities, according to Mather's bubbly and not altogether consistent exposition. In the heavenly city, the "GOLDEN RULE" shaped all exchange. There were no frauds or oppressions. Mather then made the moral application. The merchants of Massachusetts emulated Christ's glorious kingdom to the extent that they refused to cheat, trade slaves, sell liquor to Indians, overextend their credit, or squeeze the poor. The residents of Boston contributed to the victory of Protestantism by ridding their business of corruption. They even had a political mandate to sobriety. "If once this become a Country of Drunken Protestants," he scolded, then there was no reason "why we should not fail before *Popish Idolaters*." Mather concluded by urging more reform societies and the establishment of a committee to consider further laws against dishonest dealing. A prosperous, orderly market amounted to a political and millennial mandate.[134]

RELIGIOUS CONVICTION IN THE AFFAIRS OF SEWALL AND FITCH

By the late 1690s, ministers identified merchants no longer with rapacious greed, as they had in the days of Robert Keayne, but with industriousness and prudence, moral reform and Protestantism's interest in the world. They maintained that providence used overseas traders to protect English liberty and spread civilization. These convictions illuminated the meaning of everyday business for provincial merchants such as Sewall and Fitch. A student of theology and public official, Sewall explicitly articulated the intersection between imperial contests, millennial beliefs, and overseas trade. Fitch, his friend and fellow member at Old South, rarely uttered a theological statement that we know of. Untrained in divinity yet a dutiful member of the congregational establishment, he nonetheless embodied the moral teaching of pastors such as Mather and Willard. Both merchants reflected versions of puritanism shaped in the aftermath of the Glorious Revolution.

Sewall's account books and letters reveal an extraordinary juxtaposition between commercial demands and religious reflections. He interspersed notes on sermons into his accounts, a mélange of standard business notations—the terms of a lease, records of debts and credits, copies of receipts for rents, accounts balanced—and brief summaries of sermons. He inscribed Scripture and short reflections next to copies of deeds or bills. Spiritual matters abutted records of exchange, revealing an intricate strategy to correlate economic and religious discourses. Devotional recitation chastened economic ambition. Fiscal notations recalled piety to pragmatic and public good. Millennial intimations suggested a collective meaning to individual exchanges. Sewall disclosed the deep theological impulses beneath the commercial development of provincial Massachusetts.[135]

Sewall framed his business with nearly constant, explicit reference to spiritual and moral dynamics. He ambled about Boston as an omnivore of Sunday sermons, Thursday lectures, and fast and thanksgiving day orations, savoring most frequently the words of Willard and the Mathers, but also tasting the offerings of Allen, Pemberton, and Colman. He sampled dozens of preachers during his travels as a magistrate, from John Danforth at nearby Dorchester to Nathaniel Rogers in distant Portsmouth. He noted when their sermons addressed matters of money and trade and frequently inscribed their teaching on the meaning of providence for the individual: that the wise man secured blessing and happiness when he trusted divine sovereignty and shaped his conduct to principles of godliness. In a 1714 trip to Portsmouth, he heard Rogers echo Mather's frequent plea to "be fruitfull, rich in good works." "'Tis no crime to be Rich," as Sewall recorded Rogers's words, "but tis a Crime to be covetous," to value wealth and social honor above service to God and charity to the poor.[136]

He communicated similar reflections to his business correspondents. Like Hull, he commanded his ship captains to attend to providential moments: to combine "diligence" in seeking the best ports and wharves or setting their sailing schedule with "care that" God "be duly worshipped by your self, and all your Company." Prayer, Sewall admonished Captain Bowe, secured a prosperous journey. Writing in 1697, he complained to a fellow merchant about shady traders on the northern frontier, one of whom had overcharged him for transporting some grain, and predicted their downfall. He attempted to place his personal ailments, and common trials such as Indian attacks and droughts, in a providential perspective. "God's Judgments are unsearchable," he admitted to a correspondent, but are nonetheless purposeful. Momentous events in the "New World," especially among the Indians, fulfilled ancient prophecies. A current drought served as "both Comfort and Affliction to us," reminding New Englanders of their need for each other—their calling to exchange goods and provide relief when able. Sewall understood providence, as his pastors had taught him, in terms of the laws by which God encouraged virtue and, when necessary, discouraged undue attachment to worldly prosperity.[137]

Sewall also complained about men such as Samuel Shrimpton and Charles Lidget, who, drunken and boisterous, careened through the town in fancy coaches or who publicly swore oaths, drank health toasts, and sang bawdy songs "to the great disturbance of the Town and grief of good people." "Such high-handed wickedness," he observed in 1686, defiled the civic order. "Good people," in contrast, spent the awful days of that year in dread of the arrival of Andros. They prayed, fasted, trained with the militia, and attended Cotton Mather's sermons. Other impieties attracted Sewall's censure because they violated true exchange, disordered social life in New England, and betrayed England.[138]

Puritan sensibilities led Sewall to denounce, among several evils, the increasingly systematic trade in African slaves. Unlike other New Englanders, he scorned the Royal African Company and resisted the rising tide of slavery in Massachusetts. After reading a petition presented to the General Court from a captured African couple in 1700, he produced New England's first antislavery tract, *The Selling of Joseph*. No biblical exegesis or design to evangelize captured Africans, he argued, justified the vice and inhumanity of the slave trade. The Middle Passage began with outright theft, severed families, and ended with "Murder." Fornication and violence spread through the whole trade. "As black as they are," Sewall wrote of slaves, they "are the Sons and Daughters of the first *Adam*, the Brethren and Sisters of the Last ADAM [Christ], and the offspring of GOD." They were as deserving of "Respect" as any wealthy merchant. By Sewall's account, pious men should shun the slave trade. Departing here from the opinion of London's political economists, he claimed that slavery blighted transatlantic commerce.[139]

Following Mather's lead, Sewall also criticized fellow merchants who fouled trade with extortion and fraud. At the end of April 1710, for example, Andrew Belcher, a fellow member with Sewall at Old South, attempted to ship six thousand bushels of New England wheat to the Caribbean after a drought had reduced the supply and raised prices beyond the reach of many residents in Boston. Reports of Belcher's intentions spread from the docks throughout an outraged town. A small group of protesters rowed out at night and cut the rudder of the ship laden with Belcher's grain before it could sail. The next day fifty men gathered at the dock, ready to return to the ship and confiscate the wheat. Cooler heads dissuaded them. Belcher nonetheless demanded a special trial for "the Rioters." After an inconclusive and confused court session, Pemberton—Sewall's and Belcher's pastor at Old South—asked for Sewall's opinion on the matter. Sewall's response, that "twas an ill office in Capt. Belchar to send away so great a quantity of Wheat . . . in this scarce time," knocked Pemberton back on his heels. The two engaged in a heated debate. Pemberton called the protesters "evil" and "seditious." Sewall parried with Scripture, to the effect that "he that withholds Corn, the people will justly curse him" (Proverbs 11:26). Sewall knew that cutting rudders and threatening a ship were horribly illegal acts, but he was enough of an old-style puritan to sympathize with needy neighbors over and against a wealthy merchant quite indifferent to their plight.[140]

Along with mercantile colleagues such as Bromfield, Sewall assumed positions of lay leadership in Mather's voluntary reform societies. They promoted night watches and other visitations and pestered constables and other magistrates to enforce royal proclamations against vice. Preaching at the opening of the new Town House in 1713, Mather read the queen's proclamation against immoralities and urged magistrates and juries to enforce laws against the same; Sewall attended the event and approved of Mather's performance. He also took part in poor relief, donating five hundred acres of the Hull-Sewall estate in Rhode Island to the foundation of a public school and giving an equal amount of land to Harvard for indigent scholars.[141]

Throughout his commercial and political activities, Sewall pondered the meaning of the empire and biblical prophecy. He kept abreast of political and commercial news from the metropolis, scouring the latest editions of the *London Gazette*. Some news flashes sparked Sewall to millennial speculations, which he regularly included in his correspondence. Writing to Thomas Glouer in 1686, he bounced from an account of his debts to Glouer and a receipt for cotton cloth and books to news from France—he "grieved for the afflictions" initiated by the Revocation of the Edict of Nantes—and a report that there had been a fast day in Boston in response to an outbreak of smallpox. He informed another business partner in 1688 that the mounting crisis in the provincial government and rumors of attacks from French Canada portended apocalyptic battles. In a single letter to John Ive of London, Sewall gave notice of receipts and news of cargo, reported on the capture of a New England mariner off the coast of North Africa, speculated on the place of the Turks in the fulfillment of prophecies in the book of Revelation, and ended with queries about the disposition of several masts for a ship.[142]

The intersection of contemporary politics and millennial prophecies gave him an important clue to his affairs. During the Dominion and the reign of William and Mary, Sewall, unlike many of his contemporaries, wondered whether devotion to the Crown betrayed the political needs and covenantal obligations of Massachusetts. Biblical eschatology, however, eventually reconciled his puritan convictions to imperial identities. Throughout much of the 1690s, he slowly built a case (he was a judge, after all) that the sixth vial of the book of Revelation would be poured out in Mexico. To put it mildly, it was an idiosyncratic opinion. It nonetheless confirmed a belief, held by Mather and many others, that the powers of Antichrist and Christ would clash in an apocalyptic battle on North American soil. He read standard puritan biblical commentaries by Joseph Mede and Thomas Brightman, histories of the Spanish in Mexico, and the latest news reports from Europe to piece together his conclusion. He laid out his ideas in letters to pastors—one to Edward Taylor of Westfield in 1696, another to John Wise of Ipswich in 1698—and published his first essay on the topic, *Phaenomena quaedam Apocalyptica*, in 1697.[143]

Sixteen years after that essay, Sewall advanced his theses in his 1713 *Proposals Touching the Accomplishment of Prophesies*. He reiterated his previous argument: the books of Daniel and Revelation predicted that crucial events preceding the millennial return of Christ would occur in North America. In the midst of a digression on Revelation 11:8, which mentioned "the great city" where all mankind would witness the first signs of last things, Sewall alluded to political economy. He argued that the text referred to the capital of a transoceanic empire and a widely admired metropolis, which must indicate London, the administrative capital of a regime that stretched from the British Isles to America. As for the "greatness" of London, Sewall contended that the 1707 Act of Union (of English and Scottish parliaments) had elevated it to jurisdictional prominence far surpassing other European cities. For his evidence, he cited none other than William Petty: "if the Elaborat Calculations of my Learned Country man *Sir William Petty* be Credited, LONDON, the Metropolis, is not only a Great City; but it excels in Greatness, if compar'd with *Paris* or *Rome*. And if the Regal Style in its Completeness [GREAT BRITAIN, FRANCE, and IRELAND] be regarded; it will certainly be allow'd to be a Great Jurisdiction" (the bracketed material is part of the quotation). Petty was no biblical exegete, but his calculations provided Sewall with scientific evidence for the fulfillment of prophecy in America. Sewall had discovered a perfect congruence between political economy and the most intensely providential worldview.[144]

Sewall's speculations reflected an imperial ideology that incorporated Massachusetts merchants into the contest for transatlantic empire. Spanish colonies provided Rome with gold. French Canada provided the pope with Indian converts and territory. The Bible gave New Englanders a mandate to combat these instruments of Antichrist. Boston's merchants ought to acquire land, extend and enrich England's commercial interests, support evangelization of the Indians, and reinforce a Protestant bulwark against Catholic powers. Like Mather's *Theopolis Americana*, which indeed drew on Sewall's notes, Sewall's millennialism asserted a similar program of commercial, political, and religious empire in America.[145]

Sewall, and other Boston merchants who were less theologically explicit but equally dedicated to British Protestantism, enacted the ideal of the patriotic merchant in different venues, including the Company for Propagation of the Gospel in New England. Founded in 1649 by prosperous London merchants, this so-called New England Company supported missionary work among the Indians in New England. During Sewall's lifetime, the company's governors in England included Sir Henry Ashurst and Robert Boyle, the prestigious leader of the Royal Society and moderate Anglican who took an interest in translations of religious tracts into Algonquian. In New England the company found its greatest supporters and contributors among a wide array of Boston merchants, including Belcher, Brattle, Oliver, Dummer, Grove Hirst, Eliakim Hutchinson, and Samuel Lynde. Old South traders such as Sewall, Bromfield, and Fitch were especially prominent. Sewall acted as a commissioner in 1698, and soon thereafter as the provincial secretary and treasurer, corresponding with Ashurst and other London directors.[146]

Merchant commissioners and donors conducted the business of the company with fiscal ingenuity and imperial, along with evangelistic, aims. They sent dozens of letters between London and Boston, conveying thousands of pounds gathered from successful traders who found moral satisfaction and a buffer against the French in the company's work. Commissioners secured donations to add to the existing endowment and sent them to the trustees in London, who approved of expenditures for missionaries' salaries, books, and scholarships to train more missionaries at Harvard. They invested the company's funds in land, buying real estate on the northern frontier and leasing it to tenants or purchasing houses and plots in settled areas, which they used for collateral and rents. They also lent the company's money at interest, using the proceeds for annual expenses. Sewall supervised these activities in a professional manner, asking the missionaries to keep close accounts of their expenditures and evangelistic successes (which were few and far between) and providing precise tabulations of the value of the company's stock. He also encouraged the missionaries to protect their Indian flocks "from the Cousenages and Extortions of Such Englishmen as may Treat them in those Ways of the Oppressour." The frontier, no less than Boston, Sewall opined, should be cleansed of unjust trade.[147]

The commissioners and trustees frequently justified their work with reference to the competition between France and England for Indian allies. Sewall suggested to Ashurst that the commissioners in England agitate for firm boundaries to control English expansion into Indian territories. Ashurst agreed, contending that such restrictions signified a "Prudent Conduct and Zeal for the Publiq service" because they would reduce Indian antipathy toward the English, promote the gospel among the Indians, and make them more pliable allies against the French. Ashurst also urged the New England commissioners to "improve" the land "reserved to the Indians": to build roads, harvest timber, trade with natives, and erect public buildings. Commerce served diplomacy and evangelization. Writing to Sewall in 1714, Ashurst also conveyed the latest news from the royal court to Sewall, assuring him that the accession of George portended great victories for Britain. Sewall had interpreted biblical prophecy to mean that the conversion of Native Americans along with the defeat of Catholic powers in America would presage eschatological victories for Christ, and he took his part in its fulfillment. For him and his colleagues, the New England Company offered an ideal instrument to extend their commercial skills, along with hard-won profits, to evangelical, imperial, and, ultimately, millennial terrain.[148]

Sewall illuminates the mentality of the godly merchant in this period especially because his ministerial training allowed him to articulate connections, between religious ideas and commercial activities, that his business colleagues often expressed only vaguely or indirectly. Other Boston merchants took notes on sermons, absorbed the latest pronouncements on providence and empire coming from the town's pulpits and presses, and devoted themselves to the church and social reform efforts even though they left no theological treatises. Bromfield attended prayer meetings with Sewall and filled six huge notebooks with sermon notes, sometimes interspersing them among accounts, like Sewall. Bromfield also had close ties to Mather. While in London for business, he secured the publication of Mather's *Magnalia*. Mather admired Bromfield for his theological sentiments, support for other publications, and devotional habits; Cotton and Increase dedicated two publications to him.[149]

Thomas Fitch too was a pious New Englander. He apparently did not leave notes on sermons, a spiritual diary, or extensive written moral reflections, but he joined Sewall and Bromfield in many of their activities. We can infer his religious sensibilities from his public practices. He belonged to that network of Old South merchants, including Sewall and Bromfield, who succeeded in overseas and domestic markets yet refrained from the heavily Anglicized and cosmopolitan mores of men such as Hutchinson and Shrimpton. A leader with Sewall at Old South, he served on many congregational committees, auditing accounts, supervising the construction of a parsonage, providing a temporary worship space, and renting and assigning pews. He donated two expensive Communion flagons to the congregation. Other members of the church treated him with deference and respect; his reputation qualified him to serve frequently as a pallbearer for Old South's most eminent members. He also assumed municipal and provincial offices. He was elected selectman four times beginning in 1703, representative to the General Court three times, and sat on the Council from 1715 to 1730. Familiar with the law as well as with financial matters, he was appointed a special justice to the Supreme Court from 1718 to 1719 and to numerous municipal committees, including one supervising poor relief and another established in 1704 to erect a schoolhouse for the town.[150]

Fitch likewise performed imperial and godly identities as a promoter of missionary and military activities on the northern frontier. He was as eager as Sewall to note political news from London. He signed on as a commissioner of the New England Company in 1705 and took a leading role in its affairs. He supported Nathaniel Gookin's work among the Indians at Natick, traveling to pray with Gookin at one of his preaching occasions there. Fitch also patronized the Society in Scotland for Propagating Christian Knowledge. He joined other Old South merchants in the provincial artillery company, becoming a captain and colonel of the Boston regiment. Working closely with the Council in its pursuit of Abenaki and French forces in the 1721–1725 skirmishes known as Father Rale's War, he took charge of sending forces and armaments from Boston to English forces in Maine and providing bounties for the scalps of Rale and his allies. He led the regiment's ceremonial procession in honor of the accession of George II in 1727. Patriotism and piety blended easily in Fitch's affairs.[151]

From one perspective, it might appear that Fitch, unlike Sewall, had jettisoned religion for the Atlantic economy or separated piety from secular business; from another vantage, however, we can interpret his business activities as perfectly congruent with Sewall's example and the exhortations of ministers such as Mather and Willard. Fitch associated with other merchants, such as Edward Bromfield and Jeremiah Dummer the elder of Boston, and George Curwin and John Turner of Salem, who embraced puritan teaching. They participated in the local congregation, held civic office, joined the militia, and patronized the poor even as they made their money through current market practices. Sewall and Fitch admittedly evidenced different sensibilities at times. On the whole, Sewall's theological interests and judicial responsibilities distanced him from the commercial agendas that remained the center of Fitch's life. Yet both men affirmed a similar set of religious beliefs. Sewall wrote about them. Fitch practiced them. Neither merchant betrayed puritanism.[152]

Fitch's associations suggest that he enacted a new cluster of ideas coming from Boston's most orthodox puritan ministers. Even as they resented a royal administration that sometimes threatened the political prerogatives of Massachusetts, they identified the interests of New England with the Protestant British Empire. Treating economic exchange as a matter of public policy and national wealth, they conflated the morality of exchange with the interests of the state. They taught that success in the market provided a hedge against Catholic powers in Europe and America. Moreover, commercially funded aggression against the French, be it Phips's ill-fated campaign or the Council's prosecution of war against Father Rale, allowed New Englanders to participate in what Mather and Sewall declared to be the beginning of a millennial contest between Christ and Catholicism.

Within this framework, Mather and Willard produced theological rationales to dispense with customary objections to usury and oppression even before Fitch began his long and eminent career. Mercantilist ideas thus played themselves out as Fitch took his commercial responsibilities to be religious duties. In these terms, he practiced nothing that his pastors condemned. He, like Sewall, never doubted the morality of his trade. He had no reason to do so.

Puritan economic teaching in this period, to reiterate, did not amount to a wholesale justification of every profit-making strategy. Ministers such as Mather and Wadsworth knew that the market brought temptations. They blasted fraud, decried overconsumption, and pleaded for attention to impoverished residents as an attempt to purify and humanize the market system. They still feared that merchants would be tempted to form their own ethos apart from true piety and patriotism. Traders lost their souls— made very bad deals, as it were—when they turned their dearest affections toward mere money. That danger, however, could no longer be identified in specific exchange practices. It became a matter of inner disposition and moral conscience—just as Mather had told Sewall on the afternoon that hailstones had destroyed Sewall's windows.

Ministers had provided Sewall and Fitch alike with an ideology that ordered and gave meaning to the fragmentary, centrifugal, and sometimes confusing, if not altogether dizzying, expansion of economic activity from 1685 through the 1720s. They made it a nearly constant refrain in their preaching from the 1710s through the 1730s: Britain promoted order, equity, and stability in civil affairs and therefore reasonably claimed to be an instrument for divine rule. They illuminated a rule of providence that covered England and New England under the same historic law, binding provincials to the home country under a common reign. Sewall and Fitch's pastors reshaped New England's history. They asserted the Englishness of New Englanders and thereby confirmed their identity with and location in the empire. These ideals transformed communal loyalties and obligations. They made patriotism, along with economic activity on behalf of the metropolis, a providential mandate.

The story of Sewall's windows, to return to our beginning, hints at other developments in the alliance between New England Protestantism and the market. Changing conceptions of providence, moral affections, and the natural order prompted further reformulations. Another set of Boston ministers and their merchant parishioners, whose careers overlapped but extended beyond the likes of Mather, Willard, Sewall, and Fitch, began to understand the market not merely as a political good but as a universal and natural imperative. They also shaped the market to religious ideas, but we can mark Mather and Sewall, Willard and Fitch, as the last generation to embody fully a puritan conception of the economy.

Chapter Five

HUGH HALL'S SCHEME

WRITING FROM BARBADOS on February 28, 1717, Hugh Hall Jr. informed Benjamin Colman, the pastor of Boston's Brattle Street Church, that he planned to embark for London to become a merchant. Born on the island in 1693, young Hugh had been raised in Boston. His grandmother Lydia had ensured him a pious education with introductions into Old South and Brattle Street churches. At Old South, he sat in the pews among Boston's merchant families—established clans such as Oliver and Savage as well as recently established traders such as David Jeffries and Thomas Fitch—and dutifully took notes on the sermons of Pastor Ebenezer Pemberton. Like his mentors Pemberton and Colman, Hall had gone to Harvard, where, under President John Leverett's influence, he immersed himself in the most recent intellectual currents from England. Hall also acquired a taste for poetry in Cambridge and laced his stylish letters with classical allusions. Impressed with Hugh's progressive religious sensibilities and cosmopolitan manners, Colman and Leverett encouraged him to enter the ministry.[1]

Hall feebly apologized to Colman for choosing commerce instead. He implied that his father, a rising businessman in Barbados, had "fixed" him "in a Merchantile way" over his own preference. Hall nonetheless relished trade. He in fact had dabbled in the exchange while at Harvard and now embraced the opportunities before him. He boasted that he could "Assume the Freedom of Signifying my speedy Intentions for London, upon a very Considerable Foundation." That foundation consisted of his father's largesse and business contacts and, more tellingly, a great "Scheme I have laid" to bring "Success." He hoped that his plans would lavish such good fortune "as upon my Return to Arrive in as Flourishing Circumstances as any my Age can produce." This did not evidence regret. It blushed pure ambition.[2]

What was Hall's "scheme"? He mentioned it several times to Boston correspondents as he readied himself for his journey, assuring his grandmother, among others, that he had in mind "a very probable Scheme for my Advancement." He omitted details. He may have referred merely to his long-simmering intention to establish himself in overseas trade with no single project in mind. More likely, he implied a specific venture. If this were the case, then Hall might have meant a speculative investment, even trading in the stock market. He asked Leverett for an introduction to the

high-powered directors of the South Sea Company, who had not yet taken
its stock to the precarious heights from which it fell in 1721.[3]

Yet again, Hall's letters reveal a different scheme. During his first months
in London, he had worked with "Industry" to impress a variety of prospec-
tive partners. He attempted to gain their confidence with a few orders of
flavored brandy and cocoa shipped to New England while he positioned
himself for more lucrative contracts. In July he announced "an happy Establishment" that he doubted "not will be Crowned with an Answerable
Success." Making contacts through London trader William Allen, he had
managed to gain what he called, in his most polite diction, "Guinea Consignments." Hall had entered the slave trade.[4]

He initially worked as a commission merchant, soliciting orders from
Massachusetts, Maryland, Virginia, and the Carolinas and selling African
captives, along with luxury goods, in behalf of traders such as Allen. He
made much of his money over the course of his career in that business.
Hall returned to Boston permanently during the early 1720s, established
himself as a prominent citizen, achieved notoriety as a man of high style,
and became a pillar in the Brattle Street Church.

Hall's entrance into the slave trade might have struck some of his contemporaries in Boston, such as Samuel Sewall, as ungodly, but it did not
elicit censure from Benjamin Colman.[5] Hall was in Boston in the spring of
1718, arriving just before Colman delivered the May election sermon before Governor Samuel Shute. Hall rarely failed to note such occasions,
followed Colman's preaching closely, and certainly heard about the performance, even if he did not attend it.[6] Celebrating the birthday of George I,
Colman urged merchants to thank God for New England's alliance with
the Crown, which had been accompanied by a bustling trade, an abundance
of commodities, and tasteful fashions. He reiterated contemporary economic theories about the importance of trade as a means of union between
the metropolis and its colonies. England, Africa, the Caribbean, and New
England contributed their share of goods and peoples in a network of "mutual dependence" that "formed for *Society*." Indeed, Colman thought that
the apostle Paul's famous metaphor of the "one body" of Christ, constituted of members with "Gifts differing according to the Grace of God"
(Ephesians 4:4–7), symbolized economic exchange within the nation. Reformed divines traditionally read the text to refer to the church. Colman
used it to represent the imperial system. He called on merchants to cultivate patriotic devotion as a religious duty.[7]

Colman also urged his audience to enhance trade in the province. To
this end, he suggested that officials continue to study currency policy: to
"find out a just Medium of Exchange" by "consulting" economic experts
on how best to secure the value of bills of credit. Meanwhile, overseas
traders ought to increase exports to match the level of imports. Above all

such technical matters, however, he implored them to embody the dispositions of gentility. Quoting liberally from a host of Stoic writers then popular among London's literati—including Cato, Cicero, and Marcus Aure-
lius—Colman chastised base "*Self-interest*," which found its voice in
disloyalty, slander against public authorities, contention, and political faction. He encouraged affection for the civic order, expressed by polite
speech, cordiality, patriotism, and fealty to the Crown and province. He
offered three instances of other merchant worthies who displayed public
mindedness: John Winthrop, Edward Hutchinson, and Jonathan Belcher.
Old guards such as Sewall hardly regarded Hutchinson and Belcher as
moral exemplars; Colman's esteem for them bespoke a different moral vocabulary, collected not from puritan divines but from metropolitan standards of sensibility, reasonableness, and the natural order of things. As for
slave trading, he said nothing on that day. He did, however, eventually
purchase slaves from Hugh Hall.[8]

Colman's sermon illustrates how religion, extended to cultural markers
such as imperial loyalties and cultural refinement, informed and gave
meaning to the activities of Boston merchants such as Hugh Hall from
the 1710s through the 1730s. Eliding the rule of providence with urbane
conceptions of reason and natural law, Colman sanctified commercial prosperity outside of customary puritan boundaries for exchange. The previous
generation of Boston pastors, most notably Samuel Willard and Cotton
Mather, accepted the economic analyses of England's political economists;
yet they retained a religious vocabulary, and a reading of providence thick
with apocalyptic expectations, that evoked traditional Reformed sensibilities. According to them, spiritual temptations attended the market system:
avarice, idolatry, irreligious manners, ungodly diversions, political corruption, and disregard of the poor. Colman, along with his contemporaries—
Thomas Foxcroft at First Church and Ebenezer Pemberton at Old
South—offered traders such as Hall a different moral language. Politeness
and sociability, loyalty and deference, formed the moral sinews of the imperial body politic, joining British citizens of different religious sensibilities.
Moreover, this discourse reflected and shaped new perceptions of Britain's
commercial system, slavery included. As a conduit for politeness, the market not only spread Protestant hegemony over Catholicism but also channeled civility and facilitated concord.

This discourse led Hall to understand his business ventures as virtuous
even as he traded slaves, paid London suppliers with specie and bills of
credit, exchanged credit for profit, and sold English-made luxuries and
Barbadian rum to Bostonians: what previous moralists condemned as exporting fiscal security and importing moral vice. Some of Hall's older colleagues, such as Fitch, engaged in many of the same practices, but Hall,
unlike Fitch, prided himself on his ambition and eagerness to accumulate

a fortune through high manners and cosmopolitan knowledge. He fancied himself ecumenical in spirit, sophisticated in literary taste, and attuned to the metropolis. Such qualities certified his social and moral reputation. They propelled Hall into the Atlantic economy with moral confidence.

Hall's career reveals the interdependence between merchants and ministers, theology and economy, as New Englanders further assembled a market culture in early America. We cannot understand Hall without paying attention to the ways in which his religious mentors located the workings of providence within the natural and political order and, in the process, validated all profitable exchange, including slavery, with transcendent purpose. New turns in New England's intellectual and religious life—a new theological language tuned to politeness and proper affections—gave merchants such as Hugh Hall the conviction that their schemes and ambitions fulfilled divine law.

Hall and Boston's Provincial Merchants

The transatlantic market system pulsed through the veins of Hugh Hall Jr., the namesake of his father and grandfather. The first Hugh Hall, a Quaker merchant who emigrated from England to Barbados, established himself in the elite quarter of Bridgetown. He also created commercial partnerships with Friends in Pennsylvania and purchased twelve hundred acres of land, named Greenfield, on the Delaware River near Philadelphia. His daughter Mary married into the Lascelles family, which included prominent sugar traders in London and Barbados.[9]

The second Hugh Hall (our subject's father, known as Hugh Hall Sr.), born in 1673 in Barbados, extended the family's business by making connections in Boston, currying the favor of colonial officials, and abandoning Quakerism for the Church of England. Dividing his time between Barbados and Boston, he married Lydia, the daughter of Boston merchant Benjamin Gibbs. Her mother, also named Lydia, was a daughter of the merchant Joshua Scottow. Lydia Scottow married, in succession, Gibbs, Anthony Checkley (the attorney general of the colony), and William Colman (the father of Benjamin). Lydia Gibbs Hall, the mother of the third Hugh, died in Philadelphia in 1699. Sending the younger Hugh to Boston to be raised by his grandmother Lydia, Hugh Hall Sr. then married a Barbados heiress. In 1719 he was appointed a judge of the Admiralty Court for Barbados. He enlarged his estate during the next decade, especially after his third marriage in 1722, when he accumulated several warehouses, two plantations, and more than thirty slaves. As a display of his prominence and pretensions, he also adopted a coat of arms for the family. In 1732 he was nominated to serve on the King's Council. Dying on a visit to Boston

shortly thereafter, where he was buried in King's Chapel ground, he bequeathed to his son Hugh a solid estate, including several slaves, Greenfield, and £500 in cash.[10] Hugh Hall Jr. thus inherited networks of commercial exchange that
linked his family to the British Atlantic market system. He grew up among
shipping, ledgers, business correspondence, credit negotiations, commercial protocols, and slavery. He was the son of an ambitious businessman
and was related to several distinguished merchant clans: Scottow, Gibbs,
and, more distantly, Colman in Boston; Lascelles in London and Barbados.
He also knew firsthand the cosmopolitan and ecumenical culture defining
commerce at the beginning of the eighteenth century. His family members
were Barbadian Quakers, Boston puritans, and Anglican converts. His father served as an official of the Crown with Anglican and elite sympathies.
Hall lived in Barbados and Boston, owned land in Philadelphia, and visited
London. His family lines were shot through with imperial identities and
commercial aspirations.

The thick religious culture of Boston at the turn of the eighteenth century equally nourished Hall. As a child, he attended Old South Church and
listened intently to local preachers. When he was thirteen years old, he
began to take notes at Boston's Sunday sermons and Thursday lectures,
summarizing and quoting from sermons by Pemberton of Old South, Benjamin Wadsworth and Thomas Bridge of First Church, Cotton Mather of
Old North, and Colman of Brattle Street. He entered Harvard in 1709,
fell under the influence of tutor Leverett and pastor Colman, received his
first degree, and remained three further years in Cambridge to complete a
master's thesis; as befitted the pen of a devout New Englander with Protestant and English loyalties, it consisted of an attack on Jesuit theology. The
family business, however, pulled on him. His father kept him engaged in
commerce by sending him some expensive clothing to sell in Boston. Benning Wentworth, his closest friend at college and future correspondent,
came from a distinguished commercial family. Wentworth, whose brother
married Hugh's sister Sarah (sent to Boston for social polishing), eventually
amassed a fortune as a merchant and governor of New Hampshire. Wentworth began his business by working with Hall to import brandy to Boston
through Barbados.[11]

A career in trade required that Hall establish his reputation as a reliable
client in overseas ventures. His family connections did not ensure him a
ready set of suppliers, creditors, or commissions. His father had not created
the sort of dynasty to impress London businessmen, who often doubted
the creditworthiness (and sophistication) of Barbadian and New England
merchants, with their bills that plummeted in value by the month. Monetary deflation in Boston made it no easier to compete with established merchants there. In the fall of 1716, Hall returned from Boston to Barbados—

suffering through a storm-battered voyage—where he plotted his course, procured letters of introduction, and gathered money (including "an handsome Aggregate" from his father). In April 1716 he left for London. Shortly after his arrival, his uncle Edward Lascelles introduced him to the Royal Exchange, showed him the Lascelles countinghouse, and hosted him at his country estate at Stoke Newington. Yet, as Hall reported to his friends and father, Edward and the other Lascelles treated him somewhat coldly, or at least condescendingly; rather than offer him commercial contacts, much less real business, they disparaged the financial and intellectual pretensions of provincial traders, implying that he was a bad risk. Hall confided to his correspondents that he was more erudite than the snobs at Stoke Newington and better read in serious literature, including current religious disputes.[12]

Hall nonetheless labored his way through available channels, probing for suitable partners and meeting London merchants. A letter from Leverett introduced him to members of the Royal Society. He conversed with members of Parliament and reflected on the recent turns in Tory-Whig disputes. He traveled to Oxford and Cambridge, met the bishop of Bristol, and visited Hampton Court. As Hall gained the confidence of a dozen or so potential business partners, including the slave trader Allen, he attempted to fashion "a frugal yet Genteel way of Living": culturally sophisticated, knowledgeable in science and commerce, and ecumenical in religious matters. He recognized that his English counterparts valued gentility as an indication of financial reliability. Moral and cultural credit signified commercial creditworthiness.[13]

Returning to Barbados in January 1718, Hall called in several debts, built a reserve of capital for new investments, and confirmed his business contacts with a burst of letters to London. During this period, he accumulated nearly 70 correspondents, including 18 in London, 24 in New England, and 10 in the Chesapeake. His efforts paid off. Hall and his father jointly received a series of slave-trading commissions from the London firm of Betteress and Allen. The Halls imported to Barbados more than six hundred Africans over the next two years, selling most of them to island planters but also placing about a third of them with Virginians such as Harry and Nathaniel Harrison, who distributed them throughout the Chesapeake and supplied Hall with pork and tobacco in return.[14]

In April 1718 Hall traveled again to New England, bringing with him his half-brother Richard, who was born in Barbados in 1705 and, after an education at Harvard, returned to Bridgetown to work with his father. In Boston, Hugh commenced a decade-long litigation over the mortgaged estate of his grandfather Benjamin Gibbs. The next year, he journeyed again to Barbados. He arranged for several consignments of slaves to be shipped to New England and began to export sugar to Boston. Sometime after July 1720, he returned permanently to Massachusetts. He joined the Brattle Street Church and married Elizabeth Pitts, the daughter of merchant John Pitts, in 1722. Hall's marriage brought him further resources—reputation, business connections, and capital—to expand his trade. John Pitts provided the Halls with a house and warehouse facilities, and Elizabeth later received legacies of £1,800 and another dwelling in town. Hugh and Elizabeth had eleven children from 1723 to 1741; four daughters (Lydia, Elizabeth, Mary, and Sarah) and two sons (Pitts and Benjamin) survived to adulthood.[15]

Hall never built his business into a titanic trading house, but he prospered nonetheless, pursuing further contacts, different products, and more customers. Throughout his career in Boston, he imported luxury items such as fine shoes, "the newest fashions," funeral wear from London (chamois gloves, fine black wool, and white scarves, along with mourning fans), whalebone for hooped petticoats, "choice leather chairs," and dozens of bureaus, tea tables, and fine cabinets. He also developed a brisk trade in small amounts of common goods, investing in nineteen shiploads in 1723 alone between London, New England, Barbados, Saint Kitts, and Virginia. He sent New England candles, soap, mutton, timber, fish, and legumes to Barbados and bought Barbadian rum and sugar. He sold slaves to clients in the Chesapeake, receiving tobacco, meat, and grain in return. He imported furniture, clocks, books (many of which Colman bought), and fine clothing from London and shipped timber, rum, and tobacco to his English suppliers. In 1729 sales of hand tools— saws, axes, bolts, chisels, and a few pistols—amounted to a fifth of his accounts. Hall's various ventures illustrated, on a small scale, a trading pattern common among Britain's Atlantic merchants: manufactured goods from England to the colonies, slaves from Africa to the Caribbean, rum from Barbados to New England, foodstuffs from New England to the Caribbean, and New England's natural products and paper credit back to England.[16]

A remarkable number of agents and customers exchanged thousands of pounds in credit and goods with Hall. For each of the years from 1728 through 1730, a period from which we have his ledgers, he figured his credit in amounts averaging £15,550 per year, given on 180 accounts. These amounts represented sales and outstanding debts to him, not pure profits. He owed thousands of pounds to his commissioners in London. He also accumulated heavy debts to his suppliers, including some twenty-one creditors in Barbados. His chief customers in Boston, who bought from £500 to £2,000 worth of goods from him annually, included the merchants and shopkeepers Benjamin Gerrish, Daniel Henchman, Edward Bromfield, and Ebenezer and John Storer. Hall also supplied other notable Boston merchants—Andrew Faneuil, Benjamin Fitch, Arthur Savage, and

John Binning—as well as the Salem merchant Samuel Brown. At his peak, Hall operated at the center of Boston's mercantile trade.[17]

Sales of luxury and common goods in themselves placed Hall among Boston's more prominent merchants; yet his importation of slaves provided him with periodic bursts of profits that were crucial to his position. He hoped, as he confided to his father, that success as one of New England's "Noted Guinea Factors" would provide a secure income above and beyond "shop trade," which sometimes languished in unpaid accounts and unsold goods. Hall in fact figured prominently in the escalation of the slave trade between Massachusetts and Barbados during the 1720s. Sometimes working through London commissions, sometimes through his father and brother, and at other times buying several slaves and marketing them on his own behalf, he sold perhaps from fifty to eighty captives a year to Barbadian, Virginian, and New England customers during the 1720s. With a net profit averaging £3 a sale, this amounted to nearly £200 annually for Hall. Added to his gains from consumer goods, this lifted Hall's income to a level required for claims to true gentility.[18]

During the 1730s and 1740s, however, Hall's business faltered. He signed on as a minor partner in a powerful trading alliance between the Pitts and Bowdoin families and imported fewer high-end luxury items. An expensive venture, slave trading slackened throughout Massachusetts during the 1740s and 1750s, and there are no indications that Hall imported slaves after 1740. He increasingly relied on his brother Richard, the trustee of the family estate. Hugh apparently began to lag behind in remittances. Richard assured Hugh's Barbadian creditors that Hugh was an honorable man despite overdue payments, but the very fact that he had to defend Hugh's "Industry and Integrity" signified a diminishing reputation. In 1735 Richard rebuffed Hugh's repeated requests for further funds from the estate, claiming that legal terms allowed him to discharge only a few remaining possessions from their father: a telescope, several paintings (including one of the royal family and one of Hall Jr. himself), and books. These were important objects—symbols of status and imperial loyalty— but they hardly fulfilled Hugh's needs for cash. London creditors such as Abraham Blydesteyn increasingly complained of his delinquency and demanded payments on short order. Hall had gained enough prestige to be appointed a justice of the peace in Suffolk County in 1739, but the Assembly dismissed him nine years later for maladministration, chiefly questionable judgments. He pursued debtors with fierce litigation during the 1740s, once demanding an attachment of goods and jail for a debtor who owed him the relatively small amount of £60—a sign of mounting desperation. During the mid-1750s, when his brother also suffered business losses, Hugh sold off much of his Boston property, including his mansion. He also cashed in his few investments in outlying land. Protracted lawsuits over unpaid debts hovered over him during the 1760s, as did outstanding fines levied by the selectmen for improper rental practices. Hall died in 1773, leaving an estate diminished by unpaid debts and legal controversies.[19]

It is Hall's rise to prominence and early successes, however, rather than his late-life decline, that occupy this chapter. They illuminate the moral world of Boston merchants who remained attached to the established congregational order from the 1710s through the 1730s, when New England's market economy flowered into a full system. Hall joined a new breed of merchants whose careers overlapped but succeeded the generation represented by Sewall, Fitch, and Bromfield. He and his cohort, who might be called postpuritan, professed loyalty to the puritan inheritance yet defined their community in new ways. They refrained from eschatological surmises about the conflict between French Catholicism and English Protestantism and replaced it with a naturalized view of providence. They identified the British Empire with a transatlantic trade of goods and civility. For Hall and his closest associates, commercial productivity and social refinement evinced interior moral goodness. Religious virtue and market cultures did not compete; they reinforced each other.

To be sure, Hall entered a diverse mercantile community in Boston. At Old South, David Jeffries, John Spooner, and Habijah Savage formed substantial businesses trading between London, Barbados, Bermuda, Maine, and Boston. Jeremiah Bumsted and Benjamin Lynde achieved modest successes. Old North had several families who traded northward with Acadia and Nova Scotia, including Clarke, Richards, and George. Brattle Street claimed a host of new merchants, three of whom worked with Hall: James and John Pitts and the very wealthy Huguenot James Bowdoin. Other merchants with midsize businesses joined Hall at Brattle Street—Grove Hirst, Stephen Minot, Isaac Smith, and Ebenezer Storer—along with a member of the eminent Savage clan, Samuel Philips Savage. A large number of Anglicans also traded in Boston. The Church of England parish, King's Chapel, received a disparate group of the town's most prominent, richest, deeply established, and politically connected overseas traders: John Nelson, the French Protestant immigrants André and Peter Faneuil, John Erving, and Thomas Hancock, who came from a long line of puritan pastors.[20]

Although Boston's overseas traders asserted themselves as civic leaders and English patriots, they did not share a single politics of empire, colonial policy, and provincial government. They took different stances on the relative powers of governor, Council, and Assembly. Merchants also expressed various degrees of ambivalence toward the Board of Trade and Whig dominance of Parliament. Hall spent most of his career during a period of Anglo-French peace (between the end of Queen Anne's War in 1713 and the commencement of King George's War in 1744), when many of New

England's merchants, Hall included, gloried in their contribution to Britain's maritime power yet avoided military service and chafed under the expanding tariffs and regulations that drained profits to London. Hall, whose family in Barbados had Tory sentiments, was not above smuggling and skirting the customs duties the Whig government imposed.[21]

For all of their religious and political differences, long-distance merchants nonetheless stood as a powerful social bloc within Boston. In terms of monetary policy, they supported measures that shortened credit and pegged the value of bills of credit, as much as possible, to the pound sterling. Hall, along with his Pitts partners, Fitch, Spooner, and Erving, agreed not to trade in Rhode Island and New Hampshire bills, which suffered even more deflation than did those of Massachusetts. They subscribed to the short-lived "merchants' notes" project of 1733, a plan to issue private notes to be circulated among merchants in New England, thereby reserving bills of credit for public use. Hall and Pitts also rejected proposals for a Land Bank in 1740, a private scheme to provide paper currency backed by mortgages. Instead they subscribed to the Silver Bank, which would have pegged the value of new notes to specie. Neither banking scheme came to fruition, but their support of the Silver Bank identified Hall and his associates with commercial and creditor interests against land-rich but cash-poor farmers and debtors.[22]

Fiscal politics reflected a common social ethos as well. Merchants depended on cultural capital gauged by metropolitan standards that mingled gentility, moral reputation, and economic diligence. The risks of overseas trade in this period, exacerbated by fluctuations in currency values and unsteady reserves of credit, compelled merchants to exercise what one observer called "a fixed opinion of the honesty and integrity, as well as ability of a person," to fulfill his obligations. Kinship, personal acquaintance, and connection to established trading houses served as one source of trust. Refined speech and epistolary elegance served as another. In the offices, coffeehouses, and exchanges where merchants met to negotiate, knowledge of literary trends, wit, and a facility with poetry indicated sophistication— as Hall learned when he met his Lascelles cousins in London. Using the rhetoric of Richard Allestree, Defoe, Addison, or Steele, who essayed the proper deportment necessary to success, reflected prudence. Proper manners exhibited sociability and attendant virtues: honesty, fairness, and reliability. Puritans such as John Hull and Samuel Sewall relied on biblical tropes, spiritual reflection, and frank, sometimes indelicate moral appeal to convey economic integrity. Hall and his contemporaries traded in the currency of civility, stamped with style and politeness.[23]

In the quotidian conduct of business—conveying accounts, corresponding with agents, arranging shipments, and contracting credit—traders transformed the codes of politeness into legal protocols and formalized language. Hall and his colleagues such as David Jeffries and John Spooner wrote straightforward business letters, devoid of moral and religious reflection and all but the most perfunctory personal notice. They increasingly communicated through agents, rather than directly to other merchants. Their letters were deferential in their address, yet they conveyed little beyond the details of goods, dates, and receipts. Securing new accounts and the best prices called for a selective and strategic disclosure of information; politeness masked secrets and potentially harmful news. Secretary's guides, published and reprinted with astonishing frequency during the first decades of the eighteenth century, recommended this epistolary style as evidence of technical mastery. Printed blank forms, sold by printers such as Daniel Henchman, further regularized commercial speech. Forms for bonds, securities, ship's manifestoes, insurance contracts, conveyance of property, power of attorney, and ledgers carried legal terminology and logic into nearly every exchange. By scripting their transactions onto such forms, which bore the name of the king and provincial government, merchants conformed to imperial and metropolitan, as well as legal, dictates.[24]

From one perspective, such formalism appeared to be anything but sociable, certainly not witty and elegant; yet, from another perspective, it represented the genteel virtues of punctuality, precision, legality, propriety, and candor. Rote and prescribed vocabulary constituted one dialect, as it were, of the language of reason and refinement. It denoted discipline. It had a transatlantic, even potentially universal, currency: a rhetorical parallel to credit instruments that maintained their fiscal value across oceans and national borders. The starchy language and printed forms deployed by merchants such as Hall represented rationality and civic competence.

Proper language translated not only into moral and financial credit, but also into cultural authority, which merchants asserted through control of Boston's architecture and art. The town's population, rising from seven thousand in 1690 to twelve thousand in 1720, compelled construction of new highways, streets, and houses, especially in the North End. A 1705 earthquake and the great 1711 fire, which gutted whole blocks, including First Church and the Town House, especially sparked new buildings during the 1710s and 1720s. Merchants led the construction boom, erecting elegant and large homes that competed with church meetinghouses for visual space. Merchants also directed the building committees and raised funds for public structures such as the new Town House. Sewall predictably admired its costly windows, which illuminated legislative and judicial chambers. No longer used as a marketplace, the Town House now featured full-length portraits of Queen Anne, George I, and George II: faces of empire appearing in the midst of provincial affairs. Influenced by English tastes, as well as by the fear of further conflagrations, overseas traders promoted brick construction for several new churches and Georgian architectural design. The 1712 First Church structure, stylish and large, embodied these tastes, as did the New North Church (established in 1722 as an offshoot of the crowded Old North), the aptly named New Brick meetinghouse (1724), and the rebuilt Old South Church (1729).[25]

Other construction projects enhanced the commercial prospects of the town, further shaping an urban and maritime order dominated by traders. Nothing matched the Long Wharf, completed in 1713, for sheer size and transatlantic symbolism. Further improvements followed. By 1720 the selectmen had overseen the erection of two public docks and several wharves, built the first lighthouse in the New World, repaved and widened major roads, especially the transverse over the Neck, mapped and planned streets and lanes, and issued new civic codes to regularize traffic. Fourteen new shipyards helped to produce two hundred vessels annually at an average cost of nearly £2,000 each. The elaborate festivals, sometimes replete with mock baptisms, that attended launches of larger ships horrified latter-day puritans such as Cotton Mather but nonetheless epitomized the town's dependence on trade. Boston accommodated an astonishing fifty-eight wharves, along with hundreds of warehouses. A proliferation of taverns in the period gave merchants a space to gossip and flaunt their literary fluency. Several new coffeehouses offered London-like venues to negotiate deals and exchange news and rumors affecting the market.[26]

Commercial structures, moreover, patterned space in Boston on the demands of consumption. General dry-goods stores, specialty shops, and dozens of bookstores clustered in different streets. Whole neighborhoods evolved into distinct wholesale and retail districts. In addition, half of the town's shops (chiefly those offering so-called wet goods, that is, imported groceries, wine, liquor, and tobacco) were located on or near the Long Wharf. The first cross street up from the dock into town carried the name Merchants Row. Boston presented itself as a provincial center in Britain's economic empire, as fully dependent on trade and attuned by its cultural mandates as was London. The town belonged to merchants.[27]

During the 1720s, several artists, chiefly patronized by well-to-do merchants, celebrated Boston's reconstruction in a series of maps, engravings, and landscape paintings. English ship captain John Bonner produced *A New Plan of the Great Town of Boston* in 1722 (figure 5.1). Engraved by Francis Dewing and first published in London, it featured the waterfront: a disproportionately large Long Wharf with several oversize ships moored at its side and others in the harbor, wharves and docks with the names of their merchant owners (Oliver, Belcher, and Clarke), and shipyards. The map emphasized quick transport across overly wide thoroughfares, including Orange Street on the Neck. Bonner also gave attention to Boston's eleven churches, listing them prominently as integral to civic and commer-

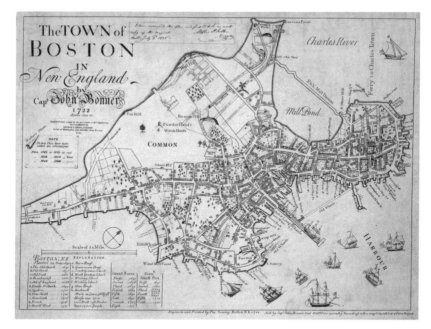

Figure 5.1. *The Town of Boston in New England by Capt. John Bonner, 1722.* Facsimile map engraved and published by George G. Smith, 1835. Bonner stressed commercial movement through wide roads and plentiful shipping while also listing churches, fires, and smallpox outbreaks in the lower left. Courtesy of the Massachusetts Historical Society.

cial culture. The Bonner map was a popular and much-used image for the town's identity, republished and updated in Boston as late as twenty years after its first appearance.[28]

London-born map publisher William Burgis bound imperial, commercial, and religious themes into his engravings, which followed closely on Bonner's map. In 1723 he produced, from the vantage of an offshore island, *A North East View of the Great Town of Boston*, first published in London. The title of Burgis's engraving and a note below the visual image emphasized "the great Trade of this place." Disproportionately tall steeples atop the new churches patronized by merchants—King's Chapel, New North, New Brick, Brattle Street, and Old South—penetrate the skyline. The steeples, a Georgian architectural emblem, suggest a rich establishment that maintained civic order with an ecumenical spirit and cosmopolitan taste. Moral and religious themes constitute the background. At the center of the view, a fantastically elongated Long Wharf, replete with shops and cranes, dominates the harbor. At the front, dozens of vessels crowd the harbor: dinghies, shallops, midsize and large merchantmen, and warships

Figure 5.2. *A South East View of the Great Town of Boston*. Engraving by William Burgis, printed by William Price, 1743. This revision of an earlier engraving by Burgis offers a perspective of Boston that features trading vessels, the Long Wharf, and church steeples. Courtesy of the American Antiquarian Society.

blazing canon. Nearly every vessel flies the Union Jack. Later paintings, by John Smibert, and another by Burgis—his 1743 *A South East View of Great Town of Boston*—present similar perspectives (figure 5.2). These works advertised Boston as an entrepôt for the Atlantic trade, a haven for the Crown and its colonial empire, and a cultured, religiously cosmopolitan society all at once.[29]

Overseas traders also attempted to shape the contours of municipal politics. As Hall set up his business in Boston, many of the town's merchants formed a campaign to exercise greater control over local marketplaces. As early as 1708, Sewall, Elisha Cooke, and other civic leaders complained that country peddlers, itinerant dealers, hucksters, and small shopkeepers violated commercial laws with impunity: selling during prohibited hours, purveying inferior goods, cheating customers, reselling goods (sometimes purchased earlier in the same day from respectable wholesalers) at exorbitant markups, and failing to follow statutory regulations for essential foodstuffs. In 1715 several selectmen called for a municipal corporation, or permanent city government, and a regulated public market. Critics of the measure, representing peddlers, small shopkeepers, and artisans who sold wares out of temporary stalls, argued that incorporation would rob the town meeting of its authority, install paid officials prone to bribery, and raise taxes. Further complaints about fraud, and fears of a growing incivility on the town's streets, including occasional grain riots, persuaded the selectmen to appoint local inspectors and reconsider the issue.[30]

Established traders such as John Colman supported incorporation and the organization of public markets regulated by the city. Colman's brother and Hall's pastor, Benjamin, spoke for merchants such as Hall when he voiced *Some Reasons . . . for Setting Up Markets* in 1719. "Wisdom and prudence," as he put it, dictated regulation on purely pragmatic grounds. Set hours for exchange would save time, which "is so much money." Confined locations would lead to competition, hence industriousness, by forcing artisans and country traders to sell side by side in full public view. Markets would encourage a transparent and knowledgeable approach to trade. They would also promote decency and "comely Order," ridding the streets of wandering peddlers "hawking and sauntering about Town" in search of unsuspecting customers. The absence of a marketplace, according to him, embarrassed the town's overseas merchants, whose foreign partners were shocked as much by the hurly-burly of exchange in the town as by the feebleness of provincial bills of credit. A regulated marketplace would strengthen the integration of the countryside into Boston's market. It would hasten Boston's transformation into a rational order, controlled by knowledgeable businessmen, unsullied by small-time fraud, and attractive to merchants from throughout the Atlantic world.[31]

Boston's debate over markets continued unresolved through the 1730s. Having approved the establishment of three marketplaces, the town meeting abandoned the project after three years. Under the influence of Peter and Andrew Faneuil, the town's officials eventually agreed to stricter enforcement of existing laws while refusing to institute set marketplaces. Peter Faneuil signaled his confidence in the measure by constructing, and offering to the town in 1742, a large market house for voluntary use. His gesture represented the social aspirations of the merchant community. Designed by John Smibert, a well-known London artist who arrived in Boston in 1729, Faneuil's building incorporated Georgian fashion and expensive bricks: decency and prowess. It signified merchants' claims to civic leadership based on the twin foundations of economic expertise and cultural sophistication (figure 5.3).[32]

Boston's traders expressed these ideals also through their promotion of and participation in an expanding consumer culture. As they accelerated the pace of imports through the first decades of the eighteenth century, they introduced luxury items, including the European linen, chamois gloves, petticoat hoops, watches, and furniture that Hall marketed, on an unprecedented scale. "A Gentleman from *London*," as one visitor put it in reference to fine goods and entertainments, "would almost think himself at home in *Boston*." Such a compliment would have insulted an earlier generation of puritans, who sometimes revered refined objects such as silver Communion ware as emblems of spiritual taste, but deemed most imported luxuries extravagances that bespoke ostentation, pretension, and indulgence. During the first decades of the eighteenth century, an increasing number of Bostonians came to regard luxuries as their rewards for eco-

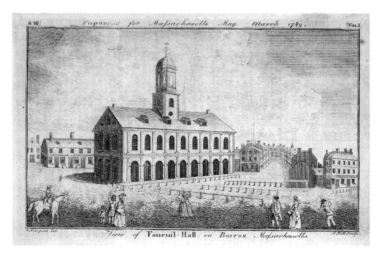

Figure 5.3. *View of Faneuil Hall, in Boston, Massachusetts.* Published image of engraving by S. Hill, after W. Pierpont. From *Massachusetts Magazine* 1, no. 3 (March 1789). The symmetrical design, arched windows, rectangular shape, and brick construction reflect Georgian style, bringing commercial exchange into the sphere of cosmopolitan sensibilities. Courtesy of the Massachusetts Historical Society.

nomic competence, material indications of a comfortable, polite, and therefore respectable life. A new set of moral mandates accordingly energized consumer culture in this period. In England the Royal Society promoted industries linking technical innovation to luxury production (porcelain, enameled tableware, watches, and scientific instruments) as a boon to the British economy. Political economists such as Petty, Barbon, and North validated consumer appetites as natural incentives to industriousness and domestic production, which enriched the nation's economy. Ecumenical and progressive religious writers overturned customary objections with observations that gentility—enacted through good manners and tasteful consumption—positioned citizens to assist their less fortunate neighbors by example and generosity.[33]

Merchants displayed their own consumer virtues in the domain of family and home. Elites such as Thomas Hutchinson, Andrew Faneuil, and William Clarke built imposing, three-story brick mansions in Georgian style (Clarke's house had twenty-six rooms), setting a trend that even less wealthy Bostonians partly imitated. Hall enhanced his house, the Pitts mansion, with £650 worth of renovations. Merchants furnished the inside of their houses with tokens of technological advances such as clocks and scientific instruments such as Hall's telescope. Hall also collected silver plate, nineteen sets of arms, and escutcheons (decorative, armorial shields, one of which presumably exhibited the Hall coat of arms). These objects represented their owners' aspirations to scientific sophistication and metropolitan taste. They bespoke of being English.[34]

Painted and engraved portraits also adorned the inside of houses. Portraiture artists in Hall's lifetime emphasized domestic themes, highlighting the comfort and wealth of commercial families. Many merchants, along with ministers, favored the work of Smibert. He also stamped au courant designs on architecture throughout the town. Smibert joined Old South Church, became active in charitable projects led by merchants such as John Erving, and was a founding member of the progressive West Church in 1736. New religious ideas, the latest styles, and commercial themes met in his work. He painted dozens of merchants and their families, including Hancock, Henchman, Oliver, Sewall, Belcher, and Peter Faneuil. In 1733 Hall commissioned from Smibert a portrait of his wife, Elizabeth, dressed in a fine violet-colored gown and seated before an idyllic pastoral scene. In 1758 Hall employed John Singleton Copley, a rising star popular among other Brattle Street merchants such as Bowdoin, Smith, and Storer. Copley's elegant portrait of Hall, done in pastels, reflected progressive techniques (figure 5.4). Peter Pelham, the stepfather of Copley, produced mezzotints (engravings from which printed copies were made) of painted portraits, most notably of Pastors Colman and Mather in large wigs that were deemed tasteful. He sold his prints to those who could not afford paintings but who nonetheless desired a semblance of gentility in their modest homes. Pelham also ran a finishing school for aspiring young gentlemen, teaching them politeness as an acquired talent. Merchants, furthermore, commissioned decorative panels and landscapes for their homes, accomplished by New England painters who emulated English schools. By 1750 Hall owned more than sixty oil paintings and mezzotints, evidence of his taste and prestige.[35]

Even in the rituals of death, families gave merchants a venue to exhibit their wealth, refinement, and social authority. Elaborate funerals dictated special and often expensive dress, from scarves to rings. The bereaved sometimes sent hundreds of mourning gloves to invited guests. Hall not only sold funeral clothing but also received a special pair of gloves from Samuel Sewall Jr., to don during the funeral of Hugh Hall Sr. Merchants also commissioned large, elaborate gravestones and other burial monuments for family members. There is no evidence of a gravestone for Hugh Hall, but his writings reveal a concerted devotion to lineage and posterity. He compiled a detailed genealogy going back to the English Halls. Like other merchants of the period, he named his children not after biblical heroes but after fellow family members (Lydia, Pitts, Hugh, Gibbs). The longevity of his family and estate symbolized mercantile power in an increasingly commercialized town.[36]

Figure 5.4. *Hugh Hall.* Pastel on paper by John Singleton Copley, 1758. Courtesy the Metropolitan Museum of Art, Purchase, Estate of George Strichman and Sandra Strichman Gifts; Bequest of Vera Ruth Miller, in memory of her father, Henry Miller, Bequest of Josephine N. Hopper, John Stewart Kennedy Fund, and Gifts of Yvonne Moën Cumerford, Berry B. Tracy, and Mr. and Mrs. Jeremiah Milbank, by exchange; Mr. and Mrs. Leonard L. Milberg Gift, and funds from various donors, 1996 (1996.279). Image © The Metropolitan Museum of Art.

Within this highly cultured arena, Boston's transatlantic merchants competed for profits in trying conditions. During the late 1710s and 1720s, Hall complained about the lack of bills of credit in Massachusetts, their sinking value, the unreliability of bills of exchange (sometimes worth only 70 percent of their face value), and the dearth of specie. It was hard enough to track prices for various goods or to depend on the judgment of agents in such matters. New Boston newspapers, such as the *Boston Gazette* and *New England Courant*, helped by publishing London stock prices and current retail prices in town; by the 1740s some indications of the price convergences and predictability that characterized a mature market system began to appear. Yet New England merchants such as Hall struggled to recover the ever-rising costs of insurance, storage, packing fees, customs, unpaid debts, interest, and unsold goods.[37]

Hall negotiated the problems of overseas exchange with shifting strategies. He often funneled his payments to London through Barbados, sending sugar and rum as remittances that held their value and were more esteemed than provincial bills. As he put it to a prominent London trader, "although it's Circular and by Consequence you are kept longer out of Your Effects, yet I think it has a much more Plausible Aspect of Proffit, considering . . . the Low Rate the Bills of Credit there have sunk to." Indeed, he continued, the value of Massachusetts bills of credit and bills of exchange had fallen so low that the province verged on "as Chimerical a Trade as that of Carolina." When an Annapolis merchant sent Hall tobacco, beer, and bills of exchange, Hall countered by remitting only a small amount of rum in return, given the high discount on Maryland bills and high price of rum at the time. Spanish currency and other forms of silver served Hall better, when he could obtain them. He sent hundreds of ounces of precious metal to London in exchange for the luxury items on which he made a stout profit, despite previous condemnations of such practices by Mather, Sewall, and Willard.[38]

The more Hall labored to secure credit, the more he advertised himself as trustworthy by virtue of his moral character. And the more he linked his character to commercial reliability, the more he fastened on refinement, honesty, and diligence—propriety, accuracy, and punctuality—as fundamental ethical standards. Old-fashioned puritans subordinated what they labeled merely civil manners to the Christian dispositions of faith and charity. Hall never mentioned faith and charity (or humility and self-sacrifice, for that matter). For him, "honesty and integrity," a repeated refrain, infused economic ambition and new exchange methods with moral goodness. At every point in his affairs, Hall appealed to them to assert his worth, judge his partners and customers, and vindicate his actions, even as they sometimes hid his liabilities.[39]

Hall assured potential commissioners and suppliers that he could be trusted for substantial orders and prompt payment, that, as he wrote to John Marriott of London, "we are Resolved none shall be more Honourable and Punctual in their Payments." Again, he professed to a friend in Boston, Timothy Prout, that he was "Resolved none shall discharge themselves with more Fidelity, Industry, and Integrity," and he knew that "Quick Remittances" were "the very Essence of Fidelity" and good "Character."

Likewise, he informed Boston's Joseph Parsons that he would not deal with suppliers who lacked moral probity, that is, "Specious Persons" who provided shoddy goods and behaved in an unseemly fashion. "We suppose it Needless," he warned Benjamin Dawson of London, "when we deal with Men of a Clear Character to Urge their Integrity in the species sent for, not only because their Moral Principles Oblidge them to it, but their Interest very forcibly Enjoins it." In the world of trade, prudence, timeliness, and protocol constituted moral goodness. Hall accordingly admired the "Deportment" of well-established traders.[40]

Competence denoted economic virtue as well. Seeking consignments from Parsons, he advertised his "Capacity" and his knowledge of the market; "at every Opportunity that shall propitiously Occur," he wrote, he would "studiously Promote your Interests here." Even when informing his Virginia client, Henry Harrison, about the going rate for pork in Boston, his language conflated economic sagacity with virtue; he was "Morally Assured" that "the Fate of a future Markett" for pork would not fall. He parried the thrusts of his Lascelles cousins with similar assertions. They thought he was inexperienced and naive; he was "determined not to be outbid by Industry and Integrity," and his "Capacity of Acquitting my self with Approbation."[41]

Hall overlaid technical expertise with Addisonian style in order to impress friends and possible partners. When competitors for his commissions from London belittled him as a provincial rube, he fired back with stinging satire. Attempting to charm London merchants, he publicized his intelligence with contemporary flair. When informing James Bunyard of his return to Boston from London, he celebrated a swift voyage with classical allusion: "by the good Favour of Eolus [the custodian of the winds]," he was "safely Carried thro the Dominions of Neptune." To induce the confidence of Benning Wentworth in a business partnership in 1717, Hall impressed on Wentworth his own "great Proficients in Politeness." He commented on Defoe's latest essays, parodied Whig-Tory shouting matches, and satirized a fashion among London's ladies to "paint" constellations or geometric figures on their faces according to political sentiment. Hall offered such observations as tokens of civility, which served as social currency.[42]

Hall even rested his most troublesome trade on the virtues of politeness. He knew that slave trading was brutal and slavery deadly. In February 1718 he reported to Samuel Betteress, who had employed him on one of his first large commissions, that poor conditions on one ship had incited an "Insurrection among the Negroes," which the captain violently suppressed. Smallpox, respiratory infections ("the flux"), and eye diseases spread throughout the vessel. By the time it reached Barbados, Hall had received ninety-four captives, many of them sick or wounded. He sold seventy-one at reduced rates; the rest remained on board, quarantined and too blind or incapacitated to put on the market. Hall's puritan elders in Boston, such as Sewall and Cotton Mather, disapproved of the slave trade as practiced in these conditions: marred by violence, destructive of families, and negligent of the souls of enslaved peoples.[43]

Hall himself complained to Benjamin Colman in 1720 that Anglican clerics in Barbados regarded Africans as having "no more Souls than Brutes" and refused to convert "our Poor Negroes here." Later he noted the "poverty and its attendant miseries" of the slave community in Boston and developed his own ameliorative scheme. He observed that only a handful of the thousand children of slaves in Boston attended the free public schools available to them. He ruminated on the possibility of establishing a separate school for "black children," funded in part by a "card-manufactury" where the children would work and learn useful trades such as leather preparation and machine operation. "In this mode," his wrote, "the children of blacks" would "be initiated and at the same time acquire a habit of industry."[44]

Yet, the occasional plans for education and the regrets over spiritual neglect aside, Hall still understood slave trading to be fraught with difficulties that compelled a narrow focus on costs, profits, sales, and fees. Piracy, currency disputes, and shifting regulations—chiefly concerning monopolies over certain sectors of the slave trade—interrupted business. The trade itself was complex. Hall exchanged massive amounts of credit among several slave commissioners, forty-seven suppliers, and hundreds of buyers, from individuals purchasing a single servant in New England to secondary traders or brokers in the Chesapeake. He dealt with dozens of ship captains, who brought him cargo from different areas of Africa (he mentioned Madagascar, Angola, and the Guinea coast) or from Barbados; the price of each slave depended on age, health, disposition, sex, and place of origin. A single shipment of slaves involved multilateral complications. In one 1729 period, for example, he marketed more than seventy slaves, delivered by seven ship captains: most on consignment for and prearrangement with Allen, several at auction (most likely at Long Wharf), and a few through private sales (figure 5.5). He managed the paperwork for customs, bought politely phrased advertisements in Boston newspapers, arranged for transport outside Boston, and negotiated fees for dockworkers who guarded slaves. He had to reimburse buyers whose slaves had died; half of the ten souls he sent to Connecticut in 1729 perished before they arrived. Slaving was a risky and expensive venture. Traders responded by treating their human cargo objectively, as disposable property. It was no wonder, as Hugh's brother Richard remarked from Barbados, that captives were "looked upon here as the most valuable species of property," with "all the properties of real es-

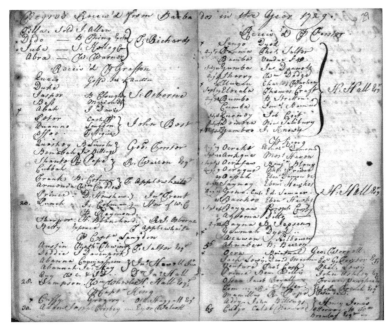

Figure 5.5. Account book of Hugh Hall, 1728–29. Original from Hugh Hall Papers. These pages from 1729 list slaves received from Barbados. The left column names the captives. The middle column names buyers—Benjamin Colman's name appears eighteen lines from the top on the left page. The right column lists transporters or the original owners for whom Hall acted as agent. Courtesy of the Massachusetts Historical Society.

tate." Richard thought it mere prudence to treat them humanely because they were "very useful as well as valuable."[45]

The language of civility transformed what in New England had been a dubious practice into an exercise in propriety—or at least deflected the moral dilemmas of slave trading to the background. Pleading for business with an Irish slave trader, Hall asserted his "Fidelity, Industry, and Integrity" as preeminent qualifications. Even as he narrated the horror of the disease-ridden 1718 shipment on consignment from Betteress, he presented himself as polite, optimistic, and diligent. He assured Betteress that "Honour, Industry, and Integrity" would compel him to market his cargo at the highest price possible. Worried that Betteress would chafe at the low selling prices, he assured his London employer that "it was a great happiness" that he managed to sell what he did, given that Betteress did not provide a shipboard physician. Hall later defended himself against Betteress's accusations, backed by rumors from Barbados, that he was shiftless and unreliable. "I have by my Education laid a Foundation for the Strictest

Morality," he insisted, and "I always Act from the Golden Law of Equity," performing for his employers "with the same Strenuous Endeavours" as he would for his own investments.[46]

Diligence and honesty, in other words, confirmed his moral integrity, and his integrity merited further slave commissions. Economic politeness injected respectability into Hall's slave trading. In contrast, the "Petty Traders" of Barbados, who were "a little above their Mechanical Fraternity," had not the slightest justification for casting aspersions on a social and intellectual superior such as himself. It was, he wrote in another letter to Betteress, a "Barbarous and Rascally Method" for his competitors to disparage him. He informed another London slave trader that he had a "good Foundation for Strict Piety as well as Undisguised Probity" and could market slaves with great advantage to potential partners. When Barbadian competitors continued to damage Hall's reputation and secure his slave consignments for themselves, Hall glowered with self-righteousness "against such Ungentlemanlike and ungenerous supplanters." In Hall's community, true barbarism was theft of commissions, not slavery. True virtue amounted to sophistication, honesty, and diligence—to good credit.[47]

Rational Protestantism and the Meaning of Commerce

Religious sentiment shaped Hall's understanding of social credit as much as it had his predecessors in Boston. His story did not turn on secularization: the triumph of profits over piety or the separation of economic exchange from spiritual dictates. He participated in a religious community that intermingled teaching on social deportment, on political loyalties, and on the rule of providence over worldly affairs. To understand his moral world, we must probe a series of fundamental intellectual changes that legitimated civility as a religious virtue and gave meaning to commerce by describing it as a natural law.

The establishment of new churches within the congregational order provided venues for moral innovation in Boston during Hall's lifetime.[48] Organized in 1699, Brattle Street Church (also Brattle Square or the Manifesto Church) was the most visible, influential, and contested of these establishments. A coalition of merchants and progressive clergy configured plans for the new congregation in 1697. Thomas Brattle donated the land, just north of the Town House, and joined other wealthy "undertakers": John Colman, Thomas Clarke, John Mico, Benjamin Davis, and Thomas Cooper. Several of the undertakers previously belonged to Old South. Resisting the sacramental orthodoxy of Willard and Cotton Mather, they joined forces with a cadre of ministers who proposed progressive, tolerant, and ecumenical practices, including liberal access to the Lord's Supper. Affiliated with Harvard, these divines included Brattle's brother William, pastor of the Cambridge church; John Leverett, Brattle's classmate, sometime astronomer, and future president of the college; and Ebenezer Pemberton, a close associate of Leverett and fellow tutor at the time. The undertakers called Benjamin Colman, brother of John and student of Brattle and Leverett, to the pulpit in 1699.[49]

With its cosmopolitan culture and liberal religious ethos, Brattle Street received a new generation of merchants, many of them transfers from Old South, among them Brattle himself, Samuel Sewall Jr., Andrew Belcher, William Jeffries, John Pitts, John Spooner, Grove Hirst, and Hugh Hall. Merchant leaders administered the congregation by professional business protocols, including strict account keeping and auditing. They also funded a magnificent new meetinghouse built in Georgian style.[50]

Benjamin Colman understood Brattle Street to be an instrument for inner piety and civil gentility, religious decorum and devotion to the empire. His father, a well-to-do London shopkeeper, immigrated to Boston and sent him to Harvard, where he acquired a taste for scientific publications and liberal Anglican writers. During a journey to London, interrupted by a brief stint as a captive of French privateers, he made close connections among England's liberal, quasi-deist Presbyterians. He developed an affective preaching style fixed on rhetorical precision and literary allusion. He emphasized religious toleration, public benevolence, and proper social deportment over dogmatic detail. He also initiated a lifelong correspondence with eminent Anglican divines. When called to Brattle Street, he sought ordination by English Presbyterians, thereby skirting Boston conservatives. Colman's travels fully acculturated him to the intellectual and political domains of overseas merchants (figure 5.6).[51]

In 1699 the founders of Brattle Street Church published their agenda in a controversial work written by Colman and titled *A Manifesto*. They subscribed to the Westminster Confession of Faith, which legitimated, along with Reformed doctrine, a Presbyterian polity—collective ministerial authority and the ideal of a national church—rather than the New England way of independent congregations. They also professed their adherence to the principles of the 1691 Heads of Agreement. A concord among English Presbyterians and Congregationalists, it promoted ecumenical cooperation, religious toleration, and fealty to the national government, including acceptance of the legal prerogatives of the Church of England.[52]

The rest of the principles of the *Manifesto* specified innovations in worship and discipline. Colman emphasized the importance of sacramental piety: a family-centered devotion that reaffirmed the household as a repository for reputation and wealth. The *Manifesto* offered baptism "to any Child referred to us by any professed Christian," exceeding even the Half-

Figure 5.6. *The Reverend Benjamin Colman, D. D.* Mezzotint engraving by Peter Pelham, after a painting by John Smibert, 1735. Courtesy of the Massachusetts Historical Society.

way Covenant in its liberality. It rejected the practice, prevalent among other Boston churches, of demanding written relations of faith for admission to the Lord's Supper. Brattle Street required communicants only to confer with the pastor and receive his approval. It thinned discipline to mutual counsel among members, rather than censure and admonition; such counsel was to be guided by "the Law of nature": candor, charity, and decorum. When Colman conducted worship for this "Manifesto Church," he instituted Anglican-like liturgical practices that his predecessors in Boston pulpits quite pointedly rejected, including set readings from Scripture without pastoral comment. One wag posted, on the door of the new church, doggerel that satirized the cultural and social pretensions represented by Colman's innovations:

> Our Churches turn genteel
> Our parsons grow trim with Wealth, Wine and Wig
> And their heads are covered with meal [wig powder].

The satire was not far from the point, at least in terms of contemporary sensibilities. The undertakers of Brattle Street vowed to participate fully in the congregational order and sponsor cooperation among the town's churches, yet they transposed congregational polity into politeness, as befitted the agendas of cosmopolitan merchants. Brattle Street initiated a postpuritan congregational order in Boston.[53]

Members of Boston's old religious guard initially resisted the new congregation, which they deemed to hold "too lax admission to the sacraments" along with a "discipline" that "seemeth to us too slender and remiss." Willard and Sewall criticized Brattle Street for poaching members from Old South and Colman for preaching sermons that displaced Calvinist grace with rational duties. Colman's irenic skills, however, eased Brattle Street into Boston's congregational order soon after the initial protests. Leaders of Old South brokered a rapprochement between Brattle Street and other congregations. Cotton Mather, who admired stylish urbanity as much as Colman did, eventually, even if tepidly, accepted Brattle Street and recognized Colman as a colleague. All parties appeared to recognize the value of a congregation that appealed to cosmopolitan sensibilities.[54]

Further developments among the churches confirmed the Brattle Street model as integral to, even if controversial in, the congregational order. Members of Old South split over the successor to Willard in 1707, eventually choosing Pemberton. Sewall and Mather derided Pemberton for his putatively Arminian theology. They also denounced his social manners as pretentious, such as when he used the term "gentlemen" rather than the customary "brethren" to address his parishioners. Conservatives at Old South hired Joseph Sewall as a colleague to Pemberton in 1713, hoping to moderate his influence. With Pemberton's death in 1717, Old

South called Thomas Prince to join Sewall. Prince promoted a relatively orthodox theology, but he was as cosmopolitan as his merchant parishioners. Educated at Harvard, he traveled to Barbados, London, and Rotterdam before returning to his native Boston. In London he curried friendships with Anglican and dissenting clergy alike, embraced the ideals of Protestant ecumenism, and adopted urbane habits such as a fine wig and fashionable clothing. Well-read in current literature, he developed a polished and witty writing style that combined scientific analyses of nature with evangelistic appeals.[55]

The establishment of other churches mirrored changes at Brattle Street and Old South. After a period of relatively slow church building throughout Massachusetts during Queen Anne's War, three new congregations were founded in the town from 1713 through 1730. In 1713 many parishioners of the overcrowded Old North Church started New North Church. A 1717 split at Old South created New South. An ordination controversy at New North in 1721 occasioned yet another North End church, the New Brick, whose new pastor, Peter Thacher, echoed Colman's preaching. The New South and New Brick churches moved toward open sacramental policies, progressive and rational preaching, and an ecumenical worship style. Even stodgy First Church began to adopt progressive practices, under the influence of pastors who embraced a moderate Calvinist theology and Colman's ecumenical spirit at the same time: Benjamin Wadsworth, Thomas Bridge, and Thomas Foxcroft. The elegant new brick meetinghouse of First Church represented the union of piety, fashion, and wealth.[56]

In this diverse, and increasingly liberal, institutional context, Boston's religious leaders inculcated discipline as conformity to reasonable, Protestant, and British standards of civility. Ministers did not recover puritan rules for the economy, much less rehabilitate long-lost practices of corporate censure in the churches. They took various positions on problems such as grain shortages, currency supply, market regulations, and relationships with the home government. Yet throughout their pronouncements, they all used common criteria to gauge the morality of commerce. They relied not only on political economy but also on a moral discourse derived from the British Enlightenment of their period.[57]

In particular, they adopted moderate expressions of the Enlightenment, which affirmed the necessity of a reasoned Protestantism to the commonweal. So used, the term "Enlightenment" serves here as shorthand for two emphases within a broad-based cultural movement during the first decades of the eighteenth century. First, British essayists, poets, and novelists popularized the natural philosophy of Newton, who had described nature as a system integrated into a regular pattern by universal physical laws. Second, they transformed such confidence about the intelligibility of the natural world into practical instruction. Moral philosophy, to wit, appeared as a corollary to natural philosophy: the description of universal laws, perceived by reason, that bound all people into an orderly and regular society.[58]

Proponents of this moderate Enlightenment frequently transposed philosophical debates about ethics, Christian doctrine, and the very nature of reason into moral advice. Serial publications and newspapers included excerpts from Locke, Newton, Boyle, the third Earl of Shaftesbury, Samuel Clarke, and Archbishop John Tillotson. Drawing on their formal treatises, writers such as Addison, Steele, Defoe, and Pope essayed the pragmatic implications of their ideas, including the means to success in a free market. They also described the political corollary of the Newtonian universe: a constitutional regime—moderate, stable, and benevolent—embodied by the Hanoverian government.[59]

Shaftesbury was among the most provocative of these writers. He gained notoriety as a defender of sociability—collective moral loyalties—against the likes of Thomas Hobbes and Bernard Mandeville, who were reputed to confirm philosophical materialism and moral hedonism, or ruthless self-interestedness, in social affairs.[60] A deist, Shaftesbury elided Newton's cosmology with Stoic natural philosophy, arguing that the social order tended by design to balance and harmony. Individuals fitted into this order, securing their happiness and public success, as they heeded innate affections for benevolence, or sympathy. Public communities reinforced this instinct for virtue by honoring sociability and shaming vicious self-interestedness. Admired especially by Addison, and excerpted in *The Tatler*, *The Spectator*, and the *Guardian*, Shaftesbury promoted "Good-Breeding," as he put it, as a means of moral education. Proper demeanor, decorum, plain and intelligible speech, polite conversation, moderation, urbanity, and cordial gesture not only revealed social dispositions but also trained them. Social presentation, by Shaftesbury's account, made inner character legible. By implication, commercial and polite performance provided material means to happiness, cultivated civility, enforced webs of social dependencies, and brought individuals pursuing their natural instincts into a sociable union.[61]

For many orthodox Protestants, Shaftesbury's formulations were useful—they refuted selfish materialism—yet also distressing. They epitomized a trend among the genteel to reject fundamental Christian tenets for the sake of natural sentiment. In England moderate and liberal Anglicans resisted Shaftesbury's deism by contending that natural morality reinforced, rather than contradicted, customary Christian teaching. The English bishop Tillotson, a latitudinarian, and his more conservative, fiercely anti-Catholic colleague Edward Stillingfleet appeared particularly deft at correlating self-improvement with Protestant creed. An inspired preacher whose sermons were avidly consumed on both sides of the Atlantic, Tillotson offered a pragmatic, irenic, and reasonable Christianity. Coming from a dissenting family background, he espoused a broad-based Protestant

union held together by toleration, simplified doctrine, resistance to Catholicism, and universal moral duties. He stressed the revelation of divine
truth in the natural order as an important parallel to Scripture, and even
as superior to Scripture when it came to convincing skeptics.[62]

Tillotson maintained that Protestant belief was reasonable because it
accorded with natural affections and desires for happiness. The titles of his
most popular sermons illustrate his strategy to show the rationality and the
"profit" of religion: "The Wisdom of Being Religious," "The Advantages
of Religion to Societies," and "The Advantage of Religion to Particular
Persons." Because religion, as Tillotson put it, offered the "present pleasure" of moral contentment and the "assurance of a future reward," it produced inner tranquillity and "satisfaction." It thereby tamed irrational passions and bred self-control, moderation, and toleration. In sum, it
generated benevolence. According to Tillotson, Jesus himself displayed
"Constancy and Resolution in that which was good, without Stiffness or
Conceit, and Peremptoriness of Humor"; "his Virtues were shining without Vanity, Heroical without anything of Transport, and very extraordinary
without being in the least extravagant." The Savior incarnated politeness.
Excepting the sacraments and belief in the mediation of Christ, Tillotson
concluded, "all the duties of Christian religion which respect God are no
other but what natural light prompts men to," which is to say promote
human well-being. True religion made for sociability and good reputation.
Christian teaching—derived from the Bible or from reflection on nature—
gave people duties that thus accrued to their happiness.[63]

Tillotson and other latitudinarian writers modeled a rational defense of
orthodoxy in the midst of the Enlightenment; they provided ministers of
the congregational order in Boston with a strategy to combat skepticism
and persuade their parishioners of the civility of Christian devotion. Progressives in Massachusetts imported his works at a brisk clip after 1690.
Even the otherwise conservative Increase Mather boasted that Tillotson
was "as precious and as valued amongst the people of New England" as he
was in England for his apologetic usefulness. The archbishop's sermons,
compiled in fourteen volumes, sold well in Boston, purchased by Harvard
students, merchants, and pastors. Cotton Mather and Pemberton owned
copies of serial publications—so-called genteel periodicals such as *History
of the Works of the Learned*, *Weekly Memorials for the Ingenious*, and *The Spectator*—that offered bits of Tillotson at every turn. Thomas Robie—a Cambridge preacher, tutor at Harvard, Fellow of the Royal Society, natural
philosopher, and Boston's most famous almanac writer—cribbed most of
his sermons from Tillotson. Ebenezer Pemberton purchased his collected
works. Colman cited him more than he did any other divine.[64]

Bostonians collected a hodgepodge of other publications from the British Enlightenment in this period. They favored periodicals such as *The*

Spectator and *The London Magazine*, anti-Catholic polemicists such as Stillingfleet, disciples of Tillotson such as John Wilkins, and theologians who expounded on the natural evidences for providence. Ministers in the town used them against what they perceived to be the potential for infidelity among their fellow citizens. Merchants such as Hall not only acquainted themselves with dangerous ideas in London but also had access in Massachusetts to an increasing number of English publications that jabbed at traditional Christianity. Periodicals published in Boston for the first time, such as Benjamin Franklin's *New-England Courant* (1717–1723), and, two decades later, *The American Magazine*, imitated *The Spectator* and reprinted essays from *The Gentleman's Magazine;* they brought satire, wit, scientific news, international affairs, and assaults on Reformed religion to the streets of Boston. Pemberton and Colman deployed the very language of such critiques, arguing that Christianity was more reasonable and virtuous than the skepticism of its detractors.[65]

A succession of benefactors and tutors at Harvard attempted to align its curriculum with this rational defense of Christianity. Patron Thomas Hollis loaded the college library with deistic and latitudinarian books. He established a professorship of divinity and natural philosophy, designed to demonstrate a correlation between Christian doctrine and the new cosmology. Beginning in the 1680s, tutors John Leverett, Charles Morton, and William Brattle adjusted the teaching of ethics from an Aristotelian model compatible with puritan divinity to, in succession, Cartesianism, the sentimentalist, affective morality of Tillotson and Shaftesbury, and the natural-law theories of Grotius and Pufendorf. William's brother Thomas, who excelled as a mathematician and astronomer (Newton included some of his observations on comets in *The Principia*), took on students as a private tutor, teaching them that the clarity and universality of mathematical language made it an ideal vehicle to assert the wisdom of providence. Thomas Brattle, along with Smibert, gave architectural expression to these ideals in simple, symmetrical, and spacious designs for college buildings and for new Brattle Street and Old South meetinghouses. Through textbooks, lectures, and even its architecture, Harvard trained students such as Hall to confirm Christianity in the vernacular of rational moral philosophy.[66]

Intellectual currents from England flowed through Harvard, as it were, into the parishes of Boston, where many pastors made selective use of writers such as Tillotson to engage a cultural discourse defined by debates between latitudinarian Anglicans and deists, moral-sense ethicists such as Shaftesbury and Hobbesians, Cartesian rationalists and Newtonian empiricists. Massachusetts ministers made sense of the intellectual swirl in different ways. Conservatives, such as Old North's Joshua Gee and New North's John Webb (we might also include Cotton Mather, but he often defied definition in such terms), rebuffed ecumenical and latitudinarian ideas.

Outside Boston, John Hancock of Braintree and John Barnard of Mar-
blehead verged on a nearly deistic fervor for reason apart from supernatural
revelation. Despite different theological emphases among them, the majority of Boston preachers stood somewhere in the middle: Wadsworth and
Foxcroft of First Church; Pemberton, Joseph Sewall, and Prince of Old
South; Colman and William Cooper of Brattle Street; and Brattle and Nathaniel Appleton of Cambridge. In their Sunday sermons and public sermons and lectures, they made repeated references to the wonders of the
Newtonian cosmos, the compatibility between divine revelation and philosophical reason, the utility of scientific advancement, the virtues of equanimity and inner contentment, the value of practical performance for the
civil society, and the preeminence of the British Empire for liberty and
civility—all as a defense of Christian belief and motive for conversion.[67]

Colman, the most influential among the orthodox liberals, described
their agenda as soundly Tillotsonian. He struck the new moral philosophy,
with its mandates to industry, self-control, and refinement, to spark conversion. His appeals may at first glance appear merely as reiterations of
the social agendas of Boston's urban elite: commercial advancement and
political stability.[68] Yet he mustered that language for transcendent purposes; he fashioned reasonableness and civility to serve piety. In a 1717
lecture after their funerals, he eulogized William Brattle and Pemberton
in such terms. They preached repentance, Christ, and a godly life with
refinement, industry, and prudence. Attentive to the latest philosophical
and scientific advances, according to Colman, Brattle drew reasons for
belief out of the cosmic order. He exhibited the finest sociability; he
"was *Wise* and *Discreet*; *Humane, Affable, Courteous* and *Obliging*; *Free, Open,
Sincere* and *Upright, Tender, Compassionate* and *Bountiful*." For his part,
Pemberton preached with "*Logic*" and reason; yet his sermons "were *Practical, Pathetical* and very *Moving*; *Illuminating, Affecting, Convincing*." He inspired morality without dogmatism. He inculcated patriotism, the "Sincere
and Ardent" love of one's "*Country*." Both Brattle and Pemberton had "a
Catholick and Enlarged Soul."[69]

In his most formal statement on the cultivation of piety as a rational
duty, a 1723 lecture aptly entitled *God Deals with Us as Rational Creatures*,
Colman asserted a firm congruence between natural laws, an innate moral
conscience, and belief. The use of "right reason" to discern "the law and
light of Nature" revealed duties to God, human sinfulness, and the need
for repentance. Even apart from the Bible—or the sacramental, church
community, for that matter—every individual ought to "reason with
himself," to "stand in awe and commune with thy own heart" and
"hear God's reasonings, and use" his or her "own reasoning faculty."
Conversion to Christ stemmed from the reasonable exercise of moral

"Conscience within " Even Shaftesbury's idea of sentiment could lead to Christ if rightly corrected.[70]

In less formal, weekly sermons to their parishioners, Colman and his colleagues also derived evangelical appeals from the most current moral categories. The merchant Edward Bromfield Jr. recorded such applications time and again in his sermon notebooks. By his hearing, Pemberton, Colman, Cooper, and Joseph Sewall issued a steady stream of denunciations "against impolite behaviors," as he tersely summarized one of Cooper's performances. They contrasted the virtues of piety, such as contentment and cheerfulness, with the sins of social disruption, such as swearing, slander, and disorderliness. Another parishioner from Old South noted the same moralizations from Pemberton: the importance of deliberation, perception and judging one's place in the social world, and acting industriously in performance of rational duties. The final exhortations in these sermons, however, were dependably evangelical: flee worldliness, attend to the soul, and trust in Christ. These were reasonable, and self-advancing, responses to the natural order.[71]

As they replaced puritan languages with idioms of the British Enlightenment, Boston's clergy redefined the meaning of providence. According to leaders of the Great Migration such as Cotton and Winthrop, providence ruled society through the gathered church and its peculiar discipline. Spokesmen during the 1660s and 1670s such as Increase Mather extended the conception of providence to New England as a covenanted social order, including commercial and legal institutions designed to promote civil prosperity. Writing during the next four decades, Cotton Mather and Samuel Sewall located the workings of providence chiefly in the political and economic events shaping the new British Empire: the struggle for Protestant and English hegemony across the Atlantic world. The generation of Benjamin Colman and Ebenezer Pemberton, pastors to merchants such as Hugh Hall during the 1710s, 1720s, and 1730s, diffused providence through the matrices of nature: God ruled humanity through a universal, which is to say natural, law.

Ideas about providence admittedly overlapped between generations and varied among different contemporaries; Boston Protestants absorbed contested ideas about divine power and mundane events.[72] Yet they accepted a common mandate to correlate providence with the natural order as described by empirical science. A succession of English writers with latitudinarian sentiments attempted to demonstrate that only a personal deity could have designed and held together the delicately balanced Newtonian cosmos. As such, nature revealed the existence of a benevolent Creator. It also revealed the glories of stability and moderation, the very virtues Whigs associated with England's new constitutional monarchy. Through the 1710s, popular writers such as the essayist Richard Bentley, the geologist

John Woodward, and the poet Richard Blackmore, along with so-called physicotheologians such as William Derham, William Whiston, and John Ray, celebrated the natural order, from planetary orbits and comets to the seemingly inexhaustible fecundity of the earth, as a divinely created text. It disclosed God's intention for the state and society. Nature guided human reflection and action.[73]

In Boston, Cotton Mather set a precedent for new understandings of providence in a succession of essays, culminating in his 1721 *The Christian Philosopher*. In that work, Mather departed from an earlier providential narrative, most notably written by his father. Increase had cataloged prodigies and portents in New England's history—comets, amazing deliverances from storms at sea, earthquakes, and appearances of the devil—to provide empirical evidence of supernatural forces that propelled history. Cotton Mather had produced interpretations along these lines in his early career, but shifting cultural concerns compelled him eventually to deemphasize extraordinary events. Enchanted by Newton and other scientific heroes such as Leeuwenhoek and Huygens, Mather focused on natural wonders. Rather than describe supernatural events, he compiled *curiosa*: New World phenomena such as exotic species, geological oddities, and astronomical peculiarities. The Royal Society granted him membership in 1713 for his frequent correspondence about natural philosophy.[74]

Although he returned time and again to chiliastic predictions about the end of history, Mather described a cosmos rationally ordered within history. His *Christian Philosopher* sounded thoroughly Newtonian notes: God had designed the universe as an "immense *Machine*" or an "*Engine* in all its *Motions*" that gave "so glorious a Spectacle" of divine power. "Whatever is natural is delightful," Mather gushed, "and has a tendency to Good." Depending on the formulations of Whiston, Ray, Derham, and Boyle, Mather explained nature as a society wondrously engineered by design rather than by miracle. He affirmed that "the Light of Reason is the Work of God" and "the Law of Reason is the Law of God."[75]

Other Bostonians, following Mather's example, relied on vocabularies of "natural religion" and "the dictate of nature." They absorbed natural theologies such as Boyle's *Christian Virtuoso*, Durham's *Astro-Theology*, and Whiston's *New Theory of the Earth*. These works gave confidence to Pemberton, Wadsworth, Foxcroft, and Prince that they could decode current events without resorting to biblical typology or apocalypticism. Reason discerned divine intentions because providence worked chiefly through secondary causes. Although Boston presses still produced the occasional piece filled with miraculous portents, and many rural New Englanders still detected supernatural powers in odd phenomena such as two-headed snakes, popular publications such as Robie's almanacs insisted on the regularity of providence and scientific explanations for current affairs.[76]

New paradigms for providence allowed congregational ministers to describe God's activity as rational and therefore credible. They asserted that God's ways conformed to verifiable sequences by design. Although they insisted that supernatural intervention propelled the momentous events of scriptural history—the creation and preservation of Israel, the coming of Christ, redemption, and the Last Judgment—they nonetheless argued that God worked by intelligible and benevolent design within contemporary history. Minimizing miracles and moral rules that contradicted reason, they largely restricted the work of providence to the creation and observation, as it were, of an otherwise self-regulating system. Providence thus served as a rubric to interpret events that had quite natural causes. It set ordinary life in meaningful patterns.[77]

Colman produced a major statement along these lines: four lectures prefaced by Pemberton and filled with citations to Tillotson and other latitudinarian bishops. Published in 1715 under the misleading title *A Humble Discourse of the Incomprehensibleness of God*, Colman's treatise contained an ambitious explanation of the comprehensibility of God's work. Emphasizing the goodness and beauty of the created order, he centered his lectures on the evidence for providence in the design of the cosmos and the human mind. Without any mention of miracles, he maintained that providence ruled human societies as it did the natural system, regulating events through natural law to promote integration and balance, produce prosperity, and restrain vice. Following Colman, Thomas Prince instructed New Englanders to interpret even unusual events such as comets and earthquakes in a similar manner. One could attribute earthquakes to natural laws—the explosion of sulfurous vapors in underground caverns, for example—yet conclude that God included them in the design of the world to induce conversions.[78]

Writers on both sides of the Atlantic probed the meaning of the economy as a subset of this cosmic order. They described commerce as a series of natural exchanges that, by the law of nature, coalesced into a balanced system. This reading prompted pastors and merchants to imagine the natural dynamics of exchange as a divinely sanctioned, moral good. Innate desires brought people together into networks of trade that depended on mutuality, confirming the natural integration of variety into a whole; as Foxcroft put it, nature "impresses men with a deep sense of the bonds and benefits of society; and so excites them to feel the good of others" as they pursued their own economic good, "rendering their work daily more and more natural." God designed the market as a system that ran by moral laws.[79]

One commentator after another—from Tillotson to Defoe, Addison, and Steele, to their admirers in Boston churches—validated the market of their day as a moral order that rewarded virtue, punished vice, and contained natural incentives to virtue. They maintained that success in Britain's commercial system required constancy, frugality, moderation, and fairness, and thereby moderated dangerous, violent, and antisocial passions. Defoe praised the "Beauty and Concern of Providence" for creating a sytem in which commercial prosperity stemmed from moral exertion. "Nothing obeys the Course of Nature more exactly than Trade," he contended, because "Causes and Consequences follow as directly as Day and Night." An unencumbered market lavished riches on the honest and hardworking and impoverished the antisocial and lazy. It inculcated personal responsibility and virtue. Just as the political economists had contended, the market appeared less as a construct of human cupidity than as an expression of natural moral law.[80]

Defoe gave perhaps the fullest explanation of this providential reading of the economy, and its implications for daily exchange, in his widely read *The Complete English Tradesman* (London, 1726). Written to validate the callings of merchants and shopkeepers—and to deflate the pretensions of England's landed aristocracy—Defoe's moral essay cum handbook reminded its readers that natural laws of cause and effect ran through every turn in business. Providence rewarded sagacity and diligence with success and punished ignorance and sloth with failure, as a matter of course, a moral law. Aspiring businessmen ought therefore to learn the "arcane" and peculiar "language" of trade, just as divines mastered doctrine, and compile a *"lexicum technicum"* of commercial and legal terms. They were to devote themselves tirelessly to their ledgers. "Books," he advised, "like a Christian conscience, should always be kept clean and clear." He maintained that tradesmen ought to sell any commodity, including slaves, that commanded a profit, make any business decision that secured their reputation, invest in their shops, and subordinate all other pursuits, including religious meetings and even marriage, to establish themselves. They were to revere their customers as "idols," pursue debtors in court with moral fervor, and show themselves honest, diligent, and impeccable. Defoe's tone rose to religious heights. He insisted that "trade is a business *for* life" and "must, I say, be worked at, not played with." No preacher sounded more serious.[81]

Defoe predicted that these virtues would be rewarded with public honor and economic satisfaction. The energetic trader would benefit Britain and merit the title true patriot, because "the greatest trading country in the world" depended completely on the "knowledge of the world" gained by her merchants. Transposing Barbon and North into contemporary idioms of sociability, Defoe extolled the politeness, the learning, and the money that merchants brought home. Civic virtues and economic prosperity worked in tandem. Moral education bred honesty and industriousness (as Hall so often claimed for himself); honesty built reputation; reputation secured credit; credit brought profits; and profits funded the means of

politeness, from education to tasteful consumer goods. The nation flourished because Englishmen were, as other writers claimed, "a polite and
commercial people."[82]

In accepting the discourse of natural theology, progressives within Boston's congregational order aligned their economic teaching with the logic
represented by Defoe's *English Tradesman*.[83] They took it as their task not
to critique the market but to illumine the moral laws that determined its
course and outcomes. Arguing against their own tradition, they rejected
older puritan economic ideas as irrationally critical of commerce. They
also articulated an alternative to the sheer materialism of Hobbes and Mandeville, which robbed exchange of providential purpose. They set out to
explain the dispositions and actions, the moral affections and behaviors,
that brought success and meaning in the transatlantic market. In the process, they fashioned an economic morality more attuned to rational laws
of reward and punishment, effort and desert, than to older Protestant notions of the mysteriousness—the unpredictability, grace, and inequity—of
economic life. Like Defoe, they emphasized the necessity for knowledge,
technique, and industriousness as the means by which providence superintended the economic order.

Boston's ministers admittedly differed in their formulations. Mather and
Wadsworth, more so than Pemberton, Colman, and Foxcroft, worried that
the mercantilist icons of empire, wealth, and liberty, so wondrously portrayed by Burgis and essayed by Addison and Defoe, tempted parishioners
to compromise their Christian identity. It was all too easy to submerge
providence beneath economic mandates. Wadsworth and Mather especially returned to conventional motifs in the 1710s: market temptations to
deception, materialism, miserliness, and oppression.[84] The younger generation of ministers at First Church, Old South, and Brattle Street analyzed
economic problems more readily in the context of cosmopolitan agendas.
Less anxious than their older colleagues about the loss of corporate Christian identity, they urged individuals toward a universal moral discipline: an
affective, individual, and interior consent to the cultural and commercial
laws of nature as the laws of God.

Pemberton dosed his merchant parishioners weekly with this discipline.
He often cited Locke on the value of labor to establish character, and he
once proposed that Boston form a committee to conduct an annual review
of each resident's productivity, with the threat of removal to the idle. In
his regular Sunday sermons, he emphasized the maintenance of social order
by industriousness and the rewards people earned by their diligence. Appealing frequently to "the God of nature" and the "infinite wisdom" of
design, he claimed that "there is a stated rule whereby God exercises his
government in the distribution either of prosperity or adversity," a
"method to entail prosperity on their posterity" that was "not infallible

but" nonetheless "the best probable." That method, which intelligent people understood ("it implies the approbation of our understandings," as he
put in another sermon), consisted partly in the cultivation of inner virtue.
One merchant heard Pemberton maintain that "virtue, wisdom, reputation
increases wealth and outward prosperity" by the "wise and sovereign institution of God." In other sermons, Pemberton admonished his parishioners
to avoid frivolous socializing, dalliance, and other diversions; like Defoe,
he advised constant assiduity. "Do your own business," he scolded. He
promised prosperity in return for such effort. Other pastors figured the
same equation in their weekly preaching. They issued evangelical appeals,
but their moralizing on nature and diligence contained straightforward assertions of a natural law of reward and punishment in economic matters.[85]

Boston's progressives interpreted political governance in Boston and
London through natural law as well. When it came to economic and political matters, they maintained that providential rule ran through universal
principles of causation, rather than through peculiar interventions in
worldly affairs. In a 1705 lecture, Pemberton used natural analogies, rather
than sacred history, to explain the problems of depreciated currency, high
rates of taxation, and partisan politics in Massachusetts. He described New
England as a body politic, subject to the "Natural" and "Moral" principles
governing the fate of all other governments. Just as disease produced symptoms in the biological body, so moral failure caused symptoms in the political body. "Immoralities," as Pemberton put it, inevitably "strike at the very
Vitals of the Body Politick." Large public debts—that is, recent emissions
of underfunded bills of credit—revealed dishonesty, the bane of commercial reputation. Unfair and increasing taxation, like bad court judgments,
manifested injustice. Cheating in the marketplace—the common lament
that prompted calls for a regulated market—indicated indolence. Political
divisions and contentions, along with slander against the government,
stemmed from envy, base self-interest, and prejudice. Vice invited further
ruin. Pemberton's list of moral causes and social effects conformed to economic reason and pragmatic judgment.[86]

Preachers often linked corporate calamity to immorality, but they did not
ascribe current problems to betrayals of historic rules and departures from
previous generations. They made little reference to biblical and creedal
standards. The antidotes consisted not only in policy but also in the cultivation of the proper cosmopolitan virtues such as honesty, industry, legal propriety, and patriotism. The fate of the province, Prince held, depended on
natural virtues, not on the particular religious positions of its citizens or
adherence to bygone proscriptions against market behaviors. He thus urged
the governor, Council, and Assembly to promote "every Publick and Private
Virtue"—to inculcate toleration, moderation, and justice—because providence worked to "smile upon Persons of Wisdom and Credit."[87]

Pemberton, Prince, and their colleagues extended this logic to national politics. They dispensed with the providentialist narratives of the 1690s, 1700s, and 1710s, which previous pastors had infused with prophetic significance. As they abandoned supernatural motifs, they validated the ordinary means of Britain's power. Political sagacity, economic competence, legal facility, and diplomatic success—all grounded on the virtues of a constitutional monarchy—served the cause of God throughout the British Atlantic.

Foxcroft proposed this reading in his 1727 sermon on the succession of George II. He suggested analogies between recent monarchs and Israelite leaders: William III as Moses, George I as David. He explained them, however, as mere resemblances, rather than literal and extraordinary equivalents. By natural design, "Providence" sustained any regime that ruled according to principles of virtue and toppled any regime that violated the moral law. Generously quoting from liberal Anglican apologists, Foxcroft argued that "the *Hanover Succession*" had triumphed because it promoted liberty and toleration. George I had preserved peace in Europe, restored and extended Britain's trade through prudent treaties, and fixed the public treasury. He thereby had restored "the public *Faith*": a tellingly religious idiom for confidence in the Bank of England. Foxcroft concluded by urging the citizens of Boston to locate themselves in the scope of the Hanoverian dynasty: to mourn the loss of George I as their loss, honor the new king as their king, pray for the nation's trade, defer to the judgments of Lieutenant Governor William Dummer (a favorite of London), and express gratitude for a sovereign whose virtues secured their well-being.[88]

Foxcroft, along with Colman, explained the relationship among natural law, providence, and the government in a somewhat haphazard fashion; Prince devoted himself to a full elucidation. One year after Foxcroft's sermon on the succession of George II, Prince spoke on the arrival of the new governor, William Burnet. In his lecture, Prince argued that God once ruled ancient Israel by special providences and covenantal promises but now supervised "every" Protestant "Kingdom, Country and Community," regardless of "Sects or Parties," by general providence: secondary means, or natural principles, of political prosperity. Just as God preserved the cosmos through the "invisible" yet powerful laws that Newton illuminated, so God appointed political rulers to follow universal principles of virtue; these were the secondary means through which providence guided states.[89]

In his 1730 election sermon, a celebration of the centenary of Boston's founding, Prince expanded his interpretation. He maintained that the biblical record revealed a peculiar covenant for ancient Israel. God blessed Moses with "natural powers" and political excellencies, but the covenant was fulfilled especially through the miraculous conquest of Canaan. New England was different. Providence superintended all current societies through secondary means only: the moral law and ordinary civic virtues. Prince put this quite clearly: "the Works of the LORD for Them [Israel] were of a *miraculous* Nature, they were the visible Operations of GOD beside the Course of natural Causes; whereas his Righteous Acts" for New England were done "by his invisible tho' real Influence according to the Course of *Nature*, which is nothing else but the usual manner of acting and ruling the World." God "might if He pleased" have led New England through miracle, but God chose instead to "operate agreeable to the *Course of Nature*."[90]

Prince likened Massachusetts to Israel in that it had just and wise rulers—Winthrop and John Cotton in parallel to Moses and Aaron—"excepting miracles." New England's success derived from its quite mundane strengths: the "Patience" and heroism of civic rulers who embodied "love of country" and desire for "order" and "liberty." Reinterpreting the first generation as devotees of the Crown, Prince described them as tolerant and ecumenical, always deferential to the monarch and established church. They led a "sober, civil, charitable quiet, loyal People" through toil and trouble to the current prosperity. "The usual Course of Providence among" the colonists, Prince announced, ran not through ruptures in natural historical causation but through ordinary human efforts. Provincial rulers who understood "our Constitution, Genius, Circumstance, and chief Concern and Interest," and, above all, monarchs who exhibited "Virtue, Learning, Power and Figure," shielded New England from its foes.[91]

Prince had long aspired to write a full history of New England, and in 1736 he produced his first version, *A Chronological History of New-England*. It represented a clear break from previous accounts: the wonder-working providences of Johnson, the jeremiads of the second generation, and Mather's overwrought and fantastic *Magnalia*. Prince set New England's story within a universal framework, only the latest chapter in a political narrative beginning with Adam and running through the Israelite kings to the first Saxon ruler (Egbert) and subsequent English monarchs. Rather than refer to biblical prophecy or acts of God, he authored a straightforward, even pedestrian political account. Quoting selectively from Bradford, he narrated the founding of Plymouth and Boston, probing for "the orderly Succession" of events. His dedication and preface suggested his history's culmination in the "ILLUSTRIOUS HOUSE" of Hanover, which had spread "British Happiness" around the globe. Prince identified Massachusetts with a natural order reflected in the imperial system and its networks of exchange. Given this thrust toward commercial empire, Boston's merchants responded by supporting the *Chronological History*. Thirty-four New England traders subscribed to its publication, including Hugh Hall and his closest associates in Boston: Belcher, Bowdoin, the younger Bromfield, Lynde, Storer, and John and David Jeffries.[92]

Ideas about nature and history had important implications for everyday business. Just as Boston ministers took cues from English latitudinarians on the reasonableness of Christianity—the congruence between natural law, civility, and orthodox doctrine—so too they echoed English writers who fashioned commercial imperatives from rational Protestantism. Divines such as Tillotson legitimated market-driven techniques as they stressed reasoned moral affections rather than conformity to traditional rules. His ethics reflected a long trend in Anglican teaching away from highly scripted duties that bounded commerce. Devotional writers from the Restoration period, who were immensely popular through the 1720s and widely read by Boston merchants, also emphasized the importance of inner moral states over external regulation. Richard Allestree's *Whole Duty of Man* and *Gentleman's Calling* focused on care for the interior life: moderation, patience, and equanimity. In his *Alarm to Unconverted Sinners*, a best seller reprinted in Boston in 1716, Joseph Alleine counseled temperance, humility, and gravity as the chief means to conversion.[93]

This Christianized version of Stoic moralism suited an economic ethos oriented to private virtue within a rational market system. Tillotson suggested that genuine piety, or inner virtue, in fact, cohered with commercial ambition. Making no reference to customary restrictions on commerce, including slave trading, he advised businessmen to pursue riches according to their reason. In his most extensive comments on trade, he maintained that "the Business of Religion" was "no hindrance to a Man's thriving in his Temporal Estate." Rather, religion was "apt to promote and advance" wealth because piety inculcated diligence and prudence. Christianity nurtured inner contentment, for example, which prompted justice and honesty, and those virtues "are the best way to establish a clear and solid Reputation, and good Esteem among Men, which is an unspeakable advantage in Business, and, at the long run, one of the best and most lasting Instruments of Prosperity and Success." Religious verities played out in civility, social refinement, and economic power.[94]

Boston preachers such as Colman followed suit. They urged a generous spirit and issued warnings against avaricious materialism, but often defined "virtue" in terms of genteel dispositions rather than obedience to biblically laden rules. As a result, they refrained from denunciation of profitable exchange practices: usurious lending rates, market-driven prices, luxury commodities, and aggressive litigation. As Boston merchants listened to their sermons, they heard exhortations to reasonableness, patriotism, and inner regulation without reference to older puritan commands. The God of the natural order cared more about sociability and sincerity than about peculiar covenantal obligations.

The lesson—that good manners bred moral approval and commercial success—was not lost on men such as Hugh Hall, nor was the implication that inner, affective virtues eclipsed conformity to older rules for economic behavior. Pemberton and Colman's ideal merchants maintained inner tranquillity, and therefore godliness, even in the midst of fantastic wealth. Previous lists of forbidden practices, including wearing wigs, dancing, consuming luxuries, as well as usury and oppression, did not translate into this moral discourse. Colman celebrated polite virtues such as cheerfulness and "Civil Mirth" as religious expression, just one of many accessions to the new sociability also displayed in elegant homes, civic ceremonies, and coffeehouses. For the preachers of the 1710s and 1720s, even the word "covetousness," which launched previous puritans into lengthy excoriations of avaricious behaviors, provoked observations chiefly on contentment. Joseph Sewall's lecture on the topic in 1718 focused on individuals' affections: the dangers of heightened material passions, "discontentment," "an immoderate Solicitude of Mind about getting," and an "excessive grief" at "Wordly losses." He argued that a more Stoical disposition conformed to true spirituality. Even when Sewall, Colman, and Foxcroft promoted philanthropy, they transformed what had been labeled "almsgiving" into "beneficence": a sign of gentility, high social status, and cosmopolitan manners.[95]

Other Boston pastors enunciated similar views. Among them, Thomas Foxcroft of First Church most explicitly argued that genteel behavior stemmed from inner virtue and conformed individuals to natural law. Discoursing on Colossians 3:12 ("put on kindness"), Foxcroft launched into a full-bored exposition of politeness. According to him, the apostle Paul meant that our "*Deportment towards others*" ought to display "a certain Placedness, Civility, Courteousness, Sweetness and Easiness in our Behaviour, whereby we willingly accommodate our selves to them for their Good." As Foxcroft elucidated this "accommodation," he did not make traditional pleadings for almsgiving and forgiveness of debts. He promoted proper gesture, from doffing one's hat and bowing to the "Civilities of common Converse," including "proper Titles of Respect." Just as Tillotson's Jesus incarnated refinement, so too did Foxcroft's Jesus, who was "free, familiar, open, affable, friendly." Dismissing puritan reserve as severe and "sour," Foxcroft suggested that conviviality and decency surmounted mere appearance. They made genuine social connection, "a commerce or Reciprocation of Good Deeds, a mutual Giving and Accepting of Kindness." As such, politeness "indicates a certain *Greatness* and noble *Generosity* of Soul," a "singular Amiableness." It was, in sum, benevolent. It revealed an inner conformity to sentiments that were "entirely consonant to the genuine Dictates of natural Reason." As the final step in this Enlightenment logic, Foxcroft promised that "this Virtue" was so "*approved of men*," that is, functioned as social credit, that it provided more "Excellency of Power" in "Business" than did any other tactic.[96]

Orthodox ministers took care to distinguish purely mundane sagacity—the sort of secularized technique recommended by Mandeville and flaunted in the Exchange Alley of London—from real moral wisdom. Metropolitan mores easily could degenerate into pure avarice. Pemberton advised the father of a young merchant about to embark for Europe to teach his child to follow his "Natural Instinct" and "the fundamental principle of Self-love" in his affairs; but only if the son realized that trust in divine providence, rather than profit mongering, effected contentment, courage, and endurance in business, and thereby enhanced the chances for commercial success.[97]

Mather, who alternated between older puritan ideals and the latest moral advances, exhorted merchants in a 1714 lecture to resist temptations to selfishness during economic downturns; they should trust that God would bless acts of charity. In an election sermon from the same year, Connecticut's Samuel Whitman warned businessmen against drawing the wrong conclusion from the fact that "Vile Men" did often "flow in Wealth." In the long run, he insisted, "the way to the Paradise of Temporal Prosperity, lieth thro' the Temple of Vertue." God designed the law of nature to reward genuine moral goodness—charity and piety along with diligence and knowledge—not Mandeville's self-directed and narrow-minded avarice.[98]

These and other oft-repeated warnings strengthened ministers' claims that commercial achievement could be made morally pure and turned to providential purposes. The good merchant avoided get-rich schemes and risky ventures; he worked hard and wisely for the commonweal. Linking polite virtues with science and commerce, Colman asserted that businessmen ought to grasp the natural connection between diligence and success. All people participated in a natural system that God designed for constant motion and interaction. "As the *Wheels* of a *Clock* or *Watch*, when set in order and wound up, are manifestly design'd by the *Artificer* for *Motion*," Colman claimed, using a perfectly Newtonian metaphor, "so much more is MAN *curiously wro't* and artfully designed by GOD his *Maker*, for an exact and regular, constant Course of Action," for "*Diligence* and *Dispatch* of Business." The Newtonian cosmos reflected a moral law. "Diligence" was "the Universal Example" scripted in "All Nature"; from the fiery cosmos to rushing streams of water, "diligence is necessary to *Proficiency* in any thing; it is the Way of GOD's *Blessing*." Hard work won profits, just as religious exertion won spiritual benefits. Two years later, Wadsworth extended this rationale to explain the rise of poverty in Boston. Idleness, "the Mother of all Vices," had corrupted so many people that the whole economic order teetered. A return to hard work, promoted by employment projects and stricter enforcement of laws against idleness, would, he promised, save Boston's economy. It was a moral surety.[99]

GENTILITY, THE EMPIRE, AND PIETY IN THE AFFAIRS OF HALL

Accepting a naturalized understanding of providence as a rationale for Christian belief, Boston's postpuritan preachers followed the logic of natural philosophy to a nearly complete validation of the market in their day. To be sure, ministers did not speak of "the market" as an abstraction, a fixed system or economic order in sociological terms. Yet they indirectly asserted its worth as they endorsed crucial components in the merchants' vocation: confidence in the design of commerce, an incentive to follow the law of reward for hard work and refinement, trust in the latest techniques of exchange as divine mandates, and moral purpose in the promotion of the British Empire of liberty, Protestantism, and politeness.

Colman outdid all of his colleagues in promoting these values. In his 1719 address to the General Assembly, *The Blessing of Zebulun and Issachar*, he urged an end to partisan quarrels between merchant and farming interests in the Assembly. His sermon rested on an exposition of Deuteronomy 33:18–19, which contains Moses's blessing on two of Israel's twelve tribes: Zebulun, a coastal people who made their living from "trade and merchandize," and Issachar, inland herders and farmers. Colman valorized commerce in remarkable ways as he explained his text. Cotton Mather had also invested commerce with religious purpose in his 1709 address to the Assembly, published as *Theopolis Americana*. He attributed the importance of mercantile wealth to the looming Armageddon between Protestant states and Catholic powers. In contrast, Colman's oration lacked all sense of apocalyptic urgency and sectarian identity. Dissolving the discrete identities of Reformed religion in cosmopolitan waters, he claimed that merchants conveyed civility, urbanity, and ecumenical piety along with their profits. They accordingly contributed to a natural social order—a system without cataclysmic providential intervention—of "mutual dependence" between colony and metropolis, countryside and city.[100]

Colman's cultural assertions provided a thoroughgoing commendation of Boston's transatlantic merchants. He strained to give members of Issachar, the farmers, their due. Settled into a single location and customary beliefs, festivals, and rituals, they preserved tradition. Hardy and honorable, they suffered through drought and freeze to produce essential goods. Massachusetts farmers contributed to the common good by providing food, stabilizing the political order, and reminding reformers of previous puritan ways. Colman made a modest concession to rural conservatives alienated from the progressive practices of the merchants who gathered to celebrate sacramental innovations at churches such as Brattle Street.[101]

By Colman's reading, Moses assigned to "Happy Zebulun"—the dynamic urbanites who traded goods and excelled in military arts—"a double portion of Joy and prosperity." The application to New England was clear. Maritime traders, exchanging their codfish and whale oil and traveling from New England to the West Indies and London, "have ordinarily more knowledge of the Necessities of other places," "keep correspondence with them," and share "Interests among them." In other words, they knew other parts of the empire and spoke the universal language of reason and propriety. Merchants, therefore, unlike inland settlers, could "propagate religion abroad by their Merchandize, and proselyte strangers at home." Colman admitted that profane manners, drunkenness, and vile speech filled "*Seaport* Towns," by which he surely meant Boston; but he admonished countryside critics that "there is sometimes a *singular* spirit of piety and charity in populous trading Towns," demonstrated in missionary societies, publications, and charitable ventures. Drawing on the naturalistic metaphor of the body politic, Colman further linked religious evangelism, cultural propagation, and economic exchange: Boston was "the *Center* of the *Province*" just as London was "of the *Kingdom*"; and "as the *Heart* lies in the midst of the body, and is continually receiving and transmitting the blood," so Boston sent her merchants throughout the transatlantic imperial body.[102]

Exuding optimism, Colman celebrated "abundance" not merely as an instrument for piety but also as a cause for "joy," worship, and reverence toward a beneficent providence. Merchants, those "Happy People! *prosperous* and *pious*," deserved to "be enrich by their commerce and traffick" as a reward for their contributions to Britain. The merchant rightly anticipated "by the favour of God a rich return," spurred on by "joyful hopes" of the "riches importing to him." Abundant profits gave merchants occasion to honor "the direction of Providence in their dealings." He sympathized with traders, who faced constant risk. Ships sank. Ventures failed. Perishable goods rotted. Fires gutted wharves and warehouses. Yet providence gave "direction," as Colman explained, in the form of moral rules to inculcate diligence and honesty. Providence also gave prudential guidance, such as the importance of learning the language of the market (what Defoe called the "*lexicum technicum*") and working through competent ship captains. Finally, recognition of providence evoked the reasonableness of donations to charity. Riches, Colman concluded, were like divine loans, repaid through contributions and public service. Speaking the merchant's vernacular, Colman warned them that profits accrued as so many outstanding bonds and bills, due to a fastidious, divine creditor who kept precise accounts and demanded his "yearly *Usury*." Punctual repayment ensured further credit. Colman could not have legitimated the cultural and economic practices of merchants more clearly. God himself was a polite but strict usurer.[103]

Other pastors followed suit, inserting encomiums to overseas traders here and there in their sermons and lectures, usually reminding their pa-

rishioners of the natural law that required diligence and intelligence from
businessmen. Prince even produced *Vade Mecum*, a handbook of trade that
made success all the easier for Boston merchants and their customers. Crib-
bing from other handbooks and secretary's guides, Old South's pastor presented tables of goods and prices, mathematical instruction and currency
rates, dates of court sessions, and the names of streets in Boston, as a matter
of aesthetic and moral accomplishment. "The *Figures* are much more neat
and beautiful," he claimed, "than those in the like Tables Published in *Great
Britain*," and therefore suited to be of "great Use and Entertainment to
many." The numerous charts and tables of conversion—giving the worth
of so many farthings, shillings, and pounds, correlating measures of commodities (for example, firkins, hogsheads, and gallons) with standard
prices, and orienting travelers to the streets of Boston—served a high purpose. Prince explained that a table of simple and compound interest rates
instructed merchants on how to exchange credit to the best effect. Rather
than condemn usury, as did humanists and puritans, he taught how best to
practice it. He did not bother to distinguish between godly and ungodly
profits from loans or mortgages. From his account, "the Person to whom
Money is due" could equally be called "Creditor, sometimes Usurer, sometimes Mortgager," without shame. Without a hint of moral scruple, Prince
gave advice for taking debtors to court, charging interest, and determining
prices according to the market. His charts and numbers facilitated profitable commerce, and "with the Flourishing of Liberty and Commerce, universal Charity, good Neighbourhood, and every other Virtue that by
the Divine Blessing tends to make" their users "prosperous and happy"
followed. Sagacious dealing in the market, as providence decreed, made
for society.[104]

Prince also framed his *Vade Mecum* to assert patriotic duty. He reminded
merchants of the glories of the English monarchy, listing kings and queens
all the way back to the Saxon Egbert; in this respect, his handbook flowed
directly from his *Chronological History* and, by implication, from his understanding of providence. When inventorying the towns, counties, and court
sessions from New England, through the middle colonies, to Maryland
and Virginia, he identified them equally as parts of the "*British Provinces*
in AMERICA," linked by commercial and legal continuities into an empire
sustained and defined by commerce. His sentiments echoed those of New
Englanders and Londoners who boasted that no Catholic nation could
compete with Britain for wealth: as the *Boston News-Letter* published it,
reprinting an editorial from London, "the Protestants have the Trade and
the Money, let Hell and Rome do their worst." Prince made his contributions to that trade through his sermons, scientific meditations, and guide
to commerce.[105]

Colman and Prince, along with their colleagues, gave merchants confidence that they were moral paragons and servants of providence as they obeyed the laws of trade. Men such as Hall, who fashioned themselves into the genteel as they engaged in previously censured business practices, appeared as patriots and as contributors to the commonweal. In the enlightened precincts of Scotland and England, politeness came to serve as an image for claims that commerce itself, aside from religious or political agendas, encouraged refinement and therefore civil society: the competition for profits prodded individuals to propriety, civility, and discipline. As David Hume put it, "*industry, knowledge,* and *humanity,* are linked together by an indissoluble chain, and are found, from experience as well as reason, to be peculiar to the more polished."[106]

Boston's ministers did not secularize this claim like later moralists such as Hume, but they nonetheless used it in the encomiums they heaped on Boston's new merchants and civil leaders. For Pemberton, John Walley, a wealthy trader, member of the Council, and justice of the Superior Court of Judicature, exemplified the conjunction of economic prowess, political pragmatism, and virtuous gentility. In his funeral sermon for Walley, Pemberton marveled at how Walley had used business and political skills that worked by laws of "*Natural Causality*" as well as of "*Moral Virtue*" to "Advance" the "Happiness" and "Truely valuable Interests of the People." Profits, politeness, and national glory connected in loops of corporate purpose for men such as Walley; pursuing their own riches, they "put many great Advantages into a Peoples hands, to advance" the nation's "Strength, Excellency and Glory." Pemberton omitted mention of the old-fashioned notion that good rulers identified themselves chiefly with the church congregation and adherence to Reformed dictates. Civil society encompassed all other loyalties. Making "the Publick Prosperity their great View," then, great men like Walley used religious and civic institutions "to Promote good Manners among a Generation," which, along with "Civility, Modesty, Diligence, Sobriety, Religion and Devotion are" the "true excellency" of their country. Addison, Defoe, and even Hume did not put it much differently.[107]

Colman commended powerful merchants in equally Tillotsonian terms. In 1720 he eulogized Governor Joseph Dudley—whom Sewall and the Mathers fairly despised for what they thought were his betrayals to New England's political prerogatives—as a man of cosmopolitan sentiment. Colman honored him for his refinement and diligence. "Made for *business,*" Dudley had presented himself in London as an emblem of New England's identification with the metropolis. He displayed such politeness, conversed with such learning, and exhibited such taste for ceremony and ritual that "the highest Prelates of the Church of England" recognized his formidableness. Colman heaped praise on one of his favorite parishioners, Grove

Hirst, the merchant and son-in-law of Samuel Sewall, for his "great *Indus-try and Diligence*" in spite of personal misfortune. In yet another postfuneral lecture, Colman acclaimed the deceased merchant David Stoddard as a man of quiet inner temperament, personal kindness, and excellent conver-sation; Stoddard was "courteous and greateful" and always "ready to oblige." Such civilities amounted to moral vindication—"a blameless life" in Colman's terms.[108]

Just as Old South had its Walley, and Brattle Street its Hirst and Stod-dard, so First Church had its Penn Townsend to evoke the eulogies of Foxcroft. By Foxcroft's reckoning, Townsend, a merchant and member of the Council like Walley, displayed skill and ingenuity in business ventures. He was prompted by a fantastic blend of pragmatic and moral virtues: sci-entific curiosity, an interest in technique, investment in public-works proj-ects, sociable affections, politeness, and piety. He accumulated wealth and sustained wise fiscal policies that steadied New Englanders' credit overseas, adding "to their Reputation in the World." Discountenancing "Idleness, Luxury, Debauchery and Filthiness," he also designed employ-ment projects for the province and promoted a "Reformation of Manners." Men such as Townsend reflected the virtues of the monarchy itself. They were good rulers because they knew how to make the province rich; they could "contrive" the "wisest Expedients to promote the public Interests." Townsend studied "to project and put in Execution wise Schemes for advancing *Trade*."[109]

Foxcroft's invocation of "schemes" to garner wealth with patriotic and providential purpose spoke to postpuritan merchants such as Hugh Hall. Hall in fact fashioned himself after his pastors' worldviews. We might mis-interpret him to have been a type of secular protocapitalist, driven by a Protestant ethos shorn of theology. Immune from church censure and ap-parently oblivious to the moral ideals of classic puritanism, he imported expensive and fashionable items, sold sugar and rum to his compatriots, sent hard-won currency and bills of credit overseas, sued his debtors, con-tributed to the unsettling fluctuation of fiscal values and prices, and dealt in slaves.[110] He engaged in nearly every market practice that evoked con-demnation from previous moralists such as Cotton, Shepard, Willard, and Increase Mather. None of this appeared to trouble his conscience. Unlike Robert Keayne, John Hull, and Samuel Sewall, he expressed little moral anxiety and none of the fidgety ambivalence of his predecessors. He made no resolutions to modesty. He understood commercial ambition to be a matter of politeness, and aggressive technique a cause for pride.

Yet Hall was thoroughly religious. The ideas about commerce and gen-tility, providence and moral law, preached by Pemberton, Colman, Fox-croft, and Prince, shaped his understanding of business. They informed his daily routines. He did not embrace the combative zeal for Protestant empire, heated by eschatological conviction, that drove Sewall and Fitch. He did, however, accept the assertion that trade within the transatlantic British Empire formed networks of sociability. He believed that commerce in the open market coalesced into civil society. He thought that economic expertise merited riches. He in sum embodied religious ideals shaped to science and natural law, a Tillotsonian morality of inner affections, and the language of refinement.

Hall did not write at length about his theological ideas, but he left telling evidence of his attempts to follow the dictates of his teachers at Harvard and Boston's progressive ministers. He practiced a broad-minded, ecumenical Protestantism. A mainstay and lay leader at Brattle Street, he had his children Lydia, Elizabeth, and Pitts baptized by Colman and his colleague William Cooper. He left the Manifesto church for a period, helping to found the West Church in 1736 along with the artist Smibert; he contributed donations and leadership to the erection of its new meetinghouse. He hosted Foxcroft and Prince at his home when they gathered to pray for and bless the new congregation. Fostering a liberal ethos, West Church hired the Scottish Presbyterian William Hooper as its pastor, who, before defecting to Anglicanism in 1746 and becoming rector of Trinity Church in Boston, baptized Hall's sons Hugh and Benjamin. The liberal Jonathan Mayhew succeeded Hooper there, by which time Hall had returned to Brattle Street. In a further gesture to his ecumenical sentiments, he also made gifts to Christ Church (founded in 1722), King's Chapel, and visiting priests. Hall nonetheless developed his closest friendships with fellow merchants at Old South and Brattle Street, especially Brattle, Hirst, and Bromfield the younger. Close to the Leverett and Bromfield families, he served as a pallbearer for their parents—one more indication of the close ties among merchant leaders and their families.[111]

Indebted to his early training under Leverett, Pemberton, and Colman, Hall maintained his interest in their instruction as he built his business. He thanked Colman for his "Tender Affection" and returned the favor by "the high Veneration" he had for Colman and his ideas. He sought Leverett's counsel on several matters and explained that his business designs flowed from "the happy Influences of your good Government." He listened intently to Pemberton as well. Hall's detailed notes on the sermons of Pemberton, Colman, Mather, and others replicate the language used in their published works. Speaking to merchants in their vernacular, by Hall's record, Pemberton described conversion as "the greatest gain" and unbelief as the accumulation of insurmountable debts written with "Gods pen of Iron with the point of a diamond" on eternal ledgers. Pemberton urged spiritual striving as an analog to strenuous effort in business; a diligent use of time was a "good investment," which was "not other than the merchant assures us."[112]

Theological publications equally interested Hall. He purchased copies of Colman's and Mather's printed sermons from Daniel Henchman (in whose shop he also could have sampled almanacs and the latest diatribes against the South Sea Company), bought Mather's *Magnalia* on another occasion, and subscribed to Prince's *Chronological History*. He displayed his cosmopolitan sentiments by donating to Harvard several books, including the major theological work of William Beveredge, the Anglican bishop and a leader of the Promotion of the Gospel in Foreign Parts. Hall praised Beveredge to Leverett as a "Noble" defender of orthodoxy against skepticism. The title of his opus, which Hall noted as "A Compleat System of Divinity," aptly evoked Willard's *Compleat Body of Divinity*, as though Beveredge marked an improvement on Willard: a rational theology emanating from the metropolis for a new generation of students in America.[113]

Hall, in other words, identified completely with the rational and imperial worldview of his religious mentors, from his first visit to London, where he hobnobbed with latitudinarian Anglicans, to his mature years in Boston, when he supported Church of England parishes. Certainly his ecumenical sensibilities rose from family connections: his father's and brother's memberships in the national church and his eagerness to appear properly genteel in their eyes.[114] Yet he also followed the example of ministers such as Colman and Pemberton. They recommended Tillotson to the people of Boston, corresponded with bishops, and adopted low versions of Anglican liturgical and sacramental practices. All British Protestants, from their perspective, belonged to a religious culture defined by common allegiances to Christian belief expressed as reasonable, civil, and patriotic. For them, the word "virtue" captured the ethos of this refined piety.

Such language filled Hall's letters to family and friends. At times, his correspondence with college mates—cluttered by classical allusions and amateur verse—echoed the deistic poetry printed in *The Gentleman's Magazine*.[115] More frequently, Hall resonated with Colman and Pemberton's version of Christian virtue. He thanked his father for sending him to Harvard, which provided him with the best moral training. He asserted his good reputation by resisting the "Unjust and Unchristian Insinuations" of his unbelieving, "Malicious" competitors in England. Writing from Barbados, he informed his Boston friend Elisa Calandar that he had not sunk into a pit of godlessness on the island. Engaging "men of the highest Distinction" and "the best Character," he had "found several not only of Strict Morality, but of true Devotion," so that those New Englanders "who think that here a Christian and a Gentleman are Inconsistent and Opossatives in the same Person" were "mistaken." Barbados may have been "Represented [as] such a Mighty Colossus of Vice, yet great Professors of Religion may find many Worthy of their Imitation and Converse." Hall closed with a profession of providence: "the Views I have of Great Success in Merchantile Affairs" would only come to pass if granted "thro' Divine blessing."[116]

He similarly assured Mary and Edward Bromfield, perhaps the most devout of his mercantile friends, of his piety. He had, as he wrote to Mary from London, "always set an higher Value upon" wholesome social exchange—what he called "that Faciousness [or ease] of Converse"—illuminated by "bright Rays of Vertue and Piety" and prompted by a "good Innate Disposition," than upon profane wit and fancy. When Hall, then in Barbados, had received no correspondence from Edward, he attempted to shore up their relationship by similar professions of Tillotsonian virtue. His "great Success," overseas travel, cosmopolitan socializing, and commercial ventures, by his account, had not corrupted him; indeed, they indicated diligence, Stoic-like reasonableness, a well-focused mind, and godly energies. Hall thus explained himself in idioms borrowed from Colman: "the true spirit of Christianity, Tends to an Alacrity of Heart, and that is the Business of Vertue, to Regulate, and not Extirpate the Affections of the Mind." He had not, he insisted, "lost my Religion, and my Morals," but rather had asserted them in trade. To William Welsteed he professed the same devotion in blunter terms: "I have not Changed my Religion, or Bartered my Moralls, but am in status quo." He could claim as much because his pastors had taught him that commercial ambition, tempered by politeness and moral sincerity, accorded with the laws of providence.[117]

Hall had learned those lessons well. His tutors, pastors, and favorite authors—the proponents of rational Protestantism—identified religious sincerity not by conformity to church-decreed rules but by affections and demeanors that signaled a spiritual understanding of natural forces. Hall detected providence not in portents or miracles but in the ordinary cause and effect running through nature: weather and waves, diligence and success, pious sentiments and social reputation. He accordingly interpreted his affairs as indications of a divine design of the natural order, and therefore of the need for redemption in Christ. A particularly violent storm, suffered on an early voyage from Boston to Barbados, provoked evangelical sentiments, which he recorded in poetic form:

Think O my Soul, Devoutly think,
How with Affrighted Eyes;
Thou saws't the Wide Extended Deep,
In all its Horrors Rise. . . .
The Storm Alayed the Winds Retir'd,'
Obedient to thy Will;
The Sea that Roar'd at thy Command,
At thy Command was still
Therefore in Dangers, Fears and Death;

Thy Goodness I'll Adore,
And Praise Thee for thy Mercies Past,
and humbly, hope for more.
O! That my Life henceforth might be,
A Sacrifice to Thee;
And when sore Death shall be my Doom,
Christs Death may make me Free.[118]

Hall's poem reflected contemporary literary sensibilities (he described it
as being "in so Easy and Familiar a Style") and progressive, Bostonian Protestantism. He expressed the same sentiments in prosaic form to his aunt
Mary Lascelles. He had, he told her, "Rational Assurances" that his ventures would succeed, but if his "most Plausible Schemes should be Un-
hinged, or the most Smiling Projections should be Ennervated," he hoped
that failure would move him "to Consider the hand that does it" and "Influence" him "to a Quiet and Easy Resignation." Stoic moral dispositions
led, as Hall had been instructed, to his "almost continually Contemplating
a Future State," which he trusted "Springs from a sure Principle of Love
and Reverence to the Divine Being, and not from a Base Servile Fear."[119]

Hall also absorbed his pastors' ideas about the political and social context
for providential action: the empire and the spread of civility and the gospel
through its transatlantic domain. Hall shared imperial loyalties with his
family. He took pride in his father's appointment as judge of the vice admiralty in Barbados. His brother Richard, appointed a magistrate and member of the Assembly of Barbados, compiled the laws of the colony into an
influential treatise on colonial administration. It extolled British dominion,
including the colonial bureaucracy required to maintain English liberties
in the Caribbean. Barbadian imports and exports indicated "what value this
and the other English Sugar Colonies are to Great Britain, not only by
supplying it with sugar" and tax receipts, "but also by employing and supporting a great number of mariners and manufactures." It was the same
argument, transposed to Barbados, that Boston's ministers had made for
New England: its legal and social institutions replicated England's, and its
commerce served the nation.[120]

Hugh Hall encountered other versions of imperial pieties, less defined
by administrative and legal matters than was Richard's, but more brightly
colored by moral and political devotion. Attuned to transatlantic politics,
Hugh repeatedly noted affairs from the metropolis, shared rumors of wars
and parliamentary politics with his brother, and exchanged news about the
king's manifestos. Like other merchants, he recorded daily occurrences—
the weather, business exchanges, governmental meetings, activity in Boston's harbor—in almanacs that contained summaries of scientific discoveries, excerpts from moral essays, and celebrations of the monarchy. One of

his almanacs, from 1723, began with a paean to King George, who was "form'd a Prince of mighty State, great Actions brave to do, that true Religion may be spread in every Nation through," which "strikes a dread on *Popish* crues [naval crews]." Every time Hall opened his almanac-diary, he faced a version of Colman's and Prince's politics. In the same almanac he logged the departure of the Massachusetts governor for England, movements of the king, arrivals of ships from Virginia, Barbados, and London, and his latest rental contracts. In such cases, he literally inscribed his affairs in the narrative of imperial events. Each shipment represented a further strand in the networks that sustained the nation's glory.[121]

Projecting himself into Britain's polite and commercial ascendance, Hall asserted his metropolitan credentials. Gentility and politeness expressed his cultural equality with vicious competitors and uppity cousins in London; his investments in Britain's commerce, including slave trading, contributed to the commonwealth. As he wrote to a friend in London in 1718, he was actively engaged in "setting" his "Heredity Estate and like the rest of Mankind strenuously Cultivating" his "Interest in Order to an happy Establishment in the World," and he did so with nationalistic fervor. "Boston N. England," he boasted, was an "Epitome of your Noble Metropolis London." He frequently referred to "our Nation." Like London's political economists, he understood trade as a tool of Britain's "contests" for empire. In 1719 he exchanged patriotic optimism, along with commercial accounts, with Boston's John Binning. On rumors of impending war with Spain, he scoffed that King Philip "must be either non compos Mentes" to send Spanish "Naval Powers" against the British, "or be Conscious that his Haughtiness Meritts the Chastisement of his Georgian Majesty" Hall was confident that the British navy would destroy Philip's fleet ("he is Drenched with another English Sea Pill," Hall wrote) and that Philip would soon "upon any Terms Sue for Peace, and to Cry Peccari for his Hostilities to our Merchants."[122]

By Hall's account, he and other Boston merchants personified devotion to the Crown. His frequent notes on public ceremonies in Boston, including the proclamation of George I as king and the fasts and thanksgiving days observed in Colman's church for royal successions, bespoke an identification of province with metropolis. As he wrote to John Timbs in London, Boston's merchants were unfailingly loyal subjects, even more so than Londoners. He sent no political news to Timbs from Boston because there were no great tumults, "no Contests" like those in England, to disturb the happiness and political equanimity between Massachusetts and the Crown. "Our King and Parliament," he claimed, "Agree very well here." As Hall minimized political quarrels within the province and restiveness against imperial trade restrictions, he revealed ideals that Boston's preachers had recommended. They had taught him to imagine a British Atlantic community fortified by loyalty to a Protestant and virtuous monarch.[123]

Aspiring to membership in that community, Hall embraced the cultural mandates—the scientific techniques and philosophic rationality—that underlay Britain's economic and political power. Like other amateur devotees of the Enlightenment, Hall brought an empirical curiosity to his world. He used his telescope to make celestial observations and exchanged with his father various explanations for natural wonders such as the eruption of a volcano on the island of Saint Vincent. He made meticulous weather observations in his diaries, setting out a system of shorthand and astrological symbols to log each morning's, noon's, and evening's weather in precise tables with notations. Some of this might have been expected from a merchant tracking his ships and dates for voyages, but Hall made it a relentless pattern for every day. He composed handwritten diaries to mimic the printed almanacs he sometimes used, replete with lined columns and notations of significant political dates, such as the birthday of the king.[124]

Hall's observations and enumerations of the physical world—the arena for divine providence—stood in place of the biblical notes and autobiographical meditations made by puritan diarists such as Hull and Sewall. His reflections were detailed, systematic, and mathematical, an appropriation of the same norms that shaped England's mercantilist tradition along with its scientific advances. Indeed, Hall sometimes wrote like a political economist. His diaries included precise tables of the annual values for Massachusetts currency. He recorded the amount of bills issued by the provincial government, along with the number of citizens and towns and the exchange rate for London silver, as a means to track the overall economic condition of the province.[125]

The development of towns in Massachusetts, Barbados, and Pennsylvania gave Hall evidence of the spread of English civility across the Atlantic. Making a survey in the 1710s that his brother Richard later used for his treatise on Barbados, Hall described the island's parishes, defined parish boundaries, tabulated black and white populations, and counted different mills, kilns, and roads. In mercantilist fashion, he listed cumulative taxes and incomes for the island. He also commented on building styles, construction materials, the layout of villages, large estates, churches, and—always alert to imperial presence—forts and battlements. The calculating habit stuck with him. Several years later, when visiting the family estate outside Philadelphia, he again surveyed his demographic and economic surroundings, from population numbers in the province to the 240 towns he counted. He commended Philadelphia, "the Capital and a fine city," as being nearly as metropolitan as was Boston, with its 2,200 houses, five nicely regulated marketplaces (unlike the scene in Boston), hundreds of "sail vessels" on its river, and sturdy brick architecture.[126]

Hall accepted rationality and technique, empirical observation and the triumph of British culture, as the proper way to interpret the world. By his reading, they did not contradict Christianity. They confirmed it. Just as he marveled at the economic ties between London and the colonies, he esteemed the moral and religious virtues that accompanied cultural and economic expertise. He extolled the people of Philadelphia for being "prudent, Frugal, and Industrious." They supported two almshouses and a free public school. Moreover, they were politely tolerant; Hall admired the "eleven places of public worship," including Anglican, Presbyterian, Quaker, Baptist, Lutheran, Moravian, and Dutch Calvinist. His diaries were, in effect, expressions of a merchant who believed his pastors. He was convinced that the cultivation of the New World into a polite, commercial, and urbane society served God.[127]

For Hall, as for Colman, Foxcroft, and Pemberton, politeness and refinement conveyed this bundle of evangelical affections, civil accomplishments, commercial ambitions, imperial loyalties, and religious reasonableness. Addison and Steele, Shaftesbury and Hume, fashioned the virtues of politeness, diligence, and sociability into secular replacements for Christianity: a moral discourse that stood for all civilized, which was to say British, people in place of divisive orthodoxies. Hall's teachers had freighted those same virtues, and the same implications for progress in the market, with Christian notions of providence. They conveyed to Hall an affective spirituality. Properly used, they led to evangelical conviction, as he himself confessed. They also provided a religious rationale for, and important contribution to, the market culture in early America. They expressed a natural and divinely sanctioned law of economic reward for diligence, skill, and self-composure in free exchange, and impoverishment for indolence, ignorance, and uncontrolled passion.[128]

Hall said as much throughout his private meditations and correspondence to family and close friends. He confided to a friend in Boston that his frequent thoughts on "true Gentility" would form him for success, and he believed that he had achieved a "Genteel way of Living" as a qualification for prosperity. He informed his father of his schemes for self-promotion and strategies to employ gentility, all couched in the language of honor: he would meet, he wrote in 1718, "Gentlemen of the best Figure and Reputation here in whose good Graces I shall Endeavour to be well Interested by the most Oblidging and Genteel Deportment I am Master of," all of which "will Prove very Serviceable to all my Designs." He promised his grandmother Lydia that his politeness and sense of obligation would yield high returns on his ventures. Hall attempted to impress his contemporaries with his moral sturdiness and devotion to natural religion; he was, as he told another young merchant, "a man of Reason or Religion." Writing to Robert Smith, an aspiring attorney in Boston, Hall claimed that he never suffered "Nonsense, and Anarchy, which is one's Continual Entertainment" on board merchant vessels, but rather burnished his reputation for intelligence and probity. He dismissed sea fables and upheld his manners despite shipboard temptations.[129]

As did many of his contemporaries, Hall understood friendship as a realm of sociability created by a sense of moral and cultural superiority. He chastised old acquaintances who lagged in their correspondence, shared excerpts from the latest belles lettres, and insisted that friends cultivate virtuous civility, that they, as he wrote to Wentworth, show themselves lettered yet eschew the "Sparkling Drapery, Eternal Cringes, and Unlimited Impertinences" brandished by frivolous and impious dandies. He had, as he informed John Timbs, a "Wonderful Ambition" to "Merit the Character of Heroick Gentility" and urged Timbs to emulate him in this regard.[130]

Hall presented himself, in the fashion of Shaftesbury, as a polite and proper man for whom deep sentiment and even effusive affection formed social bonds. The language of sensibility, conveyed through rational preaching, so influenced Hall that he used it also as an idiom for his most personal reflections. Accordingly, he expressed his remorse on the death of his thirty-six-year-old daughter Lydia in 1762 in verse form:

Come from the Body of Clay my dear
See where thy Father Stands
His soul he shed out Tear by Tear
And Wrings his wretched Hands.

Hall tied these poetic lines, conveying a sentimental aesthetic as a measure of politeness, to pious convictions of the afterlife:

Since then my Love, my Souls Delight
Thou canst not come to me
Rather than live without thy Light
I'll find the way to thee.[131]

Heroic gentility, reason and religion, polite and spiritual sentiment: these were the very terms of the discourse that Hall's pastors had taught him to use. They conveyed convictions that providence worked through natural forces, from the physical world to economic exchange and individual feeling, to form civil society. They were, for Hall, a language that infused his daily affairs with transcendent purpose, even as he constructed schemes for the market that would have shocked his predecessors in puritan Boston.

We know little else of Hall's thoughts during the period that he wrote his mournful poem on the death of his daughter, whose name, Lydia, represented three generations of the Hall family. By then, his business had so declined that the absence of manuscript evidence merely reflects the sad silence of a businessman retired to disappointing modesty and obscurity. We have no idea how Hall understood the events of the 1740s, when religious devotion overflowed into the revivals sometimes known as the Great Awakening and a massive economic crisis hit Massachusetts; the 1750s, when the relative peace among Europe's dynastic powers collapsed and imperial warfare dominated social affairs in New England; or the 1760s, when Boston's economic fortunes rose, and then alarmingly fell, in the context of increasingly disturbed relations between province and empire. A shadowy figure, Hall observed—perhaps with detachment, perhaps resentment—a younger collection of overseas merchants who belonged to the Brattle Street Church: Ebenezer Storer, Isaac Smith, and Samuel Philips Savage. Boston's religious and civic leaders dealt with a new set of issues in the province, while later economic thinkers in London and Edinburgh absorbed mercantilist ideas into a fully formed ideology of the free market. Adam Smith was writing when Hall was alive, but Hall probably never heard of the Scottish moralist.

That silence may also stand for a suitable coda in the transformation of the relationship between religion and commerce in early Boston. Hall represents those merchants who helped to construct the final pieces of a genuine market culture in New England. That culture consisted of a complex of fiscal policies, commercial practices, legal protocols, social institutions, and moral ideas that finally eclipsed older puritan ideals. It waxed in small increments, not as a burst of capitalistic enthusiasm in any one generation but as the accretion of daily practices and regular religious reflection made over a very long period of time. The market grew in small steps. Nothing in Hall's story suggests that it developed apart from the transformation of Boston's religious life: from a late puritanism shaped to defend the Protestant interest in New England into a postpuritan Protestantism intended to defend Christianity itself against the assaults of a skepticism parlayed into rationality and politeness.

Later moralists and preachers in the religious establishment of the eighteenth century would contest different strategies and practices to succeed and remain pious in the market, but they would not contest the market itself as a system of economic exchange. By the 1740s, it was a given: God had made the laws of commerce; they were instruments of providence. No one seriously doubted that the commodification of credit, rational pricing, civil litigation, entrepreneurial ambition, and slave trading expressed diligence and acuity. They fulfilled the vocations of overseas merchants, who maintained their moral balance through the practice of refinement and gentility. Such were the dictates of progressive and rational Christianity.

Epilogue

RELIGIOUS REVIVAL

IN THE FALL OF 1740, Samuel Philips Savage, a young member of a mercantile dynasty in Boston, jumped full force into the currents of religious revival. He began a correspondence with George Whitefield, the English evangelist whose preaching in the Brattle Street pulpit awed him. Traveling on business, he attended Whitefield's performances in Rhode Island and New York. On a later trip to northern New England, he celebrated an outbreak of spiritual fervor in York, Maine, which, as he recounted, shone with a "Beam of Divine Joy" falling on participants. He also began a correspondence with the itinerant revivalist Gilbert Tennent. Confessing that daily routines and anxieties often interrupted his newfound spiritual joy, he sought Tennent's counsel. He wanted to know how to reconcile his engagement "in Trade" with the "Vital Religion" that so moved his soul.[1]

We have no direct evidence of Tennent's response, but we can find a clue in two of his most popular sermons, paired under the title "The Unsearchable Riches of Christ." After urging the unregenerate to seek conversion, Tennent advised believers like Savage who had lapsed into worldliness. He observed that an "eager Chase" for mere money did not satisfy "the Desire of Happiness" that was "co-natural to the human Soul"; it brought only "anxious Cares, subtle Projects," and "unwearied Labours." Genuine conversion replaced the disappointing "Affections" of the flesh with the promise of heaven. The believer ought to rest content in "the *Riches* of *Christ's Love*," without which "ye cannot be rich" and with which "ye cannot be poor." Submission brought happiness, and happiness found expression in benevolence, compassion, and sociability: "the most *equal* and rational Life," filled with "the highest Reason and Justice." Imbued with such a temper, believers could then claim wealth and holiness. They could appreciate the clothes, food, wine, houses, liberty, and financial freedom that came with honest hard labor. Tennent said nothing about the conduct of a merchant's business. He pleaded for a spirit of humility as the key to godliness in that business.[2]

Savage's quest for contentment along with Tennent's sermons reflected the central dynamic between religion and commerce during the mid-eighteenth century: pious merchants understood their spiritual duty to reside in the cultivation of reasonable moral sentiments in the midst of a market run by natural principles. They did not doubt the prerogatives of individuals to determine the best strategies to turn a profit. They did not question the techniques of commerce. They nonetheless thought of themselves as pursuing genuine virtue. They believed that the natural desire for happiness, when directed by Christian faith, produced social affections: in Tennent's terms, the "highest Reason and Justice." This convergence between private disposition and the common good appeared to have been designed by providence itself.[3]

Tennent's reference to an "equal and rational life" echoed the sounds of the British Enlightenment: claims that people's innate drives, when guided by reason and devotion, led to equanimity, sincerity, and benevolence, and that such virtues constituted the bases for social solidarities even in the flux of exchange. In this regard, he and merchants such as Savage did not alter the fundamental terms of moral discourse that came into vogue with the ecumenical Protestantism of the 1710s and 1720s. Savage and many of his contemporaries underwent religious and political experiences unknown to older colleagues such as Hugh Hall. They and Hall nonetheless shared a common moral vocabulary that bridged piety and trade—a vocabulary informed by pastors who elaborated the meaning of postpuritan Protestantism in Boston. The cumulative transformations effected by Hull and Willard, Sewall and Mather, Hall and Colman, profoundly influenced the ministers and merchants who led New England into a free market and political independence. Religious sanction for market exchange had become a commonplace in Boston by the 1740s.

SAMUEL PHILIPS SAVAGE, ISAAC SMITH, AND ROBERT TREAT PAINE

A brief account of Savage, his fellow evangelical at Brattle Street, Isaac Smith, and one of their nonevangelical contemporaries, Robert Treat Paine, illustrates this concluding observation. These three merchants pursued their careers during the 1740s and 1750s, when New England's domestic economy (the exchange of goods within the region) showed signs of integration into a permanent commercial order. To be sure, Boston's overseas trade grew slowly relative to those of New York, Philadelphia, and Charleston in this period. Imperial warfare, from the intermittent American battles known as King George's War to the Seven Years' War in North America, alternatively lifted and depressed the economy. It enriched merchants who had a large stake in shipbuilding and wartime provisioning, such as Thomas Hancock, Benjamin Colman (nephew of the Brattle Street pastor), and John Erving. It also increased taxes, inflated prices, and impoverished urban laborers whose jobs lapsed with peace treaties. A decline in the offshore fishery during the 1740s furthermore hampered overseas trade, as did the increasing cost of doing business through Boston, with its rising fees for use of the harbor and a large number of royal navigation officers assigned to enforce tariffs and prosecute smugglers.[4]

In addition, the province's problems with monetary depreciation and price inflation reached critical levels during the late 1730s and 1740s. In 1739 and 1740, the Board of Trade demanded that the provincial government align the value of Massachusetts's currency to the English pound. For several months, the province faced the prospect of having no legal tender, provoking two schemes for private banks. Poor farmers and indebted merchants favored the Land Bank, designed to provide ready credit and stimulate internal trade. Wealthy merchants and other creditors favored a less inflationary proposal for the Silver Bank, dismissing the Land Bank as a speculative craze. With the intervention of Parliament and a grant of £183,000 to the provincial government—a reward for New England's stunning capture of the French Louisbourg fortress on Cape Breton Island in 1745—both schemes were eventually suppressed. Even this measure did not brake the depreciation of the currency. By London standards, Massachusetts notes issued in 1745 sank by 1750 to 60 percent of their original value. In 1751 Parliament's Currency Act severely restricted the amount of money issued by Massachusetts—an interference that sparked smoldering hostility to home rule.[5]

Controversies over the currency continued to disperse, through and beyond Boston, the analyses of political economists who portrayed money as a powerful instrument for economic expansion.[6] Commercial practices reflected the widespread acceptance of such promarket ideologies. Trade with London increased during the late 1740s, indicating a thorough participation in the Atlantic market. New consumer products filled Boston's shops in unprecedented quantities. The town even revoked all statutes regulating profit and credit margins in venues such as Faneuil Hall. The beginnings of a convergence of prices throughout the province, quickened by rapid transfer of capital and the spread of credit institutions and instruments, along with the complete establishment of a legal system operating according to modern protocols and professional jurisprudence, evidenced a remarkable development. The economy of Massachusetts irreversibly developed into a market system during the 1740s and 1750s.[7]

Boston merchants at midcentury thus operated within a market undergoing rapid integration. Savage inherited a large stake in that order. He was born in 1718 into a mercantile dynasty originating in the days of Robert Keayne. His great-grandfather, like Keayne, trained as a Merchant Taylor. Subsequent Savage merchants accumulated land and wharves in Boston, including an interest in Long Wharf, and held a variety of colonial appointments. Among Boston's first importers of India goods, they also constructed solid lines of business throughout the British Atlantic. The

Savage family represented the full trajectory of Boston's commercial growth from the first years of settlement through the eighteenth century.[8]

Samuel Philips Savage, the son of Arthur Savage and Faith Philips, spent his youth among merchant cousins and siblings. Raised in the Old South congregation, he joined the Brattle Street Church when he began his career. He found there a cohort of other young overseas traders, including Smith, Erving, Ebenezer Storer, and Simon Frost. Throughout his life in Boston, Savage was a mainstay at Brattle Street, an ardent devotee of Colman's and Cooper's evangelical piety, admirer and sometime associate of Jonathan Edwards, lay leader in the congregation, and defender of Brattle Street's liturgical practices. Colman performed his marriage to Sarah Tyler in 1742.[9]

Apprenticed under Joshua Winslow, he established a business partnership with David Jeffries in 1741. They exported tar and imported consumer fancies such as silk, tea, coffee, and oranges, marketing them as far south as the Jerseys and as far north as Maine. They also dealt in the provincial trade, providing goods manufactured in Boston, chiefly household wares, to merchants who sold them inland. Prospering especially through his sales of imports to New England customers, he purchased several properties in central Boston, started an insurance office in 1756, and opened a shop on Long Wharf. He achieved local prominence and served as clerk of the market and as one of Boston's first wardens. He removed to outlying Weston in 1765 but continued to influence affairs in Boston, earning a reputation for his strenuous support of the patriot cause during the 1770s. He died in 1797, leaving much of his substantial estate to four surviving children.[10]

The exchange of credit, and problems with provincial currency, inflected Savage's deals at every turn. When setting up his partnership with Jeffries, he stressed the value of ready cash over long-term credit. He demanded that they make an annual review of their ledgers so that Jeffries punctually would remit to Savage any interest due to him. A strict account keeper, he analyzed the relative worth of bills of exchange, bills of credit, and specie, angling for the most profitable transfer of capital. He often required payment in currency rather than bills of exchange, prompting one correspondent to apologize for the "scarcity of Money" that explained slow remittances. He eventually turned to insurance underwriting on shipping. Savage was as smart, informed, precise, legalistic, and demanding as any of Boston's other merchants. He operated at the center of the market system.[11]

Isaac Smith's career followed much the same trajectory. His merchant father, William, who did substantial business with Hugh Hall, bequeathed to Isaac a small fortune. Born in 1719, Isaac started his vocation by exporting codfish and importing fabrics and furniture. He turned his initial profits to financial investments. He joined other high-powered merchants, including Erving, John Hancock, James Pitts, and James Bowdoin, in several credit schemes and proposals to start a new manufactury in Boston. During the early 1740s, he also entered the lucrative market for whale oil—one shipment alone to London netted him £545 in profit—and invested in shipping. He sold dry goods and oil throughout the colonial seaboard and the West Indies. His ledgers show a large volume of commodities and credit exchanged with the London merchant James Allen, the goldsmith Samuel Edwards, and the Boston merchants Ebenezer Storer and Joseph Mico. By 1746 Smith had purchased several properties in central Boston, established his reputation as an importer of luxuries such as glass and fine fabrics, and joined the ranks of Boston's wealthy.[12]

Smith's investments in money, bonds, and other credit notes provoked him to frequent litigation. He took pride in sending English specie to his London creditors, and he frequently threatened his debtors with higher interest rates, added fees, and lawsuits. In 1746 he counted in his ledgers some ninety debtors, including Storer, a fellow church member at Brattle Street whom he sued. He was punctilious and resolute in his dealings. He fixed his attention on his accounts: keeping accurate ledgers, writing to his debtors without a hint of leniency or moral appeal, and making detailed tallies of "profits and losses" from every venture.[13]

Like Savage, Smith also conjoined hard-nosed business with evangelical piety. He served as a deacon in the Brattle Street congregation. He frequently attended sermons during his business trips, recording dozens of preaching occasions in Massachusetts, Connecticut, and Delaware. He heard Tennent at least twelve times and traveled with him from Boston through Rhode Island to Connecticut. He apparently favored the hotter sort of revivalist, writing appreciative comments after hearing the radicals James Davenport and Andrew Croswell in Boston. He contributed to a scattered network of so-called New Lights, informing correspondents of how the revivals fared in Boston and reading newspaper accounts of spiritual outbreaks elsewhere. Smith belonged to a society of Boston's merchants linked by personal ties, reliance on fiscal acumen, and evangelical activity.[14]

Robert Treat Paine was a different sort of merchant altogether: unattached to the evangelical movement, a religious moderate, and more interested in literature, law, and politics than in business. Yet he too made his early career in Boston's market. He was born in 1731 into a household where progressive religious thinking and commercial aspiration went hand in hand. His father, Thomas, a Harvard graduate and pastor in Weymouth (just south of Boston), had imbibed the same intellectual fare as had Hugh Hall: Tillotsonian theology, scientific discovery, and imperial politics. The author of two almanacs, Thomas quit the ministry in 1730 to set up trade in Boston. He built a shop and warehouse, commissioned several ships for overseas ventures, did business with other worthies such as Allen, Storer, and Hall, invested in an iron factory, and accumulated a small fortune in only a few years. He joined the Old South Church, where Robert was baptized. Although Thomas subsequently fell out of fortune—a series of bad investments, overdue loans, and disastrous voyages nearly bankrupted him by 1749—he gave Robert the finest social training: dancing school, French lessons, scientific studies at home, practice in painting and sculpture, and a library of the latest works of the English Enlightenment, John Wilkins and John Tillotson included. Robert Treat Paine was raised for commerce and gentility.[15]

He entered Harvard to study divinity in 1745, three years past the flood tide of the revivals. There he gravitated toward rational Protestantism. A future founder of the American Academy of Arts and Sciences, he collected clocks, studied mathematics and science, read literary magazines, and organized a literary society devoted to romantic letters, satirical essays, and sentimental verse. After college, he joined the Old South Church, took a school-teaching post in Lunenburg for a year, and returned to Boston to engage in trade. He joined the Society for Promoting Industry and Employing the Poor, an indication of his civic-mindedness. With his scientific and mathematical interests, he naturally turned to importing clocks and investing in bonds and other notes. He also traded staple commodities. During the early 1750s, he sailed several times to the Carolinas to buy wood products, sell brick, and trade slaves. He made a lengthy voyage to the Greenland whale grounds and Spain.[16]

Paine achieved only modest success as a merchant; he spent much of his time in unprofitable debt litigation. He eventually turned to law. After collecting a library of legal manuals, he opened an office in Maine. In 1755 he took a leave from his legal practice to preach as a chaplain for a militia regiment at Crown Point. On his return to Boston in 1757, he entered the Suffolk County Bar, specializing in commercial cases. His colleagues regarded him as a dogged litigator on behalf of creditors and disputants over land claims. He also made friends in Boston's high society, who shared his passion for dancing, the theater, and music. During the imperial-colonial crises, he supported the patriot cause. He publicly denounced the Stamp Act, assisted in the prosecution of Redcoats accused in the Boston Massacre, served as a delegate to the 1774 Continental Congress, signed the Declaration of Independence, chaired a congressional committee for munitions during the war, and was elected attorney general for Massachusetts. By the time of his death in 1814, Paine had contributed to the most important components of America's market economy: the importation and sale of consumer goods, the use of credit as a commodity, dependence on civil law to regulate exchange, and freedom from the economic regulations imposed by king and Parliament.[17]

Social Virtue and the Market

Despite their different religious experiences, Savage, Smith, and Paine measured their moral condition by the same cosmopolitan standards of sensibility and sociability. They relied on a lexicon of virtue that circulated among Moral Sense philosophers such as Shaftesbury, latitudinarian admirers of Tillotson, essayists such as Addison, and evangelical preachers. Thinkers across this wide spectrum all taught that moral decisions reflected innate dispositions or affections. They held that people inescapably were motivated by the desire for personal happiness. Reason and piety shaped this instinct to virtuous social sensibilities: sincerity and honesty, contentment and humility, a taste for beauty and intentions for benevolence.

Savage and Smith tied their affections to spiritual revival. Savage tracked his conversion in terms of inner crises and soulful delight. He confessed in 1742 that he suffered from "an odd" vacillation in "the Bent and Inclination of my Soul." He experienced "a most Charming and Attractive Beauty and Lovliness in Holyness" but sometimes felt "no Pleasure" in religious meetings.[18] Receiving a steady stream of exhortation from Cooper and Colman at Brattle Street, and inspired by visiting preachers, Smith also professed an evangelical faith centered on personal sensibilities. Jonathan Edwards inspired him with a sermon at Brattle Street that urged believers to seek spiritual pleasure before material luxuries. Sacramental occasions brought him to intense introspection on "spiritual things in a Spiritual true manner," as he wrote in one of his diary entries. In 1741, at the height of the awakening in Boston, he probed his "heart" for signs of right dispositions such as joy and peace and vicious inclinations toward "guile," insincerity, and pride. Conversion gave him an inner respite from worldly vexation.[19]

These soulful merchants accepted a line of teaching developed by Boston's preachers at the turn of the century, and transposed into evangelical piety during the 1730s and 1740s, that defined social solidarity in terms of sentiments shared among individuals, even across great distances. Moral sentiment thus shaped loyalties apart from the local community. Old South and Brattle Street churches functioned as hubs for Boston evangelicals who identified with each other as a dispersed network of like minds and hearts. Savage and Smith communicated their affections through channels of revival activity, correspondence, and commercial transaction. Savage followed Whitefield on business ventures throughout New England during the 1740s, wrote to other merchants about him, and developed a lifelong correspondence with the itinerant. He advised visiting colleagues to hear Cooper while in Boston and to read Tennent for counsel. He understood the revivals at York, Boston, New London, New York, Philadelphia, and the Jerseys as a single work of God, the creation of a new collective order. Smith's letters and diaries traced a map of evangelical networks marked by the same names—Cooper and Colman, Tennent and Whitefield—and the same events—sermons, revivals, and spiritual effusions.[20]

Robert Treat Paine did not tether his social conscience to revival—he valued conversion but rejected evangelical Calvinist doctrine—yet he too fashioned a social identity out of inner affections.[21] Echoing Shaftesbury, he claimed that rational moral sensibilities such as "true Gravity and Decency," "venerable deportment," "Honesty," and "Industry" constituted "True Virtue"; they produced "the compleatest Gentleman" and most admirable citizen. He sent his friends sober reflections on natural law and the writings of Latin moralists and Shaftesbury, along with sentimental meditations. He urged his correspondents to "expand" their "Soul" with Stoical peace of mind, religious sincerity, industriousness, and moral earnestness. He admired those "who Improv'd their reason and Cultivated their Natural powers for the rendering themselves and their fellow men Worthy the name of happy Reasonable Creatures, whose Ingenuity and Accuracy in behaviour" and "progress in knowledge made them Sociable beings and Render'd them happifying to all their Consort." Paine envisioned social solidarity more emphatically in metropolitan terms than did his evangelical contemporaries; yet for him, as much as for Savage and Smith, individuals' sense of happiness, reason, and benevolence formed the moral bonds of the commonweal.[22]

Using the same discourse to locate the individual in society, Smith, Savage, and Paine drew the same conclusions about economic matters: the market was an arena for the exercise of virtue. Commerce appeared as more than the exchange of goods. It had transformed New England from an isolated outpost to a well-governed society, increasingly well connected to other parts of the British Empire. It offered a network of social exchange—material exchange—that linked rightly motivated individuals into an expansive order. It inculcated honesty, diligence, reasonableness, and sociability. Economic justice, along with material prosperity, depended on right sensibilities, not on corporate disciplinary regimes. So conceived, the market appeared to be a corollary to evangelical and philosophical ideals of community. They did not put it in such terms, but the sum of their particular reflections was this: God designed the market system.

This perspective explains the ease with which Boston's merchants conflated religious and commercial activities. The evangelical networks of the 1740s ran parallel to, and sometimes overlapped, economic networks.[23] Savage and his business partners, particularly Frost, Jeffries, and Peter Cally, all exchanged spiritual advice along with bits of business news, invoices, and accounts. They offered prayers for each other in one moment and mentioned the prices of watches or crystal in the next. They spread revival along with their wares, exchanged religious news through rapidly produced publications, and advertised the New Birth as proficiently as they marketed the latest imports from London.[24]

Focused on their motives rather than on traditional rules for commerce, Savage, Smith, and Paine never suspected that the latest business tactics in themselves might be vicious. Savage once remarked that Christians did not sin by attending to the demands of commerce, from debt litigation to market pricing; "such is not criminal in a proper season," he informed one correspondent. To be sure, he urged others to protect "the main beat of their heart" from worldliness and to remain devout in the midst of trade. A disposition to "talk of Battles, Prizes, Expeditions, Trade, and other affairs" to the exclusion of "Spiritual Things," he warned Frost, indicated the need for repentance. Savage worried about the corruption of personal inclinations yet expressed no reservations about the hard-driving, credit-trading, and litigious practices that made for profit.[25]

Ambivalence and unease abounded in eighteenth-century merchants as much as it had in their distant predecessors, but their doubts centered on the self and its inclinations, not on clearly defined economic techniques. Smith detected no contradiction between his faith and business, as long as he refrained from base materialism. He, like his contemporaries, left no jeremiads, no millennial speculations that cut against the grain of economic and social laws, and no reflections on the economy as a morally vexed arena. It was the same with Paine. In 1755 he in fact urged New Englanders on campaign at Fort George to fulfill their duties by defending free trade. They were to "use all" their "Vigilance, Courage, Activity and Good Conduct" to protect Britain's stake in North America, which was to say "all our Rights" to property and commerce. "Are not *Liberty* and the *Sacred Priviledges* of our Country," he asked, "as dear to an *English man* as the very Bread he eats?" Paine's imperial sympathies, like those of his fellow merchant and religious rationalist at Old South, Benjamin Lynde, did not assimilate the New Lights' idea of evangelical union, but they nonetheless reflected common sentiments. Evangelical and rationalist merchants equally confided in their refinement and amiableness, along with their charitable projects and civic activism, to assert the virtue of their business dealings. Their profits and souls often rose together.[26]

Boston's ministers did more than sanction such confidence; they gave merchants the language to mediate religion and trade. Savage and Smith's pastors at Brattle Street, Colman and Cooper; Paine's pastor at Old South, Prince; other Boston worthies such as Charles Chauncy at First Church; and even popular figures from outside Boston such as Northampton's Jonathan Edwards all consented to the rational pursuit of profits in the market. They did so by accepting the moral conventions developed during the first decades of the eighteenth century. They did not modify their teaching on commerce through the 1730s, 1740s, and 1750s. They merely extended its application to the shifting political and economic events of the day.

New Lights and liberals alike, that is, affirmed the congruence of moral virtue, genuine piety, and commercial proficiency.[27] They encouraged merchants to expand their sensibilities, work industriously, become proficient in the market, and give abundant contributions for employment projects, temporary poor relief, and the ministry of their churches. So Cooper and Chauncy—foes when it came to the revivals—took quite similar positions on the moral duties of merchants. They elucidated the same list of virtues—chiefly Tillotsonian excellencies—to describe the good trader: honest, patriotic, sincere, amiable, tolerant, obliging, and benevolent. These terms represented a market culture in which politeness functioned as moral and fiscal credit-worthiness.[28]

Colman spoke for most of Boston's clergy when he extolled wealthy and rightly motivated merchants. In 1725 he delivered a sermon in that vein to one of the town's charitable societies—a performance so memorable that it was published eleven years later as *The Merchandise of a People Holiness to the Lord*. His text was Isaiah 23:18, a prophecy of doom and recovery for the ancient Mediterranean port of Tyre. Two centuries earlier, Calvin had used that passage to assail avarice and economic corruption. Colman used the text to explain the laws of the market. He contended that tenacity, diligence, and honesty produced profits and bred social cooperation, even international peace.[29]

Colman did not criticize the means by which the town's traders made their fortunes; instead he urged them to renounce degrading affections such as "Covetousness, Ambition and Pride." He, like other evangelicals, hoped that the regenerate merchant especially would be prompted to philanthropy. "Where ever the Gospel is received," he noted, "the Merchandise of the Men in *Trade*" will be "devoted to God." Or, as Colman put it in the glow of Whitefield's 1740 visit to Brattle Street, which so moved Savage, "I observe Many of a like Spirit with Them for Devotion and Liberality, that are signally prospered and blessed by God in this Town." Benevolence sanctified the practices of the successful trader. It rounded out the circle of private sentiment, commercial success, and social good.[30]

Evangelical preachers, then, moved easily through urbane Boston. They forged alliances with the town's mercantile elite through a combination of religious counsel and genteel deportment. Just as Colman had modeled the polite pastor of the 1720s—courteous, elegant, tolerant, and philosophical—so too did Cooper, his protégé at Brattle Street, and Prince, his colleague at Old South. Cooper presented himself as a man of high taste, from his polished prose to a fashionable wig, fine clothing, and expensive tableware. Smibert and Joseph Badger painted his portraits. Attuned to the latest scientific discoveries, especially in medicine, he shunned an older

supernaturalism of miracles and wonders. He replicated Newtonian explanations for strange events. His consuming habits and worldview reinforced
the coherence between religious teaching and cosmopolitan culture.[31]

The revival movement, in which Edwards, Colman, and Cooper played
such large roles, deepened evangelicals' sense—an often tacit assumption—
that free trade and piety, market behaviors and social solidarity, were compatible. Writing from Northampton, Edwards admittedly expressed some
reservations about the mercantile elite in Massachusetts. He often charged
them with partisan politics, inhumanity toward the poor, and out-and-out
selfishness. He especially worried that Boston merchants and local magnates who speculated in huge tracts of land in his Hampshire County would
deprive younger farmers of a living. Yet he meant these recriminations to
humanize the market system, not reject it. He surmised that the revivals,
along with recent scientific advances, might well spread the Protestant
commercial empire while Catholic regimes sank into economic oblivion.
He mused on the ideal economy as a worldwide market of stunning expanse
and prosperity.[32]

Many New Lights, furthermore, drew on the latest economic techniques
to convey religious agendas. Colman, Edwards, Whitefield, and Isaac
Watts operated at the center of epistolary networks that joined evangelicals
from both sides of the Atlantic, just as transatlantic merchants formed social ties through overseas correspondence. Serialized accounts of awaken-
ings, gathered and printed by Thomas Prince Jr., son of the Old South
pastor, resembled fashionable periodicals with a commercial bent. Just as
Franklin's *American Magazine* advertised Boston as a mercantile entrepôt,
provided news from European capitals, and offered excerpts of the latest
moral essays written in England, so Prince's *Christian History* advertised a
web of revivals centered in Boston, gave news of religious outpourings in
Britain and Germany, and reprinted sermons by famous preachers.
Whitefield, Cooper, and Prince used innovative advertising tactics to an-
nounce evangelical exploits. They also deployed the language of novelty,
politeness, and emotional satisfaction to recommend their spiritual activities, a striking parallel to cosmopolitan strategies to market new consumer
goods. Wealthy merchants funded a surge of publishing on behalf of revival, as well as missionary activity on the western frontier. It appeared to
contemporaries that providence worked through personal tastes, extended
networks of print and exchange, and a common culture to build social
order. Evangelicals had not capitulated their religiosity to the market; they
had found a cultural style and moral vocabulary that integrated both
spheres of life.[33]

Ministers' teaching on the specific economic problems of the province
likewise reflected a shared confidence in a market order. The policy statements of evangelicals such as Colman, Cooper, and Prince and of liberals

such as Chauncy and Jonathan Mayhew at West Church were nearly inter-
changeable. In his 1740 election sermon, Cooper disavowed any technical
"Genius" to address the fiscal problems of the province—its "*empty Treasury*" and " *embarrass'd Trade*"—so he urged the representatives to use their
expertise to encourage exchange, restore Massachusetts's credit with London, and liberate commerce from the "melancholy" effects of monetary
deflation. His disavowals aside, he hardly avoided the implication that the
representatives ought to tighten the supply of money and credit. "The
Vertue and Religion, the Liberties and Priviledges, the Trade and Riches,
the Protection and Defence of this People," he told them, "are very much
in your Hands." He covered economic expansion with the mantle of religious and political duty.[34]

Other New Light leaders such as Edwards, an authority for evangelicals
in Boston, agreed with Cooper. In the midst of the great currency crises
of the late 1740s, he assumed the mercantilist position that the government
ought to manage the supply of money to raise domestic productivity and
speed international exchange. By his reading, Massachusetts should reduce
its emissions of new currency, as the Lords of Trade demanded. He argued
that cheap money induced people to borrow heavily for speculative ventures and defraud their creditors with deflated notes for repayment. It also
tempted citizens who could otherwise ill afford luxury goods to engage in
frivolous consumption. The result—inflated prices at home and poor credit
ratings overseas—dampened trade, "on the great loss and damage of the
public society." Without saying as much, he thus leveled a critique against
the Land Bank and further paper emissions. Only fiscal discipline, he concluded, could refurbish the commerce upon which rich and poor alike depended in Massachusetts.[35]

Opponents of the revivals made the same arguments. "The will of God"
for society, as Chauncy explained in his 1747 election sermon, was "manifested by the moral fitness and reason of things." God designed the world
so that economic vices such as "idleness" and "prodigality" tended "in the
natural course of things" to the "impoverishment and ruin" of a people. In
contrast, economic virtues such as "industry" and "frugality" were "naturally connected with the flourishing of a people in every thing that tends
to make them great and happy." The good ruler, then, secured "the general
welfare and prosperity" by promoting the moral qualities necessary for
economic success, which was to say by allowing the natural law to operate
through the market: "by freeing trade, as much as possible, from all unnecessary burdens."[36]

To encourage industry and frugality, Chauncy concluded, Massachusetts's representatives ought to fund and establish public-works projects or
"manufactures" to employ the poor and stimulate industry. More important, they ought to tighten the supply of money to reverse deflation,

restore confidence in the exchange of credit, and thereby stimulate exchange. The true "oppression reigning in the land," as evidenced by defrauded creditors and overly leveraged speculation, stemmed from an excess of "*paper currency*" plain and simple. Chauncy thus blended Enlightenment conceptions of natural or moral law, rational ideas of providence, and commercial virtues to make a particular argument—in favor of monetary constriction—that reflected a more general opinion: unrestricted trade was a patriotic mandate because it prompted moral goodness and thus common prosperity. So conceived, a free market appeared to be a providential blessing.[37]

Samuel Cooper made identical claims during the mid-1750s. The son of William Cooper, Samuel underwent an evangelical conversion, inspired by Whitefield, while an undergraduate at Harvard. Succeeding his father as Colman's colleague in 1744, he entered the Brattle Street pulpit and Boston's high society with flair. He was reputed to be a man of letters, a polished orator, and a discriminating consumer of the latest fashions who gravitated toward latitudinarian sentiments. He became a friend to highly placed merchants, such as Thomas Hancock, who funded an elegant new meetinghouse for Brattle Street. As chaplain to the Assembly and Council during the French and Indian War, Cooper preached fiery sermons that linked Whig politics, anti-Catholicism, and militaristic devotion to the Crown. After the Stamp Act, he served as an informal adviser, voluminous correspondent, and anonymous propagandist on behalf of radicals. A close friend of Savage, he stayed in the merchant's home in Weston to escape possible imprisonment in 1775. During the Revolution, patriots throughout Boston regarded him as their minister. It was no wonder that he was popular among merchants such as Savage and Smith, who shared his evangelical background, moral sentiments, and loyalties to a political movement premised on commercial interests and free trade.[38]

During the mid-1750s, Cooper issued two telling statements on economic policy. In 1753 he delivered a sermon to wealthy Bostonians gathered at Brattle Street to consider an employment project for the town's indigent, a privately funded linen manufacture. Like his father and Colman, Cooper drew on the concept of "the Law of Nature," according to which individuals motivated by the instinct for happiness, or self-love, naturally served the common good. He claimed that "Self-Love may be improved as a Motive, to the Practice" of benevolence because God designed the social system to reward virtue. "If Charity seeketh not her own," Cooper promised, "yet she always finds it." He contended that the scheme would turn a profit for investors and replace public relief with productive work, reduce taxes, improve the balance of trade, reform the morals of the unemployed, and thus benefit the whole town.[39]

Cooper drew deeply from the well of evangelical affections, patriotic sentiments, and Addisonian prudence to further his case. The benefactors—creditors, actually—of the manufactury had an opportunity of "tasting the divine Pleasure, that flows from annihilating the Misery, and augmenting the Happiness of his fellow Men." If they supported the scheme, they would satisfy the dispositions of the "large-hearted and disinterested Patriot" who knew that "Designs of enlarging the Wealth and Power of his Country" depended on "enlarging it's [*sic*] commerce; by removing what obstructs it's old Channels, and pointing out new ones." Free trade, open commerce, productive work: by Cooper's reading, they accorded with the deepest sentiments of virtue and the highest aims of devotion.[40]

The next year, Cooper brought his perspective around to political issues in response to debates in the Assembly about a proposed excise. The statute, which the Assembly enacted for a short time before its repeal, was designed to defray the costs of forts on the western frontier by imposing fees on liquor, wine, and citrus fruits sold in Massachusetts. Its proponents argued that it shifted tax burdens from poor citizens, who could not afford such luxuries, to the well off. Cooper was livid. The bill, he fumed, interfered with commerce, burdened the whole system of exchange, and prohibited what for some people were the few affordable, really pleasurable incentives for hard work. It especially hurt merchants, who "by the Nature of their Business" traded New England's timber and fish for wine and entertained potential partners in the taverns that served rum and citrus punch. The excise violated personal rights and threatened an already vulnerable market in Boston. "When Trade dies," Cooper warned the legislators, "Merchants and Tradesmen" will "leave you," and there will be "hardly Commodities or People left in our Maritime Town": a dismal prospect because "many a Country has grown rich and affluent by Trade alone" and "no Country without it." Defending an open market with Whig politics, Cooper also reminded his audience that commerce powered the "Pulse of Liberty." He was so convinced of the moral and political necessity for free trade that he ended up defending what to his clerical predecessors was the one absolutely indefensible byproduct of the market, cheap liquor.[41]

Cooper's remonstrance against the excise, like Paine's evocation of the "liberty and sacred privileges" of colonial merchants, evidenced a common mind-set among evangelical Calvinists and rationalists. They deemed access to free trade a religious duty. Two decades later, many of their merchant parishioners interpreted this mandate as having revolutionary political implications. In the final year of the War for Independence, when paper was in short supply, Samuel Philips Savage used an almanac to make short notations on the sermons he heard, along with daily business transactions and scattered ledgers. The frontispiece of the almanac included a reprint of Paul Revere's famous engraving of the Boston Massacre. Underneath the image, Savage inscribed a brief note: "let it be remembered." It was a token of moral sensibility that linked Savage to Paine: the evangelical merchant to the rationalist lawyer who prosecuted British soldiers as enemies of American liberties.[42]

Conclusion

Savage, Smith, Paine, and their pastors serve merely to hint at developments after the 1730s and to make a final suggestion. When they affirmed the congruence between Christian devotion and commercial demand, they did not make a radical break with their past. They followed their immediate predecessors. Evangelicals and liberals found common ground on the moral discourse of sensibility, reason, and nature. The disassembly of puritan worldviews and rise of postpuritan religiosity created the cultural precedents for the ministers and merchants who took New England through the revivals, the coalescence of a market system, and political independence. The transformation of puritanism preceded, and therefore helped to make possible, the full fruition of a market order in early America.

This, then, returns us to the main trajectory of our narrative. The puritan founders of New England understood the market as a human construct, an artifice born of cupidity and prone to corruption. It amounted to a temporary and dangerous expedient at best. They understood Scripture, interpreted through their communities of discipline, as a universal language that transcended economic reason. All of this changed. Over the course of the seventeenth century and into the early eighteenth, ministers and merchants gradually, generation by generation, reconstituted their ideas. Focused on inner moral states such as sincerity, faith, and contentment, and on general principles such as benevolence, honesty, and frugality, they idealized the merchant who succeeded in business while remaining pious in intention. They jettisoned previous criticisms of the most salient practices of the transatlantic market: usury, market pricing, and debt litigation. They made the successful, diligent, technically proficient, and philanthropic merchant an icon of religious virtue.

By 1730 religious thinkers had transposed the very language by which they analyzed exchange. Many eighteenth-century Anglo-American moralists, often identified with the Enlightenment, pursued the language of reason because they thought that it was universally intelligible—a conduit for human community. We might surmise that they, as a corollary, also propounded a universal language of commerce: rational, mathematical, and predictable. In this sense, Boston's ministers and merchants accepted the terms of a cosmopolitan discourse settled on the rationality of the created order and the primacy of moral sentiment. They deemed the market a natural law, a divine construct, a system designed to inculcate personal virtues and thus form society. The economy had become in fact a model of integration, a system in which individuals pursued their own happiness while enhancing the public order. The market built character, taught discipline, rewarded long-range planning, and stimulated prudent risk taking. It crystallized the values of pragmatism and personal liberty. It appeared to be a universal truth, whereas the old scriptural idioms, as used by past reformers, receded into anachronism.[43]

Heavenly Merchandize has been intended neither as a cautionary tale nor as a celebration of these changes. To be sure, it might give pause to modern heirs of liberal Protestantism who lament the power of a capitalist economy. It reveals a certain irony that the founders of the progressive religious tradition served the market so well. So, too, this storyline might unsettle contemporary claimants to Reformed Christianity who revere capitalism. It discloses the discontinuities between their religious traditions and their economic ethics.

Yet terse formulations—even the brief summary offered above—can all too easily obscure the finer points of the narrative. They slight the ambiguities and hesitations of merchants and the gradual, sometimes piecemeal, nature of change: from the frustrations of Robert Keayne to the anxieties of John Hull, the imperial enthusiasms of Samuel and Thomas Fitch, and the cosmopolitan aspirations of Hugh Hall. This book has presented these complexities and continuities while still tracing and explaining innovation. In so doing, it evokes the contingency of Bostonians' decisions about commerce. It maintains that customary brakes on the market, especially puritan tradition, sometimes retarded entrepreneurial drives. It also demonstrates the fluidity of ideas and discourses, practices and disciplines: the interchange and reformulation of beliefs about faith and technique, community and empire, providence and nature, Christian identities and commercial necessities.

This account chiefly reminds us that religious beliefs and habits, rather than material instincts alone, shaped America's market culture. New economic contexts, including monetary problems, shifting balances of trade, and rising levels of poverty, to be certain, raised the very moral dilemmas to which ministers responded. Protestant teaching shifted in tandem with economic and political conditions. Boston's merchants nonetheless brought their pieties to the world of commerce. Godly conventions darted into every aspect of social life, including material production and social exchange. Such an appreciation for the versatility of New England's religious traditions finally explains the immense appeal—the moral pull— of modes of exchange so much at odds with the original puritan vision for America.

NOTES

INTRODUCTION
HEAVENLY MERCHANDIZE

1. Samuel Willard, *Heavenly Merchandize, or The Purchasing of* TRUTH *Recommended* (Boston, 1686), A3.

2. Ibid., 65; the commercial tropes and terms mentioned here appear in various places in the text.

3. In Fernand Braudel's terms, the market took shape as sites for exchange moved beyond city stalls to regional fairs, then to international ports and distant cities, where extended networks of supply and demand determined prices more than did local custom, civic code, and religious doctrine. Once dependent on commodities and coins, seventeenth-century merchants utilized a plethora of negotiable papers: bonds, bills, and increasingly complicated contracts. They developed public institutions for investment, speculation, and credit, such as banks, brokerages, and stock exchanges. The use of third parties—lawyers, agents, and law courts—to adjudicate disputes gradually displaced local negotiation over simple account books. Accounting measures in themselves became more complicated in order to rationalize rising interest rates, shifting supply and demand, and fluctuations in the values of different currencies. See Fernand Braudel, *Civilization and Capitalism, 15th–18th Century*, vol. 2, *The Wheels of Commerce*, trans. Sian Reynolds (1982; repr., Berkeley, 1992). For the importance of contingency, moral decision, and personal practice, over and against overly theorized notions of the market as a nearly independent social force, see Joyce Oldham Appleby, "The Vexed Story of Capitalism Told by American Historians," *Journal of the Early Republic* 21 (2001): 1–18; and "Value and Society," in *Colonial British America: Essays in the New History of the Early Modern Era*, ed. Jack P. Greene and J. R. Pole (Baltimore, 1984), 290–316.

4. For the relationship of political identities with commercial ones in the market, see David Wooton, "Introduction. The Republican Tradition: From Commonwealth to Common Sense," in *Republicanism, Liberty, and Commercial Society, 1649–1776*, ed. David Wooton (Stanford, Calif., 1994), 1–41.

5. For the economic motives to independence, see, for a recent version of a long-standing theme, T. H. Breen, *The Marketplace of Revolution: How Consumer Politics Shaped American Independence* (New York, 2004). On the creation of a market culture in New England by 1750, see the following: for the social and broad economic history, Margaret Ellen Newell, *From Dependency to Independence: Economic Revolution in Colonial New England* (Ithaca, N.Y., 1998); for an "empirical" economic analysis, Winifred Barr Rothenberg, *From Market-Places to a Market Economy* (Chicago, 1992), 24–55; and for legal matters, Bruce H. Mann, *Neighbors and Strangers: Law and Community in Early Connecticut* (Chapel Hill, N.C., 1987). These studies indi-

cate especially the importance of the 1720s as the turning point in the development of a market culture in New England; so my study here focuses on developments leading up to and including the first three decades of the eighteenth century, ending in an epilogue with only a brief glance at the fourth and fifth decades.

6. The use of "puritan" rather than "Puritan" is now an accepted convention among specialists who wish to avoid the connotation of a clearly defined religious party with a fixed platform: see Francis J. Bremer, *John Winthrop: America's Forgotten Founder* (New York, 2003), xvii.

7. Darrett Rutman originally suggested this line of interpretation in his "Governor Winthrop's Garden Crop: The Significance of Agriculture in the Early Commerce of Massachusetts Bay," *The William and Mary Quarterly*, 3rd ser., 20 (1963): 396–415; it has been expanded and modified especially in Stephen Innes, *Creating the Commonwealth: The Economic Culture of Puritan New England* (New York, 1995).

8. In his *New England Merchants in the Seventeenth Century* (Cambridge, Mass., 1955), Bernard Bailyn maintained that Boston's merchants had little sympathy with the farmers and preachers who consented to the corporatist ethics of leading puritans such as John Winthrop. In *Winthrop's Boston: Portrait of a Puritan Town, 1630–1649* (Chapel Hill, N.C., 1965), Darrett Rutman contended that economic interests prevented social solidarity almost from the moment that the settlers of Boston stepped ashore. He described a contest between religion and the market, ministers and merchants, and the inevitable triumph of the latter over the former by the middle of the seventeenth century. During the 1970s historians of New England towns argued that residents outside Boston held to a communal and anticommercial ethic until the eighteenth century, when urban and commercial agendas broke apart tight-knit communities. See Kenneth A. Lockridge, *A New England Town: The First Hundred Years; Dedham, Massachusetts, 1636–1736* (New York, 1970); Paul Boyer and Stephen Nissenbaum, *Salem Possessed: The Social Origins of Witchcraft* (Cambridge, Mass., 1974); and Michael Zuckerman, *Peaceable Kingdoms: New England Towns in the Eighteenth Century* (New York, 1970). In *Profits in the Wilderness: Entrepreneurship and the Founding of New England Towns in the Seventeenth Century* (Chapel Hill, N.C., 1991), John Frederick Martin maintained that the settlement and spread of New England towns must be viewed as profitable ventures in land speculation on the part of English investors and New England landholders.

9. There is an abundant literature here, much of it echoing the work of R. H. Tawney, especially his *Religion and the Rise of Capitalism: A Historical Study* (New York, 1926). In his foreword to Max Weber's *Protestant Ethic and the Spirit of Capitalism*, trans. Talcott Parsons with foreword by R. H. Tawney (New York, 1958), 1(a)–11, Tawney explicitly identified one recurrent circular argument as follows: rational market systems eclipsed puritan religiosity because puritans were inevitably driven by market rationalities rather than by religious ideals. For recent challenges to a strictly economic interpretation, see Robert Wuthnow and Tracy L. Scott, "Protestants and Economic Behavior," in *New Directions in American Religious History*, ed. Harry S. Stout and D. G. Hart (New York, 1997), 260–95, which contends for different causal paradigms and explanations according to particular cultures, political conditions, and economic factors; and the desideratum, set out by one prominent economic historian, for a reconsideration of cultural forces: David Hancock, "Rethinking *The Economy of British America*," in *The Economy of Early America: His-*

torical Perspectives and New Directions, ed. Cathy Matson (University Park, Penn., 2006), 71–106. For one economist's confirmation of the power of moral teaching over material rationality, see Deirdre N. McClosky, "Bourgeois Virtue and the History of P and S," *Journal of Economic History* 58 (1998): 297–317.

10. See, for further comment on these connections, David D. Hall, "Religion and Society: Problems and Reconsiderations," in *Colonial British America: Essays in the New History of the Early Modern Era*, ed. Jack P. Greene and J. R. Pole (Baltimore, 1984), 317–44; and Mark A. Noll, introduction to *God and Mammon: Protestants, Money, and the Market, 1790–1860*, ed. Mark A. Noll (New York, 2001), 3–29.

11. The classic text is Weber, *Protestant Ethic*. For the quotations here: Max Weber, *From Max Weber: Essays in Sociology*, trans. H. H. Gerth and C. Wright Mills (New York, 1946), 331; and *Economy and Society*, ed. Gunter Roth and Claus Wittich (Berkeley, Calif., 1978), 636–37, cited and quoted in Robert N. Bellah's "Max Weber and World-Denying Love: A Look at the Historical Sociology of Religion," *Journal of the American Academy of Religion* 67 (1999): 277–304 (quotations are from 297 and 297n26).

12. Weber, *Protestant Ethic*, 47–78.

13. For contemporary evaluations of Weber, suitably nuanced and appreciative, see the essays in William H. Swatos, Jr. and Lutz Kaelber's *The Protestant Ethic Turns 100: Essays on the Centenary of the Weber Thesis* (Boulder, Col., 2005).

14. The pervasiveness of this sort of reduction of the Weber thesis may be seen in recent, synthetic studies on the modern economy, such as Walter Russell Mead's *God and Gold: Britain, America, and the Making of the Modern World* (New York, 2007), 234–47; David S. Landes' *The Wealth and Poverty of Nations: Why Some Are So Rich and Some So Poor* (New York, 1998), 168–85; and Benjamin M. Friedman's *The Moral Consequences of Economic Growth* (New York, 2005), esp. 15–47. It also appears in histories of American business, such as Kenneth Hopper and William Hopper's *Puritan Gift: Triumph, Collapse and Revival of an American Dream* (New York, 2007), esp. 1–45. For a different critique of this use of the Weber thesis, see Rodney Stark, *The Victory of Reason: How Christianity Led to Freedom, Capitalism, and Western Success* (New York, 2005).

15. In his *Farmers and Fishermen: Two Centuries of Work in Essex County, Massachusetts, 1630–1850* (Chapel Hill, N.C., 1994), Daniel Vickers maintains that a desire for economic competence and independence, abetted by puritan theology, developed into a capitalist notion of labor and production. In her *From Dependency to Independence*, Newell explains early New England's economic history from the standpoint of prodevelopment policies. She contends, along Weberian lines, that puritanism provided a rational and even economically scientific worldview that freed New Englanders from adherence to regressive policies. Modifying Weber and drawing on R. H. Tawney, Stephen Innes has essayed a close link between puritan ethics and capitalism, contending that puritan moral ideas, especially focused on self-discipline, eventuated in the rejection of external, corporate measure against all but illegal activities in the market; Innes, *Creating the Commonwealth*. For the parallel literature on English puritanism, see Christopher Hill, *Society and Puritanism in Pre-Revolutionary England* (London, 1958; repr., New York, 1997); and David Little, *Religion, Order, and Law: A Study in Pre-revolutionary England* (New York, 1969).

16. Perry Miller held that a static Puritan ideal disintegrated under the force of late seventeenth-century social forces: Perry Miller, *The New England Mind: From Colony to Province* (Cambridge, Mass., 1953), 19–57; and Miller, *Nature's Nation* (Cambridge, Mass., 1967), 14–49. Stephen Foster has argued that after the imposition of royal control over trade in New England during the 1660s and the revocation of Massachusetts's charter in 1684, the potential individualism of puritanism was manifested in a widespread concession to market ethics: Stephen Foster, *Their Solitary Way: The Puritan Social Ethic in the First Century of Settlement in New England* (New Haven, Conn., 1971); and Foster, *The Long Argument: English Puritanism and the Shaping of New England Culture, 1570–1700* (Chapel Hill, N.C., 1991). Charles Cohen has followed suit with Foster: Charles L. Cohen, "Puritanism," in *Encyclopedia of the North American Colonies*, ed. Jacob Ernest Cooke et al., 3 vols. (New York, 1993), 3:577–93.

17. In contrast to the literature on New England, many studies of radical Protestantism in England have highlighted the complex and shifting dynamics of puritanism and the market. Consider the following examples—only a few from a massive body of literature: David Harris Sacks, *The Widening Gate: Bristol and the Atlantic Economy, 1450–1700* (Berkeley, Calif., 1991); Robert Brenner, *Merchants and Revolution: Commercial Change, Political Conflict, and London's Overseas Traders, 1550–1653* (Princeton, N.J., 1993); Joan Thirsk, *Economic Policy and Projects: The Development of a Consumer Society in Early Modern England* (Oxford, 1978); William Hunt, *The Puritan Moment: The Coming of Revolution to an English County* (Cambridge, Mass., 1983); and Gordon Marshall, *Presbyteries and Profits: Calvinism and the Development of Capitalism in Scotland, 1560–1707* (Oxford, 1980). The two most impressive syntheses on the economy and religion in early modern England also suggest variation, transformation, and the inadequacy of a simplistic correlation between puritan and market sensibilities: Craig Muldrew, *The Economy of Obligation: The Culture of Credit and Social Relations in Early Modern England* (New York, 1998); and Keith Wrightson, *Earthly Necessities: Economic Lives in Early Modern Britain* (New Haven, Conn., 2000).

18. In her study of eighteenth-century maritime communities in Massachusetts, Christine Leigh Heyrman has suggested that Calvinists could well find commercial growth to be compatible with the religious values of social cohesion: Christine Leigh Heyrman, *Commerce and Culture: The Maritime Communities of Colonial Massachusetts, 1690–1750* (New York, 1984). Karen Ordahl Kupperman has highlighted the economically progressive nature of New England—its liberalism—in comparison with the puritan colony of Providence Island: Karen Ordahl Kupperman, *Providence Island, 1630–1641: The Other Puritan Colony* (New York, 1993). In *The Origins of American Capitalism: Collected Essays* (Boston, 1991), esp. "The Weber Thesis Revisited: The Protestant Ethic and the Reality of Capitalism," 35–70, James A. Henretta identifies the need to explore differences between early puritanism and its later iterations. Mark Peterson has argued that puritan leaders of the 1660s through the 1730s sought to use the market as a means for profits to be used for the spread of religion; they took economic expansion as a corollary to religious growth: Mark Peterson, *The Price of Redemption: The Spiritual Economy of Puritan New England* (Stanford, Calif., 1997). My *Heavenly Merchandize* explores the territory mapped by Henretta and elaborates on, with some differences, the account Peterson suggested.

19. Weber, *Protestant Ethic*, 181. See especially Miller, *From Colony to Province*; and for a revision and extension into the eighteenth century, Richard Bushman, *From Puritan to Yankee: Character and the Social Order in Connecticut, 1690–1765* (Cambridge, Mass., 1967).

20. For this history into the nineteenth century, see the essays in *The Market Revolution in America*, ed. Melvyn Stokes (Charlottesville, Va., 1996); and Stewart Davenport, *Friends of Unrighteous Mammon: Northern Christians and Market Capitalism, 1815–1860* (Chicago, 2008). For an influential study of parallel vexations in Britain, see Boyd Hilton, *The Age of Atonement: The Influence of Evangelicalism on Social and Economic Thought, 1785–1865* (Oxford, 1991).

21. Among many recent books, the following stand out as examples of the current discussion: on the sanctification of technique, Robert H. Nelson, *Economics as Religion: From Samuelson to Chicago and Beyond* (University Park, Penn., 2001); on theology and economic morality, Kathryn Tanner, *Economy of Grace* (Minneapolis, 2005); on church teachings and economic dilemmas, Ronald H. Preston, *Religion and the Ambiguities of Capitalism* (London, 1991); on economic vocation, Douglas J. Schuurman, *Vocation: Discerning Our Callings in Life* (Grand Rapids, Mich., 2004); and on religion and the market economy, Rebecca M. Blank and William McGurn, *Is the Market Moral? A Dialogue on Religion, Economics, and Justice* (Washington, D.C., 2004).

CHAPTER ONE
ROBERT KEAYNE'S GIFT

1. Robert Keayne, "The Last Will and Testament of Me, Robert Keayne," published as "The Apologia of Robert Keayne," ed. Bernard Bailyn, *Publications of the Colonial Society of Massachusetts*, vol. 42, *Transactions, 1952–1956*; reprinted as *The Apologia of Robert Keayne* (New York, 1965), 6 11, 79. Hereafter cited as Keayne, *Apologia*.

2. Ibid., 6–10; quote from 7. Should this plan be unfeasible, Keayne suggested, then the courtrooms, armory, and granary could be situated elsewhere. One building could house the exchange and conduit, and meeting rooms for church elders and merchants could be added to the side of the existing meetinghouse.

3. Walter Kendall Watkins, "Subscription List for Building the First Town House," *Bostonian Society Publications* 3 (1888?): 105–49; for the list of witnesses, see Keayne, *Apologia*, 93.

4. For details about the Town House, see Josiah Henry Benton, *The Story of the Old Boston Town House, 1658–1711* (Boston: privately printed, 1908), 5–14, 58–85; for the water conduit story, see O. A. Roberts, *History of the . . . Ancient and Honorable Artillery Company of Massachusetts*, 4 vols., 1:304 (Boston, 1895).

5. Keayne, *Apologia*, 16. For this reading of the architecture as a humanist statement, see Robert Blair St. George, *Conversing by Signs: Poetics of Implication in Colonial New England Culture* (Chapel Hill, N.C., 1998), 61–66. For the subscribers, see Watkins, "Subscription List."

6. Keayne, *Apologia*, 7.

7. For the facts of Keayne's biography, here and following, see Bernard Bailyn, "The *Apologia* of Robert Keayne," *The William and Mary Quarterly*, 3rd ser., 7 (1950): 568–87; and Roberts, *Artillery Company* 1:12–21. For Keayne's connection to Winthrop in London, see Francis J. Bremer, "The Heritage of John Winthrop: Religion along the Stour Valley, 1548–1630," *New England Quarterly* 70 (1997): 515–47.

8. Keayne, *Apologia*, 82; Bailyn, *"Apologia* of Robert Keayne," 570–72; and Helle M. Alpert, "Robert Keayne: Notes of Sermons by John Cotton and Proceedings of the First Church of Boston from 23 November 1639 to 1 June 1640" (PhD diss., Tufts University, 1974), 383–85. For the *Defence*, see Alison Games, *Migration and the Origins of the English Atlantic World* (Cambridge, Mass., 1999), 142.

9. Bailyn, *"Apologia* of Robert Keayne"; and Alpert, "Robert Keayne," 385.

10. See Bailyn, *"Apologia* of Robert Keayne."

11. See Alpert, "Robert Keayne," 393–96.

12. Keayne, *Apologia*, 1, 4.

13. For the review of accounts in the company, see Charles Mathew Clode, *Memorials of the Guild of Merchant Taylors* (London, 1875), 221. See, for bookkeeping and moral trust, Muldrew, *Economy of Obligation*, 123–47.

14. Gerard Malynes, *Consuetudo: Vel, Lex Mercatoria* (1622; repr., London, 1656), 1, 3. For the importance of personal networks of trust among merchants, see Muldrew, *Economy of Obligation*.

15. Browne's work was published under the name I B; I have used here and below John Browne, *The Marchants Avizo*, ed. Patrick McGrath (Cambridge, Mass., 1957); quotations from 10, 16. Information about Browne, the role of these manuals in merchant training, and publication data are provided in McGrath's introduction and in Eric H. Ash's " 'A Note and a Caveat for the Merchant': Mercantile Advisors in Elizabethan England," *Sixteenth Century Journal* 33 (2002): 1–31.

16. The oaths are reproduced in Clode's *Memorials*, 202–33; quotes from 130–31, 231. For charities, see Clode's *Memorials*, 297–309.

17. Nigel Victor Sleigh-Johnson, "The Merchant Taylors Company of London, 1580–1645 with Special Reference to Government and Politics" (PhD diss., London University, 1989), esp. 144–86; Charles Mathew Clode, *The Early History of the Guild of Merchant Taylors of the Fraternity of St. John the Baptist, London*, 2 vols. (London, 1888), 1:214–55. In Keayne's day, the Merchant Taylors' Company, consisting of cloth merchants, tailors, and overseas traders, was organized into ascending ranks: apprentices; the "bachelors," "yeomanry company," and freeman members, to which Keayne and Heyfield belonged; and the elite company of elder members and officers, called the "livery." For membership lists and the organization, see Sleigh-Johnson, "Merchant Taylors," 101–43, 421–33.

18. Clode, *Memorials*, 130, 147–82.

19. Ibid., 541; Clode, *History* 1:256, 334–39. Keayne might well have been keenly interested in the pageant for Swynnerton. He was about to become a yeoman member; his master, Heyfield, was a yeoman; and the yeomen company was responsible for pageants on behalf of guild members who became lord mayors; see Sleigh-Johnson, "Merchant Taylors," 257.

20. John Stowe, *The Survey of London: Contayning the Originall, Increase, Moderne Estate, and Government of that City* (London, 1598; 3rd ed., 1633), esp. 94–103, 673–

79. For Stowe's tight connections with the Merchant Taylors, see Clode, *History* 1:264–65 and 2:298–304. A merchant tailor like Keayne, Stowe wrote his book to valorize merchants who gave money for civic projects such as hospitals, religious lectureships, and poor relief.

21. See Charles J. Robinson, *A Register of the Scholars admitted into Merchant Taylors' School* (Lewes, England, 1882–1883), 2 vols., 1:81, 108; F.W.M. Draper, *Four Centuries of Merchant Taylors' School, 1561–1961* (London, 1962); and John Gawsworth, *The Poets of Merchant Taylor's School* (London, 1934), which lists poet graduates and presents selections from their works.

22. For the Renaissance, see Lisa Jardine, *Worldly Goods: A New History of the Renaissance* (New York, 1996). For northern humanism, see Quentin Skinner, *The Foundations of Modern Political Thought*, 2 vols., vol. 1, *The Renaissance* (New York, 1978), 175–80, 244–62. For the humanist magistracy in the Netherlands, see Simon Schama, *The Embarrassment of Riches: An Interpretation of Dutch Culture in the Golden Age* (Berkeley, Calif., 1988), 69–125.

23. For civic humanism, see J.G.A. Pocock, *The Machiavellian Moment: Florentine Political Thought and the Atlantic Republican Tradition* (Princeton, N.J., 1975), 333–60, 423–61; Andrew Fitzmaurice, *Humanism and America: An Intellectual History of English Colonisation, 1500–1625* (New York, 2003); and Andrew Fitzmaurice, "The Commercial Ideology of Colonization in Jacobean England: Robert Johnson, Giovanni Botero, and the Pursuit of Greatness," *The William and Mary Quarterly*, 3rd ser., 64 (2007): 791–820. The language of merchant-cum-citizen comes from Cicero's *De Officiis* 1.7, a favorite text of humanist moralists.

24. Wrightson, *Earthly Necessities*, 150–213.

25. Thomas Decker, *The Seven deadly Sins of London* [1606], ed. Edward Arber (London, 1879), 22. For Lodge, Lupton, and other humanists on usury, see Lorna Hutson, *The Usurer's Daughter: Male Friendship and Fictions of Women in Sixteenth-Century England* (New York, 1994), 115–51. For lending rates in London, see Peter Earle, *The Making of the English Middle Class: Business, Society and Family Life in London, 1660–1730* (London, 1989), 50, 118.

26. Thomas Wilson, *A Discourse uppon usurye* (London, 1572); Gerard Malynes, *Saint George for England, Allegorically described* (London, 1601); Malynes, *Lex Mercatoria*, 217–26; and for Holinshed's *Chronicles* (London, 1577, 1587), Annabel Patterson, *Reading Holinshed's "Chronicles"* (Chicago, 1994), 73–98.

27. Wrightson, *Earthly Necessities*, 202–9.

28. Keayne, *Apologia*, 68, 71, 73.

29. Ibid., 29–32, 43; Alpert, "Robert Keayne," 407–8. In his *New England Merchants*, 35–39, Bernard Bailyn shows that at least four of the eighteen English-trained merchants who immigrated to Boston belonged to guilds, including Savage. Smith's portrait of Savage is discussed in Lillian B. Miller's "Puritan Portrait: Its Function in Old and New England," pp. 153–84 in *Seventeenth-Century New England*, ed. David D. Hall and David Grayson Allen (Boston, 1984), esp. 172–78.

30. Keayne, *Apologia*, 3, 11; see 10–14; Alpert, "Robert Keayne," 386.

31. Keayne, *Apologia*, 10–14, 18–21; Alpert, "Robert Keayne," 383.

32. Winthrop, quoted in Bailyn's *"Apologia* of Robert Keayne," 572; Keayne, *Apologia*, 22–23, 38–39, 44–45, 86; Alpert, "Robert Keayne," 383. The dispute with Eliot is recorded also in *Records of the Governor and Company of the Massachusetts Bay*

in New England, ed. Nathaniel B. Shurtleff, 12 vols. in 6 (1853–1854; repr., New York, 1968), 2:283, 3:181–82, 188–89, and 4(1):6–7.

33. Keayne, *Apologia*, 90.

34. Thomas Heywood, *The Second Part of, If you know me not you know nobodie* (London 1606; Chadwyck-Healey English Verse Full-Text Database, 1994); quote from line 515. For the historical Gresham, see F. R. Salter, *Sir Thomas Gresham (1518–1579)* (London, 1925). That the titles "doctor" and "preacher" evoked puritans is evidenced in Keayne's sermon notes (cited in note 39) which use these to refer to dissenting ministers. Stowe, like Heywood, contrasted the godly businessman with contemporary merchants who practiced usury, misspent their money on gambling, food, and entertainment, and neglected their civic duty; see *Survey of London*, 94–103, 673–79, 94–103, 673–79.

35. Heywood, in *If you know me not*, quotes from lines 545 and 1199; details from 805–9, 1126–59, 1194–97, 1529–44, and 2045.

36. Keayne, *Apologia*, 1.

37. In his *Worlds of Wonder, Days of Judgment: Popular Religious Belief in Early New England* (New York, 1989), David D. Hall portrays the variety within puritanism and points especially to a theologically eclectic, everyday piety. Janice Knight, in *Orthodoxies in Massachusetts: Rereading American Puritanism* (Cambridge, Mass., 1994), emphasizes two major strains within puritan divinity. For Miller, see Perry Miller, *Orthodoxy in Massachusetts, 1630–1650: A Genetic Study* (Cambridge, Mass., 1933).

38. For puritans in London, see Valerie Pearl, *London and the Outbreak of the Puritan Revolution* (Oxford, 1961); and Paul S. Seaver, *The Puritan Lectureships: The Politics of Religious Dissent, 1560–1662* (Stanford, Calif., 1970).

39. Robert Keayne, "Robert Keayne Sermon Notes," Papers 1 (1627–28, London), which is followed by Keayne's later notes in Boston, Papers 2 (1639–42 and 1643–46, Boston), Massachusetts Historical Society, Boston. I have used my transcriptions, but for other transcriptions and historical commentary, see Susan M. Ortmann, "Gadding About London in Search of a Proper Sermon: How Robert Keayne's Sermon Notes from 1627–28 Inform Us about the Religious and Political Issues Facing the London Puritan Community" (MA thesis, Millersville University of Pennsylvania, 2004). See also "Keayne's Notes of Sermons, 1627–1628," *Proceedings of the Massachusetts Historical Society*, 2nd ser., 50 (1916–17): 204–7; and Sargent Bush Jr., ed., *The Correspondence of John Cotton* (Chapel Hill, N.C., 2001), 331–34. For the Paul's Cross sermons, see Millar McClure, *The Paul's Cross Sermons, 1534–1642* (Toronto, 1958).

40. Keayne, "Sermon Notes," 1: examples, in order used here, from December 22, 1627; February 10, 1628, August 24, 1628; and July 15, 1627. For the puritan culture of the Word and how the manifold scriptural allusions in puritan writings keyed their interpretation of experience and their program of social reformation, see William Hunt, *The Puritan Moment: The Coming of Revolution in an English County* (Cambridge, Mass., 1983), esp. 113–29; Theodore Dwight Bozeman, *To Live Ancient Lives: The Primitivist Dimension in Puritanism* (Chapel Hill, N.C., 1988); and John S. Coolidge, *The Pauline Renaissance in England: Puritanism and the Bible* (Oxford, 1980).

41. Keayne, "Sermon Notes," 1: August 9, 1627; see the notes in "Keayne's Notes on Sermons," 205. I have quoted here, with comparison to Keayne's notes, from Richard Sibbes's "Art of Contentment," in *The Saints Cordials: As they were delivered in sundry sermons*, ed. Sibbes et al. (London, 1629), 7–8, 10. For the Cotton sermons, see Alpert, "Robert Keayne," 117–19, 161–62.

42. William Jackson, *The Celestiall husbandrie* (London, 1616), 30–31; Keayne, "Sermon Notes," 1: February 29, 1628, and December 22, 1627. See Samuel Clarke, *The Lives of Two and Twenty English Divines*, in *Generall Martyrologie* (London, 1660), which recounts Richard Greenham's preaching against engrossing and his remarkable attempt to form a local grain cooperative to keep down prices, 14–16; and the denunciation of notaries and lawyers in Thomas Decker's *Seven deadly Sins of London* [1606], ed. Edward Arber (London, 1879), 22.

43. As the following evidence implies, too much has been made of the technical concessions to some forms of increase in credit, for example, lending as a form of commercial investment, in puritan and other Calvinist writers. I refer here especially to the highly speculative book by Benjamin N. Nelson, *The Idea of Usury: From Tribal Brotherhood to Universal Otherhood* (Princeton, 1949). Still problematic, but more nuanced, is Norman Jones's *God and the Moneylenders: Usury and Law in Early Modern England* (Oxford, 1989), which provides a helpful description of counselors to the state and their justifications for usury in this period.

44. Thomas Hooker, "The Faithful Covenanter," in *Thomas Hooker: Writings in England and Holland, 1626–1633*, ed. George H. Williams et al. (Cambridge, Mass., 1975), 212–17; and Thomas Shepard, "The Ten Virgins," in *Works*, ed. John A. Albro, 3 vols. (Boston, 1853), 2:129–30; and Richard Greenham, *The Workes of . . . Richard Greenham*, 4th ed. (London, 1605), 41–42. On Greenham's reputation, see Samuel Clarke, *The Lives of Two and Twenty English Divines*, published as part of Clarke's *Generall Martyrologie* (London, 1660), 14–16.

45. William Pemberton, *The Godly Merchant* (London, 1613), 117. For usury's association with nearly all forms of commercial transactions and credit, see anon., *The Death of Usury* (Cambridge, 1594); for the general sense of inhumane exchange practices, see Nathanael Homes, *Usury is injury* (London, 1640).

46. Miles Mosse, *The Arraignment and conviction of usurie* (London, 1595), 58–60.

47. Homes, *Usury is injury*, 5; William Burton, *A sermon preached in the Cathedrall Church in Norwich* (n.p., 1589), G1v–G2r; and John Grent, *The Burthen of Tyre* (London, 1627), 7, 10. For further evidence of puritan preaching against usury in all its forms, see Mark Valeri, "Puritans and the Issue of Usury," *The William and Mary Quarterly*, 3rd ser., 54 (1997): 747–68.

48. For use of these terms, see his *Apologia*, 52–59. Antoine Marcourt, in *The Boke of Marchauntes* (London, 1539), and Jackson, in *Celestiall husbandrie*, repeatedly linked merchants to Catholics, as did dozens of other works. For Calvin, see Mark Valeri, "Religion, Economy, and Discipline in Calvin's Geneva," *Sixteenth Century Journal* 28 (1997): 123–42.

49. John Field, *A godly exhortation, by occasion of the late judgement of God shewed at Parris-garden* (London, 1583), sig. B1a, B2b, B3a; George Webbe, *Gods Contro-versie with England* (London, 1609), 58; Jean-Christophe Agnew, *Worlds Apart: The*

Market and the Theater in Anglo-American Thought, 1550–1750 (New York, 1986), 9–56.

50. Alpert, "Robert Keayne," 48, 65, 161–62; Keayne, "Sermon Notes," 1: August 20, 1627, May 18, 1628; Sibbes, "Art of Contentment," 15–17; and Sibbes, "Judgements Reason," in *Saints Cordials,* ed. Sibbes et al., 45.

51. Hunt, *Puritan Moment,* 113–41; Bremer, "Heritage of John Winthrop"; David Underdown, *Fire from Heaven: Life in an English Town in the Seventeenth Century* (New Haven, Conn., 1992), 33–34; and Diarmaid McCulloch, *Suffolk and the Tudors: Politics and Religion in an English County, 1500–1600* (Oxford, 1986).

52. The Geneva Bible (1560), facsimile ed., introduction by Lloyd E. Berry (Madison, Wis., 1969), 91r, 237v. For a recent study of the influence of the Geneva Bible on puritan social perspectives, see Michael G. Ditmore, "A Prophetess in Her Own Country: An Exegesis of Anne Hutchinson's 'Immediate Revelations,' " *The William and Mary Quarterly,* 3rd ser., 57 (2000): 349–92. For the language of decoding the text, see Hunt, *Puritan Moment,* 117.

53. Keayne, *Apologia,* 28. Dod and the importance of his work are discussed in William Haller's *Rise of Puritanism* (New York, 1938), 120–27.

54. Lewis Bayly, *The Practice of Piety* (1612?; 5th ed., London, 1723), 291, 327–28. For spiritual writers in England and economics, see Haller, *Rise of Puritanism,* 128–72. For the contrast between rational investment and consumption on one hand and almsgiving on the other, see the examples in Christine Leigh Heyrman's "A Model of Christian Charity: The Rich and Poor in New England, 1630–1730" (PhD diss., Yale University, 1977), esp. 7–21. For puritan devotional reading in general, the currency of these works among New Englanders, and reference to Keayne, see Charles E. Hambrick-Stowe, *The Practice of Piety: Puritan Devotional Disciplines in Seventeenth-Century New England* (Chapel Hill, N.C., 1982), esp. 49 (on Bayly) and 159–60 (on Keayne).

55. John Field, *Godly Prayers and Meditations . . . for the use of private families* (London, 1583; 1601), 138b–39a; Edward Dering, *A briefe and necessary Catechisme or instruction verye needefull to bee known of all householders* (London, 1575), n.p. (on the eighth commandment); Dering, *A Shorte Catechisme for Householders* (London, 1583); and John Mayer, *The English Catechisme* (London, 1621), 376–79.

56. Hall, *Worlds of Wonder,* 49–50, 121–39; Alexandra Walsham, *Providence in Early Modern England* (New York, 1999), 8–64, 76–77, 94, 107–8.

57. For humanist critiques of the economic conservatism of puritans, see Laura Caroline Stevenson, *Praise and Paradox: Merchants and Craftsmen in Elizabethan Popular Literature* (Cambridge, 1984); and Helen C. White, *Social Criticism in Popular Religious Literature of the Sixteenth Century* (New York, 1944), 189–254. For early puritans and their humanist leanings, see Margo Todd, *Christian Humanism and the Puritan Social Order* (New York, 1987). For the Netherlands, see Schama, *Embarrassment of Riches,* 69–220, 323–30; and Charles H. Parker, *The Reformation of Community: Social Welfare and Calvinist Charity in Holland, 1572–1620* (New York, 1998), which show a genuine ideological rift between state-oriented humanists and Calvinist clergy. In many ways, the discursive division here is represented as a whole in the twofold division of Quentin Skinner's *Foundations of Modern Political Thought,* 2 vols., vol. 1, *The Renaissance,* vol. 2, *The Age of Reformation* (New York, 1978).

58. Sleigh-Johnson, "Merchant Taylors," 10, 107, 147–89.
59. Winthrop, quoted in Bailyn's *"Apologia* of Robert Keayne," 571.

CHAPTER TWO
ROBERT KEAYNE'S TRIALS

1. John Winthrop, *The Journal of John Winthrop, 1630–1649*, abr. ed., ed. Richard S. Dunn and Laetitia Yeandle (Cambridge, Mass., 1996), 163–65 (hereafter Winthrop, *Journal*). Winthrop numbered five reasons in his journal; I have elided and reordered two of them.
2. Ibid., 164–65. Winthrop's account of Keayne's self-defense closely resembles Keayne's own recollection in the "Apologia," 45–48, 52–55. Keayne also defended himself on the grounds that his accusers misrepresented the facts of the case; he paid more for the nails in question than they said he had and had lied to the court out of envious spite. See also Bailyn, *"Apologia* of Robert Keayne," 574; Richard D. Pierce, ed., *The Records of the First Church in Boston, 1630–1868*, vol. 39 of the *Publications of the Colonial Society of Massachusetts* (Boston, 1961), 25 (hereafter cited as *First Church Records*); and Innes, *Creating the Commonwealth*, 184–85. For background on Winthrop and Keayne, see Bremer, *John Winthrop*, 301–22.
3. Winthrop, *Journal*, 165–66.
4. *First Church Records*, liv, 25.
5. Robert Keayne, "Robert Keayne Sermon Notes," Papers 2 (1639–42 and 1643–46, Boston), Massachusetts Historical Society, Boston, quoted in Alpert's "Robert Keayne," 103, 110.
6. For an exploration of financial techniques such as bookkeeping, which suggests that they were implicated in broader cultural patterns, see Naomi R. Lamoreaux, "Rethinking the Transition to Capitalism in the Early American Northeast," *Journal of American History* 90 (2003): 437–61.
7. Bailyn, in *New England Merchants*, provides the standard overview of the period. For merchant groups in England, see Brenner, *Merchants and Revolution*, 92–195; and Sacks, *Widening Gate*. For a close study of a London artisan and peddler, see Paul S. Seaver, *Wallington's World: A Puritan Artisan in Seventeenth-Century London* (Stanford, Calif., 1985).
8. Bailyn, *New England Merchants*, 34–39, 94–98. For subscribers to the Town House, see Watkins, "Subscription List," 105–49. On the Boston topography, see Walter Muir Whitehill and Lawrence W. Kennedy, *Boston: A Topographical History*, 3rd ed. (Cambridge, Mass., 2000), 18–21. Phyllis Whitman Hunter has documented a cultural clustering of merchants also in Salem: *Purchasing Identity in the Atlantic World: Massachusetts Merchants, 1670–1780* (Ithaca, N.Y., 2001), 38–43.
9. Bailyn, *New England Merchants*, 34–36.
10. Louise A. Breen, *Transgressing the Bounds: Subversive Enterprises among the Puritan Elite in Massachusetts, 1630–1692* (New York, 2001); and Bailyn, *New England Merchants*, 38–39, 87–88.
11. Brenner, *Merchants and Revolution*, 148, 182. Cobblers outside Boston evoked the term "free trade" in the 1640s to urge the General Court to discourage schemes

by Boston shoemakers to regulate the production and sale of shoes in the city: Rutman, *Winthrop's Boston*, 249–50. For commercial innovations in the seventeenth century, see Braudel, *Wheels of Commerce*, 81–230.

12. Bills of credit were promissory notes. Originally signed by two financial parties, they included amounts owed and terms of payment. Merchants often exchanged them as a form of tender, passing them through third, fourth, and even fifth parties until they came due or were rewritten.

13. Bailyn, *New England Merchants*, 44–49.

14. Ibid., 92–97, 105–11.

15. Ibid., 79–85.

16. For the background to New England antinomianism and nomenclature, see Philip F. Gura, *A Glimpse of Sion's Glory: Puritan Radicalism in New England, 1620–1660* (Middletown, Conn., 1984); for the theological origins, see Theodore Dwight Bozeman, *The Precisionist Strain: Disciplinary Religion and Antinomian Backlash in Puritanism to 1638* (Chapel Hill, N.C., 2004).

17. Standard accounts are David D. Hall, ed., *The Antinomian Controversy, 1636–1638* (Middletown, Conn., 1968), esp. 6–11; and Michael P. Winship, *Making Heretics: Militant Protestantism and Free Grace in Massachusetts* (Princeton, N.J., 2002); the numbers come from Winship, 190.

18. John Winthrop, *A Short Story of the Rise, reign, and ruine of the Antinomians, Familists and Libertines* (London, 1644), in *Antinomian Controversy*, ed. Hall, 201–310, esp. 204, 241. Hutchinson's "special revelations" were in effect the coming to mind of certain scriptural texts and their meaning; see Ditmore, "Prophetess in Her Own Country." For antinomian theology, see William K. B. Stoever, *"A Faire and Easie Way to Heaven": Covenant Theology and Antinomianism in Early Massachusetts* (Middletown, Conn., 1978). For antinomian and orthodox readings of Scripture, see Lisa M. Gordis, *Opening Scripture: Bible Reading and Interpretive Authority in Puritan New England* (Chicago, 2003).

19. No statistical profile is quite complete, given the rapid mobility of merchants in and out of Boston and swift changes in economic occupations, but it is clear that many merchants of the first generation, excepting Keayne, expressed sympathies with antinomianism, including, besides those listed earlier, Joshua Hewes, William Tyng, Thomas Clark, Valentine Hill, and Francis Norton. See Bailyn, *New England Merchants*, 40, 128–43; Emery Battis, *Saints and Sectaries: Anne Hutchinson and the Antinomian Controversy in the Massachusetts Bay Colony* (Chapel Hill, N.C., 1962), esp. 101–2, 268, 273–75; and Winship, *Making Heretics*, 198.

20. Breen, *Transgressing the Bounds*, 5, 6, 47, 57–114. Breen shows (82) that Winthrop resented Underhill's claims to humanist virtue because Underhill expressed more loyalty to England than to New England.

21. Winthrop, *Journal*, 135, 331–32; Arthur Tyndal to Winthrop, November 10, 1629, cited in Rutman's *Winthrop's Boston*, 136; Innes cites the General Court statute in *Creating the Commonwealth*, 102; Breen, *Transgressing the Bounds*, 24, 30–31, 45, 103; and Daren Staloff, *The Making of an American Thinking Class: Intellectuals and Intelligentsia in Puritan Massachusetts* (New York, 1998), 40–54.

22. Winthrop, "A Short Story," in *Antinomian Controversy*, ed. Hall, 201–2, 259, 299; Peter Bulkeley, *The Gospel Covenant* (London, 1646), quoted and cited in *Glimpse of Sion's Glory*, by Gura, 22–23; Thomas Shepard, *The Parable of the Ten*

Virgins Open and Applied (London, 1695), quoted and cited in *Making Heretics*, by Winship, 75; and Shepard, *Theses Sabbaticae, or The Doctrine of the Sabbath* (London 1649), quoted and cited in *Glimpse of Sion's Glory*, by Gura, 84.

23. The full title of Johnson's work was *A History of New England from the English Planting in the Yeere 1628, until the Yeere 1652: Wonder-working Providence of Sion's Saviour in New England* (London, 1654). See Ormond Seavey, "Edward Johnson and the American Puritan Sense of History," *Prospects* 14 (1989): 1–29.

24. Johnson, *Wonder-working Providence*, ed. J. Franklin Jameson (New York, 1937), 70–71, 247–48, 254.

25. Nathaniel Ward, election sermon quoted and cited in *Builders of the Bay Colony*, by Samuel Eliot Morison (1930; repr., Cambridge, Mass., 1964), 225; and Theodore de la Guard [Nathaniel Ward], *The Simple Cobler of Aggawam in America* (London, 1647; 5th ed., Boston, 1713), 3, 5, 8–9, 25, 30, 77.

26. The connections between antinomianism and merchants, in such terms, are explored in Louise Breen's *Transgressing the Bounds* and in Richard Archer's *Fissures in the Rock: New England in the Seventeenth Century* (Hanover, N.H., 2001).

27. Malynes, *Lex Mercatoria*, 4; quoted in Breen's *Transgressing the Bounds*, 51. Breen suggests that Malynes' discussion of the mysteries of economic exchange, especially the shifting value of money, resonated with antinomian claims to secret spiritual knowledge (50–55). For humanists on commerce and colonization, see Fitzmaurice, *Humanism and America*.

28. Morison, *Builders of the Bay Colony*, 337–75; Stephen Innes, *Labor in a New Land: Economy and Society in Seventeenth-Century Springfield* (Princeton, N.J., 1983), 4–14.

29. Hooker, quoted in Morison's *Builders of the Bay Colony*, 353.

30. Pynchon, quoted ibid., 350, 354; see 350–55 for the narrative here.

31. No surprise, then, that one of the earliest outbreaks of witchcraft accusations—signifying strong social tensions—came from Springfield in the very year that Pynchon returned to England: John Putnam Demos, *Entertaining Satan: Witchcraft and the Culture of Early New England* (New York, 1982), 246–312.

32. Gura, *Glimpse of Sion's Glory*, 304–8 (Pynchon quote on 308).

33. John Cotton et al. to Ministers in England, summer 1651, in *Correspondence of John Cotton*, ed. Bush, 455; Gura, *Glimpse of Sion's Glory*, 309–14.

34. Keayne, *Apologia*, 1–2.

35. Ibid., 82, 16–17 (in order of quotations); see 3–6, 26–27, 32–33, 41–43.

36. Keayne, notes on "Proceedings of the Boston Church against the Exiles," in *Antinomian Controversy*, ed. Hall, 394 (see 390–92); Alpert, "Robert Keayne," 387.

37. Keayne, *Apologia*, 52; see 48–59 for his self-defense as summarized here. Bernard Baylin characterized Keayne's economic mind-set as quantitative and calculating, a suitable corollary to merchant pragmatism: Bailyn, "*Apologia* of Robert Keayne," 577–79.

38. John Cotton, *The Way of Life* (London, 1641), 208.

39. George Gifford, *The Country Divinity* (London, 1598), quoted in Hunt's *Puritan Moment*, 130. Ample evidence for puritan critiques of new modes of exchange may be found in Hunt's *Puritan Moment*, for example, 33, 79, 115.

40. The secondary literature that places discipline at the heart of Reformed communities is immense and includes Charles Littleton's "Ecclesiastical Discipline in

the French Church in London and the Creation of Community," *Archiv für Reformationsgeschichte* 92 (2001): 232–63; Charles Parker, "Two Generations of Discipline: Moral Reform in Delft before and after the Synod of Dort," *Archiv für Reformationsgeschichte* 92 (2001): 215–31; Judith Pollmann, "Off the Record: Problems in the Quantification of Calvinist Church Discipline," *Sixteenth Century Journal* 33 (2002): 423–38; and Richard J. Ross, "Puritan Godly Discipline in Comparative Perspective: Legal Pluralism and the Sources of 'Intensity,' " *American Historical Review* 113 (2008): 975–1002. For connections between discipline and economic regulation in England, see especially Hunt, *Puritan Moment*, 102, 146; and Margaret Spufford, *Contrasting Communities: English Villagers in the Sixteenth and Seventeenth Centuries* (New York, 1974), 344–50.

41. John Cotton, *The Way of Life* (London, 1641), 455; see also 440; for Perkins, see especially Thomas Pickering's "Epistle Dedicatore" to Perkins, *The Whole Treatise of the Cases of Conscience* (London, 1628). Ames's treatise on conscience was *Conscience with the Power and Cases Thereof* (n.p., 1639). Standing for the generation of puritan divines who exercised an enormous influence on New Englanders such as Cotton, Perkins insisted that genuine preaching, Bible study, and godly conversation fostered solidarity: David D. Hall, *The Faithful Shepherd: A History of the New England Ministry in the Seventeenth Century* (Chapel Hill, N.C., 1972), 48–66. For puritan biblicism, see the classic study by John S. Coolidge, *The Pauline Renaissance in England: Puritanism and the Bible* (Oxford, 1980); and Bozeman, *To Live Ancient Lives.*

42. Arthur Dent, *The Plaine Mans Path-way to Heaven* (London, 1601), 198–99. See the selections and discussion of Perkins, Dent, and Greenham in Laura Caroline Stevenson's *Praise and Paradox: Merchants and Craftsmen in Elizabethan Popular Literature* (Cambridge, 1984), 131–58.

43. John White, *The Planter's Plea, or The Grounds of Plantations Examined* (London, 1630; repr., Rockport, Mass., 1930), 19; Hooker, *The Saints Guide* (London, 1645), 12, 14, 54–55, 108–9. For the devotional writers mentioned here, and others, see Hunt, *Puritan Moment*, 127–28, 137–38; and Seaver, *Wallingford's World*, 136.

44. Ames, quoted and cited in Battis's *Saints and Sectaries*, 98; anon., *A Godlie Treatice*, quoted and cited in Muldrew's *Economy of Obligation*, 45; John Knewstub, *The Lectures of John Knewstub, upon the twentieth chapter of Exodus* (London, 1578), 127, quoted in Bremer's "Stour Valley," 535; and Samuel Clarke, *Lives of Two and Twenty English Divines*, 14–15. Similar attitudes may be seen in the tract of the Bildeston (Suffolk) preacher Thomas Carew, "Caveat for craftsmen and clothiers," in *Certaine godly and necessarie sermons* (London, 1603), discussed in Patrick Collinson's "Christian Socialism in Elizabethan Suffolk: Thomas Carew and his *Caveat for Clothiers*," in *Counties and Communities: Essays on East Anglian History*, ed. Carole Rawcliffe, Roger Virgoe, and Richard Wilson (Norwich, England, 1996), 161–78.

45. Perkins, *The Workes of that famous and worthy minister of Christ, in the University of Cambridge*, vol. 1 (Cambridge, 1608), 734; see, for sections on usury, 63–64, 316–95, and 734–35.

46. William Ames, *Conscience with the Power and Cases Thereof* (n.p., 1639), sig. A2, pp. 236–44; quote on 240; John Cotton, "Of Usury, for answer to Mr. Sanderson's judgment," University College Library, University of London, ms. 38ff., 13v–17v, quote on 17v. For the usury and the Dutch church, see Albert Hyma,

"Calvinism and Capitalism in the Netherlands, 1555–1700," *Journal of Modern History* 10 (1938): 321–43.

47. Shepard, "Ten Virgins," in *Works* 2:129–30; Richard Rogers, *Seven Treatises*, 3rd ed., 195, quoted and cited in Hunt's *Puritan Moment*, 138; Bezaleel Carter, *Christ his last will, and John his legacy* (London, 1621), 56–86, discussed and cited in Collinson's "Christian Socialism," 161–78; Underdown, *Fire From Heaven* (for Chubb), 33–34; Thomas Hooker, "The Faithful Covenanter," in *Thomas Hooker*, ed. Williams et al., 211, 215–17. For further evidence, for example, from Perkins, see Helen C. White, *Social Criticism in Popular Religious Literature of the Sixteenth Century* (New York, 1944), 224–54.

48. Seaver, *Wallington's World*, 129–30 (quotation from Wallington's private manuscript journal, about his fellow woodworkers); Todd, *Christian Humanism*, 155 (from Wallington's mss., about seeing God in his business). For Wallington's reading, attendance at sermons, and business dealings, see Seaver, *Wallington's World*, 14–66, 118–31. For Gifford in Maldon and Hooker in Chelmsford, see Hunt, *Puritan Moment*, 140–41; for Shepard and loan practices, see Andrew Delbanco's *Puritan Ordeal* (Cambridge, Mass., 1989), 60.

49. Michael McDonald, "An Early Seventeenth-Century Defence of Usury," *Historical Research* 60 (1987): 353–60; Robert Tittler, "Money-lending in the West Midlands: The activities of Joyce Jeffries, 1638–1649," *Historical Research* 67 (1994): 249–63; Delbanco, *Puritan Ordeal*, 61.

50. Winthrop, copy of "Common Grevances Groaninge for Reformation," in *Winthrop Papers*, ed. Samuel Eliot Morison et al., 6 vols. (Boston, 1929–92), 1:295–310. For letters in which Winthrop also complains about the lack of reform, see his letters in Rutman's *Winthrop's Boston*, 6–7; and Bailyn, *New England Merchants*, 20–22. Francis Bacon, *The Essayes or Counsels, Civill and Morall* [written 1597–1625, first pub. 1625], ed. Michael Kiernan (Cambridge, Mass., 1985), 126–28. For the history of usury statutes in England, see Jones, *God and the Moneylenders*, which shows that under the Stuarts and the advice of mercantilist advisers such as Thomas Mun and Edward Misselden, Parliament rescinded even the bare remnants of Elizabethan usury law.

51. The earl of Leicester to Matthew Parker, 1569, in *Documentary Annals of the Reformed Church of England*, ed. Edward Cardwell, 2 vols. (Oxford, 1844), 1:351; Walter Travers, *A Defence of the Ecclesiastical Discipline ordayned of God to be used in his Church* (London, 1588), 136. Ecclesiatical court records from the period, parish records, and episcopal visitation records show only a handful of presentments or charges for usury, engrossing, extortion, and oppression: see especially W.P.M. Kennedy, ed., *Elizabethan Episcopal Administration: An Essay in Society and Politics*, 3 vols. (London, 1924), 1:iii–ccxix, for statistics. For the general pattern of the courts, see Martin Ingram, *Church Courts, Sex and Marriage in England, 1570–1640* (New York, 1987); and Ronald A. Marchant, *The Church Under the Law: Justice, Administration and Discipline in the Diocese of York, 1560–1740* (Cambridge, 1969), 174–77, 214–21.

52. John Cotton, *The Keyes of the Kingdom of Heaven* (London, 1644), 6, 41–42; see also Cotton, *On the Holinesse of Church-Members* (London, 1650). See Ingram, *Church Courts*, and John Addy, *Sin and Society in the Seventeenth Century* (New York, 1989). Churchwarden, archdeacon, and episcopal court records recount only a few

economic cases: sabbath violations and faulty (or fraudulent) record keeping of parish finances. In his "Puritans and the Church Courts, 1560–1640," in *The Culture of English Puritanism, 1560–1700*, ed. Christopher Durston and Jacqueline Eales (London, 1996), 58–91, Martin Ingram suggests that Puritan complaints after 1580 were overstated, but he also shows that puritan insistence on local, visible, zealous, and regular discipline differed greatly from Anglican campaigns to reform the courts from the top down. For two of many examples of puritan complaints that linked episcopacy, moral hypocrisy, deceit, avarice, and usury, see Thomas White, *A Sermon Preached at Pawles Crosse . . . November 1577* (London, 1578), 45, 51; and [John Udall], *The State of the Church of England* (n.p., n.d. [ca. 1593]), a satiric dialogue that includes a usurer who loved bishops for their indifference and hated puritans for their interference. Puritan charges of usury among priests were often accurate; see B. A. Holderners, "The Clergy as Money-Lenders in England, 1550–1700," in *Princes and Paupers in the English Church, 1500–1800*, ed. Rosemary O'Day and Felicity Heal (Totowa, N.J., 1981), 195–209.

53. William Fulke, *A briefe and plaine declaration, concerning . . . the Discipline and reformation of the Church of Englande* (London, 1584), 84.

54. The list of Marian exiles in Geneva, many of whom had connections to New England, amounted to a *Who's Who* of nascent puritanism: Christina Hollowell Garrett, *The Marian Exiles: A Study in the Origins of Elizabethan Puritanism* (Cambridge, 1938); and Charles Martin, *Les Protestants Anglais réfugés à Genève au temps de Calvin, 1555–1560* (Geneva, 1915); Patrick Collinson, *The Elizabethan Puritan Movement* (Berkeley, Calif., 1967), 114–41. Most puritan luminaries resided in Geneva from 1555 through 1558, when Calvin especially turned his energies to commentary on prices, wages, rents, usury, and other dynamics of exchange and to prodding the Genevan Consistory into a sweeping campaign to restrict usury, engrossing, and profiteering; see Valeri, "Religion, Economy, and Discipline in Calvin's Geneva." From 1548 to 1630, 136 separate editions of Calvin's works appeared in England, most of them in the 1570s and 1580s, including *The Laws and Statutes of Geneva*, trans. Robert Fills (London, 1562); and James Spottswood, *The Execution of Neschech* (Edinburgh, 1616), an argument against usury with several selections from Calvin on the topic. For the popularity of Calvin in England, see P. G. Lake, "Calvinism and the English Church, 1570–1635," *Past and Present* 114 (1987): 32–76. The dean of Exeter, Matthew Sutcliffe, ridiculed Thomas Cartwright for his incessant appeals to the Genevan system: Matthew Sutcliffe, *A Treatise of Ecclesiastical Discipline* (London, 1590), sig. B2r, 1–10, 86, 94, 135, 158.

55. For Northampton and Norwich, see M. M. Knappen, *Tudor Puritanism: A Chapter in the History of Idealism* (Chicago, 1939; repr., New York, 1963), 409–11; Collinson, *Elizabethan Puritan Movement*, 323–29; Robert Bolton, *Two Sermons Preached at Northampton at Two Severall Assises There* (London, 1639); Bremer, "Stour Valley," 527–31; and Bremer, *John Winthrop*, 67–123. For Dedham, see Dedham Classis, "Minute Book, 1582–1589," in *The Presbyterian Movement in the Reign of Queen Elizabeth as Illustrated by the Minute Book of the Dedham Classis, 1582–1589*, ed. Roland G. Usher (London, 1905), 59, 71, 97–100. For St. Michael's Cornhill, see Bremer, "Stour Valley," 517–25.

56. For Bildeston and Bury Saint Edmunds, see Collinson, "Christian Socialism"; for Boxford, see Bremer, "Stour Valley," 538; for Dorchester, see Underdown,

Fire from Heaven. For a broader perspective on puritan control over the local economy, see McCulloch, *Suffolk and the Tudors*.

57. John Winthrop, "A Modell of Christian Charity," in *Winthrop Papers*, ed. Morison, 2:282–95; White, *Planter's Plea*, passim; William Bradford, *Of Plymouth Plantation, 1620–1647*, ed. Samuel Eliot Morison (New York, 1959), 16–17. Like his Massachusetts Bay counterparts, Bradford was equally vexed by merchants who claimed to be true believers and civic leaders but who had allegiances to an international network of trading partners and commercial contacts who included religious radicals; see Michelle Burnham, "Merchants, Money, and the Economics of 'Plain Style' in William Bradford's *Of Plymouth Plantation*," *American Literature* 72 (2000): 695–720. For arguments about motives, see Virginia DeJohn Anderson, "Migrants and Motives: Religion and the Settlement of New England, 1630–1640," *The New England Quarterly* 58 (1985): 339–83; and David Cressy, *Coming Over: Migration and Communication between England and New England in the Seventeenth Century* (Cambridge, 1987).

58. John White, *Planter's Plea*, 34; for White on production, 2–5.

59. Winthrop, "General Observations on the Plantation of New England," in *Winthrop Papers* 2:111–24, esp. 114–16; and *The Journal of John Winthrop, 1630–1649*, ed. Richard S. Dunn, James Savage, and Laetitia Yeandle (Cambridge, Mass., 1996), 588, 317, 416. Hereafter cited as *Journal of John Winthrop*, ed. Dunn, Savage, and Yeandle. Shepard reminded his congregation that the "end of coming hither" to New England was the institution of the "ordinances of God," chief among which were, as English puritans had taught, preaching and teaching, admonition and excommunication, and proper rule by the government and its courts: Shepard, "Ten Virgins," in *Works* 2:376. For a discussion of the humanist agendas to which Shepard and Winthrop may well have referred, see Fitzmaurice, *Humanism and America*.

60. "The Cambridge Platform," in *The Creeds and Platforms of Congregationalism*, ed. Williston Walker, introduction by Douglas Horton (1893; repr., Boston, 1960), 209, 218; Thomas Hooker, "The Carnal Hypocrite" (ca. 1626), in *Thomas Hooker*, ed. Williams et al., 100, 103, 110; Winthrop, "Modell of Christian Charity," in *Winthrop Papers* 2:294.

61. Hooker, *Foure learned and godly treatises* (London, 1638), 49, 55–56, 60, 63, 216, 218; Hooker also argued that the Christian ought to refrain from "unnecessary communion" or personal friendship with ungodly men while he allowed believers to reform wicked neighbors, participate in civic affairs, perform acts of charity, and provide hospitality (food and lodging) even to unsaintly visitors: *Foure treatises*, 63–64, 72–73.

62. John Cotton, *God's Promise to His Plantation* (London, 1630), 12, 19. For one typical recommendation for the maintenance of household comforts, see White, *Planter's Plea*, 19. For puritan investors, see Martin, *Profits in the Wilderness*; for ideas about vocation and industriousness, Innes, *Creating the Commonwealth*, 39–63, 107–59.

63. Winthrop, "Modell of Christian Charity," in *Winthrop Papers* 2:284, 292. By "the Apostles times," Winthrop referred to the community of property in Acts 4:34–35.

64. Heyrman, "Model of Christian Charity," 7–21. To be sure, Winthrop gave merchants their due, allowing them to invest in commercial ventures and reap re-

wards from their risks. Yet, following his teachers, he urged his companions to consider the needs of their immediate communities; see also "Modell," 285–87.

65. Keayne, "Sermon Notes" 2, quoted in Alpert's "Robert Keayne," 48, 65.

66. Ibid., 169, 180, 228, 259.

67. Ibid., 226–27. A quarter of a century later, Michael Wigglesworth recovered this acerbic rhetoric in his popular *The Day of Doom*, 2nd ed. (Cambridge, Mass., 1666), for example, stanzas 32–37, 93–94, as a protest against changing mores in Boston.

68. Winthrop, *Journal*, 106, 111–12.

69. Geere's will is printed in the *New England Historical and Genealogical Register* 37 (1883), 229. For John Dane, see "John Dane's Narrative, 1682," in *New England Historical and Genealogical Register* 8 (1854), 154, cited in Virginia DeJohn Anderson's *New England's Generation: The Great Migration and the Formation of Society and Culture in the Seventeenth Century* (New York, 1991), 41–42. For Cudworth, see Johnson, *Wonder-Working Providence*, cited in Bozeman's *To Live Ancient Lives*, 113.

70. Cotton, *Keyes of the Kingdom of Heaven*, 41–42. For general reflections on discipline, see Cotton, *The True Constitution of a Particular visible Church* (London, 1642), 2–3; and Thomas Hooker, *A Survey of the Summe of Church-Discipline* (London, 1648), 36–40.

71. Hooker, *Foure learned and godly treatises*, 55; Cotton's words in the case of the tailor are quoted and cited in James F. Cooper Jr.'s "Confession and Trial of Richard Wayte, Boston, 1640," *The William and Mary Quarterly*, 3rd ser., 44 (1987): 310–32, quote on 326. For elders and the system of censures, see Cotton, *True Constitution*, 2–3. A full portrait of the workings of discipline, with evidence of the signal importance of Cotton and Hooker, is provided in James F. Cooper Jr.'s *Tenacious of Their Liberties: The Congregationalists in Colonial Massachusetts* (New York, 1999), esp. 59–62 for details on meetings.

72. *First Church Records* 39:20 (for Parker); the statistical profile comes from *First Church Records* 39:12–160. A similar set of disciplinary procedures may be found, in a rural context with different economic problems, in John Fiske's *Notebook of the Reverend John Fiske, 1644–1676*, ed. Robert G. Pope, *Publications of the Colonial Society of Massachusetts*, vol. 47 (Boston, 1974).

73. *First Church Records* 39:28, 42–46, 49. Likewise, the Roxbury church excommunicated Hannah Webb in 1642 for the "grosse sins" not merely of selling her bread at too high a price but also for "lying and shifting" in the public market: "The Reverend John Eliot's Record of Church Members, Roxbury, Mass.," published in *A Report of the Record Commissioners containing the Roxbury Land and Church Records* (Boston, 1881), 73–100; quote on 83. Hereafter cited as *Roxbury Church Records*.

74. Keayne, sermon notes, Massachusetts Historical Society, vol. 2, September 13, 1640, and February 1, 1641. Two versions of Keayne's notes on Hibbens have been published in part: *Proceedings of the Massachusetts Historical Society*, 2nd ser., vol. 4, March 1889, 313–16 (hereafter cited as "Keayne" in *PMHS*); and, from a transcription by Anita Rutman, in "Church Trial of Mistress Ann Hibbens," in *Root of Bitterness: Documents of the Social History of American Women*, ed. Nancy Cott (New York, 1972), 47–58.

75. Keayne, sermon notes, September 13, 1640; the quote may be found also in "Church Trial," ed. Cott, 50.

76. Keayne, sermon notes, Februray 1, 1641; Cott, ed., "Church Trial," 49; *First Church Records* 39:31–33. The words of excommunication are included in "Keayne" in *PMHS*, 316.

77. Keayne's notes, a survey of the facts and trial, and the background on Wayte are provided in Cooper."Confession and Trial of Richard Wayte"; quotes on 316, 318.

78. Ibid., 332.

79. [John Davenport], *Discourse about Civil Government* (1637). I have used a later edition that was misattributed to John Cotton (Boston, 1663); see esp. 7, 11. Thomas Shepard, "For a Time of Liberty," in *Works* 3:346–47. Winthrop, *Journal*, June 1641, 359–60. On puritan attempts to square English law with the Bible, see George Lee Haskins, *Law and Authority in Early Massachusetts: A Study in Tradition and Design* (1960; repr., Hamden, Conn., 1968); and Bozeman, *To Live Ancient Lives*, 160–92. For a study of the general theory of church and state, see T. H. Breen, *The Good Ruler: A Study of Puritan Political Ideas in New England, 1630–1730* (New Haven, Conn., 1970). On the flexible and pragmatic application of rules in local context, see Jane Kamensky, *Governing the Tongue: The Politics of Speech in Early New England* (New York, 1997). For Winthrop's perspective, see Bremer, *John Winthrop*, 203–322.

80. For the brief narrative here and in the following paragraph, see Haskins, *Law and Authority*, 25–42; Rutman, *Winthrop's Boston*, 234–35; Bailyn, *New England Merchants*, 48–49; and the essays by Thomas G. Barnes and George L. Haskins in *Law in Colonial Massachusetts, 1630–1800*, ed. Daniel R. Coquillette, vol. 62 of *Publications of the Colonial Society of Massachusetts* (Boston, 1984), 3–55.

81. The nomenclature for these courts changed after 1692. The Court of Assistants became the Superior Court of Judicature (the court of appeal). The county or Quarterly Courts became Courts of Common Pleas and dealt with civil matters; General Sessions of the Peace, somewhat like criminal courts, were then added at a county level.

82. On Ward's and Cotton's constitutional efforts, see Simon P. Newman, "Nathaniel Ward, 1580–1652: An Elizabethan Puritan in a Jacobean World," *Essex Institute Historical Collections* 127 (1991): 313–26. For various readings of the relative influence of common law, local judicial customs, and the Bible, see James S. Hart and Richard J. Ross, "The Ancient Constitution in the Old World and the New," in *The World of John Winthrop: Essays on England and New England, 1588–1649*, ed. Francis J. Bremer and Lynn A. Botelho (Boston, 2005), 237–89; John Phillip Reid, *Rule of Law: The Jurisprudence of Liberty in the Seventeenth and Eighteenth Centuries* (DeKalb, Ill., 2004), 3–79; and William E. Nelson, *Americanization of the Common Law: The Impact of Legal Change in Massachusetts Society, 1760–1830* (Athens, Ga., 1999), 11–45.

83. Thomas Lechford, *Plain Dealing*, cited in Bozeman's *To Live Ancient Lives*, 188. For the legal regimen and English law, see Bozeman, *To Live Ancient Lives*, 177; for a survey of statutes, see Bailyn, *New England Merchants*, 13–14, 33–34, 104–6; and Rutman, *Winthrop's Boston*, 181, 207, 222–23. On sumptuary laws and poor relief, see Newell, *From Dependency to Independence*, 48; Heyrman, "A Model of Christian Charity"; and Charles R. Lee, "Public Poor Relief and the Massachusetts Community, 1620–1715," *New England Quarterly* 55 (1982): 564–85.

84. Jesper Rosenmeier, "John Cotton on Usury," *The William and Mary Quarterly*, 3rd ser., 47 (1990): 548–65, esp. 557–58; Winthrop, *Journal*, 308; Massachusetts Bay Colony, *The Book of the General Lawes and Libertyes* (Cambridge, Mass., 1648), 43, 51; Shurtleff, ed., *Records* 1:160.

85. Winthrop, *Journal of John Winthrop*, ed. Dunn, Savage, and Yeandle, 102, 308, 430; Winthrop, *Winthrop's Journal: "History of New England," 1630–1649*, ed. James Kendall Hosmer, 2 vols. (New York, 1908), 1:152, 169; Battis, *Saints and Sectaries*, 96–100; Innes, *Creating the Commonwealth*, 102, 121, 147, 177–79.

86. Massachusetts Bay Colony, *Book of the General Lawes*, 43, 51; Shurtleff, ed., *Records* 1:160; Rutman, *Winthrop's Boston*, 239. Contrary to the common claim that such laws were abolished by the end of the 1650s, the court continued to revert to strict regulations of prices and wages through the 1670s, especially in response to demands from religious leaders: see, for example, Shurtleff, ed., *Records* 5:62–63, which reenacts such restrictions after the moral declamations of the famous Reforming Synod of 1679. See, for cites on post-1650 regulations, Innes, *Creating the Commonwealth*, 177–79.

87. E. N. Hartley, *Ironworks on the Saugus: The Lynn and Braintree Ventures of the Company of Undertakers of the Ironworks in New England* (Norman, Okla., 1957); and Innes, *Creating the Commonwealth*, 237–70.

88. Shurtleff, ed., *Records* 3:93 (see also 31, 59–61, 92, 142); Saugus Iron Works, "A Collection of Papers Relating to the Suit between Mr. John Gifford the Agent for the Undertakers of the Iron Works and the Inhabitants of the Massachusetts Bay Colony" (typescript, Baker Business Library, Harvard University), 2, 4, 24, 28–41, 239.

89. Massachusetts Bay, Court of Assistants, *Records of the Court of Assistants of Colony of the Massachusetts Bay, 1630–1692*, ed. John Noble and John Cronin, 3 vols. (Boston, 1901–28), 2:passim.

90. Arthur Prentice Rugg, "A Famous Colonial Litigation: The Case between Richard Sherman and Capt. Robert Keayne, 1642," *Proceedings of the American Antiquarian Society*, n.s., 30 (1921): 217–50 (the case against Palmer and quote on 236). For the other cases cited here, see Innes, *Creating the Commonwealth*, 178; Brenton, *Old Boston Town House*, 15–27; and Essex County, Quarterly Courts, *Records and Files of the Quarterly Courts of Essex County, Massachusetts*, ed. George Francis Dow, 9 vols. (Salem, Mass., 1911–75), 2:118–19, 146. For a thoroughgoing study of the contrast between puritan rigor and Anglican laxity about such matters in England, see David Underdown, *Revel, Riot, and Rebellion: Popular Politics and Culture in England, 1603–1660* (Oxford, 1987).

91. John Winthrop, "John Winthrop's Discourse on Arbitrary Government," in *Winthrop Papers* 4:468–82 (quotations on 475–76). During the early 1640s, Winthrop contended that he (as governor) and members of the Court of Assistants should have personal, discretionary powers to apply Scripture to legal cases as they saw fit. For the intimate, personal, and informal procedures, especially in relation to the courts in England, see David Thomas Konig, "Community Custom and the Common Law: Social Change and the Development of Land Law in Seventeenth-Century Massachusetts," *The American Journal of Legal History* 18 (1974): 137–77; and David H. Flaherty, *Privacy in Colonial New England* (Charlottesville, Va., 1972). Puritans took these neighborly, collective, Calvinist ideals to an extreme in New

Haven, where citizens settled economic disputes by neighborly arbitration and judges dispensed spiritual advice while eschewing legal precedents: Cornelia Hughes Dayton, "Was There a Calvinist Type of Patriarchy? New Haven Colony Reconsidered in the Early Modern Context," in *The Many Legalities of Early America*, ed. Christopher L. Tomlins and Bruce H. Mann (Chapel Hill, N.C., 2001), 337–56; and *Women before the Bar: Gender, Law, and Society in Connecticut, 1639–1789* (Chapel Hill, N.C., 1995), 29–30.

92. Rugg, "A Famous Colonial Litigation," which includes a transcript of the proceedings.

93. Ibid., 231–33. For equity courts, their reliance on moral discretion that superseded legal technicalities, and their origin in religious tradition in contrast to common law, see Mary Sarah Bilder, "Salamanders and Sons of God: The Culture of Appeal in Early New England," in *The Many Legalities of Early America*, ed. Tomlins and Mann, 47–77.

94. [Davenport], *Discourse about Civil Government*, 14–15.

95. Ibid., 12, 20, 23. For similar judgments by Cotton, on the inappropriateness of custom, common law, and natural law as sources of political principles, see his letter to William Fennes, Lord Saye and Sele, after March 1636, in *Correspondence of John Cotton*, ed. Bush, 244–46. Such opinion also runs throughout Cotton's preaching. (Perkins and Ames mentioned "natural law" as a source for ethics, but by that term they meant the moral law revealed to ancient Israel, chiefly in the form of the Ten Commandments. This law was duplicated in the natural order of things and imprinted on the consciences of human beings. Because of the universal, sinful state of humanity, however, all moral precepts derived from nature apart from Scripture were unreliable at best, misguided at worst. They carried little authority.) Civic humanists and English legal theorists of the period increasingly turned toward classical and contemporary iterations of the natural law as the conceptual framework for legislation and jurisprudence. Puritans resisted. As Shepard put the issue, "it is not now *lex nata*" (natural law) "but *lex data*" (revealed law), "which is the rule of moral duties" because only "the whole Scriptures contain the perfect rule of all moral actions"; Thomas Shepard, "The Morality of the Sabbath," in *Works* 3:44. The leaders of Harvard College during the 1630s and early 1650s reinforced this subordination of natural law to Scripture: Norman Fiering, *Moral Philosophy at Seventeenth-Century Harvard: A Discipline in Transition* (Chapel Hill, N.C., 1981), 10–103.

96. For Winthrop's opinion of lawyers, see Winthrop, *Journal of John Winthrop*, ed. Dunn, Savage, and Yeandle, 345, 360; for Cotton, see Rutman, *Winthrop's Boston*, 233–34.

97. Hooker to Shepard, November 2, 1640, in "Life of Thomas Shepard," by John A. Albro, vii–cxcii, in *The Sincere Convert and the Sound Believer*, by Thomas Shepard (1853; repr., Morgan, Penn., 1999), cxliv.

98. Winthrop, *Journal*, 345. For a typical argument against civil litigation, see [Davenport], *Discourse about Government*, 19–21.

99. Rutman, *Winthrop's Boston*, 154–55; Roger Thompson, *Sex in Middlesex: Popular Mores in a Massachusetts County, 1649–1699* (Amherst, Mass., 1986), 169; *First Church Records* 39:52; David Thomas Konig, *Law and Society in Puritan Massachusetts: Essex County, 1629–1692* (Chapel Hill, N.C., 1979).

CHAPTER THREE
JOHN HULL'S ACCOUNTS

1. Hull to Hubbard, March 5, 1680, in "The Diaries of John Hull," with appendixes and letters, annotated by Samuel Jennison, *Transactions of the American Antiquarian Society*, vol. 3 (Boston, 1857; repr., New York, 1971), 137. Pastoral salaries are discussed in Hall's *Faithful Shepherd*, 185–94.

2. Hull to Hubbard, March 5, 1680. For statistics on court cases and economic changes in this period, see note 78 in this chapter.

3. Hull to Henry Foxwell, 1674, in "Diaries of John Hull," 136; Hull to Hubbard, March 5, 1680, in "Diaries of John Hull," 137. The copy of Cotton's catechism available on the Readex electronic version of Early American Imprints, series 1: Evans, 1638–1800, shows Hull's autograph; John Cotton, *Spiritual Milk for Boston Babes* (Cambridge, Mass., 1656).

4. William Hubbard, *The Happiness of a People in the Wisdome of their Rulers* (Boston, 1676), 26, 37, 45, 62.

5. William Hubbard, *Of a Well-Ordered Conversation* (Boston, 1684), 97; see 97–103 for the full exposition of providence and commerce. The elegy for Dennison, and Dennison's piece, *Irenicon*, were published along with *Of a Well-Ordered Conversation*. In *A Narrative of the Troubles with the Indians* (Boston, 1677), which treats the Pequot War and King Philip's War, Hubbard stressed the rule of providence. For the final disposition of the debt case, see the annotation in "Diaries of John Hull," 138.

6. For details about Hull and his business in this and the following paragraphs, see Hermann Frederick Clarke, "John Hull—Colonial Merchant, 1624–1683," *Proceedings of the American Antiquarian Society* 46 (1936): 197–218; Morison, *Builders of the Bay Colony*, 135–82; and Hermann Frederick Clarke, *John Hull: A Builder of the Bay Colony* (1940; repr., Wolfeboro, N.H., 1993), esp. 133 (for Hull's apprentices). For John Hull's education in England and his father's affairs, see Clarke, *John Hull*, 5, 9, 25. The number of Boston silversmiths is noted in Carl Bridenbaugh's *Cities in the Wilderness: The First Century of Urban Life in America, 1625–1742* (New York, 1938), 43. Hull called himself a goldsmith, using the customary appellation.

7. "Diaries of John Hull," 145.

8. For Hull and the mint, see Louis Jordan, *John Hull, the Mint and the Economics of Massachusetts Coinage* (Lebanon, N.H., 2002).

9. In addition to Clarke, "John Hull," and Clarke, *John Hull*, 102–3, 171, see Newell, *From Dependency to Independence*, 86–92; and Baylin, *New England Merchants*, 131, 151.

10. Clarke, *John Hull*, 85–91; William Davis Miller, "The Narragansett Planters," *Proceedings of the American Antiquarian Society* 43 (1934): 49–115.

11. See John Hull, "Account for Sales for Severals," 1673, Hull Manuscripts, Massachusetts Historical Society, Boston; Jordan, *John Hull*, 20–26, 179–216; for the effects of inflation, Barbara McLean Ward, "Boston Artisan Entrepreneurs of the Goldsmithing Trade in the Decades before the Revolution," in *Entrepreneurs: The Boston Business Community, 1700–1850*, ed. Conrad Edick Wright and Kathryn P. Viens (Boston, 1977), 23–37.

12. William B. Weeden, *Economic and Social History of New England, 1620–1787*, 2 vols. (1890; repr., New York, 1963), 1:159; Clarke, *John Hull*, 101, 165, 186, 191; Bailyn, *New England Merchants*, 186 (for the overvaluation of currency).

13. Hull died without a will and probate inventory. The figure here is given in Clarke's *John Hull*, 191. For Shrimpton, see Hunter, *Purchasing Identity*, 28, 73. For the persistence of personal modes of exchange in rural areas, see Michael Merrill, "Cash Is Good to Eat: Self-Sufficiency and Exchange in the Rural Economy of the United States," *Radical History Review* 3 (1977): 42–71; James Henretta, "Families and Farms: *Mentalité* in Pre-Industrial America," *The William and Mary Quarterly*, 3rd ser., 35 (1978): 3–32; and Bettye Hobbs Pruitt, "Self-Sufficiency and the Agricultural Economy of Eighteenth-Century Massachusetts," *The William and Mary Quarterly*, 3rd ser., 41 (1984): 333–64.

14. For the growth of commerce in Massachusetts in the context of England's transatlantic empire, see Carla Gardina Pestana, *The English Atlantic in the Age of Revolution, 1640–1661* (Cambridge, Mass., 2004); David Hancock, " 'A World of Business to Do': William Freeman and the Foundations of England's Commercial Empire, 1645–1707," *The William and Mary Quarterly*, 3rd ser., 57 (2000): 3–34; Jack P. Greene, *Interpreting Early America: Historiographical Essays* (Charlottesville, Va., 1996), 240–80; and Gloria L. Main and Jackson T. Main, "The Red Queen in New England," *The William and Mary Quarterly*, 3rd ser., 56 (1999): 121–47. For the interdependence of agricultural production, internal trade, and overseas exchange, see James E. McWilliams, "Beyond Declension: Economic Adaptation and the Pursuit of Export Markets in the Massachusetts Bay Region, 1630–1700," in *Culture and Identities in Colonial British America*, ed. Robert Olwell and Alan Tully (Baltimore, 2006): 121–46, esp. 121–24. For other details mentioned here, see Bailyn, *New England Merchants*, 98; Newell, *From Dependency to Independence*, 77–78; and Weeden, *Economic and Social History* 1:165–212.

15. The hypothetical case constructed here, illustrating economic integration in the hands of merchants, takes its cue from Daniel Vickers, "The Northern Colonies: Economy and Society, 1600–1775," in *The Cambridge Economic History of the United States*, ed. Stanley L. Engerman and Robert E. Gallman, vol. 1, *The Colonial Era* (New York, 1996), 209–48.

16. For the Navigation Acts and political fallout, see Bailyn, *New England Merchants*, 112–67.

17. Muldrew, *Economy of Obligation*, 111, 174; Newell, *From Dependency to Independence*, 72–83, 101–17; Stuart Bruchey, "The Colonial Merchant," in *The Encyclopedia of the North American Colonies*, ed. Jacob Ernest Cooke, 3 vols. (New York, 1993), 1:577–89; and Vickers, *Farmers and Fishermen*, 85–142. The example from Hull's letterbook can be found in "Diaries of John Hull," 416–18.

18. For the multiplication of negotiable instruments and rising importance of legal adjudication according to new versions of the common law, see James Milnes Holden, *The History of Negotiable Instruments in English Law* (London, 1955), 30–65.

19. The quote from Baily comes from Arthur B. Ellis, *History of the First Church in Boston, 1630–1880* (Boston, 1881), 154. Copies of *The Act of Tonnage* and Roberts's *Merchants Mappe* can be found in the library of the Mather family (a Boston clerical dynasty) at the American Antiquarian society, Worcester, Massachusetts;

for the other works mentioned here and the spread of professional legal culture through books in New England, see Mary Sarah Bilder, *The Transatlantic Constitution: Colonial Legal Culture and the Empire* (Cambridge, Mass., 2004), 15–30. For the Usher book-selling numbers, see Bridenbaugh, *Cities in the Wilderness*, 129–30.

20. Samuel Tompson notebook, "Magnum in Parvo, or The Pen's Perfection," 1678, American Antiquarian Society. According to Tompson's notes, a bill of exchange ought to include "I _____ do owe and am indebted unto _____ the sum of _____ currant money of England to be paid unto the said _____ [or] his Heirs . . . to the which payment will and truely to be made I do bind my self . . . in the penalty or sum of _____ of like money, firmly by these presents." For other legal and secretarial manuals available, see Hugh Amory, "Under the Exchange: The Unprofitable Business of Michael Perry, a Seventeenth-Century Boston Bookseller," *Proceedings of the American Antiquarian Society* 103 (1993): 31–60.

21. In *A New Discourse on Trade* (London, 1668), a frequently reprinted tract, Child urged lower interest rates on purely pragmatic grounds: ready credit would spur English merchants to compete more aggressively with the Dutch. For Child's economic arguments in other publications, see William Letwin, *Sir Josiah Child, Merchant Economist, with a reprint of Brief Observations concerning trade, and interest of money (1668)* (Cambridge, Mass., 1959). At least one New England pastor, John Higginson of Salem, knew Child firsthand; see "Higginson Letters," *Massachusetts Historical Society Collections*, 3rd ser., 7 (1838): 196–221. Most of this paragraph rests on Joyce Oldham Appleby's *Economic Thought and Ideology in Seventeenth-Century England* (Princeton, N.J., 1978). For mathematical analysis, empirical social science, and calculation, especially in regard to William Petty, see Patricia Cline Cohen, *A Calculating People: The Spread of Numeracy in Early America* (New York, 1999), 32–33.

22. Appleby, *Economic Thought*, 24–128; for Misselden's critique of religious dissent and of Malynes' humanist assumptions, see also Andrea Finkelstein, "Gerard de Malynes and Edward Misselden: The Learned Library of the Seventeenth-Century Merchant," *Book History* 3 (2000): 1–20.

23. Edward Misselden, *The Circle of Commerce* (London, 1623), 17, 132, 134. For the literature in defense of merchants in this period, see Steve Pincus, "Neither Machiavellian Moment nor Possessive Individualism: Commercial Society and the Defenders of the English Commonwealth," *American Historical Review* 103 (1998): 705–36.

24. Thomas Sprat, *History of the Royal Society* (London, 1667), 86–88; James Howel, *Londinopolis: An Historicall Discourse or Perlustration of the City of London* (London, 1668), 396–99. For Dryden, Waller, and the general reputation of merchants, see John McVeagh, *Tradefull Merchants: The Portrayal of the Capitalist in Literature* (London, 1981), 33–52.

25. For the economic dominance of Boston, see John J. McCusker, "Measuring Colonial Gross Domestic Product: An Introduction," *The William and Mary Quarterly*, 3rd ser., 56 (1999): 3–8; and David W. Galenson, "The Settlement and Growth of the Colonies: Population, Labor, and Economic Development," in *Cambridge Economic History*, ed. Engerman and Gallman, 1:135–207, esp. 200–201. For infrastructure, shipbuilding, and Boston as the hub of credit, see Weeden, *Economic and*

Social History 1:232–67; Newell, *From Dependency to Independence*, 72–93; Bailyn, *New England Merchants*, 98; Whitehill and Kennedy, *Boston*, 15–38; and Hunter, *Purchasing Identity*, 9–10. For cultural production, see Hugh Amory, "Printing and Bookselling in New England, 1638–1713," in *A History of the Book in America*, ed. Hugh Amory and David D. Hall, vol. 1, *The Colonial Book in the Atlantic World* (New York, 2000), 99–103; and Wayne Craven, *Colonial American Portraiture: The Economic, Religious, Social, Cultural, Philosophical, Scientific, and Aesthetic Foundations* (New York, 1986), 64–77.

26. Bailyn, *New England Merchants*, 75–111; Raymond D. Irwin, "Cast Out from the 'City upon a Hill': Antinomian Exiles in Rhode Island, 1638–1650," *Rhode Island History* 52 (1994): 3–19.

27. Bailyn, *New England Merchants*, 110–67, 192–93; Newell, *From Dependency to Independence*, 90. One hundred and thirty-four New Englanders signed the 1664 petition of loyalty: twenty-five were from Boston and thirteen of those were recently arrived merchants who became Anglicans (Bailyn, *New England Merchants*, 124). For Wharton, see Viola F. Barnes, "Richard Wharton: A Seventeenth Century New England Colonial," *Publications of the Colonial Society of Massachusetts*, vol. 26, *Transactions, 1924–1926* (Boston, 1927), 238–70.

28. Bailyn, *New England Merchants*, 135–37; Barnes, "Richard Wharton," 239–40; Hunter, *Purchasing Identity*, 28–30.

29. "Diaries of John Hull," 153; Bailyn, *New England Merchants*, 151, 152, 193; Clarke, *Robert Hull*, 97–98, 140, 184 (for Hull's political allegiances). For puritan merchants and their opposition to religious toleration, see E. Brooks Holifield, "On Toleration in Massachusetts," *Church History* 38 (1969): 188–200.

30. For Sewall, see Hall, *Worlds of Wonder*, 213–38. For Curwin, see Hunter, *Purchasing Identity*, 42. For Scottow, see Julie Helen Otto, "Lydia and Her Daughters: A Boston Matrilineal Case Study," *NEHGS Nexus* 9 (1992): 24–29; and Mary Beth Norton, *In the Devil's Snare: The Salem Witchcraft Crisis of 1692* (New York, 2002), 88, 129, 142.

31. The key texts, including the Cambridge Platform, with detailed background, are provided in Walker's *Creeds and Platforms*, 157–339. There is an abundant literature on the Halfway Covenant; this and the following paragraph relies on Robert G. Pope's *Halfway Covenant: Church Membership in Puritan New England* (Princeton, N.J., 1969); Foster, *Long Argument*, 175–230; Peterson, *Price of Redemption*, 23–50; and Cooper, *Tenacious of Their Liberties*, 88–114.

32. Robert Middlekauff, *The Mathers: Three Generations of Puritan Intellectuals, 1596–1728* (New York, 1971), 119–37.

33. Clarke, *John Hull*, 115–17, 153–59; Peterson, *Price of Redemption*, 41–49, 82–84; and Mark A. Peterson, "Puritanism and Refinement in New England: Reflections on Communion Silver," *The William and Mary Quarterly*, 3rd ser., 58 (2001): 307–46. Formal animosities between First and Third Churches ended when Hull convinced his fellow members to accept an overture of reconciliation offered by First Church in 1682, but the two congregations maintained different sacramental and disciplinary regimes through Hull's lifetime: Ellis, *History of First Church Boston*, 135.

34. Clarke, *John Hull*, 156–57; Ernest Benson Lowrie, *The Shape of the Puritan Mind: The Thought of Samuel Willard* (New Haven, Conn., 1974), 10; Bailyn, *New England Merchants*, 55, 134–38.

35. *First Church Records*, passim; Foster, *Long Argument*, 203, 231–85. For the voice of suspicion toward the magistracy, see [Davenport], *Discourse on Civil Government*, 19–23; and John Davenport, *Sermon . . . Preach'd at the Election* ([Cambridge, Mass.], 1670).

36. James A. Henretta, "Economic Development and Social Structure in Colonial Boston," *The William and Mary Quarterly*, 3rd ser., 22 (1965): 75–92; Michael G. Hall, *The Last American Puritan: The Life of Increase Mather, 1639–1723* (Middletown, Conn., 1988), 51–52, 93.

37. Hall, *Last American Puritan*, 51–53, 61–67, 93 136, 224; Kenneth Ballard Murdock, *Increase Mather: The Foremost American Puritan* (Cambridge, Mass., 1925), 125–26, 198–99; Middlekauff, *Mathers*, 65–175, for a general biography.

38. Hall, *Last American Puritan*, 141; Murdock, *Increase Mather*, 141, 181.

39. Hamilton Andrews Hill, ed., *An Historical Catalogue of the Old South Church (Third Church) Boston, 1669–1882* (Boston, 1882), 5–21, 215–315; Roberts, *Artillery Company* 1:484–88; Peterson, *Price of Redemption*, 69–74.

40. *First Church Records*, 12–160; Second Church, Boston, records, vol. 3, Massachusetts Historical Society, Boston; Third Church, records, Congregational Library, Boston. The records of the church at Cambridge are not extant before 1705. For the other congregations mentioned here, see *Roxbury Church Records*, passim; Charlestown, Massachusetts, First Church, *Records of the First Church in Charlestown, Massachusetts, 1632–1789* (Boston, 1880), i–xii; Plymouth Church Records, in *Publications of the Colonial Society of Massachusetts*, Collections, vol. 22 (Boston, 1920), 154–64. For a statistical overview, see Emil Olberholzer Jr., *Delinquent Saints: Disciplinary Action in the Early Congregational Churches of Massachusetts* (New York, 1956), 186–99.

41. John Higginson, *The Cause of God and His People in New-England* (Cambridge, Mass., 1663), 11; Samuel Whiting, *Abraham's Humble Intercession for Sodom* (Cambridge, Mass., 1666), 306–7, 312–13; Urian Oakes, *New-England Pleaded with* (Cambridge, Mass., 1673), 32–55; Hubbard, *Well-Ordered Conversation*, 97–98.

42. Jonathan Mitchel of Cambridge, for example, contrasted Boston's entrepreneurs and financiers in 1671 to godly merchants in the past, who never would have practiced "the biting" and merciless "*Usury*" that compelled poor people to repay their loans: Jonathan Mitchel, *Nehemiah on the Wall* (Cambridge, Mass., 1671), 4; Miller, *From Colony to Province*, 37, 48.

43. Hull, sermon notes, Massachusetts Historical Society. Hull listed all of the names here, along with the preaching texts, at the beginning of each entry. The quotes and specific references here are from Hull's notes on Thacher, sermon on Ezekiel 22, January 24, 1672; Thacher, Matt. 25:33, July 11, 1671; Oakes, Ps. 122:1, January 20, 1672; Willard, 2 Chron. 32:25, November 15, 1677; and Willard, Ecc. 1:12–13, December 26, 1678. See Clarke, *John Hull*, 72, for Hull's methods of sermon note taking; 153–59, 162, 184 for Hull's clerical friendships.

44. Hull, sermon notes, Thacher, Matt. 25:33, July 11, 1671; Oakes, Ps. 122:1.

45. Clarke, *John Hull*, 148.

46. "Diaries of John Hull," 141, 146, 161 (for the quotations); 19, 143, 150, 155 (for the other examples here). Problems with Dutch privateers arose during the three Anglo-Dutch Wars (1652–54, 1664–67, 1672–74).

47. "Diaries of John Hull," 208, 220.

48. For politeness as opposed to puritan moral rhetoric in commercial transactions, see Philip H. Round, *By Nature and Custom Cursed: Transatlantic Civil Discourse and New England Cultural Production, 1620–1660* (Hanover, N.H., 1999); for moral commentary rather than strict business accounts, see Cohen, *Numeracy*, 47–50, 79.

49. Hull to Allin, cited in Newell's *From Dependency to Independence*, 103; Clarke, "John Hull," 211. For one instance of Hull's move from commercial details to signs of the times, see his April 29, 1674, letter to Allin, "The Letterbook of John Hull," American Antiquarian Society, Worcester, Massachusetts. For further examples, see Newell, *From Dependency to Independence*, 92–93.

50. Hull to Rook, May 21, 1683, Hull "Letterbook." For other letters to ship captains, see Newell, *From Dependency to Independence*, 92–93.

51. Hull to George and John Broughton, Hull "Letterbook," December 7, 1673.

52. Hull to Marshall, November 6, 1674, Hull "Letterbook"; Hull to Joshua Fisher, September 27, 1671, Hull "Letterbook." See Clarke, "John Hull," 213, 218; and Newell, *From Dependency to Independence*, 93, 103–4, 117.

53. "Diaries of John Hull," 212, 215; Clarke, "John Hull," 218; quote from Miller, *Colony to Province*, 43.

54. Hull to William Heifernan, September 10, 1673, Hull "Letterbook"; Clarke, *John Hull*, 64–65, 69, 103, 131–32; Newell, *From Dependency to Independence*, 86–94; Hunter, *Purchasing Identity*, 23.

55. Hull to Joshua Lamb, September 29, 1674, Hull "Letterbook"; Hull to Joshua Lamb, September 1, 1677, Hull "Letterbook"; John Josselyn, *An Account of Two Voyages to New England* (London, 1674), 180; Bailyn, *New England Merchants*, 98 (for the first Josselyn quote), 129–30; Clarke, *John Hull*, 110. For London's high interest rates on loans to New Englanders, see Bailyn, *New England Merchants*, 183. For other criticisms of Boston merchants, see Newell, *From Dependency to Independence*, 77; Bridenbaugh, *Cities in the Wilderness*, 38; and Rutman, *Winthrop's Boston*, 272. For the vices of maritime, urban Boston society, see Laurel Thatcher Ulrich, "Big Dig, Little Dig, Hidden Worlds: Boston," *Common-Place* 3, no. 4 (2003), *www.common-place.org/vol-03/no-04/boston*. Accessed June 30, 2009.

56. [John Davenport], *Discourse about Civil Government*, 23; see also 12, 20; Davenport, *Sermon Preach'd . . . at the Election*, esp. 11; John Oxenbridge, *New-England Freemen Warned* ([Cambridge, Mass.], 1673), esp. 19; James Allen, *New Englands Choicest Blessing* (Boston, 1679), 10.

57. Sacramental piety and new patterns of discipline in the late seventeenth century often enhanced the authority of ordained ministers as religious professionals, but it also accompanied the sort of division between civil and religious discipline discussed later. For ministerial authority, see Hall, *Faithful Shepherd*.

58. Increase Mather, "Journal," *Massachusetts Historical Society Proceedings* 8 (1899–1900): 340–409; quotations and other details on 343, 335, 358–59, 400; W. DeLoss Love Jr., *The Fast and Thanksgiving Days of New England* (Boston, 1895), 464–83; Hall, *Last Puritan*, 129–31; Miller, *Colony to Province*, 130–46.

59. Increase Mather, "Journal," 340, 343, 400–402.

60. Stoughton (who later entered politics as the colony's lieutenant governor and supervisor over the courts of justice) scattered covenantal language throughout his election sermon in 1668; he argued that civil rulers were near "*Gods*" by virtue of their public office: William Stoughton, *New Englands True Interest: Not to Lie* (Cambridge, Mass., 1670), 34. Oakes deployed the trope of "the New-England Israel"; Oakes, *New-England Pleaded with*, 17. See also Samuel Willard, *Useful Instructions for a Professing People* (Cambridge, Mass., 1673), 63–80.

61. Increase Mather, *The Day of Trouble* (Cambridge, Mass., 1674), 3–13.

62. Ibid., 22–23.

63. Increase Mather, *An Earnest Exhortation to the Inhabitants of New-England* (Boston, 1676), 9, 11.

64. Ibid., 3. Mather's tract on the Halfway Covenant was *The Life and Death of that Reverend Man of God, Mr. Richard Mather* (Boston, 1670); see also Middlekauff, *Mathers*, 104–16. William Hubbard's history of the Indian war was *A Narrative of the Trouble with the Indians*; his "General History of New England" was not published until 1815, in the *Massachusetts Historical Society, Collections* 2:5–6 (1815). For the jeremiad and the rise of historical consciousness, see Miller, *Colony to Province*, esp. 28–33, 51, 116; and Sacvan Bercovitch, *The American Jeremiad* (Madison, Wis., 1978). For the rise of historical narrative, see Michael P. Winship, *Seers of God: Puritan Providentialism in the Restoration and Early Enlightenment* (Baltimore, 1996), 9–73.

65. In its popularized, sometimes bowdlerized version, providence merged with centuries-old folklore: tales of wonders and supernatural prodigies that inflicted pain on the wicked or rescued repentant sinners from natural disaster. Hull's diary contained some hint or residue of this personalized, predictive, and miraculous reading of providence, which differed from the retrospective and collective readings given by Mather and other divines: Hall, *World of Wonders*, 71–116; Michael P. Winship, "Encountering Providence in the Seventeenth Century: The Experiences of a Yeoman and a Minister," *Essex Institute Historical Collections* 126 (1990): 27–36; Alexandra Walsham, *Providence in Early Modern England* (New York, 1999); and Bozeman, *To Live Ancient Lives*, 287–343. For a recent survey that limns changing notions of providence and the nation throughout this period, and their importance for social consciousness, see Nicholas Guyatt, *Providence and the Invention of the United States, 1607–1876* (New York, 2007), 1–52.

66. In his journal, essentially a recounting of events in New England through 1649, Winthrop occasionally referred to the spiritual lessons of calamities or good fortunes, to the effect that the Lord was teaching New Englanders to trust and obey, but only as a general principle; Winthrop did not speculate on the specific meaning of public events in providential terms.

67. Increase Mather, *Day of Trouble*, 26–27. For differences between Bradford and Winthrop on one hand and Increase Mather on the other, see Peter Lockwood Rumsey, *Acts of God and the People, 1620–1730* (Ann Arbor, Mich., 1986), 7–44.

68. Increase Mather, *Earnest Exhortation*, 3–4, 13. The "Provoking Evils" legislation was printed in *Several Laws and Orders . . . of the General Court* (Cambridge, Mass., 1675), 32–37. For the general narrative here and the following paragraphs, see Hall, *Last American Puritan*, 107–9; Foster, *Long Argument*, 206–30; and

Richard P. Gildrie, *The Profane, the Civil, and the Godly: The Reformation of Manners in Orthodox New England, 1679–1749* (University Park, Penn., 1994), 19–40.

69. Displeased at Mather's 1677 *Discourse* because of its implied critique of governmental laxity, the governor and members of the upper house refused to offer the usual proposal for publication; it was printed later as a separate work in Mather's *Call from Heaven to the Present and Succeeding Generations* (Boston, 1679).

70. Increase Mather, *Discourse Concerning the Danger of Apostasy*, 35, 66, 55–66. For the background to and importance of Mather's sermons at this time, see Hall, *Last American Puritan*, 113–31; Gildrie, *The Profane, the Civil, and the Godly*, 25–37.

71. Increase Mather, *Discourse Concerning the Danger of Apostasy*, 71, 72–81, 88–91.

72. Ibid., 86–87; Samuel Willard, *A Sermon . . . Occasioned by the Death of . . . John Leveret* (Boston, 1679), 6–8, 13.

73. Boston Synod, *The Necessity of Reformation* (Boston, 1679), 11; Peterson, *Price of Redemption*, 167; Hall, *Last American Puritan*, 155–56.

74. Shurtleff, ed., *Records*, vol. 4, pt. 2, passim; 5:59–63.

75. Increase Mather, *Returning unto God the Great Concernment of a Covenant People* (Boston, 1680), n.p. (the quote is from the covenant itself, printed after the sermon without pagination). For the covenant renewals of the 1680s, see David A. Weir, *Early New England: A Covenanted Society* (Grand Rapids, Mich., 2005), 191–220.

76. Samuel Willard, *The Duty of a People that have Renewed their Covenant with God* (Boston, 1680), 5, 11, and *The Only sure way to prevent threatned Calamity* (Boston, 1684), esp. 179–88. Confessions of faith and conversion narratives, often given to meet the requirements for Communion, still provided some corporate discipline in the church, but these confessions did not mention specific economic behaviors; Elizabeth Reis, "Seventeenth-Century Puritan Conversion Narratives," in *Religions of the United States in Practice*, ed. Colleen McDannell, 2 vols. (Princeton, N.J., 2001), 1:22–31.

77. Pastors in the congregational order during this period increasingly regarded their vocation as a specialized profession. They accordingly deemphasized church meetings led by the laity and moved moral oversight to private consultations with individual church members while investing civil rulers with expertise over secular business: Hall, *Faithful Shepherd*.

78. The figures come from a statistical analysis of the records of the Massachusetts Superior Court of Judicature, included in Noble and Cronin, eds., *Records of the Court of Assistants*; the Suffolk County Court of Common Pleas, published as "Records of the Suffolk County Court, 1671–1680," ed. Samuel Eliot Morison, *Publications of the Colonial Society of Massachusetts: Collections*, vols. 29–30 (Boston, 1933); the Middlesex County Court of Common Pleas, 3 vols., trans. David Pulsifer (Massachusetts State Archives, Boston); and the *Records and Files of the Quarterly Courts of Essex County, Massachusetts*, ed. Dow, vols. 2, 8. For background, see Newell, *From Dependency to Independence*, 116–20; and Muldrew, *Economy of Obligation*, 173–95. For one example of the spread westward of debt litigation, see Joseph H. Smith, ed., *Colonial Justice in Western Massachusetts (1639–1702): The Pynchon Court Record* (Cambridge, Mass., 1961), 161–63, 203–27.

79. There is an extensive literature by legal and social historians that reinforces the point: increases in numbers of economic disputes brought before the courts, changes in courtroom procedure, and the proliferation of formal legal argumentation all indicate a transition from church to a civil institution as the moral authority in society. To sample such literature, consult Peter Charles Hoffer, *Law and People in Colonial America*, rev. ed. (Batimore, 1998), 76–91; Foster, *Their Solitary Way*, 138–47; Haskins, *Law and Authority*; T. H. Breen, "Persistent Localism: English Social Change and the Shaping of New England Institutions," *The William and Mary Quarterly*, 3rd ser., 32 (1975): 3–28; Cornelia Hughes Dayton, "Turning Points and the Relevance of Colonial Legal History," *The William and Mary Quarterly*, 3rd ser., 50 (1993): 7–17; Konig, *Law and Society*; Carole Shammas, "Anglo-American Household Government in Comparative Perspective," *The William and Mary Quarterly*, 3rd ser., 52 (1995): 104–44; and Douglas Greenberg, "Crime, Law Enforcement, and Social Control in Colonial America," *American Journal of Legal History* 26 (1982): 293–325.

80. "Records of the Suffolk County Court," 78; see 65–78.

81. "Diaries of John Hull," 211–12, 237, 249; see 213–15, 233–36, 244–46. Hull continued to record ill omens when the Reforming Synod's measures had little effect: more fires, fasts, deaths of prominent leaders, and comets.

82. [Joshua Scottow], *Old Mens Tears for their Own Declensions* (Boston, 1691), 3–5, 17–19; [Joshua Scottow], *A Narrative of the Planting of the Massachusetts Colony* (Boston, 1694), 25–26, 40, 43. For Scottow's providential reading of history, see Dennis Powers, "Purpose and Design in Joshua Scottow's *Narrative*," *Early American Literataure* 18 (1983–84): 275–90.

83. In 1656 Hull and nearly twenty other merchants resolved to establish a fund to house and educate unemployed youth in Boston. In 1660 the town appointed the deacons of First Church to oversee the construction of an almshouse, funded by bequests from merchants, including Hull. During the 1670s, the number of indigent residents in Boston increased markedly, especially from the flood of northern refugees during King Philip's War. From this point on, poor relief in Boston depended on a mélange of voluntary contributions taken in congregations, the beneficent campaigns of well-do-do donors, and, after the colonial government enacted its first poor law in 1671, tax revenues: Foster, *Their Solitary Way*, 138–47; Bridenbaugh, *Cities in the Wilderness*, 81–82; and Lee, "Public Poor Relief."

84. Clarke, *John Hull*, 115–17, 180–85; Rugg, "Famous Colonial Litigation," 229.

85. "Diaries of John Hull," 167–68; Hull to the General Court, ca. 1681, quoted and cited in *John Hull*, by Clarke, 191–92.

86. Cotton Mather, *Magnalia Christi Americana* (1702; repr., Hartford, Conn., 1852), 2 vols., 1:316.

87. Samuel Willard, *The High Esteem which God hath of the Death of His Saints* (Boston, 1683), 16–17.

88. Samuel Willard, *The Righteous Man's Death* (Boston, 1684), printed as part of *The Child's Portion* (Boston, 1684), 160–61; Hubbard, *Well-Ordered Conversation*, 135–59.

89. *A Rich Treasure at an Easy Rate* (1657; 1683; 3rd ed., Boston, 1763), 23–26.

90. In Nathaniel Hawthorne, *Hawthorne's Works*, Concord Edition, 25 vols. (Boston, 1899), 12:41.

91. M. Halsey Thomas, ed., *The Diary of Samuel Sewall, 1674–1729*, 2 vols. (New York, 1973), 1:15 (hereafter cited as Sewall, *Diary*).

CHAPTER FOUR
SAMUEL SEWALL'S WINDOWS

1. Sewall, *Diary* 1:330. The "bleake" quotation is cited in the entry for Sewall in John Langdon Sibley and Clifford K. Shipton, eds., *Sibley's Harvard Graduates*, 17 vols. (Cambridge, Mass., 1881–1975) [hereafter cited as *Harvard Graduates*], 2:348. For houses and bodies, with reference to demonic attack and Sewall's house, see St. George, *Conversing by Signs*, 115–203; and Marion Nelson [Winship], "Safety and Danger in a Puritan Home: Life in the Hull-Sewall House, 1676–1717," in *The American Home: Material Culture, Domestic Space, and Family Life*, ed. Eleanor McD. Thompson (Hanover, N.H., 1998), 257–71.

2. Sewall, *Diary* 1:330, 340. For Renaissance-Netherlandish style of the period in London and Boston, with reference to the details here about Cunnable, the quoins, and other features of Sewall's house that signified spiritual forces, see Abbott Lowell Cummings, "The Beginnings of Provincial Renaissance Architecture in Boston, 1690–1725," *Journal of the Society of Architectural Historians* 42 (1983): 43–53, esp. 48–49; and St. George, *Conversing by Signs*, 190. For windows as eyes, see St. George, *Conversing by Signs*, 141–50. The glass panes were quite small and would have constituted between ten and twenty windows.

3. Sewall, *Diary* 1:330.

4. Ibid. 1:330–31.

5. Cotton Mather, *Durable Riches* (Boston, 1695), 2, 5, 12–13.

6. Ibid., 3, 18–19, 24 (second pagination). "The True Way of Thriving" restarts pagination at 1 following the first lecture, "The True Cause of Loosing."

7. Sewall, *Diary* 1:331–39.

8. For an important study of one of Sewall's contemporaries, who operated in the same imperial context with different religious loyalties, see Richard R. Johnson, *John Nelson Merchant Adventurer: A Life between Empires* (New York, 1991).

9. The basic biography is provided by Ola Elizabeth Winslow, *Samuel Sewall of Boston* (New York, 1964).

10. See Charles G. Steffan, "The Sewall Children in Colonial New England," *The New England Historical and Genealogical Register* [hereafter *NEHGR*] 131 (1977): 163–72.

11. Sewall's letters were printed as "Letterbook of Samuel Sewall," *Massachusetts Historical Society, Collections*, 6th ser., 1 (Boston, 1886), and 2 (Boston, 1887). For his trade in commodities, see Sewall to Edward Hull, February 13, 1688, "Letterbook" 1:2–3; Sewall to Edward Hull, July 15, 1686, "Letterbook" 1:32–33; and Sewall to John Ive, July 15, 1686, "Letterbook" 1:34. For his books, see Sewall to John Love, January 7, 1713, "Letterbook" 2:10–11; Sewall to Thomas Bridge, August 30, 1702, "Letterbook" 1:273; Sewall to Cotton Mather, February 3, 1713, "Letterbook" 2:15.

12. Sewall, *Diary* 1:202–3; Sewall, "Memoranda," February 1720, "Letterbook" 2:105–6. For the spiritual meaning of material refinement, see Peterson, "Puritanism and Refinement."

13. Sewall to Joshua Raymon, June 9, 1687, "Letterbook" 1:47–48 (for Block Island); Sewall, *Diary* 1:401–2, 409–10 (for the Panama venture). Sewall's Maine property and work on the witchcraft court placed him in the company of other eminent merchants such as John Richards, Wait Winthrop, and William Stoughton; see Emerson W. Baker and James Fences, "Maine, Indian Land Speculation, and the Essex County Witchcraft Outbreak of 1692," *Maine History* 40 (2001): 158–89, esp. 167–69.

14. The quotation is taken from Sewall to William Hutchinson and William Pulford, August 24, 1686, "Letterbook" 1:37. For some of many references to problems with credit and the value of specie, see Sewall to Nathaniel Man, November 10, 1687, "Letterbook" 1:64–65; Sewall to Nathaniel Barns, March 8, 1690, "Letterbook" 1:108–9; Sewall to John Leverett, July 22, 1695, "Letterbook" 1:156–57; Sewall to Charles Blinco, May 6, 1696, "Letterbook" 1:161–62; and Sewall to Samuel Shepard, February 21, 1705, "Letterbook" 1:309–10.

15. Sewall to Cotton Mather, December 10, 1706, "Letterbook" 1:341–45.

16. No sustained study of Fitch has been published. The biographical details provided here and below come from probate and other records, artillery company records, and church records, along with the extant writings of Fitch; Thomas Fitch, Letterbook, 1703–11, American Antiquarian Society (hereafter cited as AAS letterbook); Thomas Fitch, Letterbook, 1723–34, Massachusetts Historical Society (hereafter cited as MHS letterbook); and Thomas Fitch, Account Book, 1720–25, Massachusetts Historical Society (hereafter cited as Account Book). For probate records, land deeds, and scattered biographical information, see Annie Haven Thwing, ed., *Inhabitants and Estates of the Town of Boston, 1630–1800*, compact disc (New England Historical and Genealogical Society, Boston), entry for Thomas Fitch; for artillery company, O. A. Roberts, *Artillery Company* 1:324–25; for church records, Hill, *Old South Church*, passim. For Thomas Fitch the elder, see the following entries in the *NEHGR*: 16 (1862): 70, 162; 51 (1897): 280, 398; 114 (1990): 15.

17. For Fitch's estate, see Ezra Sterns, "The Descendants of Dea. Zachary Fitch of Reading," *NEHGR* 55 (1901): 291–94; for Mary Oliver, see *NEHGR* 19 (1865): 103; for John Fitch, see *Harvard Graduates* 7:133–34; for James Allen and the lavish wedding, see *Harvard Graduates* 6:159–60.

18. Fitch to William Crouch, September 21, 1703, and to Capt. Faneuil, October 30, 1704, AAS letterbook (for luxury imports and two of many examples of European dealers); Fitch, Account Book, May, August 1723 (for dealing in bonds and bills); Newall, *From Dependency to Independence*, 92.

19. Boston, Long Wharf Corporation Documents, 1713–29, Boston Public Library, Boston, meeting notes from 1713 and 1719; Fitch to Edward Shippen, June 26, 1710, AAS letterbook (in which Fitch sought advice on building and maintaining wharves). See also Hunter, *Purchasing Identity*, 85–85; Whitehill and Kennedy, *Boston*, 20–21; and *NEHGR* 67 (1913): 108.

20. Fitch to Jonathan Crouch and Samuel Arnold, August 17, 1709 (for the quotation); Fitch to Samuel Taylor, May 3, 1703 (wine and turpentine); Fitch to Henry

King, January 3, 1704 (furs); Fitch to William Crouch, May 20, 1703 (advice on fashion); Fitch to Jonathan Crouch and Samuel Arnold, February 6 and 13, 1710 (fashion and concerns about ships); and Fitch to William Brown, February 27, 1710 (relative values of notes): all from Fitch, AAS letterbook.

21. Fitch to Robert Plumsted, April 1, 1703 (for the quotation); Fitch to Jeffrey Grey, November 9, 1703 (different forms of payment sent); Fitch to John Crouch and Company, November 13, 1705 (on Fitch's preferred means of being paid); Fitch to Edward Shippen, May 29, 1704 (the Philadelphia merchant); Fitch to Capt. Faneuil, September 10, 1705 (on New York bills): all from Fitch, AAS letterbook. Fitch, Account Book, 1723 (for the Annapolis bill of exchange).

22. Fitch to John Crouch and Company, March 12, 1708, AAS letterbook; Fitch to David Jeffries, March 30, 1724, MHS letterbook.

23. Fitch to David Jeffries, March 30, 1724; Fitch to David Foxcroft, January 4, 1723; Fitch to William Wanton, September 2, 1730; Fitch to John Chandler, October 4, 1730: all from MHS letterbook. Fitch's suits for debts are recorded in the Suffolk County Court of Common Pleas, Record Books, Boston, Massachusetts, 1699–1701 (for example, *Fitch v. Joseph Royal*, ca. 1699), 1706–15 (for example, *Fitch v. James Browne*, 1709), and 1715–19 [1720] (for example, *Fitch v. William Pollard*, 1720). By 1735 90 percent of all cases on this court's docket involved causes for debt. The record books of one justice of the peace in Suffolk from 1700–1714, John Clark (a member of Cotton Mather's Old North Church), reflects the explosion of debt cases in this period; Russell K. Osgood, "John Clark, Esq., Justice of the Peace, 1667–1728," in *Law in Colonial Massachusetts*, ed. Coquillette, 107–51. A statistical sampling of the manuscript records of the Court of Appeals for the Suffolk Court, the Massachusetts Superiour Court of Judicature, Boston, Massachusetts, 1692–95 and 1715–29, further confirms of the rise of debt cases.

24. Examples of transatlantic litigation over such matters as bill of exchange transferred throughout the Atlantic abound. One of the most illustrative is *Samuel Keeling and Charles Chauncy v. Isaac Royal*, 1698, Suffolk County, Court of Common Pleas, Record Books, 1699–1701, which involved the transfer of funds between London, Barbados, and Boston. Further examples can be found in John Ballantine to the Sheriff of Suffolk County, July 1719, and John Hollis to Edward Hutchinson, February, 11, 1732, Edward Hutchinson Papers, Massachusetts Historical Society. For the rise of litigation and professionalization of legal practice, see Peter Charles Hoffer, *Law and People in Colonial America*, rev. ed. (Baltimore, 1998); Dayton, *Women before the Bar*, 47–52; Richard B. Morris, *Studies in the History of American Law*, 2nd ed. (Philadelphia, 1959), 41–67; Konig, *Law and Society in Puritan Massachusetts*, 78–116; and Mann, *Neighbors and Strangers*, 93–100. In "The Zuckerman Thesis and the Process of Legal Rationalization in Provincial Massachusetts," *The William and Mary Quarterly*, 3rd ser., 29 (1972): 443–60, David Grayson Allen provides a helpful discussion of legal rationalization, courtroom protocol, and commerce in a neighboring county (Middlesex). See also William M. Offutt, "The Atlantic Rules: The Legalistic Turn in Colonial British America," in *The Creation of the British Atlantic World*, ed. Elizabeth Mancke and Carole Shammas (Baltimore, 2005), 160–81. My language here about the replacement of personal and religious moral appeal with contractual obligation derives from Muldrew's *Economy of Obliga-*

tion, 173–95, 299, and 318; see also Craig Muldrew, "Interpreting the Market: The Ethics of Credit and Community Relations in Early Modern England," *Social History* 18 (1993): 163–83.

25. Thomas [John] Hill, *The Young Secretary's Guide*, 3rd ed. (Boston, 1703).

26. Fitch to David Foxcroft, January 4, 1723, MHS letterbook.

27. In dealing with his tenants, Fitch did use morally charged language, although in reference only to fiscal responsibilities. As he told one of his agents seeking a renter for one of his properties, he expected "every penny of the money you had of me" to improve the property for the renter, "to be prudently, frugally, and faithfully laid out on the said house and barn," Fitch to Nathaniel Walker, June 22, 1733, MHS letterbook.

28. For this and the following political narrative, I have relied on G. B. Warden, *Boston, 1689–1776* (Boston, 1970), 5–66; Richard R. Johnson, *Adjustment to Empire: The New England Colonies, 1675–1715* (New Brunswick, N.J., 1981); Bailyn, *New England Merchants*, 168–97; and Viola F. Barnes, *The Dominion of New England: A Study in British Colonial Policy* (New Haven, Conn., 1923). For the Council and Andros, see also Barnes, "Richard Wharton."

29. In addition to the above sources, see Richard S. Dunn, "The Glorious Revolution and America," in *The Oxford History of the British Empire*, ed. Nicholas Canny, vol. 1, *The Origins of Empire: British Overseas Enterprise to the Close of the Seventeenth Century* (Oxford, 1998), 445–66; David Lovejoy, *The Glorious Revolution in America* (New York, 1972); and Gary B. Nash, *The Urban Crucible: Social Change, Political Consciousness, and the Origins of the American Revolution* (Cambridge, Mass., 1979), 36–93.

30. On the economic devastations caused by war in this period, see Baker and Fences, "Maine, Indian Land Speculation"; Nash, *Urban Crucible*, 60–65; and Murdock, *Increase Mather*, 233.

31. Warden, *Boston*, 27–43.

32. For Salem and its connections to warfare, see Norton, *In the Devil's Snare*. Phips's opponents decried his ambitions as a betrayal of Whig principles and New England's interests. Increase Mather countered with further defenses of the new charter in his 1693 election sermon, *The Great Blessing of Primitive Counsellors* (Boston, 1693). Nathaniel Byfield and other Tory-minded merchants with vested interests in approval from London competed with Cooke's faction for seats in the lower House. In his 1694 sermon, *The Character of a Good Ruler* (Boston, 1694), Samuel Willard attempted to formulate a mediating position, but implied the need to reduce the executive's power in Massachusetts. For the politics, see Hall, *Last American Puritan*, 265–68.

33. See especially Warden, *Boston*, 35–59.

34. For exports and imports, see Curtis Nettles, "England's Trade with New England and New York, 1685–1720," *Publications of the Colonial Society of Massachusetts*, vol. 28, *Transactions, 1930–1933* (Boston, 1935): 322–50. For Boston's fleet, see Hunter, *Purchasing Identity*, 9–10. For economic growth and trade networks, see McCusker and Menard, *Economy of British America*, 91–111, 189–208; McCusker, "Measuring Colonial Gross Domestic Product"; and Greene, "Colonial New England in Recent Historiography," in *Interpreting Early America*, 240–80. For comparison between Boston and New York, see Cathy Matson, *Merchants and Empire:*

Trading in Colonial New York (Baltimore, 1998), 49–65. For frontier settlements, see Anderson, *New England's Generation*, 179–221. For periods of crises and the growth of poverty, see Nash, *Urban Crucible*, 55–57; Henretta, "Economic Development"; and Bridenbaugh, *Cities in the Wilderness*, 175–79.

35. Old South memberships are recorded in Hill's *Old South Church* 1:13–26, 104–18, and 219–349. For political actions, the printers, and mercantile leadership at Old South, see Peterson, *Price of Redemption*, 91–92, 139, 123–26, 163–90. Sewall's identification with a townwide, dispersed religious culture rather than with his particular congregation is evidenced in his diary throughout, and in his sermon notebooks, which show him flitting about town, between ministers and congregations.

36. Hall, *Last American Puritan*, 205–6, 213–24; Murdock, *Increase Mather*, 262–70.

37. Mather, quoted in Miller's *Colony to Province*, 162; Miller explores the replacement of covenantal idioms with Whiggish, contractual language. Mather circulated "Reasons for the Confirmation of Charters" and "New England Vindicated" in unpublished form; *A Further Vindication of New England* was published anonymously in London in 1689; *A Brief Relation on the State of New England*, published under Mather's name, appeared in London in 1689. See Hall, *Last American Puritan*, 223–48; and Murdock, *Increase Mather*, 220–35. Elizabethan puritans and their New England successors had asserted continuity between what has been called civic republicanism—including a defense of liberty, property rights, and contracts against arbitrary political authority—and Reformed polity. Mather's mere use of such idioms was not, therefore, completely innovative, but his particular deployment of them to defend New England's place in the imperial system represented an especially potent Whiggish discourse: Michael P. Winship, "Godly Republicanism and the Origins of the Massachusetts Polity," *The William and Mary Quarterly*, 3rd ser., 63 (2006): 427–62. Jeremiah Dummer, the agent for Massachusetts in London, asserted that New England's overseas commerce had enriched England despite a few unprosecuted violations of the Navigation Acts: Jer[emiah] Dummer, *A Defence of the New-England Charters* (London, 1721; repr., Boston, 1721), 10–11, 17–37, 45–46, 73.

38. Increase Mather, *A Brief Account Concerning Several of the Agents of New-England* (London, 1691), 288; quoted and discussed in Hall's *Last American Puritan*, 252. For Mather's willingness to accept religious toleration in return for commercial opportunity and protection from the French, see his diary, September 9, 1691, typescript, Mather Family Papers, American Antiquarian Society, Worcester, Massachusetts.

39. Hereafter, Cotton Mather will be referred to simply as Mather. References to his father will use "Increase Mather."

40. Cotton Mather, *The Wonderful Works of God Commemorated* (Boston, 1690), "Epistle Dedicatory" for the dedication and comments on New England's loyalties (n.p.); 31, 36, 42–43, for the effects on New England. The discussion here and below, which traces the notion of a transatlantic Protestant interest, takes its cue from Thomas S. Kidd's *Protestant Interest: New England after Puritanism* (New Haven, Conn., 2004).

41. On the continuities and discontinuities between puritan republicanism and Whig ideology, see Winship, "Godly Republicanism."

42. Emerson W. Baker and John G. Reid, *The New England Knight: Sir William Phips, 1651–1695* (Toronto, 1998), esp. 18–66; Viola F. Barnes, "The Rise of William Phips," *The New England Quarterly* 1 (1928): 271–94; and Cyrus H. Karraker, "The Treasure Expedition of Captain William Phips to the Bahama Banks," *The New England Quarterly* 5 (1932): 731–52.

43. The election sermon was Cotton Mather's *Serviceable Man* (Boston, 1690), which claimed that Phips and Nehemiah equally clamped down on oppressive usury by establishing a public treasury and gave military protection to their people: 4–5, 14–15. In his *Present State of New England* (Boston, 1690), Mather argued along these lines that support for Phips included the establishment of a public bank to fund the administration and relieve poor debtors. In his *Magnalia Chirsti Americana* 1:118–31, Mather called John Winthrop America's Nehemiah. His willingness to invest Phips with the same likeness further illustrates his elision between puritan (Winthrop) and imperial (Phips) identities. For controversies surrounding Phips, see Baker and Reid, *New England Knight*, 66–81.

44. Cotton Mather, *Optanda: Good Men Described and Good Things Propounded* (Boston, 1692), A4–5, 11, 13, 32; for Mather's defense of the charter and use of Whig categories, see 30–33, 60–63.

45. Increase Mather, *Great Blessing*, 12–17.

46. Cotton Mather, *Pietas in Patriam: The Life of His Excellency Sir William Phips* (London, 1697); printed in Mather's *Magnalia Christi Americana* 1:164–230, esp. 166–71. For Mather on Phips, see Jennifer J. Baker, *Securing the Commonwealth: Debt, Speculation, and Writing in the Making of Early America* (Baltimore, 2005), 28–42 (with reference to the pieces of eight on 37); Philip F. Gura, "Cotton Mather's *Life of Phips*: 'A Vice with the Vizard of Vertue Upon It,' " *New England Quarterly* 59 (1977): 404–57; and David Watters, "The Spectral Identity of Sir William Phips," *Early American Literature* 18 (1983–84): 219–32.

47. Cotton Mather, *Pietas in Patriam*, 173–74, 182, 203.

48. Willard, *Character of a Good Ruler*, 9, 16; 10–11, 23–25 for his critique of patronage and political faction. For Wise, see Johnson, *Adjustment to Empire*, 74–75. The shift from the jeremiad to republican politics, or from covenantal to Whiggish discourse, is ably documented and analyzed by Stephen Foster, *Long Argument*, 231–85; and Breen, *Character of the Good Ruler*.

49. Cotton Mather, *A Pillar of Gratitude* (Boston, 1700), 10–11, 18–19. Bellomont, a favorite of William and erstwhile treasurer to the queen, returned to London after only one year in Boston.

50. Ibid., 32–34.

51. See especially Eliga H. Gould, *The Persistence of Empire: British Political Culture in the Age of the American Revolution* (Chapel Hill, N.C., 2000), 3–21 (10 for the quotation from the anonymous observer); and Kidd, *Protestant Interest*.

52. Benjamin Wadsworth, *King William Lamented in America* (Boston, 1702); and Benjamin Colman, *A Sermon on the Union* (Boston, 1708), 14.

53. Benjamin Colman, *Sermon on the Union*, 3, 13, 16, 29; Benjamin Colman, *A Sermon . . . of Thanksgiving for the Suppression of the late Vile and Traiterous Rebellion* (Boston, 1716), 15, 23, 28.

54. [Ebenezer Pemberton], *A Brief Account of the State of the Province* (Boston, 1717), 2, 8.

55. Thomas Prince, *A Sermon on the Sorrowful Occasion* (Boston, 1727), 20–21.

56. Later opposition to the Walpole ministry, with its severe restrictions on colonial prerogatives and varied reactions to Whig-Tory contests in Westminster, revealed limits to the colonists' patriotism. Should toleration and ecumenical Protestantism ever lapse in England—should Jacobite Catholics ever succeed—Thomas Foxcroft warned, then New England would "have Reason" to resist the metropolis; Thomas Foxcroft, *God the Judge* (Boston, 1727), 39. For shifts from relative trust in the empire in the 1720s to contestation during the 1730s and 1740s, see David Armitage, *The Ideological Origins of the British Empire* (New York, 2000), 170–98.

57. See especially Ian Kenneth Steel, *The English Atlantic, 1675–1740: An Exploration of Communication and Community* (New York, 1986); and J. H. Eliott, *Empires of the Atlantic World: Britain and Spain in America, 1492–1830* (New Haven, Conn., 2006), 219–51. Eliott, along with P. J. Marshall, *The Making and Unmaking of Empires: Britain, India, and America, c. 1750–1783* (Oxford, 2005), stresses administrative integration in the context of Anglo-French and Anglo-Spanish contests. For an overstated, yet suggestive, reading of contemporary devotion toward the Hanovers, see Brendan McConville, *The King's Three Faces: The Rise and Fall of Royal America, 1688–1776* (Chapel Hill, N.C., 2006), 105–41. On toleration and empire, see Gould, *Persistence of Empire*, 21.

58. Ebenezer Pemberton, *The Divine Original Dignity of Government Asserted* (Boston, 1710), 79, 89, 43, 65.

59. *Ibid.*, 100–101, 33–35, 41–45.

60. Benjamin Colman, *Rulers Feeding and Guiding Their People* (Boston, 1716), 49; Thomas Prince, *Civil Rulers Raised up by God to Feed His People* (Boston, 1728), 9 (see also 10, 16–19).

61. For Petty's career and significance, see Terrence Hutchison, *Before Adam Smith: The Emergence of Political Economy, 1662–1776* (New York, 1988), 27–35; Irvine Masson and A. J. Youngson, "Sir William Petty, F. R. S.," *Notes and Records of the Royal Society of London* 15 (1960): 79–90; and Julian Hoppit, "Political Arithmetic in Eighteenth-Century England," *Economic History Review* 49 (1996): 516–40.

62. Other important political economists during the period included Samuel Fortrey, Roger Coke, Thomas Culpeper, John Houghton, and Henry Martyn. For the economic thinkers and their careers, see Appleby, *Economic Thought*, 199–241; and Hutchison, *Before Adam Smith*, 27–80.

63. A classic definition of "mercantilism" is provided by Eli Hecksher, "Mercantilism," *Encyclopedia of Social Sciences* 10 (1933): 334–39, and updated in John J. McCusker's "Mercantilism," *Encyclopedia of the North American Colonies* 1:459–65. For the philosophical background to mercantilism, see Hutchinson, *Before Adam Smith*, 135–55.

64. This and the following paragraphs on economic ideology rely heavily on Istvan Hont's *Jealousy of Trade: International Competition and the Nation-State in Historical Perspective* (Cambridge, Mass., 2005), which, focusing on Barbon and Davenant, describes the whole circle of thought as a "neo-Machiavellian political economy" (52); and Armitage, *Ideological Origins*, 146–69. For the administrative and

political aspects of empire, see John Brewer, *The Sinews of Power: War, Money, and the English State, 1688–1783* (New York, 1989). This emphasis on imperial agendas has, in part, replaced an interpretive paradigm that contrasted republican, communal, and anticommercial virtues to liberal, imperial, and royal designs: see J.G.A. Pocock, "Virtue and Commerce in the Eighteenth Century," *The Journal of Interdisciplinary History* 3 (1972): 119–34; and Wooton, "Introduction: The Republican Tradition." The imperial and Atlantic context has been highlighted in the so-called new Atlantic history: Bernard Bailyn, *Atlantic History: Concepts and Contours* (Cambridge, Mass., 2005). For transatlantic economic history, see Peter A. Coclanis, ed., *The Atlantic Economy during the Seventeenth and Eighteenth Centuries: Organization, Operation, Practice, and Personnel* (Columbia, S.C., 2005).

65. Appleby, *Economic Thought*, 242–79; and P.G.M. Dickson, *The Financial Revolution in England: A Study in the Development of Public Credit, 1688–1756* (New York, 1967), 3–14.

66. David McNally, *Political Economy and the Rise of Capitalism: A Reinterpretation* (Berkeley, Calif., 1988), 22–84; Hutchison, *Before Adam Smith*, 72–73; Appleby, *Economic Thought*, 169–84, 223–27.

67. John Locke, *Several Papers Relating to Money, Interest and Trade*, 2nd ed. (London, 1696), 1–2, 8; Dudley North, *Discourses upon Trade* (1691), in *Commerce, Culture, and Liberty: Readings on Capitalism before Adam Smith*, ed. Henry C. Clark (Indianapolis, Ind., 2003), 108, 114. For Locke and the background, see C. B. Macpherson, *The Political Theory of Possessive Individualism: Hobbes to Locke* (Oxford, 1962); and Appleby, *Economic Thought*, 199–241.

68. North, *Discourses on Trade*, 107, 119. For Barbon, see Hutchinson, *Before Adam Smith*, 73–77; for Davenant, Hont, *Jealousy of Trade*, 57–62, 186–226. The point here about natural appetites and social order is informed by Appleby's *Economic Thought*. In "Modernization Theory and the Formation of Modern Social Theories in England and America," *Comparative Studies in Society and History* 20 (1978): 259–85, Appleby describes how shifting policy positions reflected deep moral convictions about natural economic powers and the explanatory power of political economy. For the long philosophical implications hinted at here, see, among a vast literature, Albert O. Hirschman, *The Passions and the Interests: Political Arguments for Capitalism before Its Triumph* (Princeton, N.J., 1977); and Charles Taylor, *Sources of the Self: The Making of Modern Identity* (Cambridge, Mass., 1989), 211–302.

69. Perry Gauci, *The Politics of Trade: The Overseas Merchant in State and Society, 1660–1720* (New York, 2001); Tim Keirn, "Monopoly, Economic Thought, and the Royal African Company," in *Early Modern Conceptions of Property*, ed. John Brewer and Susan Staves (New York, 1996): 427–66. For Delaune, see his *Present State of London* (London, 1681), 281 (misnumbered 293)–301.

70. Gauci, *Politics of Trade*, 156–94; Hont, *Jealousy of Trade*, 240–58.

71. Dickson, *Financial Revolution*, 3–14, 21–176; Stuart Banner, *Anglo-American Securities Regulation: Cultural and Political Roots, 1690–1860* (New York, 1998), 14–40.

72. Muldrew, *Economy of Obligation*, 98, 116; Larry Neal, *The Rise of Financial Capitalism: International Capital Markets in the Age of Reason* (New York, 1990), 1–43; Edward Stringham, "The Extralegal Development of Securities Trading in Sev-

enteenth Century Amsterdam," *Quarterly Review of Economics and Finance* 43 (2003): 321–44.

73. John Carswell, *The South Sea Bubble* (1969; rev. ed., Dover, N.H., 1993); John G. Sperling, *The South Sea Company: An Historical Essay and Bibliographical Finding List* (Cambridge, Mass., 1962); Banner, *Anglo-American Securities Regulation*, 41–87. For the South Sea Company and slave trading, see Matson, *Merchants and Empire*, 123.

74. Gauci, *Politics of Trade*, 156 (for the Addison quotation), 156–94, 234–70 for merchant handbooks, serial publications, and Defoe; McVeagh, *Tradeful Merchants*, 66–67 (for the Steele quotation), 53–60 (for Steele, Centlivre, and Defoe). Appleby, in *Economic Thought*, 164, 210, shows Defoe's transmission of the ideas of Petty and Davenant. For the courage and mathematical skill of merchants, see Nuala Zahedieh, "Making Mercantilism Work: London Merchants and the Atlantic Trade in the Seventeenth Century," *Transactions of the Royal Historical Society* 9 (1999): 143–58. For popular acceptance of taking interest on credit, the relation of interest rates to the Bank of England, and the patriotic reputations of merchants in the 1710s, see Matson, *Merchants and Empire*, 67–72, 125–27.

75. The potential for conflict between colony and metropolis began to be realized during the 1720s, 1730s, and 1740s, when Parliament set the interests of home manufactures against colonial producers, but did not erupt into open political and economic dispute until the 1760s: John J. McCusker, "British Mercantilist Policies and the American Colonies," in *Cambridge Economic History*, by Engerman and Gallman, 1:337–62; John E. Crowley, *The Privileges of Independence: Neomercantilism and the American Revolution* (Baltimore, 1993); and Janet Ann Riesman, "The Origins of American Political Economy, 1690–1781" (PhD diss., Brown University, 1983).

76. For the examples of the news bits listed here, see the *Boston News Letter*, September 4–11, 1704; November 26–December 3, 1711; and September 25–October 2, 1721. For the establishment of the papers, see Bridenbaugh, *Cities in the Wilderness*, 292. For imperial and trading company news conveyed through letters, see, for only two of many sources, Josiah Child's letters in the "Higginson Letters," 196–221; and Thomas Fitch to Thomas Crouch and S. Arnold, February 6, 13, 1710, in AAS letterbook.

77. For Bromfield and Henchman, see, for one of many examples, the September 20, 1719, entry in the 1719–21 Wastebook, Henchman Family Papers, American Antiquarian Society (microfilm of the original from the New England Historical and Genealogical Society, Boston). For Gerrish's sales, see the sale catalogues: Samuel Gerrish, *Choice English Books* (Boston, 1720), and *Catalogue of Choice and Valuable Books* (Boston, 1723). For booksellers and printers, see Hugh Amory, "Printing and Bookselling in New England," in *Colonial Book*, ed. Amory and Hall; and Elizabeth Carroll Reilly, "The Wages of Piety: The Boston Book Trade of Jeremy Condy," in *Printing and Society in Early America*, ed. William L. Joyce et al. (Worcester, Mass., 1983), 83–131. For Old South's cadre of printers and publishers, see Peterson, *Price of Redemption*, 91–92, 139. For Defoe especially, see Chester Noyes Greenough, "Defoe in Boston," *Publications of the Colonial Society of Massachusetts*, vol. 28, *Transactions, 1930–1933* (Boston, 1935): 461–94.

78. T[homas] Goodman, [*Experience'd Secretary*, mistitled as] *The Young Secretary's Guide* (Boston, 1703); Hill, *Young Secretary's Guide*; James Hodder, *Hodder's*

Arithmetick, 25th ed. (Boston, 1719). The implicit presence of mercantilist ideas in almanacs and merchant's handbooks is discussed in Cohen's *Calculating People*, esp. 32–33, 77, 81–115. For letter-writing manuals, including a discussion of Hill and Goodman, see Eve Tavor Bannet, *Empire of Letters: Letter Manuals and Transatlantic Correspondence, 1680–1820* (New York, 2005), 105–39.

79. N.H., *The Compleat Tradesman*, 2nd ed. (London, 1684), 2–3, 65 (for the marginalia on the copy from the Mather family library at the American Antiquarian Society). Illustrations of other relevant titles in the Mather library include John Withers, *The Whigs Vindicated* (London, 1715); Daniel Defoe, *Caledonia, or The Pedlar turn'd Merchant* (London, 1700), and *Reasons Showing the Necessity of Large and Speedy Supplies to the Government* (London, 1691). The American Antiquarian Society holds the Davenant and Child titles mentioned here, the latter of which stressed the new meaning of usury. The catalog of the Old South Library, largely assembled by Samuel Sewall's son Joseph, lists works by Davenant, Defoe, and Locke, as well as several issues from London serials such as *The London Magazine*: [Boston, City, Public Library], *The Prince Library: A Catalogue* (Boston, 1870), 91–92, 103, 121, 113.

80. For Mather and *The Spectator* essay, see Norman S. Fiering, "The Transatlantic Republic of Letters: A Note on the Circulation of Learned Periodicals to Early Eighteenth-Century America," *The William and Mary Quarterly*, 3rd ser., 33 (1976): 642–60, 643. On Defoe, his connections to New England, correspondence with Mather, and economic views, see Paula R. Backscheider, *Daniel Defoe: His Life* (Baltimore, 1989), 48–49, 56–57, 70, 85–86, 437–66. For Mather, Defoe, and Mather's periwig, see Kenneth Silverman, *The Life and Times of Cotton Mather* (New York, 1984), 145; and Greenough, "Defoe in Boston." For Mather's authorship of *News from Robinson Cruso's Island* (Boston, 1720), see Andrew McFarland Davis, ed., *Colonial Currency Reprints, 1682–1753*, 4 vols. (1910–11; repr., New York, [1971]), 1:121–26; and Silverman, *Cotton Mather*, 320–26. For Mather's style and later New England's poets of empire, see David S. Shields, *Oracles of Empire: Poetry, Politics, and Commerce in British America, 1690–1750* (Chicago, 1990), 22–25, 110–23.

81. There is a vast literature on currency debates in provincial Massachusetts. The following discussion relies especially on the general economic history provided by Newell, *From Dependency to Independence*, 111–80; the fiscal history given in Leslie V. Brock's *Currency of the American Colonies, 1700–1764: A Study in Colonial Finance and Imperial Relations* (New York, 1975); the legal history analyzed by Claire Priest, "Currency Policies and Legal Development in Colonial New England," *Yale Law Journal* 110 (2001): 1303–1405; the literary suggestions provided by Baker, *Securing the Commonwealth*, 1–42; and, for the English background, Dickson, *Financial Revolution*. The most detailed description of the primary sources continues to be Davis, introduction to *Colonial Currency Reprints* 1:1–105; and Joseph B. Felt, *Historical Account of Massachusetts Currency* (1859; repr., New York, 1968), 46–83.

82. [John Woodbrige], *Severals Relating to the Fund* (Boston, 1682), 3, 5.

83. *A Model for Erecting a Bank of Credit* (London, 1688; repr., Boston, 1714), 1, 20, 27. John Blackwell, a newcomer to New England, authored a similar manuscript proposal, "A Discourse in Explanation of the Bank of Credit," in 1687, and, according to Davis, probably authored *A Model*: Davis, *Colonial Currency Reprints* 1:146–51, 187–88.

84. The legislation is quoted in Felt's *Historical Account*, 49–50. For the narrative in this and the following paragraph, see Felt, *Historical Account*, 46–79; Brock, *Currency of the American Colonies*, 1–34; Newall, *From Dependency to Independence*, 129–37; and Warden, *Boston*, 69–86.

85. In *From Dependency to Independence*, 165, Newall recounts the enormous rise in debt litigation in the period, illustrated by one thousand writs of attachment for debt filed in Essex County in April 1720 alone.

86. The following interpretation relies heavily on Newall's *From Dependency to Independence*, 107–80; and Felt's *Historical Account*, 65–77.

87. [John Colman], *The Distressed State of the Town of Boston* (Boston, 1720), 1–2, 7; John Colman, *The Distressed State of the Town of Boston once more Considered* (Boston, 1720), 21.

88. Amicus Patriae [John Wise], *Word of Comfort to a Melancholy Country* (Boston, 1721), in *Colonial Currency Reprints*, by Davis, 2:170, 178, 219; the tables and charts are on 178–79.

89. Wise, *Word of Comfort*, 175–76, 182; for comments on Holland and Venice, 181, 203–6.

90. [Paul Dudley], *Objections to the Bank of Credit* (Boston, 1714); *The Present Melancholy Circumstances of the Province* (Boston, 1719), 13.

91. Edward Wigglesworth, "One in the Country," *Boston News Letter*, April 18, 1720, in *Colonial Currency Reprints*, by Davis, 1:408–13; [Edward Wigglesworth], *A Letter from One in the Country to his Friend in Boston* (Boston, 1720); and [Edward Wigglesworth], *A Vindication of the Remarks of One in the Country* (Boston, 1720), 8–9, 15–16.

92. For imitations of Defoe and other literary styles, see Davis, *Currency Reprints* 2:250–77.

93. [John Higginson], *The Second Part of the South-Sea Stock* (Boston, 1721), 2, 6, 22; see 10–12 (for his reference to France and other American colonies). Higginson died in 1718, before the South Sea Company bubble burst, but the printers' decision to bring out his tract in 1721 clearly derived from the transatlantic furor over the demise of the company: Davis, *Currency Reprints* 2:332–34.

94. [Cotton Mather], *Some Considerations on the Bills of Credit* (Boston, 1691), 3, 7–9. For Mather and money, see Jennifer Jordan Baker, " 'It is uncertain where the Fates will carry me': Cotton Mather's Theology of Finance," *Arizona Quarterly* 56 (2000): 1–23.

95. Cotton Mather, *Some Considerations*, 3, 18, 21.

96. Sewall, *Diary* 2:773, 822, 934, 1023.

97. Samuel Sewall, "Address in Opposition to Issuing More Paper Money," in "Letterbook" 2:235, 238–39.

98. Fitch, quoted in Ron Michener's "Money in the American Colonies," EH.Net Encyclopedia (*http://eh.net/encyclopedia/article/michener.american.colonies.money*); accessed July 1, 2009. Felt, *Historical Account*, 72–73; Andrew McFarland Davis, "Boston 'Banks' —1681–1740—Those Who Were Interested in Them," *NEHGR* 57 (1903): 274–81; and Andrew McFarland Davis, "New Hampshire Notes—1735—Those Who Agreed Not to Receive Them," *NEHGR* 57 (1903): 387–89. The proposed "shop notes," "notes of hand," or "merchants notes" were privately signed papers paid to laborers (especially ship builders and dock-

workers) or other traders, who could redeem 50 percent of their value for bills of credit and 50 percent for goods in designated shops.

99. For the continued currency of bills of exchange, see J. Sperling, "The International Payments Mechanism in the Seventeenth and Eighteenth Centuries," *The Economic History Review*, n.s., 14 (1962): 446–68.

100. Thomas Hutchinson, quoted in Newell's *From Dependency to Independence*, 141; John Wise, quoted ibid., 163; John Colman, *Distressed State*, 16; and Joseph Sewall, quoted in Miller's *Colony to Province*, 323. For Mather's concessions, see Miller, *Colony to Province*, 308. Miller illuminates, but overstates, the replacement of the moral authority of ministers with a science of economics in *Colony to Province*, 305–29.

101. The stress here, on the religious-providential validation of political economy, offsets the argument made by others that Colman, Pemberton, and Mather had so deferred to mercantilism that they divorced religious ideas from economic affairs and completely privatized spiritual convictions: see John E. Crowley, *This Sheba, Self: The Conceptualization of Economic Life in Eighteenth-Century America* (Baltimore, 1974), esp. 34–94. For the general statement here about money as a sign and subject of moral deliberation, see Marc Shell, *Money, Language, and Thought: Literary and Philosophical Economies from the Medieval to the Modern Era* (1982; Baltimore, 1993); Baker, *Securing the Commonwealth*; Jennifer J. Baker and Eric Wertheimer, introduction to "Special Issue: Economists and Early American Literature," *Early American Literature* 41 (2006): 397–403; and Jonathan Parry and Maurice Bloch, eds., introduction to *Money and the Morality of Exchange* (New York, 1989), 1–32. For currency and wider ideological perspectives, see Joyce Appleby, "Locke, Liberalism, and the Natural Law of Money," in Appleby's *Liberalism and Republicanism in the Historical Imagination* (Cambridge, Mass., 1992), 58–89. For Boston, the metropolis, and money, see Mark A. Peterson, "Boston Pays Tribute: Autonomy and Empire in the Atlantic World, 1630–1714," in *Shaping the Stuart World, 1603–1714: The Atlantic Connection*, ed. Allan I. Macinnes and Arthur H. Williamson (Leiden, 2005), 311–55.

102. [Cotton Mather], *Thirty Important Cases* (Boston, 1699), 49; for lotteries, 62–64, 74–77. For traditional versions of the common law that proscribed trading in mortgages and other securities, see E. James Ferguson, "Currency Finance: An Interpretation of Colonial Monetary Practices," *The William and Mary Quarterly*, 3rd ser., 10 (1953): 153–80.

103. Cotton Mather, *Thirty Cases*, 49–52.

104. Willard, *A Compleat Body of Divinity* (Boston, 1726), 685, 689, 706, 720. Willard delivered the lectures quoted here in 1704. There are repeated mispaginations and repaginations in this edition.

105. Ibid., 698–701.

106. Ibid., 701; Boston, City of, *A Report of the Record Commissioners of the City of Boston, Containing the Records of Boston Selectmen, 1701–1715* (Boston, 1884), 178.

107. Willard, *Compleat Body*, 703, 706.

108. "The Churches of *New England* have no express and agreed *Catalogue* of the *Crimes*, that shall expose to *Censures*," including usury, Mather explained, because the Bible gave no guidance on such matters: [Cotton Mather], *Ratio Disciplinae Fratrum Nov-Anglorum* (Boston, 1726), 142–43. In taking these progressive

stances, Mather and Willard also echoed English moral treatises such as Robert Filmer, *Quaestion Quolibetica, or a Discourse, Whether it may bee Lawfull to take Use for Money* (London, 1653), a4r, a6r–a7v, 149; Henry Hammond, *Large Additions to the Practical Catechesime* (London, 1646), 3, 7, 9–11; and Edward Stillingfleet, *A Letter to a Deist* (London, 1677), 119–22.

109. Cotton Mather, *Fair Dealing between Debtor and Creditor* (Boston, 1716), 27. For a country preacher, see Peter Thacher, *The Fear of God Restraining Men from . . . Iniquity in Commerce* (Boston, 1720). This Thacher was the pastor in Middleborough.

110. [Edward Ward], *A Trip to New-England* (London, 1699); repr., with notes by George Parker Winship, in *Boston in 1682 and 1699* (Providence, R.I., 1905; repr., New York, 1970), 45.

111. Joshua Moodey, quoted in Miller's *Colony to Province*, 46; Ebenezer Pemberton, sermon from February 28, 1697, as noted by John Leverett, in John Leverett sermon notes, American Antiquarian Society, Worcester, Massachusetts; Cotton Mather, *Pascentius* (Boston, 1714), 11; Cotton Mather, *Durable Riches*, 27. See Cotton Mather, *The Religious Marriner* (Boston, 1700), 20–21; Cotton Mather, *True Riches* (Boston, 1724), 1; Benjamin Colman, *Industry and Diligence* (Boston, 1717), passim; and Ebenezer Pemberton, *Advice to a Son* (London, 1705), 5–8, for four of many possible illustrations.

112. Samuel Willard, *Heavenly Merchandize* (Boston, 1686).

113. Ibid., 31 (buying and selling), 45 (merchants' anxieties and the risks of trade), 51–52 (heavenly insurance and payoff).

114. Samuel Willard, *Compleat Body*, 693, 709. There are repeated and lengthy mispaginations and repaginations in this edition; the quote, to provide an additional locator, comes from sermon 202.

115. Cotton Mather, *A Christian at his Calling* (Boston, 1701), 38, 42, 48–49, 53–54.

116. Ibid., 37–42, 63–64 (for the special benefit of merchants to the commonweal), 67, 70–71; Cotton Mather, *Pascentius*, 23, 27 (for the promise of reward); Increase Mather, *Practical Truths, Tending to Promote Holiness* (Boston, 1704), 61, 63.

117. Cotton Mather, *A Very Needful Caution* (Boston, 1707), 23; Cotton Mather, *True Riches*, 18; [Cotton Mather], *A Weaned Christian* (Boston, 1704), 29–30; Samuel Willard, *Walking with God* (Boston, 1700), 46–48; and Benjamin Wadsworth, *The Saint's Prayer to Escape Temptations* (Boston, 1715), esp. 15–27.

118. Cotton Mather, "A Memorial of the Present Deplorable State of New England" (London, 1707?), *Massachusetts Historical Society Collections*, 5th ser., 6 (Boston, 1879); Cotton Mather, *Ornaments for the Daughters of Zion* (Boston, 1692); and *Hoop Petticoats, Arraigned and Condemned* (Boston, 1722). For Increase Mather, see Hall, *Last American Puritan*, 194–95, 205–6. For the other iniquities mentioned here, see Cotton Mather, *Things for a Distressed People to Think Upon* (Boston, 1696), 68–77; Benjamin Colman, *The Piety and Duty of Rulers* (Boston, 1708), 17; [Cotton Mather], *The Bostonian Ebenezer* (Boston, 1698); Wadsworth, *Fraud and Injustice*, 4–5, 13–14; Gildrie, *The Profane, the Civil, and the Godly*, 63–83; and David W. Conroy, *In Public Houses: Drink and the Revolution of Authority in Colonial Massachusetts* (Chapel Hill, N.C., 1995), 12–89.

119. Increase Mather, *Burnings Bewailed* (Boston, 1711), 21; Cotton Mather, *Advice from Taberah* (Boston, 1711), 18; Benjamin Wadsworth, *Five Sermons* (Boston, 1714), 37–59.

120. Cotton Mather, *Things for a Distressed People to Think Upon*, 11.

121. Cotton Mather, *Lex Mercatoria*, 26, 16–25 (for the lists of common sins). The title mirrored Gerard Malynes's work of a previous generation (*Lex Mercatoria, or The Ancient Law-Merchant* [London, 1622]) and reflected Mather's intention of addressing overseas merchants with European-wide standards of commercial law.

122. Cotton Mather, *Fair Dealing between Debtor and Creditor* (Boston, 1716), 8, 11–20; Cotton Mather, *The Balance of the Sanctuary* (Boston, 1727), 8–9; Wadsworth, *Blameless Christian*, 33–34; Wadsworth, *Fraud and Injustice*, 5–11, 15–16, 20–25. For Cotton Mather on the widespread debasement of public speech and promise breaking in commerce, see his *Man of his Word* (Boston, 1713) and *A Flying Roll*, 15–20. For one of many examples of similar denunciations coming from outside Boston, see the sermon by the Dorchester pastor John Danforth, *The Vile Profanations of Prosperity* (Boston, 1704).

123. The formulation in this paragraph differs from, but is informed by, Perry Miller's *Province to Colony*; and Kenneth A. Lockridge's *New England Town: The First Hundred Years; Dedham, Massachusetts, 1636–1736* (New York, 1970).

124. Samuel Willard, *The Peril of the Times Displayed* (Boston, 1700), 92; Wadsworth, *Fraud and Injustice*, 23–25. For changes at Old South and Mather's 1703 manifesto to other ministers, see Cooper, *Tenacious of Their Liberties*, 137–39. Many rural churches continued to use relations of faith—individuals' confessions recorded by the minister and delivered to the congregation—as requirements for the Lord's Supper through the 1720s, thereby sustaining a measure of coercion against economic misdeeds such as harsh credit practices. There are several such instances, for example, in "Confessions of Faith of the Members of the First Parish Church, Haverhill, Massachusetts," Haverhill Public Library, Haverhill, Massachusetts; and in "The Medfield Relations," Medfield Church, Medfield, Massachusetts. Douglas Winiarski kindly provided me with transcriptions.

125. Increase Mather, "To the Reader," in *Peril of the Times Displayed*, by Willard, 3–8. For one of many references to royal proclamations against immorality, see Massachusetts, Governor (1702–15, Dudley), *Province of the Massachusetts-Bay . . . Declaration against Profaneness and Immoralities* (Boston, 1704). The overall campaign for moral reform, with reference to royal edicts, is summarized in Joel Bernard's "Original Themes of Voluntary Moralism: The Anglo-American Reformation of Manners," in *Moral Problems in American Life: New Perspectives on Cultural History*, ed. Karen Haltunnen and Lewis Perry (Ithaca, N.Y., 1998), 15–39.

126. For Mather's maxims, see Silverman, *Cotton Mather*, 299–302; Middlekauff, *Mathers*, 222–30.

127. [Cotton Mather], *Methods and Motives for Societies to Suppress Disorders* [Boston, 1703], 5; Cotton Mather, *Bonifacius: An Essay upon the Good* [Boston, 1710], ed. David Levin (Cambridge, Mass., 1966), esp. 107–19. In *The Pourtraiture of a Good Man* (Boston, 1702), Mather portrayed the civic man as engaged in helping neighbors in need. In *The Faithful Monitor* (Boston, 1704), Mather provided the night watchers with a list of the latest provincial laws against immoralities and their attendant punishments. By the time of his *Advice from the Watch tower* (Boston, 1713),

Mather appeared to have lost his enthusiasm for reform societies and emphasized instead the renewal of personal piety and family discipline. For Bromfield, and the background to the societies, see Bernard, "Original Themes of Voluntary Moralism," esp. 28–32.

128. Cotton Mather, Benjamin Wadsworth, and Benjamin Colman, *Testimony against Evil Customs* (Boston, [1719]); Benjamin Wadsworth, *Vicious Courses Procuring Poverty* (Boston, 1719), 9. This and the following paragraphs depend in part on Heyrman's "Model of Christian Charity."

129. Bridenbaugh, *Cities in the Wilderness*, 233–35; Lee, "Public Poor Relief"; Boston, City of, *A Report of the Record Commissioners of the City of Boston, Containing the Boston Records from 1701 to 1728* (Boston, 1883), 24–26, 128–30, 147–48. The rationales for employment schemes are illustrated in Massachusetts Bay, Province, "Act for Encouraging the Linnen Manufacture, and the making of Canvus or Duck," *Acts and Laws*, May 30, 1722 (Boston, 1722). For a standard narrative on social welfare in this period, with attention to taxes and works projects, see Nash, *Urban Crucible*, 76–88.

130. Benjamin Colman to Robert Woodrow, November 6, 1725, quoted in Heryman's "Model of Christian Charity," 138. For the contrast between such optimism and previous criticisms of commerce, see Nash, *Urban Crucible*, 76–88.

131. Boston, Old South Church, manuscript records; Boston, Old North Church, manuscript records. The formation and work of the interchurch charitable association, including detailed financial accounts, are recorded in the manuscript records of the Boston Churches, Second Church, Quarterly Charitable Lecture, Massachusetts Historical Society, Boston. Alarmed at the high number of destitute residents who attended his church—he counted some eighty in 1712—Mather especially pursued wealthy benefactors and donated his own money and books to relief efforts: Bridenbaugh, *Cities in the Wilderness*, 235; and, for one telling example of a convert-turned-benefactor, David Levin, *Cotton Mather: The Young Life of the Lord's Remembrancer, 1661–1703* (Cambridge, Mass., 1978), 97–98. For further elucidation of the administration of poor relief in the churches, see Heyrman, "Model of Christian Charity," 199–216.

132. Samuel Willard, *Reformation the Great Duty of an Afflicted People* (Boston, 1694), 29–30, 47; see A2, 7, and 65 for Willard's despair over previous modes of discipline.

133. Cotton Mather, *Theopolis Americana: An Essay on the Golden Street of the Holy City; Publishing, a Testimony against the Corruptions of the Market-Place* (Boston, 1710), A3, 47, 50; see 43–50.

134. Ibid., 6, 16, 36, 49; see 16–36. Mather held household slaves, suggesting that his denunciations of slave trading amounted either to self-contradiction or, more likely, to an attack on large-scale, unnecessarily cruel, and violent slaving. He promoted the conversion of captive Africans and the benevolent treatment of them: Silverman, *Cotton Mather*, 263–65.

135. Sewall, account book, Samuel Sewall Papers, Massachusetts Historical Society, Boston (hereafter cited as account book), numerous entries from 1689 to 1690 and 1698 to 1702; see, for example, the entries from February 22, 1689, and June 30, 1690.

136. Sewall recorded his attendance at sermons throughout the *Diary*. His sermon notes are contained among his extant account books. His notes on Rogers's sermon are given in an entry from 1714.

137. Sewall to Nicholas Bowe, November 14, 1687, "Letterbook" 1:66–67; Sewall to [an unnamed correspondent], July 12, 1697, "Letterbook" 1:187.

138. Sewall, *Diary* 1:121, 116–22.

139. [Samuel Sewall], *The Selling of Joseph* (Boston, 1700), 3; for the couple's petition, see Sewall, *Diary* 1:432–33. For the context of Sewall's tract, see Mark A. Peterson, "*The Selling of Joseph*: Bostonians, Antislavery, and the Protestant International, 1689–1733," *Massachusetts Historical Review* 4 (2002): 1–22. For the rise of slavery and Sewall's critique, see William A. Pettigrew, "Free to Enslave: Politics and the Escalation of Britain's Transatlantic Slave Trade, 1688–1714," *The William and Mary Quarterly*, 3rd ser., 64 (2007): 3–38.

140. Sewall, *Diary* 2:637–38. Two years later, when Sewall was not in town, a more serious incident erupted, a real riot of two hundred men who broke into a warehouse on the Boston Common looking for a load of Belcher's grain rumored to be shipped to Curaçao; Sewall, *Diary* 2:715.

141. Bernard, "Original Themes of Voluntary Moralism," 33–35; *Harvard Graduates* 2:351.

142. Sewall to Thomas Glouer, July 15, 1686, "Letterbook" 1:31; Sewall to Nathaniel Barns, October 26, 1688, "Letterbook" 1:90; Sewall to John Ive, March 30, 1687, "Letterbook" 1:45; see a similar sort of letter five years later, with news of Indian attacks on York in Maine: Sewall to John Ive, February 19, 1692, "Letterbook" 1:128–30. For Sewall's reading of the *London Gazette*, see the invoice in the "Letterbook" 1:16; and Sewall to John Ive, September 4, 1686, "Letterbook" 1:38.

143. Sewall to Edward Taylor, October 28, 1696, "Letterbook" 1:171–78; Sewall to John Wise, April 12, 1698, "Letterbook" 1:196–99; Samuel Sewall, *Phaenomena quaedam Apocalyptica . . . or, Some few Lines towards a Description of the New Heaven* (Boston, 1697). As Richard Cogley shows in "Samuel Sewall and the Mexican Millennium: The Exception which Proves the Rule about Millenarianism in New England, 1630–1730" (typescript), Mather argued, along with most of his colleagues, that the millennium began in Palestine and spread to America, whereas Sewall bafflingly maintained that it would be initiated in Mexico. For Sewall's shifting attitudes toward the British monarchy, see McConville, *King's Three Faces*, 39–56.

144. Samuel Sewall, *Proposals Touching the Accomplishment of Prophesies* (Boston, 1713), 11. It appears likely that Sewall made reference (without citation) to two publications of William Petty: *Two Essays in Political Arithmetick concerning London and Paris* (London, 1687) and *Observations on the Cities of London and Rome* (London, 1687).

145. There are other illustrations of how Sewall took millennial prophecies to legitimate commercial and imperial programs. In 1699, for example, he informed Nathaniel Higginson, a New England merchant in Madras, that the most likely place for the millennium was North America, implying that Higginson would do well to return home: "you may lay out yourself and your Estate to more advantage for the glory of God, in N. E. then any where else in the whole Universe." Sewall to Nathaniel Higginson, November 18, 1699, "Letterbook" 1:216. Anti-Catholic

sympathies further linked Boston to England, where similar rhetoric was common-place throughout the eighteenth century: J.C.D. Clark, *English Society, 1660–1832: Religion, Ideology, and Politics in the Ancien Regime* (New York, 2000).

146. For the history of the New England Company, see William Kellaway, *The New England Company, 1649–1776: Missionary Society to the American Indians* (London, 1961). For the names here, see Vesta Lee Gordon, *Guide to the Microfilm Edition of the Letter Book, 1688–1761, of the Company for Propagation of the Gospel in New England* (Charlottesville, Va., 1969), 6–8; and the "Trustees Proposal," ca. 1712, in "Letter Book, 1688–1776, of the Company for Propagation of the Gospel in New England," microfilm edition, 118, at the University of Virginia Library, Charlottesville, Virginia (hereafter cited as NEC).

147. Sewall (for the New England Company) to Josiah Cotton, February 10, 1713, Ayer Collection, ms. 181, Newberry Library, Chicago. Kellaway, in *New England Company*, provides an overview of finances; for land investments and scholarships, see the "Trustees Proposal," ca. 1712, NEC, 118–20.

148. Ashurst to Sewall, November 1, 1701, NEC, 30–32; Ashurst to John Leverett, 1713, NEC, 123; Ashurst to Sewall, August 3, 1714, NEC, 140–41.

149. Bromfield noted some four hundred sermons, the bulk of which came from Willard, Mather, and Pemberton; Bromfield sermon notebooks, Massachusetts Historical Society, Boston, 1682–1698, 1713–1721; he began by combining sermon notes and accounts in 1713. For Mather, the *Magnalia*, and Bromfield, see Cotton Mather, *Diary of Cotton Mather*, 2 vols. (New York, [1957]), 1:400, 410, 445, 558; the two sermons dedicated to Bromfield are in Cotton Mather's *Memoria Wilsoniana* (Boston, 1695) and Increase Mather's *Discourse Concerning the Maintenance Due to Those that Preach the Gospel* (Boston, 1706). For Old South merchants, see also Peterson, *Price of Redemption*, 79–85. For further reflections on Sewall's spiritual sensibilities, see Hall, *Worlds of Wonder*, 213–38.

150. Hill, *Old South Church* 1:282, 284, 291, 294, 298, 303, 310, 311, 334, 338; Roberts, *Artillery Records* 1·324–25.

151. Roberts, *Artillery Records* 1:324–25; Fitch to Thomas Wilks, January 11, 1726, MHS letterbook (for one example of notations on British politics); *NEHGR* 33 (1879): 177 (for the schoolhouse); "Diary of Jeremiah Bumsted of Boston, 1722–1727," *NEHGR* 15 (1861): 193–204, 305–15, 314 (for the ceremonial proclamation of George II); "Letters of Col. Thomas Westbrook and others," *NEHGR* 46 (1892): 25; and *NEHGR* 48 (1894): 187 (for Fitch and Father Rale's War); Gordon, *Guide to the Microfilm Edition of the Letter Book*, 6–8.

152. Curwin's career and close association with Sewall, Bromfield, and Fitch are demonstrated in his correspondence in the Curwin Family Manuscript Collection, American Antiquarian Society, box 1, folder 4; box 2, folder 1. For Turner, see Lorinda B. R. Goodwin, *An Archaeology of Manners: The Polite World of the Merchant Elite of Colonial Massachusetts* (New York, 1999), 67–76. Dummer's career is detailed in Herman Frederick Clarke and Henry Wilder Foote's *Jeremiah Dummer: Colonial Craftsman and Merchant, 1645–1718* (1935; repr., New York, 1970), 28–73. For one suggestion that Fitch had divorced religion from business, see Newell, *From Dependency to Independence*, 104. For Hutchinson's and Shrimpton's offenses to Sewall, see Hunter, *Purchasing Identity*, 71–106.

CHAPTER FIVE
HUGH HALL'S SCHEME

1. Hugh Hall to Benjamin Colman, February 28, 1717, in Hugh Hall, letterbook, 1716–20, Houghton Library, Harvard University, Cambridge, Massachusetts (hereafter cited as Hall letterbook). Information about Hall's family and life is taken from his letters and other writings, and from four short biographical sketches: John Wentworth, biographical appendix to "Letters of Hugh Hall to Benning Wentworth," *NEHGR* 42 (1888): 300–307; Samuel Eliot Morison, "Letterbook of Hugh Hall, Merchant of Barbados, 1716–1720," *Publications of the Colonial Society of Massachusetts*, vol. 32, *Transactions, 1933–1937* (Boston, 1937), 514–22; *Harvard Graduates* 6:11–18; and S. D. Smith, *Slavery, Family and Gentry Capitalism in the British Atlantic: The World of the Lascelles, 1648–1834* (New York, 2006), 11–42. No sustained study of Hall has been published. Hall's extensive notes on the Sunday-morning sermons of Pemberton at Old South, made when he was a young teenager, attest to his precocious devotion; he also noted lecture sermons by Colman at other times during the week: Hugh Hall, sermon notebook, 1706–9, Massachusetts Historical Society, Boston. The merchant membership at Old South during these years is recorded in Hill's *Old South Church*, 5–25. Grandmother Lydia, the widow of merchant Benjamin Gibbs, rented a pew at Old South. She changed her membership to Brattle Street after her marriage to Anthony Checkley and kept her membership there after her third marriage, to William Colman. A 1710 sketch of the pew assignments for the church confirms, in striking fashion, the names listed here, along with other merchant families such as Scottow, Stoddard, Sheafe, Wharton, and Sewall; Boston, Third Church, "Plan of Old South Pews," 1710, Congregational Library, Boston. On the curriculum at Harvard, latitudinarian theology, Brattle and Leverett, and Pemberton's attraction to Tillotson, see Norman Fiering, "The First American Enlightenment: Tillotson, Leverett, and Philosophical Anglicanism," *New England Quarterly* 54 (1981): 307–44.

2. Hall to Lydia Colman, March 6, 1717, Hall letterbook.

3. Hall to John Leverett, February 28, 1717, Hall letterbook.

4. Hall to Timothy Prout, March 6, 1717, Hall letterbook (for one of his accounts of his "industry" in pursuing his scheme); Hall to Hugh Hall Sr., July 16, 1717, Hall letterbook (for his initial, modest dealings in London); and Hall to J. Haragan, July 16, 1717, Hall letterbook (for the first announcement of the Guinea consignment).

5. As noted in chapters 3 and 4, John Hull, Increase Mather, and Samuel Sewall expressed moral unease about slave trading, despite the fact that previous puritans, including John Winthrop and the settlers of Providence Island, experimented with slaving ventures. For puritan ambivalence about slavery, see Smith, *Slavery, Family and Gentry Capitalism*, 18; Robert E. Desrochers Jr., "Slave-for-Sale Advertisements and Slavery in Massachusetts, 1704–1781," *The William and Mary Quarterly*, 3rd ser., 59 (2002): 623–64; Peterson, "*Selling of Joseph*"; and Wendy Anne Warren, " 'The Cause of her Grief': The Rape of a Slave in Early New England," *Journal of American History* 93 (2007): 1031–49.

6. During the 1710s, Hall kept a daily diary with brief notations on weather and public events, recording fast and thanksgiving days, election days, the arrival

of Shute in 1716, ordinations, and other such occasions. There is, however, no extant diary from the spring of 1718; see Hugh Hall Jr., diary, 1714–17 (with scattered entries through 1762), New York Public Library, New York (hereafter cited as diary), November 1715 and March, May, and July 1716, for the examples listed here.

7. Benjamin Colman, *The Religious Regards We Owe to our Country* (Boston, 1718), 15, 17, 45.

8. Ibid., 29, 37, 40; see 21–23 (for the Stoics), 41 (for treatment of bills of credit), and 47 (for Winthrop, Hutchinson, and Belcher). Hall charted several shipments of slaves, and listed many by name, in his diaries and account book; for sales to Colman and Colman's brother John, see Hugh Hall, account book, 1728–33, Massachusetts Historical Society, Boston, (hereafter cited as account book), 28. John Colman himself later sold slaves; see Robert E. Desrochers, "Slave-for-Sale Advertisements," 623.

9. This and the following paragraph rely on Smith, *Slavery, Family and Gentry Capitalism*, 26, 29–32; Wentworth, appendix to "Letters of Hugh Hall to Benning Wentworth"; *Harvard Graduates* 6:11–18; and "The Checkley Family," *NEHGR* 2 (1848): 351. For the family property in Philadelphia, see E. M. Shilstone,foreword to Richard Hall's *General Account of the First Settlement and of the Trade and Constitution of the Island of Barbados* (Barbados, 1924), iii, vi (a published transcription of a 1755 manuscript authored by Richard Hall and his son, Richard junior); and Richard Hall to Hugh Hall Jr., July 8, 1733, Hugh Hall Papers, Massachusetts Historical Society, Boston. For another example of a Barbadian family with connections to New England, see Larry Gragg, *A Quest for Security: The Life of Samuel Parris, 1653–1720* (New York, 1990), 2–21.

10. In heraldic terms, the Hall coat of arms features three talbots' (hunting hounds') heads eclipsed by nine crosses: Morison, "Letter-book of Hugh Hall," 514–15. For Richard Hall, and the second Hugh's conversion to Anglicanism, see *Harvard Graduates* 8:54–58. For Quakers in Barbados, and their tentative relationships to the government there, see Barbara Ritter Dailey, "The Early Quaker Mission and the Settlement of Meetings in Barbados, 1655–1700," *The Journal of the Barbados Museum and Historical Society* 39 (1991): 24–46.

11. Hugh Hall, sermon notebook, passim; *Harvard Graduates* 6:11–12; Smith, *Slavery, Family and Gentry Capitalism*, 30, 41; Hugh Hall Sr. to Hall, April 22, 1711, Hugh Hall correspondence, 1711–50, James W. Bleecker Papers, New York Historical Society, New York (hereafter Bleeker Papers); and, for Wentworth, *Harvard Graduates* 6:113–14.

12. Hall to Lydia Colman, March 6, 1717, Hall letterbook; Smith, *Slavery, Family and Gentry Capitalism*, 12, 33–34.

13. Hall to Lydia Colman, March 6, 1717, Hall letterbook. Hall recounted his various meetings in his letter to Hugh Hall Sr., September 9, 1717, Hall letterbook. He also noted his movements in England in his diary, April through September 1717. See also Smith, *Slavery, Family and Gentry Capitalism*, 12, 33–34.

14. Hall's travels can be tracked through his letterbook; see the short biographies listed in note 1 of this chapter, and especially Smith, *Slavery, Family and Gentry Capitalism*, 12–14, 16, 34, for the details mentioned here.

15. *Harvard Graduates* 6:15–16. Hall's contestant in litigation was John Richards, a parishioner of the Old North Church, to whom Checkly (while married to Hall's grandmother Lydia) had mortgaged much of the Gibbs estate.

16. Joseph Laurenton to Hall, July 11, 1723, NYHS; Hall to Samuel Fitch, March 10, 1718, Hall letterbook; Joseph Paice to Hugh Hall, February 14, 1731, Hugh Hall correspondence, Bleecker Papers; Hall to Richard Bowaton, January 28, 1719, Hall letterbook; Hall to John Binning, April 7, 1720, Hall letterbook; Hugh Hall, account book, Massachusetts Historical Society, Boston, 4–5, 6, 10, 60; Hall, 1729 inventory of sales, Hugh Hall Papers, Massachusetts Historical Society (MHS). Morison, in "Letter-book of Hugh Hall," summarizes Hall's trading arrangements and shows how they represented larger patterns.

17. Hugh Hall, letterbook, passim; Hall, account book, MHS, 13, 19, 20, 23, 31, 41, 45, 49; Smith, *Slavery, Family and Gentry Capitalism*, 16–17. Hall's papers mention only part of his outstanding debts, for example, £2,000 owed for consignments in 1729.

18. Hall to Hugh Hall Sr., July 9, 1718, Hall letterbook. For the Boston-Barbados connection, with a useful set of citations on New England slavery, see Pettigrew, "Free to Enslave"; for Hall's relationship to Barbados slave traders, see Smith, *Slavery, Family and Gentry Capitalism*, 19, 22–26. For typical annual imports and commissions by Hall, see 14, 16. For the profits mentioned here, I have averaged the annual sales to sixty-five, figured a price of £50 per slave (the most frequently mentioned price), and approximated a 6 percent profit. (Hall's commission was typically 5 percent; his profits from direct sales probably would have averaged 7 percent). Profit margins varied according to conditions not mentioned in his papers: costs of insurance and handling, percentage of the sale price actually paid, refunds for slaves who died or were incapacitated soon after their sale, and so on. I have consulted here the figures compiled by David Hancock, *Citizens of the World: London Merchants and the Integration of the British Atlantic Community, 1735–1785* (New York, 1995), 419–24; and Desrochers, "Slave-for-Sale Advertisements," 642. On income levels and gentility in this period, see Margaretta M. Lovell, *Art in a Season of Revolution: Painters, Artisans, and Patrons in Early America* (Philadelphia, 2005), 6–7.

19. Richard Hall to Hugh Hall, July 8 and September 4, 1733, Hugh Hall Papers, Massachusetts Historical Society; Richard Hall to Hugh Hall, September 18, 1735, Hall Papers; John and Abraham Blydesteyn to Hall, July 4, 1740, Bleecker Papers; the lawsuits are described in a 1744 summons for Benjamin Williams, and a 1750 summons for Thomas Paine, Bleecker Papers; Hugh Hall, account book, MHS, 17 (for Hall's outlying lands); Hugh Hall, diary (for scattered accounts of Hall's diminishing estate); *Harvard Graduates* 6:16–17. See also Smith, *Slavery, Family and Gentry Capitalism*, 17, 41–42. For the decline in slave importation during the 1740s and 1750s, see Desrochers, "Slave-for-Sale Advertisements."

20. Bailyn, *New England Merchants*, 195; Bridenbaugh, *Cities in the Wilderness*, 187–88; Jon Butler, *The Huguenots in America: A Refugee People in New World Society* (Cambridge, Mass., 1983), 71–90; John F. Bosher, "Huguenot Merchants and the Protestant International in the Seventeenth Century," *The William and Mary Quarterly*, 3rd ser., 52 (1995): 77–102; Lawrence Park, "The Savage Family," *NEHGR* 67 (1913): 198–215, 309–13; and Johnson, *John Nelson*.

21. For the political ambivalence of merchants in this period, especially in regard to new navigation laws, see Matson, *Merchants and Empire*, 123–27; and Weeden, *Economic and Social History* 1:373–75. Governor Joseph Dudley (1702–15) elicited strong support and dissent. Hall smuggled some brandy to Boston during his early trading days, fussed over the paperwork necessary to avoid import duties on slaves passing through his hands to other colonies, hinted at an evasion of customs, and timed his shipments of slaves to Virginia to gaps in duty regulation: *Harvard Graduates* 6:113; Smith, *Slavery, Family and Gentry Capitalism*, 42; Hall to Samuel Brown, February 19, 1720, Hall letterbook; and Hall to Henry Harrison, February 25, 1719, Hall letterbook.

22. Davis, "Boston 'Banks' " and "New Hampshire Notes."

23. The quotation is from A. A. Sykes's *Letter to a Friend* (London, 1717), cited in Peter Mathias's "Risk, Credit and Kinship in Early Modern Enterprise," in *The Early Modern Atlantic Economy*, ed. John J. McCusker and Kenneth Morgan (New York, 2000), 15–35 (quotation on 29). For the general observations here about credit and trust, see Mathias, "Risk, Credit and Kinship"; Jacob M. Price, *Capital and Credit in British Overseas Trade: The View from the Chesapeake, 1700–1776* (Cambridge, Mass., 1980); and David Hancock, " 'A Revolution in the Trade': Wine Distribution and the Development of the Infrastructure of the Atlantic Market Economy, 1703–1807," in *Early Modern Atlantic Economy*, by McCusker and Morgan, 105–53. For civility, literary sophistication, sociability, and commercial reputation, see David S. Shields, *Civil Tongues and Polite Letters in British America* (Chapel Hill, N.C., 1997); Michal J. Rozbicki, *The Complete Colonial Gentleman: Cultural Legitimacy in Plantation America* (Charlottesville, Va., 1998) (with extended reference to Allestree and Defoe); and, on contrasts with puritan rhetoric, Round, *By Nature and Custom Cursed.*

24. The formality of business correspondence may be seen in the letters of John and David Jeffries, Jeffries Family Papers, Massachusetts Historical Society, esp. vols. 1–5, 9, 12–15; in the letterbook of John Spooner, 1741–42, American Antiquarian Society; in Hall's letters in the Bleecker Papers; and in the discussion of Thomas Fitch in chapter 4. For secretary's guides, politeness, and strategic candor, see Toby L. Ditz, "Secret Selves, Credible Personas: The Problematic of Trust and Public Display in the Writing of Eighteenth-Century Philadelphia Merchants," in *Possible Pasts: Becoming Colonial in Early America, ed.* Robert Blair St. George (Ithaca, N.Y., 2000), 219–42. For the printed forms, including the examples listed here, I have relied on the collection of blank forms, 1700 to 1776, otherwise uncatalogued, from the American Antiquarian Society, and on the daybook of Daniel Henchman, 1719–1750, microfilm copy at the American Antiquarian Society (for example, April 27, 1726). Hall's papers in the Bleecker Papers include several printed and completed legal forms: summonses for Hall's defendants in causes of debt. Each form is issued under the name of George II and the County of Suffolk. See also Konstantin Derks, "Letter Writing, Stationary Supplies, and Consumer Modernity in the Eighteenth-Century Atlantic World," *Early American Literature* 41 (2006): 473–94.

25. Whitehill and Kennedy, *Boston*, 15–46; Bridenbaugh, *Cities in the Wilderness*, 147, 152–59, 168; Hall, *Last American Puritan*, 332; Silverman, *Cotton Mather*, 279–

80; Richard H. Saunders, *John Smibert: Colonial America's First Portrait Painter* (New Haven, Conn., 1995), 63; Sewall, *Diary* 2:713–14.

26. Hunter, *Purchasing Identity*, 85–88; Bridenbaugh, *Cities in the Wilderness*, 171–72, 184 (for the Cotton Mather anecdote); Warden, *Boston*, 67–68; Weeden, *Economic and Social History* 1:368; and Silverman, *Cotton Mather*, 279–81. For taverns and coffeehouses as social spaces, see Conroy, *In Public Houses*. As Addison claimed of London's clubs and coffeehouses, they provided a venue where conversation translated philosophical and political abstractions into pragmatic and everyday opinion: Roy Porter, *The Creation of the Modern World: The Untold Story of the British Enlightenment* (New York, 2000), 11.

27. For neighborhoods, retail and wholesale differentiation, and commercial clustering, see Gayle Sawtelle, "The Geography of Shop- and Storekeeping in Eighteenth-Century Boston" (paper presented at the Tenth Annual Conference of the Omohundro Institute of Early American History and Culture, June 2004, and kindly shared with me).

28. For the Bonner map and Burgis engravings described in the following paragraph, see Alex Krieger and David Cobb with Amy Turner, *Mapping Boston* (Cambridge, Mass., 1999), 37–47, 175–79, which provides evidence of a community of cartographers, landscape painters, and portrait artists, all oriented toward commercial enterprise, including John Smibert and Peter Pelham, who are discussed later. See also Peter Benes, *New England Prospect: A Loan Exhibition of Maps at the Currier Gallery of Art* (Boston, 1981), 50–53, 101–6.

29. Benes, *New England Prospect*, 50–51, 103–6; and Saunders, *John Smibert*, 62. As propaganda, the Burgis perspectives, or views, advertised Boston's preeminence among colonial ports when, in fact, the pace of Massachusetts's economic growth in this period, relative to the middle and southern colonies, was slowing; see McCusker and Menard, *Economy of British America*, 91–111, 189–208; and Edwin J. Perkins, *The Economy of Colonial America*, 2nd ed. (New York, 1988), 212–38.

30. Criticisms of market proposals included *A Dialogue between a Boston Man and a Countrey Man* (Boston, 1714[5]); and *Some Considerations Against the Setting Up of a Market in this Town* (Boston, 1733). For the relevant selectmen records, see Boston, City of, *A Report of the Record Commissioners of the City of Boston, Containing the Records of Boston Selectmen, 1701–1715* (Boston, 1884), 29, 101–4, 193–95. See also Bridenbaugh, *Cities in the Wilderness*, 144; and Nash, *Urban Crucible*, 76–80. For the debates about incorporation and marketplaces, see Bridenbaugh, *Cities in the Wilderness*, 194; Warden, *Boston*, 73–79; and especially Jonathan McClellan Beagle, " 'The Cradle of Liberty': Faneuil Hall and the Political Culture of Eighteenth-Century Boston" (PhD diss., University of New Hampshire, 2003).

31. Benjamin Colman, *Some Reasons and Arguments Offered to the Good People of Boston . . . for Setting Up Markets in Boston* (Boston, 1719), 1, 3, 5; see 4–6 for the arguments about knowledgeable exchange and 13 for the opinions of foreign merchants. In a letter to Robert Wodrow, January 23, 1719, Colman also expressed his abhorrence of what he described as a vile concoction of profaneness, fraud, theft, irreligion, and incivility in common exchange: *Proceedings of the Massachusetts Historical Society* 77 (1965): 108.

32. Whitehill and Kennedy, *Boston*, 41; Beagle, " 'Cradle of Liberty' "; and Abram English Brown, *Faneuil Hall and Faneuil Hall Market, or Peter Faneuil and His Gift* (Boston, 1900).

33. The quote is given in Silverman's *Cotton Mather*, 281. For the general observations here, see Newall, *From Dependency to Independence*, 96, 101; Hunter, *Purchasing Identity*, 107–46; John E. Crowley, "The Sensibility of Comfort," *American Historical Review* 104 (1999): 749–82; Linda Levy Peck, *Consuming Splendor: Society and Culture in Seventeenth-Century England* (New York, 2005); and Goodwin, *Archaeology of Manners*. There is an abundant literature, replete with theoretical controversies, about consumer culture, puritanism, and liberal religion in this period. The most convincing arguments, on which much of this paragraph rests, include Peterson, "Puritanism and Refinement"; Jean-Christophe Agnew, "Coming up for Air: Consumer Culture in Historical Perspective," in *Consumption and the World of Goods*, ed. John Brewer and Roy Porter (New York, 1993), 19–39; the essays in *The Birth of Consumer Society*, by Neil McKendrick, John Brewer, and J. H. Plumb (Bloomington, Ind., 1982); and Colin Campbell, *The Romantic Ethic and the Spirit of Modern Consumerism* (New York, 1987).

34. St. George, *Conversing by Signs*, 84–87; Cummings, "Beginning of Provincial Renaissance Architecture"; Saunders, *John Smibert*, 62; Craven, *Colonial American Portraiture*, 139; Richard L. Bushman, *The Refinement of America: Persons, Houses, Cities* (New York, 1992); and Hall, account book, 64.

35. Lovell, *Art in a Season of Revolution*, 13, 24, 48, 90–91, 116–17; Saunders, *John Smibert*, 61–107 (179 for the portrait of Elizabeth Hall); Craven, *Colonial American Portraiture*, 101–11, 140–48, 165–77; Carrie Rebora et al., *John Singleton Copley in America* (New York, 1995), 127–36, 254–55 (128 for the pastel portrait of Hall); Hall, diary, 1750; Smith, *Slavery, Family and Gentry Capitalism*, 40–41.

36. For the gloves sent to Hall, see "Extracts from Interleaved Almanacs for the Years 1724 and 1732, in the Handwriting of Samuel Sewall, Jr.," *NEHGR* 16 (1862): 70; Hall's genealogical inscriptions are in his diary. On funerals, see Hunter *Purchasing Identity*, 73, 120–21; for gravestones, Sally M. Promey, "Seeing the Self 'In Frame': Early New England Material Practice and Puritan Piety," *Material Religion* 1 (2005): 10–47. Promey suggests a transition in headstone and gravestone art during Hall's lifetime: seventeenth-century puritans erected simple headstones inscribed with Scripture and stark emblems of mortality such as skulls, whereas many of Boston's merchants from Hull's generation had gravestones decorated with carvings of the Hebrew temple or ethereal beings, which evoked Old Testament motifs conveying the endurance of tribal and familial lines.

37. For Hall's complaints, see Hall to Hugh Hall Sr., July 31, 1718, and September 9, 1718, Hall letterbook; and Hall to Joseph Parsons, February 12, 1718, Hall letterbook, for three of many examples. As an example of extraneous fees attached to imports, Abraham Blydesteyn of London charged Hall fees for packing, commission, customs, shipping, insurance, and bills of lading, all on a modest order of tea, paper, silk, and cambric; John and Abraham Blydesteyn to Hall, April 30, 1743, Bleeker Papers correspondence. To illustrate further complications: Hall once instructed an agent in London to insure a shipment for 16 percent above the real value of goods in order to cover, in case of loss, the inevitable disputes with the insurer and extra interest he would have to pay his creditor/suppliers while

he waited for a settlement (Hall to Benjamin Dawson, March 8, 1718, Hall letterbook). For newspapers, increasing facility with pricing, and the "market" as a
dependable system, see Stuart Bruchey, "The Colonial Merchant," in *Encyclopedia of
the North American Colonies*, ed. Cooke, 1:577–89; Warden, *Boston*, 89; and Matson,
Merchant and Empire, 49–65. The 30 percent discount on bills reflects common
trends and official evaluation by the Bank of England. During the 1740s, monetary
deflation reached alarming levels: Massachusetts bills lost as much as 70 percent of
their worth relative to the pound sterling; John J. McCusker, *Money and Exchange
in Europe and America, 1600–1775* (Chapel Hill, N.C., 1978), 131–37. In 1750
new provincial issues, pegged to silver, provided some relief. For the definition
and importance of price convergence, see Rothenberg, *From Market-Places to a
Market Economy*.

  38. Hall to Phillip Nisbett, January 15, 1719, Hall letterbook; Hall to Carroll
and Garrett, July 11, 1719, Hall letterbook; Hall to Joseph Laurenton, February 2,
1723, Bleecker Papers.

  39. Hall to John Marriott, February 1718, Hall letterbook.

  40. The following citations are to Hall's letters from the Hall letterbook: to John
Marriott, February 1718; to Timothy Prout, March 6, 1717; to Joseph Parsons,
February 28, 1717; and to Benjamin Dawson, March 8, 1718.

  41. The following citations are to Hall's letters from the Hall letterbook: to
Joseph Parsons, November 6, 1716; to Henry Harrison, May 3, 1720; to Edwards
Lascelles, December 6, 1716; and to Edward Cordwent, July 15, 1718.

  42. Hall to James Bunyard, January 20, 1718, Hall letterbook; and Hall to Benning Wentworth, July 16, 1717, Hall letterbook.

  43. Hall to Samuel Betteress, February 1718, Hall letterbook; Hall provided a
similar report in a March 13, 1718, letter to Betteress, Hall letterbook.

  44. Hall to Benjamin Colman, March 30, 1720, quoted and cited in Smith's
Slavery, Family and Gentry Capitalism, 39; Hall, MHS account book, 27. For a
broader statement on the moral ambiguity and paternalistic concern of slave traders
for slaves, see Hancock, *Citizens of the World*, 203–4.

  45. Hall to Samuel Betteress, February 1718, Hall letterbook; Hall provided a
similar report in a March 13, 1718, letter to Betteress, Hall letterbook. Hall, account book, MHS, 5, 28–31, 34 (for trading complexities); Hall to Samuel Betteress, June 22, 1719, and to Mssrs. Harrison, October 15, 1719, Hall letterbook (for
origin of slaves); Desrochers, "Slave-for-Sale Advertisements," 625, 651 (for Hall's
advertising). The quotation by Richard Hall comes from Hall's *General Account*,
64–65. For the Long Wharf as the likely venue for slave auctions, see Desrochers,
"Slave-for-Sale Advertisements," 627. For the external interruptions mentioned
here, with reference to Hall, see Virginia Bever Platt, "The East India Company
and the Madagascar Slave Trade," *The William and Mary Quarterly*, 3rd ser., 26
(1969): 548–77.

  46. The following citations are to letters from Hall in the Hall letterbook: to
J. Haragan, July 16, 1717; to Samuel Betteress, February 1718 (with a similar report
in a March 13, 1718, letter to Betteress); and to Samuel Betteress, September 2,
1718.

  47. The following citations are to letters from Hall in the Hall letterbook: to
Samuel Betteress, September 2, 1718; to Samuel Betteress, March 29, 1718; to

James Bunyard, October 14, 1718; and to Thomas Cocke, May 30, 1720. The same language and themes appear in other letters as well.

48. The nomenclature for church order in this period is vexed. The "established order" does not quite fit. All of the congregations discussed here were part of the order established by the General Court of Massachusetts but were regarded by the royal government as dissenters from the national church. Nor does the appellation "puritan" quite work. These congregations affirmed a puritan polity of church governance, joined in the Massachusetts synods, and claimed to be adherents of Reformed theology, but they varied widely in their interpretation of that theology. The more ecumenical, rationalistic, and sympathetic to Anglican mores they became, the more they might be called postpuritan. The label Congregationalist is anachronistic, conveying later denominational developments after independence. I settle on "congregational" for lack of a better name.

49. For general treatments of the founding of Brattle Street Church, see Anthony Gregg Roeber, " 'Her Merchandize . . . Shall Be Holiness to the Lord': The Progress and Decline of Puritan Gentility at the Brattle Street Church, Boston, 1715–1745," *NEHGR* 131 (1977): 175–94; Samuel Kirkland Lothrop, *A History of the Church in Brattle Square, Boston* (Boston, 1951), 4–53; Miller, *Colony to Province*, 240–74; and Hall, *Last American Puritan*, 292–301. For William Brattle and John Leverett, see *Harvard Graduates* 3:180–207.

50. Church membership lists are taken from Robert S. Dunkle and Ann S. Lainhart, transcribers, *The Records of the Churches of Boston*, compact disc, New England Historical and Genealogical Society (Boston, 2002). For business procedures in the church, see Boston, Brattle Street Church, *The Manifesto Church: Records of the Church in Brattle Square, Boston, 1699–1872* (Boston, 1902), 17–23. For the meetinghouse, see Silverman, *Cotton Mather*, 146–47.

51. *Harvard Graduates* 4:120–37; John Corrigan, *The Prism of Piety: Catholic Congregational Clergy at the Beginning of the Enlightenment* (New York, 1991), 10, 19–21; Roeber, " 'Her Merchandize . . . Shall Be Holiness to the Lord,' " 179–83.

52. [Benjamin Colman], *A Manifesto or Declaration, Set forth by the Undertakers of the New Church* [Boston, 1699], 1. For a discussion of the Westminster Confession and of [United Ministers], *Heads of Agreement* (London, 1691), including the text of the latter, see Walker, *Creeds and Platforms of Congregationalism*, 440–62.

53. [Benjamin Colman], *A Manifesto*, 3; the doggerel is quoted in Roeber's " 'Her Merchandize . . . Shall Be Holiness to the Lord,' " 175.

54. Lothrop, *History of the Church in Brattle Square*, 28–32, 40–62 (32 for the quote); Silverman, *Cotton Mather*, 140–56; Ellis, *History of the First Church*, 99–100; Hill, *Old South*, 327; Hall, *Last American Puritan*, 289–91. The Mathers, as Silverman shows, linked Colman's supposed laxity to the open sacramental policies of the formidable Solomon Stoddard, minister in Northampton and predecessor of Jonathan Edwards.

55. Corrigan, *Prism of Piety*, 24–25; Cooper, *Tenacious of Their Liberties*, 183–84; *Harvard Graduates* 5:341–68 (for Prince).

56. Silverman, *Cotton Mather*, 225–56, 332–34; Ellis, *First Church*, 162–69, 176–77, 184. For the establishment of new churches, see Joseph S. Clark, *A Historical Sketch of the Congregational Churches in Massachusetts from 1620 to 1858* (Boston, 1858), passim.

57. Heyrman, "Model of Christian Charity," 110–11, 202–16. J.C.D. Clark documents the spread of this discourse of providence and empire in Britain and America in this period: *The Language of Liberty, 1660–1832: Political Discourse and Social Dynamics in the Anglo-American World* (New York, 1994), 46–282.

58. Among the various iterations of the Enlightenment, the focus here especially is on the so-called moderate Enlightenment as described by Henry F. May, *The Enlightenment in America* (New York, 1976), 3–101.

59. For the popularization of Newton and pragmatic morality, see Porter, *Creation of the Modern World*. For political corollaries, see Margaret C. Jacob, *The Radical Enlightenment: Pantheists, Freemasons, and Republicans* (Boston, 1981); and Jacob, *The Newtonians and the English Revolution, 1689–1720* (New York, 1990). Porter provides a prodigious bibliography of recent works on the Enlightenment and reviews historiographical debates. His account stresses secularization, especially anti-Calvinist critiques, rather than the interplay between postpuritan theology and the Enlightenment emphasized here. Porter shows especially the development of highly pragmatic and antireligious polemic during the 1740s and 1750s.

60. See G. G. Hundert, *The Enlightenment's Fable: Barnard Mandeville and the Discovery of Society* (Cambridge, 1994).

61. Shaftesbury's full name was Anthony Ashley Cooper, third Earl of Shaftesbury; his most popular treatise was *Characteristics of Men, Manners, Opinions, Times* (London, 1711); the quote is from that work and is cited in Porter's *Creation of the Modern World*, 54. Samuel Clarke's most widely read attack on Hobbes, the 1704 Boyle Lectures, was *A Demonstration of the Being and Attributes of God* (London, 1705). For Shaftesbury's reliance on Netwon and Stoic philosophy, see Stanley Grean, *Shaftesbury's Philosophy of Religion and Ethics: A Study in Enthusiasm* (Athens, Ohio, 1967). For the popularity of Shaftesbury, see Stephen Copley, "Commerce, Conversation and Politeness in the Early Eighteenth-Century Periodical," *British Journal for Eighteenth-Century Studies* 18 (1995): 63–77; and Porter, *Creation of the Modern World*, 54, 96, 196, 265. There is a large literature on sympathy and compassion as moral vocabularies in this period, including Norman S. Fiering's "Irresistible Compassion: An Aspect of Eighteenth-Century Sympathy and Humanitarianism," *Journal of the History of Ideas* 27 (1976): 195–218; and Graham John Barker-Benfield's *Culture of Sensibility: Sex and Society in Eighteenth-Century Britain* (Chicago, 1992). For the connections among the moral discourse of sensibility, the culture of politeness, and the market economy, see Hirschman, *Passions and Interests*; and Porter, *Creation of the Modern World*, 158, 179, and 263–83.

62. Fiering, "The First American Enlightenment"; and Gerard Reedy, "Interpreting Tillotson," *Harvard Theological Review* 86 (1993): 81–103.

63. John Tillotson, *The Works of the Most Reverend Dr. John Tilloston* (London, 1728), title page, 41; Tillotson, quoted in Porter's *Creation of the Modern World*, 102–3.

64. Fiering, "First American Enlightenment," 319 for the Mather quote; Fiering, "Transatlantic Republic of Letters," 642 for "genteel periodical"; Elizabeth Carroll Reilly, "The Wages of Piety: The Boston Book Trade of Jeremy Condy," in *Printing and Society in Early America*, ed. William L. Joyce et al. (Worcester, Mass., 1983), 83–131 (for sales figures). Pemberton's library is cataloged in [Samuel Gerrish], *A Catalogue of Curious and Valuable Books Belonging to the late Reverend*

and Learned Mr. Ebenezer Pemberton (Boston, 1717); for other pastors, see [Samuel Gerrish], *A Catalogue of Rare and Valuable Books Being the greatest part of the Library of the late Reverend and Learned Mr. Joshua Moodey, and . . . Daniel Gookin* (Boston, 1718). London presses produced numerous editions of John Tillotson's *Works of the Most Reverend Dr. John Tillotson* (for example, 1696, 1701, 1704, 1712, and 1717), with some 50 to 250 sermons and discourses in each, sometimes published as ten or fourteen volumes bound in two books.

65. In addition to Fiering's "First American Enlightenment" and "Transatlantic Republic of Letters," see the catalog of the library begun at Old South Church: Boston, Public Library, *The Prince Library* (Boston, 1870), 121, 125, 135–36; and Corrigan, *Prism of Piety,* 27–31, 55–61. Wilkins, a son-in-law of Tillotson, eventually leaned toward deism. For Boston booksellers and serial publications, see Hugh Amory, "Reinventing the Colonial Book," in *Colonial Book,* ed. Amory and Hall, 26–54; and Stephen Botein, "The Anglo-American Book Trade before 1776: Personnel and Strategies," in *Printing and Society in Early America,* ed. William L. Joyce et al., 48–82.

66. Annabel Patterson, *Early Modern Liberalism* (Cambridge, 1997), 27–61 (for Hollis); Norman Fiering, *Moral Philosophy at Seventeenth-Century Harvard: A Discipline in Transition* (Chapel Hill, N.C., 1981) (for the curriculum); Arthur Orlo Norton, "Harvard Text-Books and Reference Books of the Seventeenth Century," *Publications of the Colonial Society of Massachusetts,* vol. 28, *Transactions, 1930–1933* (Boston, 1935), 361–438; Rick Kennedy, "Thomas Brattle and the Scientific Provincialism of New England, 1680–1717," *The New England Quarterly* 63 (1990): 584–600; Rick Kennedy, "Thomas Brattle, Mathematician-Architect in the Transition of the New England Mind, 1690–1600," *Winterthur Portfolio* 24 (1989): 231–45. The college tutors shared a camaraderie of cosmopolitan, scientific, and imperial sensibility: Fiering, "First American Enlightenment." Leverett and Morton had ties to Defoe and latitudinarian writers. William Brattle, the son of a wealthy merchant, became pastor of the Cambridge church in 1696; he was perhaps the least scientifically versed of his cohort. Thomas Brattle was treasurer at the college, auditor of the town's accounts, and supervisor of the construction of a fort on Castle Island. His Stoughton Hall provided a precedent for later building at Harvard, particularly Smibert's neoclassical, Georgian design for the college chapel: Lovell, *Art in a Season of Revolution,* 184–224.

67. For this typology, see Corrigan, *Prism of Piety.*

68. See especially Teresa Toulouse, " 'Syllabical Idolatry': Benjamin Colman and the Rhetoric of Balance," *Early American Literature* 18 (1983–84): 257–74.

69. Benjamin Colman, *A Sermon at the Lecture in Boston, After the Funerals of those Excellent and Learned Divines,* with the running title of *Industry and Diligence in the Work of Religion* (Boston, 1717), 28, 34, 36, 39, 40. Colman made similar observations about Brattle and Pemberton and added a dedication to Thomas Hollis (enshrining the progressive circle at Harvard), in his "Dedicatory Letter" to Ebenezer Pemberton, *Sermons and Discourses on Several Occasions* (London, 1727), i–iv.

70. Benjamin Colman, *God Deals with Us as Rational Creatures* (Boston, 1723), 8, 18, 22.

71. Edward Bromfield Jr., sermon notes, vol. 11, notes on Cooper's sermon on Ephesians 4:1, 1718, Bromfied Family Papers, Massachusetts Historical Society,

Boston; Samuel Philips sermon notes, Pemberton on 1 Thess. 4:11, April 1704, Samuel Philips Papers, Massachusetts Historical Society. These are only two of dozens of examples in these notebooks, which, although noted as Samuel Philips Papers, are of questionable authorship.

72. The details of formal debates about divine power and world events, such as between Cartesians and Newtonians, influenced Bostonians less than did an overriding and increasingly popular cultural mandate to correlate Christian teaching to the natural order. For these debates, see Fiering, "First American Enlightenment"; and Margaret C. Jacob, "Christianity and the Newtonian Worldview," in *God and Nature: Historical Essays on the Encounter between Christianity and Science*, ed. David C. Lindberg and Ronald L. Numbers (Berkeley, Calif., 1986), 238–55.

73. See Porter, *Creation of the Modern World*, 105, 131–40, 299, 301–3; Jacob, "Christianity and the Newtonian Worldview"; Gary B. Deason, "Reformation Theology and the Mechanistic Conception of Nature," in *God and Nature*, ed. Lindberg and Numbers, 167–91; and, for the relationship between natural and supernatural causation, Vladimir Janković, *Reading the Skies: A Cultural History of English Weather, 1650–1820* (Chicago, 2000), 33–77.

74. Cotton Mather, *The Christian Philosopher* (London, 1721); and Increase Mather, *An Essay for the Recording of Illustrious Providences* (Boston, 1684). See also Increase Mather, *The Doctrine of Divine Providence Opened and Applied* (Boston, 1684). For background and details on Mather's views, Hall, *Last American Puritan*, 167–73; Miller, *Colony to Province*, 143; and Middlekauff, *The Mathers*, 140–54.

75. Cotton Mather, *Christian Philosopher*, quoted in Silverman's *Cotton Mather*, 250–51, and in Winship's *Seers of God*, 105; the last quotation from Mather, from a 1711 diary entry, is given in an essay that provides further evidence of the spread of natural theology: Pershing Vartanian, "Cotton Mather and the Puritan Transition into the Enlightenment," *Early American Literature* 7 (1973): 213–24, quote on 221. For Mather's views on providence and nature, see Winton U. Solberg, introduction to Cotton Mather's *Christian Philosopher* (1721; repr., Urbana, Ill., 1994), xix–cxx; Silverman, *Cotton Mather*, 247–51; Middlekauff, *Mathers*, 283–304; Rumsey, *Acts of God*; William E. Burns, *An Age of Wonders: Prodigies, Politics, and Providence in England, 1657–1727* (Manchester, U.K., 2004), 57–80; Peter Julie Sievers, "Drowned Pens and Shaking Hands: Sea Providence Narratives in Seventeenth-Century New England," *The William and Mary Quarterly*, 3rd ser., 63 (2006): 743–76; and especially Winship, *Seers of God*, 21–106.

76. For the popularity of natural theology, see Corrigan, *Prism of Piety*, 55–61 (the two quotations, from Colman and Foxcroft, are cited on 61); Rumsey, *Acts of God and People*, 117–42; and Vartanian, "Cotton Mather and the Puritan Transition." For Robie and other almanacs, see Hall, *World of Wonders*, 108; and Kidd, *Protestant Interest*, 86–87. For further evidence, see Erik R. Seeman, *Pious Persuasions: Laity and Clergy in Eighteenth-Century New England* (Baltimore, 1999), 116–46.

77. The term "natural theology" and its subject, "natural law," thus took on a different meaning for Pemberton, Colman, and their colleagues than it did for their predecessors. Earlier puritans used the rubric to assert the duplication in nature of a divine law more reliably encoded in Scripture. Natural law did not imply for them any limitation to God's direct intervention in physical or moral affairs. For the

importance of natural law as a rubric in this period, see T. J. Hochstrasser, *Natural Law Theories in the Early Enlightenment* (Cambridge, 2000), 1–23; and Taylor, *Sources of the Self*, 230–72. For puritan uses of natural law, see Lowrie, *Shape of the Puritan Mind*, 27–29. For puritan views of providence, natural law, and morality, see Winship, *Seers of God*, 36–50; Maxine Van de Wetering, "Moralizing in Puritan Natural Science: Mysteriousness in Earthquake Sermons," *Journal of the History of Ideas* 43 (1982): 417–38; and J.C.D. Clark, "Providence, Predestination and Progress, or Did the Enlightenment Fail?" *Albion* 35 (2004): 559–89.

78. Benjamin Colman, *A Humble Discourse of the Incomprehensibleness of God* (Boston, 1715), 11; see esp. 49–76; Thomas Prince, *An Account of a Strange Appearance in the Heavens* (Boston, 1719), which he called a "Piece of *Natural History*," 2; and Thomas Prince, *Earthquakes the Works of God* (Boston, 1727). Colman's remarks on sociability echo the work of natural law theorists such as Samuel Pufendorf; see Hochstrasser, *Natural Law Theories*, 62–71.

79. Foxcroft, quoted in Corrigan's *Prism of Piety*, 94. For providence and exchange, see Jacob Viner, *The Role of Providence in the Social Order: An Essay in Intellectual History* (Philadelphia, 1972). On the relationship between Newton's cosmos and theories of the market, see Porter, *Creation of the Modern World*, 383–96.

80. Daniel Defoe, *The Review*, 1706 and 1713, quoted in Porter's *Creation of the Modern World*, 384. For the spread of ideas of personal moral accountability among American merchants, attached to ideals of honor, see Toby L. Ditz, "Shipwrecked, or Masculinity Imperiled: Mercantile Representations of Failure and the Gendered Self in Eighteenth Century Philadelphia," *Journal of American History* 81 (1994): 51–80.

81. Defoe, *The Complete English Tradesman* (London, 1726; Edinburgh, 1839), 22, 26, 28, 32, 58, 62, 153; 52–87 for the subordination of all other affairs to business; 96–102 for treatment of debtors. I have used the Project Gutenberg eBook electronic version, which provides text and pagination from the Edinburgh edition.

82. Ibid., 173, 175, 179–80; the oft-cited phrase "polite and commercial people" is discussed in Paul Langford's *Polite and Commercial People: England, 1727–1783* (New York, 1989).

83. Porter, in *Creation of the Modern World*, 205–29, mistakes all naturalized understandings of economic exchange for pure secularization, whereas this claim emphasizes the theological purposes that lay embedded in the promotion of a natural and rational discourse of providence in postpuritan Boston.

84. See especially Wadsworth, *Saint's Prayer*. Wadsworth encouraged parents to inculcate "*Good Manners* (a Civil, Kind, Handsome, Courteous Behaviour, is a Christian Duty and Ornament)" yet criticized the "*Nice Invented Modes of Gesture, Compliment and Behavior*" that stood for polite "Skill" in cosmopolitan circles. He also chastised merchants for "an Expensive-way of living" adopted to "make some figure" in the world: Wadsworth, *Fraud and Injustice*, 27.

85. Pemberton sermons, noted in John Leverett sermon notes, February 28, 1697 (for the reasonableness of the moral equation between virtue and prosperity); and noted in Samuel Philips Papers (on the method for success). Other quotes come from Pemberton's sermons as noted in Heyrman, "Model of Christian Charity," 206 (wealth and the social order); 51–51 (Locke and labor); 38–40 (the God of nature and design); 32 (on avoiding diversions and doing business); and 236 (the

contrast between vigor and sloth). For Pemberton's proposal for a labor committee, see Heyrman, "Model of Christian Charity," 46. Similar assertions can be found scattered throughout other notes on Brattle's and Wadsworth's preaching, for example, Leverett sermon notes, June 28, 1696 (Brattle); Thomas Prince notebook, 1718–1722, Boston Public Library, Boston (Sewall); and Samuel Philips Papers, notes on September 7, 1704 (Wadsworth).

86. Ebenezer Pemberton, *A Sermon Preached in the Audience of the General Assembly* (Boston, 1706), also known as *Ill-boding Symptoms*, 5, 15–17, 26–33.

87. Prince, *Civil Rulers Raised up by God*, 16–19.

88. Thomas Foxcroft, *God the Judge* (Boston, 1727), 10, 14, 27–28, 39.

89. Prince, *Civil Rulers Raised up by God*, 9–10 (2–9 for Israel; 11–13 for providence and the cosmos in general).

90. Thomas Prince, *The People of New-England Put in Mind of the Righteous Acts of the Lord* (Boston, 1730) 11, 16–17, 20. Colman's perspectives, then, changed along these lines from his earlier political preaching described in the previous chapter; see especially his *Government the Pillar of the Earth* (Boston, 1730).

91. Prince, *People of New-England*, 21, 24, 28, 35, 38, 41.

92. Thomas Prince, *A Chronological History of New-England* (Boston, 1736), dedication (no pagination); introduction, 60–61, 78, 86, 100; part 1, 8, 15, 16; part 2, 83, 87, 90, 96, 140; and "List of Subscribers."

93. Richard Allestree, *The Whole Duty of Man* (London, 1667) and *The Gentleman's Calling* (London, 1677); Joseph Alleine, *An Alarm to Unconverted Sinners* (London, 1678; Boston, 1716), esp. 25–26, 41, 78–79, 166. For the popularity of these writers in New England, see David D. Hall, "Readers and Writers in Early New England," in *Colonial Book*, ed. Amory and Hall, 117–51.

94. John Tillotson, *The Works of the Most Reverend Dr. John Tillotson* (London, 1712), 285 (see 259–88); and Tillotson as quoted in Porter's *Creation of the Modern World*, 103.

95. Benjamin Colman, *The Government and Improvement of Mirth* (Boston, 1707), A4, 60; Joseph Sewall, *A Caveat Against Covetousness* (Boston, 1718), 3–4; Benjamin Colman, *Dying in Peace in a Good Old Age* (Boston, 1730), for the ideal merchant, in this case, Simeon Stoddard. For charitable giving and gentility, see Christine Leigh Heyrman, "The Fashion among More Secure Superior People: Charity and Social Change in Provincial New England, 1700–1740," *American Quarterly* 34 (1982): 107–24.

96. Thomas Foxcroft, *A Discourse Concerning Kindness* (Boston, 1720), 17–19, 23, 27.

97. Pemberton, *Advice to a Son*, 1, 8, 23.

98. Cotton Mather, *Pascentius*, esp. 22–27; Samuel Whitman, *Practical Godliness the Way to Prosperity* (New London, Conn., 1714), 7–8.

99. Benjamin Colman, *Industry and Diligence in the Work of Religion*, 13–14, 17; Wadsworth, *Vicious Courses*, 9.

100. Benjamin Colman, *The Blessing of Zebulun and Issachar* (Boston, 1719), 3, 14 (7–10 for Colman's projection of a natural, regular order sustained by overseas commerce).

101. Ibid., 3, 17, 22–26.

102. Ibid., 4, 6, 20–21.

103. Ibid., 1, 5, 13, 15, 19, 29 (12–13 for the risks of trade).

104. [Thomas Prince], *The Vade Mecum for America* (Boston, 1731), ii, iv, 162 (on usury), and 217 (for the measures of commodities mentioned here).

105. Ibid., A2; the selection from the *News-Letter*, quoting the London *Post-Man*, is given in Kidd's *Protestant Interest*, 51–52.

106. David Hume, "Of Refinement in the Arts," quoted and cited in Gould's *Persistence of Empire*, 28; see 28–30 for the claims about commerce and sociability.

107. Ebenezer Pemberton, *A True Servant of his Generation* (Boston, 1712), 4–5, 8, 14.

108. Benjamin Colman, *Ossa Josephi* (Boston, 1720), 38, 40; Benjamin Colman, *A Funeral Sermon . . . upon the Death of . . . Grove Hirst* (Boston, 1716), 38; Benjamin Colman, *The Blameless and Inoffensive Life* (Boston, 1723), 32. Hirst, the father-in-law of Charles Chauncy—an important merchant and father of the future pastor of First Church—earned Colman's admiration especially for his combination of civic prominence and piety. Despite bouts of melancholia, Hirst read devotional literature, listened to Colman's sermons, and acted with proper decorum until his premature death. His lengthy spiritual diary, which Colman published along with the funeral oration, contained extensive meditations on providence.

109. Thomas Foxcroft, *A Brief Display of Mordecai's Excellent Character* (Boston, 1727), 11, 16.

110. In searching for profitable commodities, Hall turned to sugar products, including rum, which he imported from Barbados to Boston in the 1720s; see especially his detailed accounts of various sugars and rums listed in his note of "sale of sugars bought of C. Coddington," in his account book, MHS. Ironically, Hall also purchased from Daniel Henchman two sermons by Increase Mather, published as *Wo to Drunkards* (1673; 2nd ed., Boston, 1712), that blamed the high incidence of alcoholism in Boston on imported rum: Daniel Henchman, 1712–36 ledger, held at the New England Historical and Genealogical Society and available in microfilm as part of the Henchman Family Papers, American Antiquarian Society.

111. For the baptisms, see *Harvard Graduates* 6:16; and Dunkle and Lainhard, transcribers, *Records of the Churches of Boston*. On the founding of West Church and Hall's hosting of the prayer meeting, see Sheila McIntyre, " 'I Heare it so Variously Reported': News-Letters, Newspapers, and the Ministerial Network in New England, 1670–1730," *New England Quarterly* 71 (1998): 593–614, 610–11 on Hall. For Hall's contributions to Anglican churches and priests, see Smith, *Slavery, Family and Gentry Capitalism*, 40; and Richard Hall to Hugh Hall, August 1734, Hugh Hall correspondence, Massachusetts Historical Society. For Hall as pallbearer, see Sewall, *Diary* 2:822, 898.

112. Hall to Colman, February 28, 1717, Hall letterbook; Hall to Leverett, February 28, 1717, Hall letterbook; Hall, notes on February 6, 1709, February 13, 1709, Hugh Hall, sermon notes, Massachusetts Historical Society.

113. Daniel Henchman ledger, 1712–35; Daniel Henchman daybook, 1726–28, original at Boston Public Library, microfilm copy in the Henchman Family Papers, American Antiquarian Society; Hall, account book, Massachusetts Historical Society, 3 (for Mather's *Magnalia*); Prince, *Chronological History*, "List of Subscribers" (n.p.); and Hall to Leverett, August 2, 1717, Hall letterbook (for Beveredge).

114. Hall assured his father that he was polite enough to appreciate Anglican piety: Hall to Hugh Hall Sr., September 6, 1717, Hall letterbook.

115. For one example of deistic poetry, see the clipping from the *Boston Gazette*, Februrary 7–14, 1737, which reprints an excerpt from *The Gentleman's Magazine*, in the Pitts Family Papers, Massachusetts Historical Society. Hall's brother-in-law and partner James Pitts had collected the poem.

116. Hall to Hugh Hall Sr., October 2, 1718, Hall letterbook; Hall to Elisha Calandar, February 28, 1717, Hall letterbook.

117. Hall to Mary Bromfiled, April 1717, Hall letterbook; Hall to Edward Bromfield, February 1718, Hall letterbook; Hall to William Welsteed, February 14, 1718, Hall letterbook.

118. Hall included a copy of his poem in his letter to Mary Lascelles, June 16, 1718, Hall letterbook.

119. Ibid.

120. Hall, *A General Account . . . of Barbados*, 13–14. See the whole account and the foreword to this for other details. Richard partly relied on Hall's observations on the island, recorded in Hugh Hall, diary, New York Public Library.

121. Hugh Hall, diary, 1723, New England Historic and Genealogical Society, Boston (the diary is contained in Hall's copy of N. Whittemore's *Almanack* [Boston, 1723]); for one example of the exchange of news (in this case, rumors of war), see Richard Hall to Hugh Hall, July 11, 1734, Hugh Hall correspondence, Massachusetts Historical Society.

122. The following letters are all from the Hall letterbook: to John Timbs, May 15, 1718 (Boston as the epitome of London); to Hugh Hall Sr., October 25, 1717 (the nation's contests); to John Binning, March 20, 1719 (on Philip). For further discussion of Boston slave traders and their understanding of business as a means of identification with the metropolis, see Desrochers, "Slave-for-Sale Advertisements."

123. Hall to John Timbs, May 15, 1718. For Hall's record of the political events mentioned here, among many others, see especially his diary from 1714 to 1716. Hall left no evidence of the growing resentment of provincials who suffered from new trade regulations during the 1720s, 1730s, and 1740s, which protected home manufactures from colonial producers: John J. McCusker, "British Mercantile Policies and the American Colonies," in *Cambridge Economic History of the United States*, ed. Engerman and Gallman, vol. 1, *Colonial Era*, 337–62. Hall's story, then, belongs to a larger history of the Atlantic world, recent descriptions of which are identified in Eric Slauter's "History, Literature, and the Atlantic World," *The William and Mary Quartertly*, 3rd ser., 65 (2008): 135–66.

124. Hall to Hugh Hall Sr., May 15, 1718, Hall letterbook; Hall, diary, New York Public Library, passim.

125. Hall, diary. For popular appropriations of Enlightenment science, empirical curiosity, and its relation to political economy, see Porter, *Creation of the Modern World*, 149. For similar themes, and their propagation in almanacs, see Cohen, *Calculating People*, 77, 81–115.

126. Hall, diary.

127. Ibid.

128. For the secular theme and writers mentioned here, see Porter, *Creation of the Modern World*, 88, 195.

129. The following refer to letters from Hall in the Hall letterbook: to Jonathan Davis Jr., June 8, 1717; to Hugh Hall Sr., May 6, 1718; to Lydia Colman, March 6, 1717, and November 26, 1716; and to Robert Smith, March 6, 1717.

130. The following refer to letters from Hall in the Hall letterbook: to Francis Wilkes, February 28, 1717 (on friendship and correspondence); to Benning Wentworth, August 10, 1717 (the quote about frivolous language); and to John Timbs, August 15, 1718 (for heroic gentility). For other merchants, friendship, and sociability, see the comments on Defoe, Steele, and Hume in Porter's *Creation of the Modern World*, 80, 201.

131. Hall, diary.

EPILOGUE
RELIGIOUS REVIVAL

1. Samuel Philips Savage to Gilbert Tennent, February 2, 1742, Samuel P. Savage Papers, 1712–50, correspondence 1741–44, Massachusetts Historical Society, Boston. (Unless otherwise noted, all Savage papers come from this collection. Reference to his correspondence will be cited more specifically as SPS correspondence.) See Savage to Tennent, January 18 and January 30, 1742; Savage to George Whitefield, November 3, 1740; and David Jeffries to Savage, September 7 and December 11, 1741: all SPS correspondence. For the revivals at York, see Douglas L. Winiarski, " 'A Jornal of a Fue Days at York': The Great Awakening on the Northern Frontier," *Maine History* 42 (2004): 47–85 (esp. 49–50 for Savage). For Savage and his family, see Lawrence Park, "The Savage Family," *NEHGR* 67 (1913): 198–215, 309–30.

2. Gilbert Tennent, "The Unsearchable Riches of Christ," in *Sermons on Sacramental Occasions by Divers Ministers* ([Boston, 1739]), i, iii. 9, 20, 33.

3. This formulation of private instincts and social order was central, as many historians have noted, to the thought of Adam Smith and his contemporary political economists; for discussions of Smith in such terms, see Charles L. Griswold Jr., *Adam Smith and the Virtues of Enlightenment* (New York, 1999); and Emma Rothschild, *Economic Sentiments: Adam Smith, Condorcet, and the Enlightenment* (Cambridge, Mass., 2001).

4. Nash, *Urban Crucible*, 161–97; and David Hancock, "Markets, Merchants, and the Wider World of Boston Wine, 1700–1775," in *Entrepreneurs*, ed. Wright and Viens, 63–95.

5. See Newall, *From Dependency to Independence*, 214–35; George Athan Billias, *The Massachusetts Land Bankers of 1740* (Orono, Maine, 1959); and Brock, *Currency of the American Colonies*, 1–64, 130–51, 169–334.

6. The evidence for political economists and the debate over money in mid-eighteenth-century America is provided in Riesman's "Origins of American Political Economy," 88–250.

7. The timing of the development of a market economy is a much-contested issue. The evidence for the fourth and fifth decades of the eighteenth century,

merely sketched here, is presented most persuasively in Rothenberg's *From Market-Places to a Market Economy*, 25–55, 112–47 (45–46 for the details on Faneuil Hall regulations). For legal developments, see Mann, *Neighbors and Strangers*. On trade during the 1740s, see McCusker and Menard, *Economy of British America*, 35–50, 62–63, 91–111. Some rural areas continued to operate out of older principles through the eighteenth century. My argument here, taken largely from Rothenberg and Mann, concerns the point at which a market economy can be said to predominate in the major lines of trade in and out of Boston.

8. Park, "Savage Family."

9. Savage to anon., ca. 1742, SPS correspondence (on Brattle Street's liturgical practices); and Savage, July 6–7, 1741, notes and extract from unsigned letter (on Edwards). For Savage's engagement in Brattle Street, see Park, "Savage Family." For further information on Savage's evangelical interests and his relationship to Edwards, including a transcription of the unsigned letter mentioned here, see Douglas L. Winiarski, "Jonathan Edwards, Enthusiast? Radical Revivalism and the Great Awakening in the Connecticut Valley," *Church History* 74 (2005): 683–739.

10. See Park, "Savage Family," for biographical information; Peter Cally to Savage, February 10, 1742, SPS correspondence (for an example of the extent of their business); and scattered accounts (for various imports and exports).

11. Simon Frost to Savage, August 6, 1744, SPS correspondence (for the quote on money); Savage, "Articles of Agreement," with David Jeffries, July 1741; David Jeffries to Savage, November 27, 1741, SPS correspondence (for the relative value of bills and specie); and various ledgers.

12. All of the following citations refer to documents in the Smith-Carter Papers, Massachusetts Historical Society, Boston: William Smith, 1732 probate account (for the debt from Hugh Hall); Isaac Smith, accounts and ledgers, 1740–44, 1746–47 (for accounts of his imports and dealings in whale oil); Isaac Smith to Benjamin Burroughs, February 2, 1743 (for one example of the luxury items mentioned here); and Isaac Smith, loose accounts, 1740–48, which includes annual tax receipts that reflect his growing wealth. (All subsequent reference to Isaac Smith manuscripts, account books, and letters refer to the Smith-Carter Papers.) For other biographical information, including Smith's credit schemes, see Andrew H. Ward, "Notes on Ante-Revolutionary Currency and Politics," *NEHGR* (1860): 261–62; and Barbara McLean Ward, "Boston Artisan Entrepreneurs of the Goldsmithing Trade in the Decades before the Revolution," in *Entrepreneurs*, ed. Wright and Viens, 31–33.

13. Isaac Smith, account book, 1740–55, which includes the quote, separate tallies for each of his ventures, and a ledger of his debtors. Smith's impersonal style and resolution to pursue debtors may be sampled in the following letters by Smith: to Joseph Mico, December 14, 1741; to Messrs. Sedgwick and Barnard, August 28, 1742; and to Benjamin Burroughs, December 12, 1742.

14. Isaac Smith, diary, 1738–40, which includes mention of Smith's frequent travels and attendance at sermons; Smith, diary, 1741, for his attendance on Tennent; Smith, diary, 1742, for his response to Davenport and Croswell; and Isaac Smith, loose papers and diaries, 1738–43 (for correspondence about the revivals).

15. Robert Treat Paine's biography is provided in Stephen T. Riley and Edward W. Hanson, eds., introduction to *The Papers of Robert Treat Paine*, 2 vols. (Boston, 1992), 1:ix–xxviii. (These volumes hereafter are cited as *Paine*.) Informa-

tion on Thomas Paine is provided in *Harvard Graduates* 6:201-7. For the library, which was deeded to Robert and included standard works of puritan divinity (Ames, Perkins, and Samuel Willard) as well as almanacs, translations of Stoics such as Cicero and Seneca, writings by Pemberton and Thomas Prince, and other examples of the latest, most progressive divinity, see John D. Cushing, ed., "Catalogus Librorum: The Library of Thomas Paine of Boston (1694–1757)," *Proceedings of the Massachusetts Historical Society* 100 (1988): 100–127. See also the "Administration of the Estate of Thomas Paine," in *Paine* 2:189–91.

16. Robert Treat Paine to Richard Cranch, November 25, 1749, and Cranch to Paine, November 29, 1749, in *Paine* 1:76–77, 80–81 (for the clocks); Paine, "Notes, Accounts and Bank Books," cashbook from 1759, in the Robert Treat Paine Papers, Massachusetts Historical Society, Boston; and the "Agreement" and "Robert Treat Paine's Sailing Orders," 1751, along with attendant correspondence about the Carolina ventures, in *Paine* 1:128–51. See also Riley and Hanson, introduction to *Papers of Robert Treat Paine*.

17. Paine to Samuel Eliot, January 12, 1770, in *Paine* 2:458 (for the law books); Paine to Henry Snoad, November 3, 1752, in *Paine* 1:179 (for complaints about litigation). See also Riley and Hanson, introduction to *Papers of Robert Treat Paine*.

18. Savage, "The Present Frame I fell in," private meditation, 1742, SPS correspondence. Savage also reiterated revivalist idioms in his meditation "Marks of the Regenerate and Unregenerate," SPS correspondence.

19. Smith, diary, 1738–40 (mention of Edwards's sermon on Ezek. 22:14 in 1738 and of periods of sacramental introspection); Smith, "Confession of Faith," 1741; and diary, 1738–40 (for his concurrent preoccupations with business, mortality, and equanimity).

20. Among abundant examples of this perspective, with evidence for the details mentioned here, see Savage to Whitefield, November 3, 1740, SPS correspondence; Savage, personal notes, SPS correspondence; Savage, July 6–7, [ca. 1741,] notes; Savage to Tennent, January 18, 1742, January 30, 1742, and February 2, 1742, SPS correspondence, and Savage to Arthur Savage, April 20, 1741 (for sending Tennent's works and recommending Cooper), SPS correspondence. See also Winiarski, " 'A Fue Days at York.' " For Smith, see Isaac Smith, diary, 1738–43, at several places.

21. As a student in Cambridge, Paine encouraged his friends to seek conversion, what he described as "great Joy" in "the Remission of Sin" secured "for the Elect" by Christ and the "merit in his Blood"; Paine to James Freeman, in *Paine* 1:1 (on joy and forgiveness); see also Paine to James Freeman, May 11, 1746, in *Paine* 1:5. As a member of Old South later in his career, he diligently took notes on sermons, heard Whitefield, and adopted some evangelical ideas; Riley and Hanson, introduction to *Papers of Robert Treat Paine*, xviii; and for Paine's sermon notes, see Robert Treat Paine Papers, sermons, Massachusetts Historical Society. When he made his confession of faith in 1749 under Joseph Sewall's tutelage at Old South, however, he muted evangelical themes in favor of a somewhat placid orthodoxy: Paine, "Confession of Faith," in *Paine* 1:48–49.

22. The following citations all refer to *Paine*: Paine to Abigail Paine Greenleaf, March 17, 1755, 1:246–47; Paine to Samuel Quincy, May 6, 1755, 1:260; Paine to "Miss. M.M.," April 10, 1753, 1:188; and Ezekiel Dodge to Paine, May 5, 1747,

1:12. Paine frequently wrote in a Stoical vein, making explicit reference to the Stoics, inner tranquillity, religious devotion, personal happiness, scientific knowledge, and economic proficiency; see, for example, the various essays, letters, and meditations in *Paine* 1:33–35, 63–64, 79, 88–98, 126–27, 237, 245–48; and 2:169.

23. Several studies have confirmed various continuities between the Great Awakening and market sensibilities and practices. See, for example, Bushman, *From Puritan to Yankee*, which focuses on the evangelical sanction of internal affections; Susan O'Brien, "Eighteenth-Century Publishing Networks in the First Years of Transatlantic Evangelicalism," in *Evangelicalism: Comparative Studies of Popular Protestantism in North America, the British Isles, and Beyond, 1700–1990*, ed. Mark A. Noll, David W. Bebbington, and George A. Rawlyk (New York, 1994), 38–57, which describes dispersed moral networks linked by correspondence and published serials; Frank Lambert, *Inventing the "Great Awakening"* (Princeton, N.J., 1999), for the use of market strategies to promote the revivals; and Mark A. Noll, "Protestant Reasoning about Money and the Economy, 1790–1860: A Preliminary Probe," in *God and Mammon*, ed. Noll, 265–94, which surveys the general patterns of congruence between evangelical moral sentiment and modern economic behavior. To explain the coherence between Protestantism and the market, the formulation in this epilogue suggests less emphasis on the revivals and more on prerevival shifts than do the above studies.

24. The following are all from the SPS correspondence: David Jeffries to Savage, September 7, 1741; David Jeffries to Savage, November 27 and December 11, 1741; and John Blunt to Savage, December 22, 1741. There are many letters in the collection between Simon Frost and Savage. For the general point here about commercial and evangelical networks, publications, and correspondence, see Susan O'Brien, "A Transatlantic Community of Saints: The Great Awakening and the First Evangelical Network, 1735–1755," *American Historical Review* 91 (1986): 811–32.

25. Savage to Simon Frost, April 8, 1744, SPS correspondence; Savage, "Marks of the Regenerate and Unregenerate."

26. Paine, "Sermon: There is a Time for War, and a Time for Peace," November 16, 1755, in *Paine* 1:328–29, 332. Paine's attitude is reflected throughout his many writings and essays. Savage and Smith also embraced metropolitan identities. Savage sometimes interrupted letters otherwise filled with matters of exchange—payments, credits, and the prices of commodities—with professions of devotion to the Crown and prayers for victory over France. Smith made witty observations on fashion and traded political information, gossip, and battlefield reports. See Savage to Simon Frost, April 8, 1744, SPS correspondence; Smith, "An Answer to Your Answer, Sirs," 1733–34; and Smith, "A True and Impartial Account of the Celebration of the Prince of Orange's Nuptials," June 3, 1734. For Lynde, whose personal reflections echoed the moral ideas of Paine, see Benjamin Lynde, almanac diaries, for example, "Diary in Ames' Almanac," 1741, entries from February 1, 15, 26, April 19, and May 10, Massachusetts Historical Society.

27. To be sure, evangelicals' enthusiasm for latitudinarian writers waned during the 1740s, when Whitefield warned them that rational apologetics, refined morality, and Newtonian physics were incapable of bringing audiences to real conversion. See especially Thomas Foxcroft, *Some Seasonable Thoughts on Evangelic Preaching*

(Boston, 1740), title page (quoting Isaac Watts against Locke and Newton); and the general discussion of Cooper, Colman, Whitefield, and Tillotson in *Seasons of Grace: Colonial New England's Revival Tradition in Its British Context*, by Michael J. Crawford (New York, 1991), 154–55. Yet evangelicals continued to deploy Tillotsonian moral idioms when discussing commerce. The intellectual leader of evangelicals, Jonathan Edwards, relied on many of the conventions of rational moral philosophy to make his evangelical argument: Norman Fiering, *Jonathan Edwards's Moral Philosophy and Its British Context* (Chapel Hill, N.C., 1981).

28. William Cooper, *Man Humbled by Being Compar'd to a Worm* (Boston, 1732), 2, 25; cf. Charles Chauncy, *Cornelius's Character* (Boston, 1745), 18.

29. Benjamin Colman, *The Merchandise of a People Holiness to the Lord* (Boston, 1736); see ii, 2. For Calvin, see John Calvin, *Commentary on the Book of the Prophet Isaiah*, trans. William Pringle, 2 vols. (1850; repr., Grand Rapids, Mich., 1979), 1:157–58. Calvin dedicated one edition of his commentary to Elizabeth I; it was translated and published in London in 1609 and undoubtedly read by many puritan divines.

30. Colman, *Merchandize of a People*, 7, 9; see esp. 10–15; Colman, *Souls Flying to Jesus Christ Pleasant and Admirable to Behold* (Boston, 1740), 24. For an example of another evangelical, see Mark Valeri, "The Economic Thought of Jonathan Edwards," *Church History* 60 (1991): 37–54.

31. See, for example, Cooper's sermons on the reasonableness of inoculation for smallpox and the moral lessons of the great 1727 earthquake: [William Cooper], *A Letter to a Friend in the Country* (Boston, 1721), esp. 6; and William Cooper, *The Danger of a People's Loosing the Good Impressions Made by the Late Earthquake* (Boston, 1727), esp. 7–8, 11, 20. E. Brooks Holifield has documented this widespread appeal to reason and what he calls Baconian empiricism among New England clergy in this period, in *Theology in America: Christian Thought from the Age of the Puritans to the Civil War* (New Haven, Conn., 2003), 79–126. For Cooper's personal habits of consumption, see *Harvard Graduates* 5:624–31.

32. Valeri, "Economic Thought of Jonathan Edwards"; and for land speculation, Mary C. Foster, "Hampshire County, Massachusetts, 1729–1754: A Covenant Society in Transition" (PhD diss., University of Michigan, 1967), 204–7. Edwards's ruminations on the spread of Protestant trade and science, and decline in Catholic commerce, may be found in his eschatological predictions: Jonathan Edwards, *An Humble Attempt to Promote Visible Union* [Boston, 1747], in *The Works of Jonathan Edwards*, vol. 5, *Apocalyptic Writings*, ed. Stephen J. Stein (New Haven, Conn., 1977), 338–39; Edwards, *Works of Jonathan Edwards*, vol. 9, *A History of the Work of Redemption*, ed. John F. Wilson (New Haven, Conn., 1989), 483–84; and for notations on Catholic and Protestant affairs, Edwards, "Apocalyptic Notebook," in Edwards's *Apocalyptic Writings*, ed. Stein, 255–74. For an important study of how the revivals offered a form of social order in the midst of economic crises and expansion, see especially Heyrman, *Commerce and Culture*. Following Heyrman, the interpretation here contrasts with the reading given by Bushman in *From Puritan to Yankee*, who contends that the revivals sanctioned individualism and relieved the guilt of merchants who displaced communal loyalties with economic ambition. See, for a wider perspective on moral discourse and social order, T. H. Breen and Timothy Hall, "Structuring Provincial Imagination: The Rhetoric and Experience of Social

Change in Eighteenth-Century New England," *American Historical Review* 103 (1998): 1410–39.

33. See, for example, William Cooper, preface to Jonathan Edwards's *Distinguishing Marks of a Work of the Spirit of God* (Boston, 1741), which illustrates not only the link between Cooper and Edwards, but also the conviction of an extended and well-advertised moral network. For epistolary ties, see Christopher R. Reaske, introduction to Ebenezer Turell's *Life and Character of the Reverend Benjamin Colman*, D. D. (Boston, 1749; repr., New York, 1972), v–xxiii. For a more detailed dicussion of Prince's *Christian History*, which was published in Boston, and its similarity to *The American Magazine*, published in Boston, Newport, New Haven, New York, and Philadelphia, see Mark Valeri, "Jonathan Edwards, the Edwardsians, and the Sacred Cause of Free Trade," in *Jonathan Edwards at Home and Abroad: Historical Memories, Cultural Movements, Global Horizons*, ed. David W. Kling and Douglas A. Sweeney (Columbia, S.C., 2003), 85–100. For publishing and missionary work, see Peterson, *Price of Redemption*, 219–39. There is a large literature describing the relationship of the revivals to transatlantic commerce, new communication techniques, and publishing ventures, including Lambert's *Inventing the "Great Awakening"* and Crawford's *Seasons of Grace*. This literature stands in contrast to an older argument that focuses on New Light radicalism, anticommercial rhetoric, and their ties to lower-class discontent: Nash, *Urban Crucible*, 184–219.

34. William Cooper, *The Honours of Christ Demanded of the Magistrate* (Boston, 1740), 2, 40–41.

35. Jonathan Edwards, sermon on Ezek. 22:12, 1746 or 1747, Beinecke Library, Yale University, New Haven, Connecticut. Other New Lights, to be sure, supported the Land Bank. Particular positions on banks and currency policies, however, were not as significant as were the economic ideologies by which such positions were defended. A free-market political economy informed even Edwards's argument. For New Lights and the Land Bank, see Harry S. Stout, "The Great Awakening in New England Reconsidered: The New England Clergy," *Journal of Social History* 8 (1974): 21–47; and Rosalind Remer, "Old Lights and New Money: A Note on Religion, Economics, and the Social Order in 1740 Boston," *The William and Mary Quarterly*, 3rd ser., 47 (1990): 566–73.

36. Charles Chauncy, *Civil Magistrates Must Be Just* (Boston, 1747), 11, 44–45.

37. Ibid., 63–64.

38. Cooper's career, with special attention to his political activities, is documented in Charles W. Akers's *Divine Politician: Samuel Cooper and the American Revolution in Boston* (Boston, 1982).

39. Samuel Cooper, *Sermon . . . Before the Society for Encouraging Industry, and Employing the Poor* (Boston, 1753), 11, 21. Chauncy had also preached at the meeting of the Society for Encouraging Industry, and Employing the Poor in 1752, delivering a bitter condemnation of indigent residents in Boston; Charles Chauncy, *The Idle Poor Excluded from the Bread of Charity* (Boston, 1752), 17.

40. Cooper, *Sermon . . . Before the Society for Encouraging Industry*, 5, 7, and, for the reference to Addison, 29.

41. [Samuel Cooper], *The Crisis* (Boston, 1754), 9–11. The bill was published as "An Act [1754]," in *Temporary Laws* (Boston, 1754), by Massachusetts Bay, Province, 435–42.

42. The Boston Massacre print is on the frontispiece of Savage's copy of Abraham Weatherwise's *Town and Country Almanac* (Boston, 1783), cataloged as "Ledger" in the Savage Philips Papers. For the Calvinist-liberal alliance during the American Revolution, see Mark Valeri, "The New Divinity and the American Revolution," *The William and Mary Quarterly*, 3rd ser., 46 (1989): 741–69.

43. The formulation here has been informed by Muldrew's "Interpreting the Market"; Hilton's *Age of Atonement*; and Joyce Appleby's *Capitalism and a New Social Order: The Republican Vision of the 1790s* (New York, 1984).

INDEX

Note: Page numbers in italic type refer to illustrations.

ecumenism, 164, 207, 225, 226
education, 102, 205, 212
Edwards, Jonathan, 237, 240, 244–45, 305n54, 316n27
Edwards, Samuel, 238
Eliot, John, 24
Elizabeth I, queen of England, 21
Elutheria, West Indies, 43
emissions (money), 150–53
Emmons, Nathaniel, *Samuel Sewall, 115*
enclosure, 20–21, 32
Endicott, John, 94
England: Civil War in, 79; commerce and morality in, 20–22; departure from, 57; economists in, 4, 81–82, 89, 113, 131, 134–38; economy of, 21–22; Glorious Revolution in, 123, 130, 154; law in, 66; money in, 136, 138; puritanism in, 27, 50–57; Restoration in, 8, 79, 84, 85, 96, 217; rule of, 1–2, 122–34, 143, 216, 285n37, 289n75; and trade with American colonies, 79–80, 83, 122, 124–27, 132–33. *See also* imperialism
engrossing, 20, 52, 53, 55, 56
Enlightenment, 204–6, 209, 218, 230, 239, 246, 248
Erving, John, 186–87, 194, 235, 237–38
Essex County Quarterly Courts, 70, 104
evangelism, 8, 158, 170, 172, 172–74, 204, 209, 214, 221, 227, 231, 234–35, 237–38, 240–46, 316n27
exchanges, 11–13, 25–26
excise, 247
excommunication, 33, 38, 49, 50, 55, 58, 62–65, 72
extortion, 30, 31, 34

Familists, 42
Faneuil, Andrew (André), 184, 186, 192, 193
Faneuil, Peter, 186, 192, 194, 236
Faneuil Hall, 192, *193*
fashion. *See* culture
Father Rale's War (1721–1725), 175
Field, John, 31; *Admonition to Parliament* (with Wilcox), 55; *Godly Prayers and Meditations*, 34
Filmer, Robert, *Quaestion Quolibetica,* 293n108
First Church, 3, 4, 14, 15, 37–38, 48–49, 62–64, 72–74, 76–77, 86–89, 96, 116,

131, 161, 162, 180, 182, 188, 189, 204, 208, 213, 218, 224, 275n33, 280n83
Fitch, Benjamin, 184
Fitch, John, 117
Fitch, Martha, 117
Fitch, Mary, 117
Fitch, Thomas, 4, 113, 178; business career of, 116–22, 138, 141, 152, 174–77, 180, 225; civic career of, 174–75; and the poor, 166; and religion, 125, 168, 173, 174–77, 225
Fitch, Thomas (father), 116–17
Fortrey, Samuel, 287n62
Fowle, Thomas, 47
Foxcroft, David, 121
Foxcroft, Thomas, 4, 180, 204, 208, 210, 211, 213, 215, 218, 224–25, 287n56
France: as American threat, 2, 113, 122, 123, 126, 127, 143, 167–68, 175; and commerce, 81–82, 134; and money, 151; Protestantism in, 2, 50, 171
franchise, 67, 76, 123–24
Franklin, Benjamin, 7, 244; *New-England Courant,* 207
Franklin, William, 63
free market, 233, 235, 246
free trade, 41, 135, 141, 143, 242, 247
French and Indian War (1754<n>1763), 246. *See also* Seven Years' War
friendship, 232
Frost, Simon, 237, 242
Fulke, William, 55
Fund, the, 145–46
funerals, 194

Gee, Joshua, 207
Geere, Dennis, 61–62
General Assembly, 162, 167, 220
General Court of Connecticut, 46–47
General Court of Massachusetts: and Boston crisis of 1675–1676, 97; and commerce, 61, 81; and court system, 66; creation of, 65–66; criticisms of, 87; on the economy, 41; and English rule, 122–24; and Halfway Covenant, 86; Hull and, 76–78, 106; Keayne and, 14, 15, 37, 48; lawyers' role restricted by, 72; and money, 145–46, 150; and religion, 42, 44, 48, 71–72, 97, 101–2, 305n48; Sewall and, 85, 114; and slavery, 170
General Sessions of the Peace, 269n81
Geneva, Switzerland, 2, 55–56, 266n54